THE ORIGINS OF DISLIKE

THE ORIGINS
OF
DISLIKE

AMIT CHAUDHURI

OXFORD
UNIVERSITY PRESS

OXFORD
UNIVERSITY PRESS

Great Clarendon Street, Oxford, OX2 6DP,
United Kingdom

Oxford University Press is a department of the University of Oxford.
It furthers the University's objective of excellence in research, scholarship,
and education by publishing worldwide. Oxford is a registered trade mark of
Oxford University Press in the UK and in certain other countries

First Edition published in 2018

Impression: 2

Published in the United States of America by Oxford University Press
198 Madison Avenue, New York, NY 10016, United States of America

British Library Cataloguing in Publication Data
Data available

Library of Congress Control Number: 2018932396

ISBN 978–0–19–879382–3

Printed and bound in Great Britain by Clays Ltd, Elcograf S.p.A.

For Tom Paulin

Acknowledgements

I am grateful for permission to reproduce the following materials: Chapter 2, 'The Piazza and the Car Park' and Chapter 19, '*I* am Ramu', originally published in n+1 online. ('The Piazza and the Car Park' was first presented as 'The Mehrotra Campaign' at the inaugural University of East Anglia symposium on 'Literary Activism' in Calcutta.) Chapter 3, 'Poetry as Polemic', originally published as the Introduction to *The Essential Tagore* (Harvard University Press, 2011) and *Guernica*. Chapter 5, 'The Other Green', originally published as the Introduction to *Party Going* by Henry Green, *NYRB Classics* and *The Guardian*. Chapter 6, 'On the *Gita*: Krishna as Poetic Language', originally published as the Introduction in The Folio Society edition of *The Bhagavad Gita*, 2011 and the *Times Literary Supplement*. Chapter 7, 'The Alien Face of Cosmopolitanism', originally published in *New Left Review*. Chapter 8, 'Qatrina and the Books', originally published in *London Review of Books*. Chapter 10, 'The Photographer as Onlooker', originally published in MET Catalogue, New York. Chapter 11, 'The Sideways Movement', originally published in *Caravan*, 1 September 2012. Chapter 13, 'Un-machinelike', originally published in *Telegraph*, India. Chapter 14, 'Nissim Ezekiel: Poet of a Minor Literature', originally published in *A History of Indian Poetry in English* (Cambridge University Press, 2016). Chapter 18, 'On the Paragraph', originally published in *Granta*. At the time of writing this, 'Starting from Scratch: Buddhadeva Bose and the English Language' is to appear as the preface to *An Acre of Green Grass and Other English Writings* by Buddhadeva Bose, due from Oxford University Press in 2018.

I am grateful to the editors of all these publications.

'The Origins of Dislike' was first presented as a talk at the South Asia Initiative at Harvard University in 2010, and then at Yale and Warwick Universities. 'What We Do: Deprofessionalization and Legitimacy' was first presented in 2016 at the India International Centre, Delhi as part of the University of East Anglia symposium on 'Deprofessionalization'. 'Ray and Ghatak and other Filmmaking Pairs: The Structure of Asian Modernity' was the Satyajit Memorial Lecture at the Nehru Centre, London, in 2009. 'The Emergence of the Everyday: Kipling, Tagore, and Indian Regional Writing' was the John Coffin Memorial Lecture at London University, 2011, and later a public lecture at Smith College and New York University. 'Unconstitutional Spaces' was a keynote address at the Crafts of World Literature conference at Oxford University, 2012. 'Possible, Not Alternative, Histories: A Literary History Emerging from Sunlight' was first presented at the University of East Anglia symposium on 'Reassessments' at Presidency University, Calcutta, and then at King's College, London, 2017.

Although some of these talks were given at academic venues, their aim was to explore a style of discussion that isn't, strictly speaking, academic. This is in keeping with the intentions of the symposia in the 'literary activism' series organized by me on behalf of the University of East Anglia. I'm grateful to my various hosts for accommodating this departure in tone.

Thanks are due to my editor Jacqueline Norton, and to others, especially Aimee Wright and Phil Henderson, on her team, for their enthusiasm and support.

I'm beholden to a small circle of friends and colleagues, and above all to my wife Rosinka, for their help in sustaining the space from which these writings emerge.

And, of course, I'm sustained by my daughter Radha in more ways than I can say.

Contents

List of Figures

'The starting-point of critical elaboration is the consciousness of what one really is, and is "knowing thyself" as a product of the historical process to date, which has deposited in you an infinity of traces, without leaving an inventory . . . therefore it is imperative at the outset to compile such an inventory.'

Antonio Gramsci

Introduction

The title of this collection might mislead one into thinking that it's solely an exploration of 'dislike'. It isn't. It represents an attempt—undertaken repeatedly, from different vantage-points and at different moments—to understand the writer's relationship to literary history, and the way it and the writer define each other. These attempts seemed necessary to me—as a writer—as the available histories, whether they were governed by politics, ethnicity, or a reverence for literature, didn't quite account for my practice, and *why* the practice should be important to myself. I should point out that these essays don't intend to *write* literary history, or study authors. They are not an examination of events that happened seventy-five or a hundred years ago, though they might refer to such events. In that sense, they aren't defined by the proprieties of academic work. They have to do with what it means to write in the period most resistant to analysis—*now*.

This introduction is less an overview of the book's contents than a collection of thoughts arising from them. It's the preamble to a journey covering the terrain described above. The journey ends with two reflections on the literary occasioned by some time I'd spent with a friend I'd written about in my last novel, *Friend of My Youth*. Like my fiction, these essays emerge from an encounter with life.

★

Much criticism from the early to the middle of the twentieth century—over which period critical practice would be turned increasingly into academic discipline—was written by what managers in the last fifty years have been calling 'creative writers'. In spite of this, the romantic prejudice against imaginative writers who 'think' in the Anglophone world is an old one, and predates the emergence of academic disciplines to do with criticism and scholarship. As for us, we've been living in a period in which writers appear at literary festivals mainly to share the talismanic properties of their craft—to do with whether they write in longhand or on the computer; what kind of ballpoint pen they use; whether they write in the afternoon or morning. Craft is not seen to be a form of historical or intellectual practice; if writers happen to *know* anything, the knowledge is extraneous, and may or may not be put to use. This extraneous knowledge could have to do with, say, politics, anthropology, the social sciences, or climate change. The writer may be asked to comment on issues related to these disciplines or concerns. If she or he is asked to comment on craft, however, it will be because we want an account of the magical rather than the historical. Professional scholarship and sociology—I don't include 'criticism' here, since it has, in the academy, been in protracted death-throes for decades—is left to academics, who are seen somehow not to be 'writers'; that is, not one of those who dabble in craft and magic.

Once you step out of the domain of the Anglophone—that is, the literary sphere in Britain, the USA, and partly India—you realize that the nervousness about philosophy, 'theory', and criticism that marks writers (who exhibit less anxiety about espousing the sociological, the historical, or the political) is relatively absent in poets and novelists from Western and Eastern Europe, from the Middle East, and from some of the major writers who write or wrote in languages like, say, Urdu or Hindi. In 2005, at a gathering of international writers in Norwich, I discovered that the Anglophone writer's uneasiness with thought was aberrant rather than 'normal' in the literary world (here I mean 'world' more literally than figuratively). It was a curious congregation, in that the incarnation of the 'international' I encountered there emphasized to me not a worldwide family of writers, in which the unremarked-on medium of communication happened to be English, but a schism: a difference in tone between the English-speaking and non-Anglophone that had not to do simply with political or ethnic backgrounds, but the relationship with thinking. For instance, Dubravka Ugrešić had much to say on the 'new' country she belonged to, Croatia, and the historic destruction it had emerged from was implicit in what she said; but her words were not without an irony to do with how belonging to this nation and also discovering the West for the first time had led her to revise her understanding of the literary.

For writers like her, engaging with the intellectual foundations of literary practice didn't seem to be incompatible with creativity.

That politics, outside the Anglophone literary sphere, need not be extraneous to what writing or craft embody, that a writer needn't just speak or write *about* politics (that word, 'about', is a key term in Anglophone literary discourse, and is meant to enforce a dichotomy between creativity and thought, writing and event), that politics can be related to the poetics of narrative in a way that seems impossible today in mainstream English writing, became clearer to me in the aftermath of the Hindi novelist Uday Prakash's forfeiture of his Sahitya Akademi Award as a protest against state-abetted violence against writers. Prakash wasn't just saying that fiction should be free to utter political truths that were unpleasant to the present dispensation; during a discussion on television, he said that he was defending writing's 'ambivalence'. When I asked him about his use of this word, he said he had in mind Susan Sontag's essay, 'Against Interpretation', which he'd encountered years ago; he was struck by the notion that interpretation is a 'power-tool' (Prakash's word), and that it tends to make the writer culpable in 'power-centric systems'. 'Dissenting authors of every political or religious system had to face similar fate. Akhmatova, Bulgakov, Dabholkar, Kalburgi, Mandelstam and others',[1] said Prakash to me in a message. What I find instructive here are not only the overlaps that encourage us to throw out prefabricated intellectual itineraries and start mapping things anew (Hindi; fiction; the village in which Prakash grew up; his erstwhile Maoist sympathies; Sontag; 'ambivalence'), but that 'interpretation' and 'power-centric systems' should converge in Prakash's imagination in a way that would be unlikely for an Anglophone counterpart, for whom politics on the one hand and writing and criticism on the other come from very distinct realms. Writing might often be *about* politics both inside and outside the Anglophone sphere, but there's also a chance that, outside it, the 'about' may be dispensed with in a way that allows poetics and politics to flow into each other.

★

In the Anglophone literary sphere today (I can't speak authoritatively for other languages), writing is secondary. The writer may be relatively unimportant, but is the focus of more attention than writing itself. If a discussion on writing is largely a discussion on the writer, what are the terms of this discussion? How do writers assess themselves? If craft is a kind of magic, and, conversely, if writing novels is mainly dignified by the fact that it involves hard work (research; a regular discipline ensuring productivity), and if writing itself is neither an argument nor intervention—that is, a working out of ways in which a writer is at odds with, while being part of, their larger practice—then what represents a writer's struggle; how do they judge what they have done?

It would seem that most writers today refer primarily to a check-list. This check-list defines writerly ambition. Naturally, the first thing on it is publication. Almost inextricable from this basic aim, to be published, are the questions, 'Who is going to be my publisher? And where will I be published? Will it be Jonathan Cape? Will it be in London? And in New York?' If these ambitions are achieved, then the inaugural bit of the check-list is taken care of—one would now just need to ensure that the tick mark denotes a permanent state of affairs: that one *continues* to be published in a major Western metropolitan centre by an acknowledged publisher.

Then comes the hour of publication and its aftermath. Will I get reviewed? You begin by presuming that you will be reviewed everywhere. Gradually, it dawns on you that this may not be the case. Will I get coverage in the *Guardian*? In the *New Yorker*? But *who* will review me in the *New Yorker*? (This question succeeds the previous one.) I want James Wood to review me. Would Michiko Kakutani write about me in the *New York Times*? Naturally, I want these responses to be thoughtful and positive. Once these are taken care of, a substantial part of the check-list has been addressed.

Then there's the matter of prizes. I *want* to be honoured. Which prizes do I stand a chance of winning? How do I increase my chances? Tautological as this might sound, even better than lobbying is the idea of *writing* a prizewinning book. I need to get on to shortlists; and win. Which awards have I won? In the ethos surrounding fiction-writing in Britain and its former territories, it's essential I win the Booker, or am shortlisted, or at least longlisted. The position of the Booker in relation to the writer published in Britain is roughly equivalent to what the Eiffel Tower's was, according to Guy de Maupassant, to the Parisian: it seemed—indeed, seems—to follow you wherever you are. 'To escape the Eiffel Tower,' Maupassant said (as Roland Barthes pointed out), 'you have to go inside it.'[2] Similarly, the only reason any writer would want to win the Booker is to no longer be under the obligation of winning it.

Once the check-list is all ticked—as it is in, say, Ian McEwan's case, twice over—the question that echoed repeatedly in Yeats's ear remains: '"*What then? sang Plato's ghost.*"'[3]

★

Attending to, and assiduously ticking, the check-list doesn't absolve the writer from their main task: to make a case for their writing, and to argue for how it's to be read. The writer's job is not to be Jhumpa Lahiri (I use the name as a shorthand for our obsession with certain forms of acquisition: for instance, awards and column inches in the *New Yorker*). Certainly, Jhumpa Lahiri doesn't think that it's her job to be Jhumpa Lahiri, but to work out what her writing is about.

With D. H. Lawrence or Henry James we don't know or remember what the check-list was: who their publishers were, which magazines they contributed to and how much they got paid for their pieces, which awards they received, if any. But we're aware that they did not shirk the task of trying to create the parameters within which they were read, and within which we think of reading itself.

The interventionist act need not necessarily take the form of a piece of writing. It could express itself as a move to Trieste: a move from one's native location to an unexpected one is an attempt to fashion a parameter of reading and reception. The move—which could well be part of a check-list, or a meaningless gesture—could also be a variety of thought. So could *not* publishing one's writing. Here I'm thinking of Franz Kafka (who published little), Fernando Pessoa (ditto), Jibanananda Das, and Arun Kolatkar (the last two withheld some of their most important work). This is not a courtship of failure. It's an attempt on the part of these writers to fashion the terms by which they are read.

★

What is the difference between poetry and thought? The answer to this question might throw light on the writer's particular form of intervention (here, I use the word 'writer' to refer as much to academics and scholars as to poets and novelists). Of course, there's no clear answer. We believe that the provenance of the first, poetry, is at once mysterious and formalistic, and that the second, thought, is related to our rational faculties. (It might seem such debates have long been settled and rendered archaic, but the assumptions on which they are based still inform the off-guard responses of the most rigorous academic.) We also infer that each activity emerges from a particular location in ourselves—a source that either governs, controls, or validates. To dismantle the distinction between poetry and thinking first involves challenging the notion of the centre from which they arise. Two antagonists from the first half of the twentieth century, T. S. Eliot and D. H. Lawrence, undertake the challenge separately. Eliot questions Philip Sidney's assignation of the 'heart' as the locus of the poetic. 'Those who object to the "artificiality" of Milton or Dryden,' says Eliot, 'sometimes tell us to "look into our hearts and write." But that is not looking deep enough; Racine or Donne looked into a good deal more than the heart. One must look into the cerebral cortex, the nervous system, and the digestive tracts.'[4] What is notable is that Eliot doesn't appoint a new centre over the 'heart', but invokes a general pattern of redistribution, which mimics the way we must rethink terms like 'tradition', 'literature', and 'modernity': not as inert 'bodies' that are an accumulation of works and histories, but an area of shifting relations. (Eliot's early poetry too refers to the anatomy as a distribution of impulses, turning it into a metaphor for a 'tradition' that is not static, but altered by routes briefly illuminated: 'as if a magic lantern threw the nerves in patterns on a screen'.[5]) It's in entering and engaging with this area that we begin to abandon the more orthodox dividing lines separating the poetic and the intellectual. Lawrence comes to it from the opposite direction. His overt concern is not with poetry, but thought, whose recognized delineations he questions, appropriately, in a poem: 'Thought, I love thought. / But not the jiggling and twisting of already existent ideas.'[6] The poem's final line—again a statement of reallocation and redistribution—removes 'thought' from an identifiable centre: 'Thought is a man in his wholeness wholly attending.' Once we dispense with sources of validation or control—the heart for poetry, the brain for thought—we're also thrown into exploring modes of reading history that result from centres shifting from one position to the next. These readings (of culture, of history) embody a process in which the difference between thinking and poetry ceases to be a dependable one.

*

For me, the essay is a visible record of the fact that writing emerges not from a single location in oneself. I began to write a particular kind of essay in the 1990s. The aim was not to bring in an element of autobiography into a critical or intellectual project. In 2003, I find that I said to an interviewer about some essays that were deemed 'political' that '... what I've tried to allow is for the essay to be a space in which the consciousness which reads poetry or remembers a line of poetry or listens to music or goes for a walk, is also the consciousness that is inflected and threatened and endangered by the political; is also the consciousness that registers and is permeated by the political. That somehow it is not a separate ... consciousness that is hiding behind the facade of the man who remembers a line of poetry or forgets it, but that it is the same consciousness in which these various things are coming in and going out.'[7] The essay, then, is not the product of a 'separate' consciousness. My remark was my way of suggesting that the essay requires one to be 'wholly attending'. Just as Eliot uses, when speaking of poetry, corporeal metaphors for rethinking 'tradition'—the digestive tract, nerve-patterns—I believe that (since writers can't take their cultural identity for granted) a disparate series of acts leading up to, and described in, the essay—going for a walk, listening to music, responding to the political—gesture towards a desire for a new vocabulary or mapping for how we inherit, inhabit, and shape culture. The essay is not a venue in which the itineraries we've already been handed down will do.

★

This matter of 'handing down' things brings me to what, as I glance at many of the pieces in this book, constitutes an ongoing problem to which the essays repeatedly return. Whatever the cultural contexts which appear to define me or other writers and artists—to do with race, identity, class, or history—it seems that none of them is definitive. One must remake these categories, not to assert one's individualism, but because both the critical and the creative are inextricable from such a remaking—from a refashioning of notions of one's cultural inheritance. Every category is open, and we probably first become aware of this during our inevitably errant encounter with the art object, or poem. This encounter—which may take the form of viewing a Rembrandt in an art gallery, or watching a film by Satyajit Ray or Abbas Kiarostami, or, for Raghubir Singh, veering regretfully but decisively away from a body of distinguished photographic work on India—reminds us that the definitions at hand to do, for example, with history, modernity, and culture, are inadequate to explaining the artist's actions and reactions. The fact that we—both artists and all of us who respond to an artwork—feel out of place in relation to handed-down cartographical narratives that inform us what our location in the world is supposed to be becomes evident as we uncover unexpected, even inappropriate, aesthetic affinities, and experience powerful but, again, inappropriate moments of recognition—as Ray did when he first saw Kurosawa's *Rashomon*, though he realized he knew nothing of Japanese cinema—or, on the other hand, inklings of discomfiture in the presence of the canonical. The discomfiture may arise not just because of the power-relations the encounter resonates with, to do with race, class, or imperialism, but because the historical parameters of the encounter—according to which I'm placed in a culturally *appropriate* position vis-à-vis the art object—don't make full sense. This means I need to constantly refashion the narratives by which I understand my encounter with the artwork or poem, not in the light of what history tells me, but what the artwork does. At any given point, it rejects the handed-down account. This doesn't mean that the artwork is outside history; it eludes an inherited history. For instance, the films of Abbas Kiarostami are not accounted for by what I've been told about the East, the West, modernity, and Iran. After watching, for instance, *Life and Nothing More*—which not only depicts the aftermath of an earthquake but reconsiders the process of filmmaking itself—I not only have to rethink Iran, but the modern, in which Kiarostami's decisions about narrative are embedded. This leads to the question: *How do I relate the modern, and the departures in form it represents, to Iran?* Our reason for generally not asking this question when we see a film, especially an Iranian film, is because we view it for its content, and as a presentation of a culture and society, without necessarily being interested in what the history of the formal decisions—the formal agreements and disagreements—that the film emerges from tells us of that culture's history, and ours. The encounter is a critical act because it's the starting-point in our awareness of the inadequacy of the terminology, the *appropriate* vocabulary, at our disposal. Critical language is a language that's unable to rely on the givens of cultural and racial lineage. The key word here is 'givens'. Critical language is a reinvention of lineage: rather than debunking lineage, it asks us to overhaul our conception of what it is. This is equally true of creative language. The one indefatigable, modest, self-renewing moral purpose of both creative and critical language is to dismantle, and refuse to reconfirm, what we already know to be true.

★

A preoccupation runs through the book, to do with the nature of poetic language: its difference from narrative. The enquiry into literary history emerges from having been a writer identified with a genre, a culture, and a time in which the idea of narrative has dominated.

★

I have described my reinterpretation of literary histories, at one point, as a positing of 'possible' histories. These histories are, to an extent, fictionalized. I mean that they are speculative: they suggest responses—as in my account of Tarkovsky's encounter with Russian religious iconography—that can't be verified, but are possible to speculate upon.

★

I first encountered the critical spirit in my mother, in whose singing—she was a great exponent of the Tagore song—I also had my first experience of what creativity means: the rejection of the time-worn. Her observations were established by her 'strong likes and dislikes', though—since the dislike was related, among other things, to the rejection of conventional approaches to the Tagore song—her style of singing was marked by rejection too. Her creativity—which was distinguished by its immersion in tone, and a lack of ostentation—was another form of her critical self. However self-effacing a certain kind of undramatic creative temperament might be, I've always been interested in its positioning, in what it's arguing for. This is as relevant to my mother's recordings as it is to my understanding of Kiarostami's cinema.

In my mother, powerful expressions of 'liking' and 'disliking' things were related to her principal characteristic: the advocacy of life. As the cliché goes, she loved life. In art, love of life is a polemic, a kind of argumentation: against death, certainly, but also against the metaphysical. I could hear this argumentation in her singing. Its most compelling expression in contemporary narrative is the taxidermist Bagheri's long, semi-comical speech in Kiarostami's *Taste of Cherry*. Bagheri has been approached by a melancholy, middle-aged driver of a car, Badii, to assist him with his suicide. Bagheri makes a case for life to Badii inside the car before acceding to the latter's request. His speech encompasses anecdote, street directions, imprecation, special pleading, and persuasion. 'Turn right! If you look at the four seasons, each season brings fruit. In summer, there's fruit. In autumn, too. Winter brings different fruit, and spring too. No mother can fill her fridge with such a variety of fruit for her children. No mother can do as much for her children as God does for His creatures. You want to refuse all that? You want to give it all up? You want to give up on the taste of cherries? Don't. I'm your friend. I'm begging you! Turn right . . . turn right, this is the main road . . . Turn left, please.'

Even on the day she passed on in July 2016, my mother asked for a few spoonfuls of vanilla ice cream, which were given to her. She was 90. 'Dislike' is not to be confused with 'distaste'. 'Dislike' has to do with the difficult process of life and renewal; 'distaste'—or, in Bengali, '*bishwad*'—is a withdrawal from living, an extreme waning of interest, when the flavours that once diverted us begin to mean nothing. In Bengali, the other word that describes this state is *aruchi*: literally, a lack of *ruchi*, or taste (*ruchi* has the same connotations of refinement in Bengali as 'taste' does in English), but really referring here to loss of appetite. Dislike, in my mother's case, never denoted a loss of appetite. This reminds us that distaste's antinomy, 'taste', a word now hardly used, and hardly unavailable without the inflections of class, is an expression of appetite and engagement. Liking and dislike too are animated by engagement.

★

The conjunction of eating and writing—which always risks sentimentality—reminds me that, in my first novel, I slipped in Matthew Arnold's aphoristic definition of poetry ('[it] is, at bottom, a criticism of life'[8]) when describing the nature of post-lunch conversation among relatives in a house in South Calcutta: 'This kind of talk, whether at the dinner-table or in the bedroom, did not become too oppressive: it was too full of metaphors, paradoxes, wise jokes and reminiscences to be so. It was, at bottom, a criticism of life.'[9] For a certain kind of nineteenth-century English writer, poetry could be conceived of as a critical act; a rerouting of modernity's nerve centres means that it was possible for me to conflate, just over a hundred years later, Arnold's formulation with the everyday language of an East Bengali family in Calcutta in the early 1970s. But Arnold's own conflation, of poetry and criticism, was already a response to a historic shift that had opened the English, European, and Indian, writer to the world.

The blurring of the border separating the poetic and the critical in the nineteenth and twentieth centuries is related to the manner in which theories of impersonality begin to travel in that age from 'East' to 'West', and within the 'East' itself. This journey constitutes a lineage. Like the other, related lineages and journeys I discuss in this book, it's powerful precisely because I can't take it for granted through an already-decided sense of ownership. In what way do I own a lineage when I must invent it for myself? *All* histories, after all, are belated rather than timely, in the sense that they seem to come before us but are written last of all, long after the event, just as a Preface in a book (as Derrida remarked once[10]) is composed after the book is finished, but appears to precede it.

Arnold's remark is made in 'The Study of Poetry' in 1880, the year of Flaubert's death. By then, Flaubert has established in the realm of the aesthetic—in the relatively new domain of 'literary' prose which he helps create—a theory of what Arnold would call, in relation to criticism, 'disinterestedness', and what Eliot (otherwise unfailingly dismissive of Arnold), would term, in relation to poetry, 'impersonality'. In this context, to do with the idea of a work's consequence, and the curiously non-interventionist role the writer plays in his or her writing, criticism and poetry begin, in modernity, to become each other.

Flaubert's theoretical position is expressed through his literary practice in *Madame Bovary*; but, in a letter written well before Arnold broaches 'disinterestedness' in 1865 in 'The Function of Criticism at the Present Time', Flaubert writes to his mistress Louise Colet: 'An author in his book must be like God in the universe, present everywhere and visible nowhere.'[11] This is an echo of the *Upanishads*, which was translated from a Persian version (and not from the original Sanskrit) into Latin at the end of the eighteenth century by the Frenchman Abraham Hyacinthe Anquetil-Duperron, and picked up early on by Schopenhauer. The paradoxical nature of Flaubert's observation (how can one who's present everywhere be visible nowhere?) is prefigured by lines scattered through the *Upanishads*, including these from the *Isa Upanishad*—'The Spirit, without moving, is swifter than the mind; the senses cannot reach him: He is ever beyond them.

Standing still, he overtakes those who run . . . He moves, and he moves not'[12]—and the *Kena Upanishad*—'What cannot be spoken with words, but that whereby words are spoken . . . What cannot be seen with the eye, but that whereby the eye can see: Know that alone to be the Brahma, the Spirit'[13] (the translations are Juan Mascaró's).

In Calcutta, the Brahmo Samaj was founded by Raja Ram Mohan Roy and Dwarkanath Tagore in 1828, seven years after Flaubert's birth. The Samaj's impetus was provided by the *Upanishads*. For Debendranath Tagore, Dwarkanath's son and Rabindranath's father, and soon the Samaj's most active philosophical theorist, the encounter with the Sanskrit text reportedly occurred by accident when he was a teenager, grieving his grandmother's death, and accidentally discovered a page which had the opening verses of the *Isa Upanishad* on it. From this and earlier encounters with the *Upanishads* come the Brahmo Samaj's (and Debendranath's) position to do with a *niraakar* (formless, invisible) creator, a God present everywhere in his work, but nowhere visible. Chronologically, culturally, Debendranath is a progeny of both Raja Ram Mohun Roy and Anquetil-Duperron. Both Flaubert and Rabindranath, who aestheticize the notion of the invisible, nameless author in their work (Tagore will often call the creator of the universe *kobi*—poet—but hardly ever *name* him), are, chronologically, the spiritual progeny of Debendranath.

Eliot, of course, was steeped in the *Upanishads*, just as, before him, Arnold was in the *Gita* (translated into English first by Charles Wilkins with the aid of Brahmin priests towards the close of the eighteenth century). More than Kant's notion of the aesthetic, it's perhaps the *Gita*'s impact on Arnold (which he alludes to in his description of the critic as yogi in 'The Function of Criticism in the Present Time') that resulted in his notion of the 'disinterested' work of criticism, as a species of the detached but passionate action described in Krishna's exhortation to Arjuna. The notion of a passionate detachment—of being at once visible in but absent from one's work—hops from the creative to the critical to the creative from the early nineteenth to the early twentieth century, moving once again to poetry with the *Upanishads*-loving Eliot, whose study of that text is only mentioned by scholars in connection with the closing lines of *The Waste Land*, but not in the way, as a young man, he conceives of 'personality' and its negation.

What I'm tracing here briefly is not the influence of the East on the West, or the latter's discovery of the former, or the East's rediscovery of itself through its discovery of the West, but 'patterns lit upon a screen', suggested by the terms 'impersonality', 'invisibility', and 'disinterestedness'—terms defining the competing domains of criticism and poetry—that open on to a lineage including the anonymous authors of Sanskrit texts, Anquetil-Duperron, Charles Wilkins, Raja Ram Mohun Roy, Debendranath and Rabindranath Tagore, Flaubert, Arnold, Eliot, and others. This is among the various lineages that inform the decisions I take in my writing, and of which I might become aware at any given moment.

Amit Chaudhuri
1 December 2017

* * *

I

The origins of dislike

After our marriage, my wife discovered it was risky accompanying me to art galleries. In the Louvre, in 1996, I kept up a relentless commentary as we passed from one room of great Western art to another, registering, in various degrees, my intolerance (unless we entered a non-Western room, or found we were among the post-Impressionists or the moderns). I wasn't playing the 'postcolonial' card—why should I, with my wife? Besides, that would have been clear in the delight I took in the post-Impressionists; though, even here, I had to interject and point out I'd never cared for Monet's water-lilies. No, I was expressing a deep, ingrained impatience—which is not to say that, simply because it was deep, it had no cultural context or historical ancestry—while taking advantage of the fact that my wife would be a cooperative victim or listener.

What was it about Western art that I recoiled from? In what capacity exactly had I generalized when I used the term 'Western'? In many ways, all I abhorred was contained in arguably the most important rooms in the Louvre—the ones exhibiting Renaissance painting and Greek sculpture. In order to have a proper feeling for and understanding of Western art, you had to walk around these rooms with a proprietary ease—or at least ostensible respect. You didn't skulk in them in a state of antagonism. Try as I might, though, I couldn't open up to a Rembrandt. Some part of me acknowledged this both as a deficiency on my part and as an unavoidable situation—that my upbringing may have ensured that I didn't have the intellectual background, or enough connectedness to that background, to prevent myself from seeing this tradition from the outside. The matter of being 'inside' or 'outside' a certain circle—let's call it the believers in and aficionados of the Renaissance for the moment—was subterranean but present; and, with it, the business of feeling included or excluded.

In the early years of the new millennium, I saw, in Amsterdam, paintings by contemporaries of Rembrandt that seemed to me more interesting than anything I'd encountered by the great man; they were portraits of burghers of the town. Each group portrait marked the emergence of both biographical narrative and the social as we've long understood them: that each life, in fruition of past achievements, and looking towards the future, came together in a static, rehearsed moment of sociability, in what D. H. Lawrence, in the more fluid context of the novel, had called 'subtle human interrelationship'. It was as an antecedent for a certain kind of novel that I found these Dutch portraits remarkable. I was also aware, as I gazed upon these pictures, that I was constructing the pre-history of the kind of novel I didn't really care for.

★

Should I provide instances of things in the museum I couldn't bring myself to admire? A list of dislikes always seems more feral, and less related to a rational cause, than a list of things you approve of. Anyway, on my list were Titian and Rubens, varieties of Renaissance oil painting, and the very texture of Greek and Renaissance sculpture: the fold of a pleated gown, the crease between the eyebrows, the muscles impressed on a stomach all set my teeth on edge. All careful marks on stone, and to what purpose? To capture and replicate life? To demonstrate such replication was achievable? When Lawrence said of Cezanne's apples that they were not 'true-to-life', but '*more* true to life',[1] he was speaking of an art that had escaped the Renaissance's bulging, three-dimensional quality. Yet this quality was, we'd been told when we were children, one of the pinnacles of Western art: the precision and individuality of the folds and pleats on a gown.

The moment we slipped into the rooms containing Mesopotamian sculpture, I experienced a sense of release—I was moved by this regal, alien notion of gracefulness. I was also reminded a bit of the Zoroastrian figures carved into the Parsi buildings in Bombay, which I'd noticed since I was a schoolboy, but never enquired after or properly understood. But subjective association couldn't fully explain my sense of recognition in the Mesopotamian room; because I'd never been properly aware that I *liked* the Zoroastrian figures. Then my wife and I went to the part of the gallery where the Russian art that preceded the Enlightenment was displayed; here, too, I felt I was in proximity to a world at once infinitely distant and known. Moving to the icons—those repetitive images of adoration—meant coming face to face with what I'd only encountered before in Tarkovsky's *Andrei Rublev*. Harold Bloom describes a condition, an anxiety, that the writer or artist is susceptible to, probably from Romanticism onward, and certainly until postmodernity, which he terms 'belatedness':[2] the writer's intuition (experienced as a crisis) that he—Bloom's examples are male—was born at the wrong moment in history, just after the masters who are formative to him, and in an environment in which he can't put his 'natural' gifts to use. (Although 'writing naturally', qua Keats, for whom poetry must come as 'naturally as leaves to a tree or not at all',[3] is considered part of the mythology of Romanticism, 'belatedness' reminds us that the Romantic poet had also fallen irretrievably from nature.) The context of Bloom's discussion, as we know, is principally Milton and the English Romantics; but 'belatedness' has many incarnations, some of them cultural rather than ontological. Seamus Heaney's crisis in the early 1980s, when he seemed, in effect, to believe that the free world couldn't produce poets of the stature of Miroslav Holub because it lacked East Europe's repressive political history, is an odd example of 'belatedness'. Adorno's commandment that writing poetry is impossible after Auschwitz is surely a species of belatedness, since it presumes there was a time, before that historical trauma occurred, when poetry was natural and spontaneously possible. In modern India, the conflation, from the nineteenth century onwards, of the use of the mother-tongue with creative authenticity is a version of belatedness; all would be well, according to this line of thought, with the canon of Indian Anglophone writing if only its practitioners returned to their own language. Some such yearning, and the awareness of being historical latecomers, must have informed the turn initiated by a few key writers in Bengal from the 1860s onward from English to Bengali. That this didn't banish belatedness becomes clear when we find the great poet of the age, Tagore, feeling as acutely belated as any writer previously had, and longing, despite himself, to be a contemporary of the fourth-century court poet Kalidasa.

Yet it wasn't belatedness I felt in the Louvre while confronting Titian on the one hand and the Russian icon on the other. It was the superannuation of certain civilizations, of certain forms of representation and viewing the world, that I found myself participating in, while rediscovering the extant reign and encompassing dominion of others. Closest to the inviolate hegemon were the rooms related to the Renaissance; while the Mesopotamian and Russian rooms gave us a chance to come into contact with styles and views that had, essentially, been vanquished or sidelined. And yet, making one's way to the civilization that reigned, you felt an incongruous deadness, while among the superannuated world-views there was a residue that corresponded to something still vital and alive in us. In such a way, imperceptible battle-lines were drawn across the museum, and to move from one part of it to another was also to travel from an area of imprisonment to that of freedom, and then back again, through a doorway, to the imprisoning; the sense of alternating, neighbourly entrapment and escape was literal and real. The visits to these zones determined the nature of my commentary to my wife, which changed from angry, heretical, muttered invectives into sudden, easy paeans of worship, and then, in another room, in another dominion, reverted to resentful slanders.

★

That my dislike of the Renaissance wasn't a solitary failing, or an entirely personal eccentricity—that there were great Renaissance-haters before me, like John Ruskin—didn't become clear to me until later. And it took me a while to understand that uncovering the origins of dislike can be instructive—not therapeutic, in the way that discovering the root of a neurosis can cure it, but helpful in comprehending fidelities and affiliations, and especially why, often, one doesn't adhere to the expected affiliations—the expected 'likes'—according to class, colour, education, and identity. How nice it would be to like the things one is supposed to; life would be so much more comfortable, so much calmer! Dislike, then, is potentially more disruptive and disorienting than ideology or taste. Partly this might be because, for the artist or writer, it's related to an emotional state that's constantly, strategically, evolving, and this emotional state is inextricable from an intellectual position that may not have wholly been brought to light, while the intellectual position can't be seen divorced from the most important consideration of all for an artist—the question of survival. The artist argues for the survival not of a species, or a race, or a class, but of a particular practice and lineage, as well as a specific interpretation of that practice; in the interests of this mission—survival—she or he might, of course, appear, at times, to conveniently will the destruction of art itself. The polemic against art is just one of the numerous strategies with which the artist attempts to gain the upper hand in the interests of *his* brand of art. Survival and power govern the continuum of art, but not just in the institutional, socialized, and discursive sense in which Foucault and Bourdieu understood such decision-making or governance. Dislike is essential to the artist's art, and his task, of survival as a particular kind of artist.

★

To experience dislike is also to experience sudden isolation. In, and from, that isolation germinate the strategies of the artist or writer, and his or her business of forming, even fabricating, not friendships or coteries, but alliances. An alliance is an extension of an argument; it is, often, two persons united in a dislike; it's the first gesture towards inventing a tradition, or a climate, or a lineage—or, if you like, an anti-tradition or anti-lineage. The first time I properly realized that there was another who viewed the Renaissance with scepticism was when I read John Berger's Benjaminesque *Ways of Seeing*; although the section that I was most struck by, the section on oil painting, is too polemical to recall Benjamin. Berger begins with some extraordinarily categorical statements: 'Oil paintings often depict things. Things which in reality are buyable. To have a thing painted and put on a canvas is not unlike buying it and putting it in your house.'[4] As Berger quickly points out, he's taking his cue from Claude Lévi-Strauss: 'It is this avid and ambitious desire to take possession of the object for the benefit of the owner or even the spectator which seems to me to constitute one of the outstandingly original features of the art of Western civilisation.'[5] How straight-faced is that 'outstandingly original'? At any rate, according to Berger, the urge to possess, to encompass, reaches its apogee with painting in oil. (The ambiguous literary term, 'to capture', is surely related to but also subversive of the 'avid and ambitious desire to take possession of the object', in that 'to capture' or evoke a world, in a poem or story, is also to suggest the impossibility of regaining it except obliquely, and through memory.) In Chapter 5, Berger riffs on Lévi-Strauss beautifully and abrasively: here he is, for instance, on three portraits of Mary Magdalene, from the sixteenth, seventeenth, and eighteenth centuries:

The point of her story is that she so loved Christ that she repented of her past and came to accept the mortality of flesh and the immortality of the soul. Yet the way the pictures are painted contradicts the essence of this story. It is as though the transformation of her life brought about by her repentance has not taken place. The method of painting is incapable of making the renunciation she is meant to have made. She is painted as being, before she is anything else, a takeable and desirable woman.[6]

Renunciation means withdrawal or abnegation, and Berger is using it here as an aesthetic term, to gesture to the painter's, or the painting's, inability to abnegate from, to renounce, the conventions of full-on, realist representation. Berger cites a couple of exceptions in the course of his demolition drive: William Blake and a good deal of landscape painting. His reason for this seems, in both cases, to have to do with tangibility. He praises Blake for doing 'everything he could to make his figures lose substance... to be present but intangible, to glow without a definable surface ... '.[7] Of landscape painting, he points out: 'The sky has no surface and is intangible; the sky cannot be turned into a thing or given a quantity. And landscape painting begins with the problem of painting sky and distance.'[8] That is, both Blake and some of the landscape painters grapple with material resistant to being turned into (in the value-laden, pejorative meaning Berger accords to that word) objects. And so, what appears simple and buoyant (a painting by Corot) or idiosyncratic and miraculous (a scene from Blake) also, in a sense, becomes resistant and unyielding (Berger's euphemism is 'intangible'); subtly, dislike transfers itself, and gives to luminosity in painting its moral, unassimilable quality. And just as rules are proven by exceptions, so too, apparently, is dislike shaped and defined by them. Even on the odd chance that you, like me, don't care for Renaissance art, there will always be one or two painters from that period you will admire. You might find yourself being drawn to Brueghel. You might consider the enigma of Vermeer, and why he appeals to you while Rembrandt doesn't—what is it that makes Vermeer escape the Renaissance ethos? You might covertly admire Giotto, because of the echo in his figures of a Byzantine formalism. In my case, the oil paintings that absorb me from the end of the period I've been referring to are from early nineteenth-century Bengal, the Chinsura oils depicting sacred and epic subjects painted by anonymous *patuas*. These works have little of the hyper-realism of a Titian or Rubens, a hyper-realism which tells us that the world is present for us in finite but irrefutable gradations of verisimilitude and colour. With the Chinsura oils, we have the paradox of attending to a created world that shines but is unfinished, is opulent but is in the process of being made. Some of these are owned today by Aveek Sarkar, but they are, metaphorically, on loan; their aesthetic and representational mode doesn't abide by the Renaissance principle of ownership, as defined by Lévi-Strauss and recited by Berger. When a writer such as myself, a disliker of oils, admits to *liking* a certain genre of oil painting from before the advent of Impressionism, he's making a critical statement, and hinting not so much at an accommodation as to an adjustment that changes the outward reaches of what he stubbornly is.

★

The writer's life, or the artist's, is not only punctuated by epiphanies and visitations. It's constituted of moments of recognition that are directly related to one's own practice, to the kind of practitioner one is, to the sort of practice that's anathema to one's temperament, and, arising from this, of a series of decisions such as the Bourdieuan analysis seldom addresses, deeming those decisions to belong to the realm of literary mythology. When I say 'temperament', I mean something different from both the old, now discredited, literary term 'sensibility' and from the dreamy 'artistic temperament'; I mean something that, at first at least, appears intractable and not entirely within the realm of the artist's conscious understanding or volition. After all, we can't be sure why certain artists or writers are drawn to miniaturism rather than to the epic, and why the latter upsets and agitates them; we don't know why certain writers tend towards historical narrative or fantasy rather than, say, realism. Temperament, which is not entirely governable, rather than sensibility, which can be cultivated, seems to hold the key; one can't help one's temperament, or shed it or acquire another one. The matter of temperament becomes crucial to understanding why one might be working in a style or mode that lacks prestige at a particular moment in literary history: for instance, one might be writing in the epic mode when the lyric is predominant, and the epic is out of favour. To write in the epic mode is, then, suicidal at that moment; yet what I've called 'temperament' dictates that one undertake a suicidal activity. Yet writing, and the philosophy of writing, tend not towards self-destruction but self-perpetuation; so the artist's temperament attempts to ensure that temperament's survival through a number of means. A purely Bourdieuan, sociological view of the literary 'field' would tell us that writers are drawn irresistibly to centres, publications, and genres of prestige; but this is not wholly true—indeed, much of literary history and debate comprises that 'not wholly'. There are writers who might actively, and perversely, dislike and militate against the genres of prestige of the day. How do we account for this antithetical, seemingly self-destructive urge? One explanation would be to invoke class, national, and political affiliations; that certain anomalous forms of narrative or representation are used by artists of a political minority or a colonized nationality in order to assail or overthrow forms predominantly used in the hegemony. This still doesn't tell us why many writers and artist distance themselves from forms and expressions that may be conflated at a certain point of history with their political, racial, or class identity, and cultivate forms that are, in these practitioners' own context, anomalous. Art and writing is, indeed, a field of battle, but battle is not really undertaken for the purposes of either identity or metropolitan prestige, but intentions that seem, on a first examination, unfathomable. Nevertheless, an inordinate amount of energy and strategy and a considerable marshalling of resources are devoted to this ongoing battle.

Strategic thinking for a writer articulates itself as dislike and as allegiance. So Philip Larkin, who began by being an apprentice to the style and language of W. B. Yeats, makes a conscious and exhibitionistic disavowal of Yeats the moment he finds his voice, and turns with great fanfare instead to Thomas Hardy. Poor Yeats gets similar treatment later from Seamus Heaney, who chooses Patrick Kavanagh as his forebear. In this matter of artistic allegiance, the student chooses his teacher—conferring teacherhood on the earlier figure as a sort of calculated gift—rather than the other way round. The forebear may well be a relatively marginal figure, as Kavanagh was in Ireland; as Henry Green, John Updike's chosen precursor, was in England; as Hardy the poet was in comparison to Yeats—the marginality accentuating the seemingly arbitrary and temperamental nature of the allegiance, but gesturing towards and raising other questions to do with writerly intention. The allegiance may set aside nationality—Green was English, Updike American; Dante Italian, his disciple T. S. Eliot Anglo-American—in a way that's barely noticeable but again hints at argumentations and strategies of survival beyond the first impression of arbitrariness.

Tagore's case—his low tolerance of Shakespeare; his choice of the Sanskrit poet Kalidasa as precursor—might make more sense on postcolonial and racial grounds. But it doesn't really: for Tagore turns to Kalidasa not for his obviously Oriental or Indian qualities, but for being a proto-modernist and realist, a poet of suggestion and of the concrete—all very modernist concerns—in a way that, he suggests, Shakespeare wasn't. In his simultaneous concern with the concrete, the momentary, and with tradition and strategic positioning (that is, *his* relationship to these things), Tagore emphatically becomes part of a larger fabric of modernist argumentation. Decades later, the Indian poet Arvind Krishna Mehrotra makes a similar move when, long after having read Pound, he observes that the poems he discovered in, and translated from, the ancient Prakrit, reminded him, in their economy, of Pound's Confucian analects. Mehrotra's not just making an analogy here, or tracing routes along an internationalist map of literature, but forging a rhetoric of survival, uncovering lines of contact to which he too is invisibly joined—escape routes, emergency pathways, often pursued or taken advantage of in the interests and compulsions of practice. In doing so, Mehrotra is also making adjustments to the linearity of history, to the familiar story of cause and effect, to the paths and routes via which we're supposed to arrive at the contemporary.

Sometimes, a writer might identify a single precursor with disparagement on the one hand, and an acknowledgement of partnership on the other. This might well have to do with the writer's own troubled and contradictory position in relation to a tradition or practice he represents, and may even have helped shape. I have in mind Pound's dislike and adoration of Whitman: 'I have detested you long enough . . . ' he begins in 'A Pact', concluding a few lines later, ' . . . we have one sap and one root'.[9] Whitman might well be Anglophone modernist poetry's great secret, testing its limits in his open display of carnality and *joie de vivre* and his blithe lack of belatedness. There's a metaphysical, hieratic, ironic side to Pound that 'detests' the older poet; there's a physical, worldly, and exhibitionistic side that sees him as a partner. Pound's turbulent relationship with Whitman reminds us of the former's peculiar, contradictory location in modernism: as one of its high priests, but also as one of its delighters, a propagator of the image, and, via the image, an advocate of the worldly and the luminous. 'Those who know aren't up to those who love; nor those who love, to those who delight in,'[10] he remarks, translating Confucius. But it's a conviction he derives, I think, from Whitman, and it introduces an all-important element of spaciousness to modernism's apparent existential despondency. All these modulations are the compulsions of temperament, and they create literary culture as we know it.

Another instance occurs to me, this time of an unexpected case of liking rather than disliking: F. R. Leavis's odd championing of D. H. Lawrence. What compulsion draws an exemplar of the literary like

Leavis towards a dishabille outsider (and admirer of Whitman) like Lawrence? It's an intriguing move, and forces us to rethink how we often make synonymous, disdainfully, a certain idea of Leavis and a certain idea of literature. It's intriguing, too, that Leavis should identify (correctly) the significance of one of Lawrence's most revealing, and on the whole forgotten, expressions of dislike—his review of Thomas Mann's *Death in Venice*. For Lawrence, writing in 1918, Mann is the 'last sick progeny of Flaubert', and his novella an incarnation of 'Flaubertian control' and 'will-to-power'.[11] Leavis's crucial defence and reconstruction of this increasingly angular, anti-literary Lawrence points to a surprising complexity in his missionary, 'high' literary Englishness.

The examples I've cited are meant only as a reminder that an artist has no innocent likes or dislikes; that his or her decisions and choices regarding the dead and living are governed by the question of self-interest and self-preservation, where the self and its well-being and life are inextricable from a particular interpretation of a craft, and, crucially, vice versa. What's at stake is not just Bourdieuan metropolitan prestige or Foucauldian power, but a network of escape routes that are often taken advantage of in the interests of the perpetuation of a lineage or, in Berger's words, 'ways of seeing'. The poem is a provisional space, like the room of Mesopotamian sculpture in the Louvre, where some lines of contacts and affinities converge while others are left behind. These cat and mouse feints, these moments of recognition, these peripatetic wandering movements from room to room can't be contained or traced in linear, or canonical, or national histories; these connections are made laterally, or sideways, often with no regard for what came first and what later, for what's native and what foreign. To the person gripped by strategic likes and dislikes, the Russian icon might seem new, the Titian old-fashioned, just as Pound's Confucian analects and the Prakrit love poems might appear contemporaneous.

★

This brings me back to where I started, to the Renaissance painting. 'Avid' and 'ambitious' are the adjectives Lévi-Strauss uses in relation to Western art, and to its 'desire to take possession of the object for the benefit of the owner or even the spectator'.[12] While talking about a kind of art, he's gesturing, coterminously, towards a particular narrative of history that Walter Benjamin named 'historicism': a linear account of development, of the 'onward march of progress',[13] so definitive to

Western man from the Renaissance and certainly the nineteenth century onward. The Renaissance painting—which, admittedly, I'm using as much as a generalized bogey as Berger did—is a virtuoso performance: it possesses, replicates, manufactures, and perfects reality. In playing this bravura role, it presupposes a story of progress, by making possible what was previously impossible: the perfect reproduction of reality. In this feat, and in its historicist assumption—that the closer you get to reproducing reality, the more 'advanced' you are—it's the moral precursor of cloning. The so-called 'developed societies' are close to the Renaissance painting in another way: they not only perfect reality, they possess and embody it. Other societies are not only less 'developed'; they're also, consequently, somehow less real. The whole business of 'possessing', in Renaissance art, has not just to do with acquisition and desire, but perfectibility or development, using what the twentieth century called 'technology'—a secret, albeit transferrable, instrument essential to this miracle: development; reproducing the real. The 'real', especially as 'realism', is a key feature of the modern, the developed; it's a crucial component in progress. The arrival of perspective in Western art—the opening up not of space but of a new means of capturing and mimicking it—is a significant ingredient in the historicist story, and spoken of as a great stride forward in the story of art. So is, more recently—though we may scorn it—a technological advance like 3D, which takes the Renaissance image literally one step further, or outward. This is true, too, of 'special effects', which has been bringing, for several decades now, imagined universes to our doorstep, replete with historicism, presenting us not only with extraordinary futures, but a well-rounded simulacrum. At the heart of historicism lies our approach to the 'real'—the real being marked by completeness and, tautologically, by veracity. As Berger points out, the things in Renaissance painting—even, or perhaps especially, in the mythological scenes—look very real, and they do so by being ripe and heavy. The same's true of 'special effects'; that, paradoxically, objects appear more real in entirely fantastic and futuristic domains. Completeness and veracity are the end of development; memory may be smudged and unclear, but objects situated in the future of historicist time must especially draw attention to their life-like qualities.

This species of historicism not only pervades the Renaissance and the visual field, but informs literary and generic considerations. Reality, in the realist novel or film, is an accumulation, an addition, of pertinent fact, information, and detail; the novel, as a genre, most symbolizes this accumulation, completeness, and development. The short story, in Anglophone culture, and certainly in British culture today, is described in historicist terms, as a backward version of, and a stepping-stone to graduating towards, the novel. I'm not sure how this relates to non-Anglophone cultures of the written word. One can only throw up possibilities. Would Colette have been the national treasure she is in France had she been an English writer living in England? To an observer on the outside, Junichiro Tanizaki's short tales don't appear to carry less weight, metaphorically, in Japan than does his compendious novel, *The Makioka Sisters*. In an Anglophone literary culture, Tanizaki's novella, 'Portrait of Shunkin', would automatically be considered a minor achievement, and *The Makioka Sisters* his major work. 'Major' and 'minor' are historicist terms in Anglophone literary criticism, inadvertent euphemisms for developed and less developed. On first thought, I find it hard to arrive at words that have exactly the same meaning in Bengali literary language, where importance might be identified not only with achievement, but with amplification and completeness. Does this influential version of historicism, then, have less of an absolute hold on the world of the modern Indian languages, in, say, Kannada or Urdu, just as it may exercise less authority in Japanese or French? Would it be rash to suggest that an absence, in these cases, of a hierarchy between longer and shorter forms seems to have created, in the late nineteenth and twentieth centuries, literatures that had an ambiguous relationship with the ethos of nationalism?

*

Modernism has a curious relationship to historicism. On the one hand, by cherishing the fragment, by refuting totality, it dismantles the presuppositions of development. In doing so, it doesn't, crucially, look with nostalgia, at least in its aesthetic, to a past that's lost but organically whole—a sort of inversion of historicism. In its fascination with ruins and derelict objects, it makes the past constitute the present with an incongruous immediacy, the immediacy of decay; it robs linearity of its momentum. Modernism's relationship to the real—contained in a language of images and fragments—is idiosyncratic and fundamental, but not cumulative; as a consequence, it's the opposite of developmental. As a part of Western literary history, though, modernism is triumphantly appropriated by the historicism that its aesthetic rejects: it's viewed exclusively by its propagandists in terms of newness, vanguardism, and breakthroughs. There's hardly a popular critical language of modernism that emerges from the anti-historicism its artistic departures embrace.

Two critical interjections, one from within the heart of modernism, the other from the cusp of a succeeding epoch, are worth mentioning very briefly here. The first comes from Virginia Woolf's essay, 'Mr Bennett and Mrs Brown'. Alongside her famously exasperated observation about 'this appalling narrative business of the realist: getting on from lunch to dinner',[14] this essay attacks the cumulative and enumerative in the novels of Arnold Bennett and much realist writing, rejecting it as a means of arriving at the 'truth' about character and setting. Her piece itself is about sitting in a train compartment with a lady she names 'Mrs Brown', about whom she realizes that no amount of information provided about Mrs Brown's life and milieu is going to enable Woolf to imaginatively create her character. As an essay, Woolf's piece perfectly exemplifies modernism's vocabulary of a thrilled historicism—it begins with the remark, 'On or about December *1910* human character *changed*'—as well as its deep anti-historicist, anti-developmental agitation, its revolt against the sort of attempts to possess reality that, for her, Bennett's work represents, attempts that are among the Renaissance's legacies.

The other interjection I'm referring to is from Roland Barthes's *Writing Degree Zero*. Barthes reminds us, as he reflects on the genre of the novel, of its use of the *passé simple*, or the simple past tense or preterite: 'Its function is no longer that of a tense. The part it plays is to reduce reality to a point of time, and to abstract, from the depth of a multiplicity of experiences, a pure verbal act...'.[15] In other words, the simple past tense achieves in narrative what the representation of a scene does in Renaissance painting: an apogee or culmination, a transcendence of process. 'This is why,' says Barthes, 'it [the simple past tense] is the ideal instrument for every construction of a world; it is the unreal time of cosmogonies, myths, History and Novels.' Barthes's 'unreal time of...History and Novels' echoes Benjamin's 'homogeneous, empty time of history', in which the onward march of progress occurs, which we now see is also the time of the novel. 'When the historian,' says Barthes, 'states that the duc de Guise died on December 23rd, 1588, or when the novelist relates that the Marchioness went out at five o' clock, such actions emerge from a past without substance; purged of the uncertainty of existence...'[16] The other way of purging time, space, and history of that 'uncertainty' is, as in the Renaissance artwork, to replace time and space with finished objects you can literally possess in lieu of reality. In both cases—the simple past tense and the oil painting—we're talking of a mode of development that completes historical time.

★

It's possible that my feelings of dislike in the Louvre have something to do with an inchoate prejudice against historicism. It's historicism, with its message of progress and perfection, that I perhaps secretly feel I confront when I view the pleated garment in sculpture; and escape it when I move towards the stately Mesopotamian figures. Understanding the origin doesn't cure the dislike; it just brings it out into the open.

There are many reasons why a writer might make one kind of allegiance, or experience a particular sort of dislike, rather than another; however, in this context, I'm mainly interested, as I've already stated, in the artist's relationship with, and understanding of, the historical. Again, there could plausibly be several reasons as to why artists or writers treat the business of historical representation in different ways; for my purposes, I'm going to throw up some notions regarding this question that have to do with a cultural milieu's relationship with its historical inheritance.

Here, I'll take the liberty of moving into a series of speculations. It appears to me that the world of the Anglophone middle class, the Indian middle class included, is particularly informed by historicism in the way it relates to, and imagines, the past. Let me, after having made this vast generalization, mention two writers in passing. The first, William Dalrymple, is a product of British society while at once being an honorary Indian, or at the very least an honorary Delhiite. I much admire his writing for its elegance, shrewdness of judgement, and humour; still, I'm also interested in some of the narrative devices he uses when writing popular history, a genre of which he's a robust proponent. Occasionally, you notice Dalrymple catch the mood of historicism, which is so seductively present in both the British and Indian view of the past, and which has had a resurgence in narrative histories and Anglophone historical novels. In *The Last Mughal*, Dalrymple comes up repeatedly, deliberately, with the simple past tense (interspersed, in a way that doesn't disrupt his aims, with the past imperfect) in a crucial chapter, when he's describing the coming of dawn on the day of the

Sepoy Mutiny. So, 'The British were the first up: in the cantonments to the north of the Delhi Civil Lines, the bugle sounded at 3.30 am etc';[17] also, 'Two hours later, by the time the sun was beginning to rise over the Yamuna, and the poets, the courtesans, and the patrons were all heading back to bed'; and again, 'As the cantonment memsahibs awaited the return of their menfolk from the parade ground . . . '; moreover, 'As the sun rose, and as the British were returning from their morning rides and preparing for breakfast . . . '; finally, 'At the Raj Ghat Gate, the earlier-rising Hindu faithful . . . '. Did all this happen that day in 1857? Dalrymple would claim it's in the archive, and that, through his labours and his imagination, he's pieced together the doomed picture like a jigsaw puzzle. Yet what gives the account its air of having happened is the preterite, which locks the past as history. The past tense also gives to the chapter its fictionality, its air of inhabiting what Barthes called the 'unreal time of cosmogonies, myths, History and Novels', of narratives that suppress the 'uncertainty of existence' by beginning with statements like 'The Marchioness went out at five o' clock'. Dalrymple, even while using this tested method, tries to undermine that unreality through calculated repetition and incantation, whereby he senses, perhaps, that the simple past tense will lose its reliability. And yet the past tense can't help but imply: 'This is what happened'; and, moreover, 'The past is out there to be pieced together again.' This is what another writer, the novelist Amitav Ghosh, also assumes when he reveals to us how he researches every aspect of his historical novels: of how he will climb aboard the actual counterpart of a ship he's writing about, or put together, through his research, piece by piece, a horse-drawn carriage from the nineteenth century. It's as if the past is not only an entity that can be revisited, but, with adequate groundwork, possessed.

This leads me to dwell on a particular interpretation, and the recent prestige, of the word 'research' in India. Its significance in the domain of science is well known, as is the narrative it plays a role in: a scientist amasses material, hypotheses, and evidence to do with immunology or malaria, and comes up with findings. This, at least, is the lay understanding of scientific research, one that scientists haven't done much to dispute. Since the context and infrastructure for such output needs constant abetment and funding, it's right that, say, organizations like the Infosys foundation, with its grants and prizes, should be involved in funding and encouragement. Not long ago, the foundation introduced prizes for the social sciences (though it had no separate prize for history till 2012). After all, the social sciences are an important body of knowledge, and they emerge from research: archival material; fieldwork. Of course, the social sciences and history are generally—but especially in India—seen not only to be dependent on research, but legitimized by it. In this, we are children of the European Renaissance—research verifies and reproduces reality; 'thinking' is an imponderable, and in some ways closer to the 'imagination'. For instance, I once noticed that some readers view Dipesh Chakrabarty's *Provincializing Europe* with wariness, as it explores a thought-process instead of bearing the unmistakable imprimatur of archival labour. Which brings me to fiction. With the conflation, in some circles, of the Indian novel in English with a particular sort of historical novel, it isn't unusual to encounter Indian readers who praise such-and-such novelist because they 'do a lot of research'. The remark expresses a familiar sense of relief, as well as the triumphal faith our educated Anglophone classes have in the rationally verifiable. Research authenticates the novel's putative ambition of representing reality—of embodying the evolution from archival forays to fictionalization, which sometimes becomes indistinguishable from reconstruction. Indians who clearly haven't read my work sometimes ask me (as I'm a novelist): 'You must do a lot of research.' I've pondered on this query, and what I've begun to say to them is this: that I 'do research' all the time, but not for specific books or projects. That is, the imagination—at least my imagination—doesn't seem to follow the model of scientific work, from premise to fieldwork to hypothesis to published findings.

What makes one believe that the past is out there, waiting to be joined together in its various elements? Partly, it's do with a vantage-point which allows one to look back on history from a distance, as a spectator. To be such a spectator, one must be on the right side of history, and have moved on from the past one is looking at, sharing little complicity with it. The past doesn't, in other words, impinge on the historicist imagination through shame or guilt; and this lack of impingement is essential to viewing the past clearly, and putting it together into a whole. Indian middle-class self-consciousness (although, or perhaps because, it makes much of colonization, subjecthood, and indigenous elites) is, I sense, relatively free of guilt about history. It won't address complicity or aesthetic self-contradiction: that, for example, it may be drawn to something on a sensory or imaginative level which it morally disapproves of entirely. One reason for this may be (and, again, I freely speculate) that the Indian liberal bourgeoisie in India made a clean break with *sati*, making it, thankfully, an intellectual and emotional taboo that couldn't be engaged with on any level, but also, as a consequence, distancing itself from its own 'otherness'. *Sati* belongs to the past—a disgraceful past, no doubt, but one that has no power to impinge any more on the historicist consciousness of the Indian liberal. I might hazard a guess and say the same might be true of our relationship with the caste system: that it may well be a burdensome, even traumatic, political reality, but (to use a catchword reclaimed by Žižek) our superego has thoroughly (and correctly) disowned it; it's an inadmissible, if terrible, aspect of our tradition. And so, I think, the past fails to really encroach upon, to compromise, or to taint the liberal bourgeoisie in India, because it is behind us—especially the Anglophone bourgeoisie, for whom the break is most effective and clear-cut. In spite of having once been colonized, despite living in a context of profound inequity, and despite violence in Kashmir and Gujarat, the liberal Anglophone Indian feels relatively little anxiety about being on the wrong side of history. He or she might feel exercised, angry, or outraged about various things, but always from the distance that historicism provides, which allows these problems to exist outside oneself without in any way entering or issuing from the self that is outraged. When representing these problems in narrative or visual terms, in fiction or cinema, the lack of implicatedness allows the creators of those novels and films to stand back and view, or reconstruct, the landscape or event in its fullness. And while historicism gives the viewer a kind of distance, it also gives her or him a sense of ownership: that the past can be not only reconstructed, but laid claim to, as 'our' heritage or tradition. *Sati* and its defeat at the hands of the nationalist reformers is an episode in the history we own. Historicism ensures that an unbroken line leads up from the past to ourselves; history isn't foreign—it is, in a sense (like the objects or figures in the Renaissance painting were for the man who owned it), our property.

★

I've always been moved by the historical imagination in artists who represent an aberration rather than the norm. I'm thinking of the Russian filmmaker Andrey Tarkovsky, as well as a few twentieth-century Japanese writers and filmmakers. I'm no expert on film, Russia, or Japan, but I'm going to pursue this curious feeling of affinity a bit longer.

Tarkovsky is extraordinary in his distinctive approach to Russian history. This is in evidence in almost all his films, particularly in *Andrei Rublev*, his reimagining of the eponymous fourteenth-century icon-maker's life and times. The film is divided into black and white sections. There's a hint of colour at the beginning, and there are several minutes of colour at the very end, when we're shown the actual icons by the painter—strange pictures, if we're judging them through the conventions of classic Western paintings; as strange, in their way, as the Russia depicted in the film. In the course of the film's considerable duration, we realize that Rublev's Russia isn't quite Europe; its religion is partly witchcraft and mystic superstition; its politics is barbaric conquest; and it is within this context that its Christianity exists. However, this landscape is not a less evolved and, therefore, recognizable stage in the European telos; its violence and magic aren't those depicted in films like *Troy*, where the action is detailed in a burnished way, in a manner that permits us to spectate on those cruelties and heroic feats from this side of history. Tarkovsky's Russia is essentially foreign, foreign even to the notion of the historical, more 'third world' than 'Europe', and will not be contained by soothing terms like 'early modern', 'medieval', or 'historical'; Tarkovsky might study it, but, crucially, he can't lay claim to it. When I think of the Russia in *Andrei Rublev*, I'm reminded of what the East German playwright Heiner Mueller once said in an interview: 'We in the Eastern Bloc have a great Third World in our midst.'[18]

It's clear to anyone who knows Tarkovsky's oeuvre that he believed himself to be an inheritor of 'high' European culture. His films are populated with references to Western painting, and these references surface in the unlikeliest of locations—in a spaceship in *Solaris*, in an apartment in *Mirror*, the reproduction of the painting glimpsed briefly within the covers of a book. Tarkovsky's younger contemporary Aleksandr Sokurov's *Russian Ark* (filmed in a single shot in the Winter Palace of the State Hermitage Museum in St Petersburg) is a record of some of the great treasures of Western art while also incorporating enactments of scenes from Russian political history; yet *Russian Ark* could also be seen as a homage to the European métier of Tarkovsky's work. For all that, I think that Tarkovsky, upon encountering Rublev's icons—sacred pictures with repetitive outlines and stylized expressions, remarkable for their abstention from inwardness (which suffuses paintings after the Renaissance like water does wet cloth)—I believe that, on studying these icons, Tarkovsky was faced with a dilemma. He'd have been made aware that to be a Russian and to be a European are not coterminous. There's no easy passage or bridge connecting the icon to Renaissance 'high' art; even to move from one room to the other in the Louvre is to traverse a great change. To be Russian, *Andrei Rublev* instructs us, is to be 'other': a source, perhaps, of both shame and wonder. And, we realize, there's no unbroken line from medieval Russia to the Renaissance to the present historical moment which Tarkovsky occupies doubly as a great Russian and European artist; the disjunction represented by those strange icons can't be soothingly transformed into an inheritance. Tarkovsky himself responds, in the film, disjunctively, angularly, very differently from how a Renaissance painter would. Of course, the moment I've just described, of Tarkovsky confronting the icons, of coming to terms with the fact that the historical past isn't out there to be accessed in a straightforward fashion, is pure speculation, even fiction.

Perhaps I've taken the liberty of making up this piece of fiction about Tarkovsky because of an experience I had a few years ago near Bhubaneswar, when I went, accompanied by my wife and daughter, to the Sun Temple at Konark, once in ruins and then resurrected by native and colonial archaeologists. A prurient guide, ignoring my family, showed me the multiplicity of erotic sculpture occupying almost every inch of the temples, on ground level and at impossible heights—of couples copulating, and participating in an unbelievably fecund array of positions. I was filled with wonder—at the exuberance of these figures, yes, but, even more powerfully, at a culture and tradition that was fundamentally foreign. I realized I didn't know my ancestors, and also that they *weren't*, in a sense, my ancestors; and I thought I understood what Tarkovsky had felt upon viewing those icons. The wonder I felt, then, was quite different from the excitement of the popular historian or historical novelist as they piece together the past. Who were these people, having sex indefatigably, carved into stone? Were they my heritage? They seemed to be telling me something. It was a time when the Hindu right-wing was vandalizing contemporary works of art that depicted religious figures in an erotic way; M. F. Husain was under attack. The liberal intelligentsia, as a result, was invoking the sexually liberated, even profligate, antiquity of Hinduism as its inheritance, as if an unbroken path stretched from the past to the present. In Konark, though, I experienced not recognition but strangeness. Whatever the sculptures were telling me couldn't be translated into a past-to-present-to-future story.

★

What could the sculptures or icons be saying? Tagore, too, had trouble with decipherment. Obsessed with Kaildasa and the fourth century AD, he, in a poem called 'Dream', speaks of himself as one who 'once went to find / my first love / from a previous life' in a 'dream-world, in the city of Ujjain, by the River Shipra'. Finding her leads to a breakdown in communication: 'I looked at her face, / tried to speak, / but found no words. / That language was lost to me . . . '.[19] Of course, Tagore was especially interested, for reasons of affinity, and from visceral biases and prejudices to do with survival strategy, in claiming Kalidasa as both his precursor and his contemporary—rejecting, in the process, his immediate predecessor, Madhusudan Dutt, and the earlier Bengali poets, Chandidas and Vidyapati, of whose work he'd composed an enthusiastic pastiche when he was fifteen. But reading Kalidasa also tells Tagore that Kalidasa can't be possessed; that's why '*Meghdut*', Tagore's poem about Kaidasa's long poem-sequence *Meghadutam*, describes a world coming to life as he reads—'In a gloomy room I sit alone / And read the *Meghaduta* . . . / There is the Amrakuta Mountain, / There is the clear and slender Reva river, / Tumbling over stones in the Vindhya foothills . . . '[20]—and also notes, by the time he's finished both poems (the one he's reading and the one he's writing), that history will not become full and present, but will diminish and withdraw: 'The vision goes . . . I watch / the rain again / Pouring steadily all around'.[21] Tagore's affinities with Kalidasa's craft make him approach him in a way that's recuperative and proprietary; but he's aware that Kalidasa resists being appropriated—in his essay on the court poet, he points out that 'we are banished from that India', from the 'slow, measured mandrakanta metre of the *Meghadutam*', 'not just during the rains but for all time'.[22] Nothing as reassuring as colonization creates this disjunction. Tagore knows it comes from his contradictory instincts as a modern as he views the physical object (the Amrakuta and Ramagiri mountains) or Kalidasa; it is, in a way, similar to Woolf's anxiety as she faces Mrs Brown in the train compartment—that details and traits taken incrementally won't add up to a time or 'character'. Tagore's poem is probably the first literary work anywhere that expresses an aesthetic of the historical imagination that states history can be felt most powerfully only in its resistance to appropriation. In this, it's different from the narrative histories in verse written in Bengal in the nineteenth century—indeed, from his own verse narratives about history—and from romantic assessments of the ruins of the past, such as Derozio's; distinct, too, from earlier poems by Hölderlin about the departure of the gods, or from Matthew Arnold's 'Stanzas from the Grande Chartreuse', about travelling between two worlds. Tagore's temperament sees to it that the tone of the Bengal Renaissance is—not in a nationalistic or postcolonial way, but in a manner that articulates itself through dislike—counter to the ethos of the Italian Renaissance, with its hyper-production of the real and its great monuments. It's no paradox that, within the counter-naturalistic mood of this later Renaissance, one of its principal artists, Binode Behari Mukherjee, should paint in a state of semi-blindness or blindness, and go to Indian history taking not Renaissance painting as his model, but, among his various sources, images that were already irretrievably fading: the frescoes of Ajanta. As for Tagore, his unease with aesthetic appropriation, as expressed in his writings on Kalidasa, must explain in part his disquiet with and strategic disavowals and, indeed, dislike of nationalism from the 1890s onward. This incongruous dislike put him, Tagore would have known, on the wrong side of history.

*

Being on the wrong side of history is what gives to certain Japanese writers and filmmakers their anomalous aesthetic—an aesthetic of prevarication, and one that brings together pastiche and the poetic image. The Anglophone historical novel, emerging from traditions that have a more robust investment in development, is, in contrast, a different sort of beast. The reasons, in twentieth-century Japan, for national embarrassment were clear. Firstly, in the context of growing modernity and so-called Westernization in the early twentieth century, there was the imaginative ambivalence towards the samurai code and the scandal of ritual suicide—represented in films and books as tragic and heroic, but with a suggestive light and shade that's unknown to the historicist imagination, and the way in which it burnishes the past as it represents it. Again, in keeping with the speculative manner of the rest of this talk, I speculate here and guess that there was no clean break in Japan in relation to its samurai code as there was in India with regard to *sati*. The other reason has to do, of course, with the world-view that led to the Second World War, and subsequent defeat. Both facts may be pertinent to a literature and an art that lack, in their versions of history or myth, the gleaming objects viewed from a historicist distance, as well as the 'unreal time' established by the simple past tense. Kurosawa's *Rashomon*, for example, is a story from the past narrated from three perspectives that, like the icons in Tarkovsky's film, confront us but won't address us directly, coming to us, instead, from multiple, confusing directions. The frame, in the film, is not just the narrative voice, but rain—it's raining as the story is told three times. The viewer of the film, as at the end of Tagore's '*Meghdut*', watches, at the close of each episode, 'the rain again / Pouring steadily all around'.[23] Rain is the element into which the narrative's historicity vanishes. Each time we return to the present, when it's raining, we see that no one version has veracity, and that we've been impeded from possessing the past.

Examples must abound in Japanese writing of this aesthetic—where history becomes palpable only in its resistance—but I'm particularly struck by three. Two of these are stories by Junichiro Tanizaki. 'Portrait of Shunkin'[24] is, as the title indicates, a portrait, though hardly a Renaissance-type one, of an imperious and cruel musician from the end of the Meiji era in the late nineteenth century. The narrator's sources are a bland guidebook-like biography—a pastiche—and a possibly apocryphal and unreliable piecing together of the story of Shunkin's principal student, Sasuke, who also, later, became her husband. Sasuke's devotion to his teacher-wife extends to the fact that he evidently blinds himself after *she* goes blind from an infection. The narrative is light and dark; the one remaining visual representation of Shunkin is a faded, indiscernible photo. Some kind of shame or disgrace is being concealed by the narrator's evasive account of things, his bogus allusions to the biography, and his anxiousness to appease. All the while, an impulse opposite to the possessive urge of the Renaissance painting as described by Berger is at work here; indeed, it's a destructive urge, as exemplified, in the arts, by the fragment, but, here, not only narrated but, in the act of self-blinding, disturbingly reified.

Tanizaki's 'Bridge of Dreams'[25] is a tale told by a young man who's having an incestuous relationship with his stepmother, whom his father married after the young man's mother died. The relationship began alarmingly early; at the teat, as it were. At times, the narrator can't recall at which point the stepmother entered the family and merged with his true mother. The era the story is set in is invoked by judicious allusions to poems, to the crafts of the time, and calligraphy. But neither the narrator, nor the foundation of his existence, the mother-figure, will speak to us plainly about what's happening. With two mothers, one adored but dimly remembered, the other desired but enigmatic, the narrator loses his ability to lay claim to where he emerges from: it's impossible for him to own his origins. It's in this impossibility that the troubled past pulsates most in Tanizaki's story. Meanwhile, a source of shame (probably incest) is being constantly hinted at and elegantly glossed over. This source, like the proximity of the stepmother's body, actively impinges upon the narrative distance essential to historicism's clear view of heritage.

My final example comes not from Japan, but from a British writer of Japanese origin, Kazuo Ishiguro. In his second novel, and his best one, *An Artist of the Floating World*, Ishiguro is still dealing with Japanese subject-matter, and, while doing so, undermining the reassurance of the preterite, and bringing a rare note of uncertainty to the English 'period' novel. The novel assumes the form of a memoir; yet it's the perfect example of the novel of prevarication. The novel of prevarication (Richard Ford's *The Sportswriter* is another example) is different from the novel of irony: the ironicist says one thing and believes another; the prevaricator not only wants you to believe his account is true, he's keen to believe in its truth himself. Partly this is because the prevaricator wishes to *forget* the real truth, whatever that may be. The ironicist is economical, because he or she is out to imply a great deal; the prevaricator is loquacious, because he has much to conceal. The prevaricator is on the wrong side of history; no comfortingly unbroken line stretches back from him and his utterances to his cultural past or identity. History, because of the narrator's complicity in its shame, can't be viewed, in the narrative of prevarication, from a distance, in cumulative detail—in Ishiguro's novel, the evasive narrator, an old man, was a famous artist favoured by the emperor before the war. Now, after the war, we learn—from unintended slips in his story—that he's in disgrace, and lives in relative isolation, except when he's being an indulgent grandfather. He's mainly unwanted by his former students, who sometimes pretend not to see him when they pass him on the street. Ishiguro's first-person narrative's primary fictions are self-belief and bogus cheerfulness, both of which—self-belief and cheerfulness—the narrator lacks. In order to conceal complicity, a new sort of space and movement comes into play, circular, prevaricatory, which is not available to the historicist novel, with its onward movement and its conviction that history is always 'out there' in the archive, waiting to be reclaimed. The novel starts, 'If on a sunny day you climb up the steep path leading up from the little wooden bridge still referred to around here as "the Bridge of Hesitation", you will not have to walk long before the roof of my house becomes visible between the top of two gingko trees.'[26] The future conditional tense plunges the reader into a hypothetical situation far from the 'unreal time' of the preterite—and it ramifies, in the novel, into an account that's disquietingly puzzling.

2009–10

* * *

2

The piazza and the car park

It was 1989. I was a graduate student at Oxford. I had made little progress with my doctoral dissertation and I had written a novel that had almost, but not quite, found a publisher. One of the routes that had taken me, in my fiction, towards Calcutta was Irish literature—its provincialism and cosmopolitanism, its eccentricity and refinement. So I was pleased when I heard that Seamus Heaney was the likeliest candidate to win the elections for the Oxford Professorship of Poetry. Paul Muldoon's anthology, *The Faber Book of Contemporary Irish Poetry*, had reintroduced Heaney to me: the magical early poems about the transformative odd-jobs men of a prehistoric economy—'diviners' and 'thatchers'; the features of that economy: wells and anvils; the Dantesque political cosmology (Heaney's overt response to the 'troubles') of *Station Island*.

A diversion was caused by the nomination of the Rastafarian performance and dub poet Benjamin Zephaniah. It was a strategically absurd nomination, made in the political tradition that periodically produces a fringe contender from the Monster Raving Loony Party to clear the air. Meanwhile, Heaney himself had begun subtly to remake himself as a postcolonial poet since *Wintering Out* and particularly *North*. By 'postcolonial' I mean a particular allegorical aesthetic to do with power, Empire, violence, and empowerment: an allegory that, in Heaney's case, had seen him scrutinizing, since 1971, Iron Age John Does buried for centuries in the peat and Tollund men who had once been the victims of state violence; it now also involved the glamour his words imparted to bottomless bogs and to Celtic orality. There was a hint of magic realism to *North*'s politics and poetics. In retrospect, I realize this reinvention on Heaney's part was making me uneasy.

Naturally, Heaney won by a wide margin. The poet's lectures were thronged with students and Heaney's performances often had the dazzling quality of brilliant undergraduate papers. There was another narrative unfolding in these lectures, though, which would become clearer when they were collected in *The Redress of Poetry*, some of these thoughts having already been rehearsed in *The Government of the Tongue*. It had to do with Heaney's exploration of artistic delight alongside his increasing disquiet about, and premonition of, the emptiness of the poet's life in liberal democracies. Against this he had begun to counterpoise, more and more, the exemplary pressure that East European poets experienced under punitive, totalitarian regimes. Those regimes seemed to become a kind of inverse pastoral for Heaney: enclosed, isolated, and capable, paradoxically, of producing the great artists that the West no longer did. Was Heaney at a dead end? Had he been made less creative somehow, or less powerful—not only by success, but by the collapse of those regimes that had unwittingly legitimized what for him was the only great poetry being written at that time: regimes that, one by one, began to fall almost immediately after he took up the Professorship?

A decade is a long time in the life of a culture, and much changed during the 1980s. But arguably far more changed—unthinkably—between 1989 and 1993. The American writer Benjamin Kunkel said in an interview published in 2014:

> I'm now old enough to remember when the Cold War just seemed like a permanent geological feature of the world. And then it just vanished. Then people would talk about how Japan was going to be a wealthier economy than the United States in 10 years. It would have seemed totally insane that there was going to be a black president and that gay people were going to get married.[1]

Kunkel is telling us how difficult it was, and always is, to predict the outcomes that we now take so for granted that we no longer think about them; no longer, experientially, perceive a discontinuity. But perhaps he's also telling us how hard it is to remember—actually to feel the veracity of a time when it would have seemed 'insane' to make those predictions. The imminence of a changed world order and the ignorance of that imminence are only two features of that world to which Kunkel is referring—for that world also had an infinity of other features whose reality it is now almost impossible to recollect. In order to remember, we need to rely on a species of voluntary memory, that is, a willed remembering whose consequences are largely predetermined by the conceptual structures of the present; so we are led to recall large categories, but not what it would have meant to inhabit them. Kunkel is trying to imply the lived immediacy of inhabiting a moral order by one of the ways through which we can move beyond voluntary memory—by gesturing towards the unthinkable: 'It would have seemed totally insane . . .'. In this business of recollecting the world before the free market, before globalization, voluntary memory misleads, and the flicker of involuntary memory throws up an array of sensations, but doesn't, in itself, instruct us in the ethics of the vanished order, an ethics we have critiqued but whose proximity we no longer sense. So it is almost impossible now to remember—as it was impossible then to predict the fall of the Berlin Wall and the advent of President Obama—that poetry was the literary genre to which the greatest prestige accrued until the mid-1980s; that one might have spent an afternoon talking with an acquaintance about the rhythm of a writer's sentences (in my specific instance, the novelist was James Kelman, the acquaintance an English graduate student in Oxford whose name I have now forgotten). In the same way, it's hard to recall that we didn't think of success in writing mainly in relation to the market, and in relation to a particular genre, the novel, and to a specific incarnation of that genre, the first novel, possibly until 1993, when *A Suitable Boy* was published, or a year earlier, when Donna Tartt's *The Secret History* appeared. It is now difficult to understand these examples as watershed occurrences in an emerging order, and difficult to experience again the moral implications of living—as I lived then, and maybe Benjamin Kunkel, who's much younger than I am, did too—in an order that was superseded.

This might be because the brain or mind or whatever you call it—our emotional and psychological make-up—is geared to cope with death, not just our own, but especially of our loved ones, with whom we identify the founding phases in our lives. Upon a significant death, we mourn the irrevocable closure of that phase; then, pretty consistently, with the passage of time, we find it almost impossible to comprehend what it means for that person not to be alive.

This mechanism constantly translates into our experience of the everyday. In Oxford, I recall a dimly lit car park next to the cinema on George Street that was finally turned into a fake piazza in which a market now congregates on Wednesdays (Figure 2.1). I find it difficult to recall the car park except theoretically. I know very well that it was there. I have to rely on a moral variant of voluntary memory, on a willed excavation, to bring it back. This excavation—this ethical variation of voluntary memory—is increasingly important to those of us who have lived through a bygone epoch into this one. Without it, we accept the timelessness, the given-ness, of whatever is equivalent to the piazza in our present-day existence. In other words, voluntary memory—or that form of excavation—must take us towards what from our point of view is plausible, but essentially unthinkable: not just the past's ignorance of its own future, as in Kunkel's anecdote about a world presided upon by the Cold War and unable to conceive of its own contingency, but the past studied from the vantage-point of a present in which we know the Cold War to be a historical fact, but unthinkable. To truly attest today to the existence of the car park, or our habits of reading before the free market, is, to use Kunkel's word, 'insane': or uncanny. We presume, immediately upon taking on new habits, that those habits are inborn reflexes. We are shocked to hear that poets were central to the culture; that writers once deliberately distanced themselves from material success. The past, as we reacquaint ourselves with these unthinkable facts, begins to look like that rare thing: compelling science fiction—utterly new, and unsettling. Our excavation is perhaps all the more important because we have been inhabiting, for twenty-five years, an epoch in which there has been really no contesting order, no alternative economic or political model. Only through a moral variant of voluntary memory might we, who belong to a particular generation, intuit a different order and logic which isn't really recoverable, and which challenges the present one—the piazza—simply by exposing its contingency, its constructedness.

What are the features, since the 1990s, of the piazza that have almost obliterated our memory of the car park, making us doubt it existed? Let's enumerate, quickly, some obvious developments in literary culture, focussing on publishing and dissemination, and the ways in which they converged with a rewriting of the literary. I'll restrict myself to Britain, my primary location during that time, taking the developments there to be in some senses paradigmatic. For one thing, most British publishing houses, as we know, were acquired by three or four German and French conglomerates, leading to a version, in publishing, of the Blairite consensus: a faithful mimicking of the absence of true oppositionality

Figure 2.1 Piazza, George Street, Oxford, November 2017.

in British politics following the creation of New Labour in the image of the Thatcherite Tory party. Bookshop chains such as Dillons and Waterstone's emerged, at first heterogeneous in terms of their individual outlets, then becoming merged and centralized. As many of us also know, the Net Book Agreement collapsed—that is, the agreement that had protected books from being sold under an agreed minimum price. Offers and price reductions not only became possible, they determined shelf space and, thus, what was read. The books on price reductions and three-for-the-price-of-two offers were those that had been deemed commercial by marketing executives—the new, unacknowledged bosses of the editors and publishers—and bookshop chains, the new, unacknowledged bosses of the marketing executives.

What we were presented with, then, was a stylized hierarchy in which the author, at its bottom, was, like a monarch in a parliamentary democracy, celebrated or reviled—because, as with the monarchy, there was no agreement on whether the author was really *necessary*—and in which even publishers and agents played stellar roles within accommodations determined by marketing men and bookshop-chain bureaucrats. This is not to say that agents or publishers didn't *believe* in unlikely books. The shift lay here: they believed in them in the cause of their market potential. However, with the creation of a new marketing category, 'literary fiction', market potential would *only* be expressed in terms of aesthetic excellence. No publisher would claim, in their press release: 'We believe this novel is going to sell tens of thousands of copies.' They would say, instead: 'We believe this novel puts the writer in the ranks of Salman Rushdie.' Belief defines radical departures in literature and publishing: so it appeared, by a slight adjustment of language, as if the literary were being invested in.

Here was a commercial strategy that spoke in the language of literary populism: 'More and more people are reading books.' At the top was the figure the marketing men scrambled to obey: the reader. The word 'reader' possessed a mix of registers: it evoked the old world of humanistic individualism that had ensconced the act of reading, while, at once, it embraced the new, transformative populism. This populism worked so well in culture precisely because it didn't dispense with the language of the old humanism even though it rejected almost everything it had stood for; it simply embraced that language and used it *on its own terms*.

Who was the 'reader'? He or she was an average person, put together by marketing with basic techniques of realist writing (in the way Arnold Bennett, according to Woolf, created characters by making them an agglomeration of characteristics). The reader was, according to marketing, unburdened by intelligence; easily challenged by expressions of the intellect; easily diverted by a story, an adventure, a foreign place or fairy tale, or an issue or theme of importance. This reader was transparent, democratic, and resistant only to resistance, occlusion, and difficulty. Writing must assume the characteristics of the 'reader': the term for this process, in which literature took on a desirable human quality, was 'accessibility'. In order to placate the 'reader', who, despite being invented by marketing staff, disappointed them constantly, jacket designs were adjusted, and literariness programmatically marginalized. But, crucially, the notion of the 'reader' made it possible to claim that literature was thriving, so it wouldn't seem that its humanistic context had been made defunct, but, instead, renewed. There were more and more readers. New literatures were coming of age: 'like a continent finding its voice',[2] the *New York Times* had said of *Midnight's Children* more than a decade previously, though the pronouncement still seemed recent in the mid-1990s. Abundance was curiously repressive. Here, via the later incarnations of Waterstone's and the Booker Prize, with their ambition to capture readers, were early instances of what would become a typical convergence between the vocabulary used retrospectively to describe a Renaissance with the vocabulary of boom-time.

What was the academy doing at this point? By the late 1980s, critical theory and its mutations—including postcolonial theory, which would take on the responsibility of defining the increasingly important literatures of Empire—had begun to make incursions into Oxbridge and other universities. The departments of English, by now, looked with some prejudice upon value and the symbols of value, such as the canon; problematized or disowned terms such as 'classic' and 'masterpiece'; often ascribed a positive political value to orality, which it conflated with non-Western culture, and a negative one to inscription or 'good writing', which it identified with the European Enlightenment. Some of this was overdue and necessary.

Meanwhile, publishers robustly adopted the language of value—to do with the 'masterpiece' and 'classic' and 'great writer'—that had fallen out of use in its old location, fashioning it in *their own terms*. And these were terms that academics essentially accepted. They critiqued literary value in their own domain, but they were unopposed to it when it was transferred to the marketplace. Part of the reason for this was the language of the market and the language of the publishing industry were (like the language of New Labour) populist during a time of anti-elitism. Part of this had to do with the fact that publishers adopted complex semantic registers. For example: from the 1990s onwards, publishers insisted there was no reason that literary novels couldn't sell. This was an irrefutable populist message disguising a significant commercial development. What publishers meant was that, in the new mainstream category of 'literary fiction', only literary novels that sold well would be deemed valid literary novels. Academics neither exposed this semantic conflict nor challenged the way literary value had been reconfigured. When, in response to political changes in the intellectual landscape, they extended the old canon and began to teach contemporary writers, or novelists from the former colonies, they largely chose as their texts novels whose position had been already decided by the market and its instruments, such as literary prizes.

Experts, critics, and academics took on, then, the role of service-providers in the public sphere. This dawned on me in 2005, when I was spending a couple of months with my family in Cambridge. Watching TV in the evening, possibly Channel 4, we chanced upon a programme on 'The 10 best British film directors'; the list had been created on the basis of votes from viewers. As with all such exercises, it was an odd compilation, displaying the blithe disregard for history so essential to the market's radicalism. Chaplin had either been left out or occupied a pretty low rung; Kenneth Branagh might have been at the top. Each choice was discussed by a group of film critics and experts (such as Derek Malcolm) who, in another age, would have had the final say. Here, they neither interrogated the choices nor the legitimacy of the list; they solemnly weighed the results. If Channel 4 viewers had come up with a completely different list, it would have been accorded the same seriousness by the experts. They were here to perform a specific function. The programme made me realize that it's not that the market *doesn't* want the expert or the intellectual; it simply wants them *on its own terms*. The arbiter of taste and culture and the expert—whether they're a film critic, or a celebrity chef, or a Professor of English judging the Booker Prize—is a service-provider. The circumstances—such as the 'public' vote that had gone towards the list, or the six months in which the Booker judge reads 150 novels (two novels nominated by each publishing house) in order to choose the best literary novel of the year—will invariably be absurd from one point of view, and revolutionary and renovating from the point of view of the market. The expert, in a limited and predetermined way, is a requisite for this renovation. The genius of market activism lies in the fact that, unlike critical theory, it doesn't reject the terminology of literary value; it disinherits and revivifies it, and uses it as a very particular and powerful code. This accounts for its resilience.

What's interesting in this scenario is how far the logic of the market extends, encompassing what might seem to be rents in the fabrics. Take, for example, the phenomenon of 'pirated' books in urban India, more or less coterminous with the emergence of the mainstream 'literary novel' in the 1990s. 'Pirated' books are cheap copies, illegally reproduced and sold at traffic lights and on pavements. Confronting them, you have the same sense of disapproval and curiosity that you might towards contraband. In other words, the sight of 'pirated' books provokes an excitement and unease in the middle-class person that recalls, from another age, a response to the avant-garde, the out-of-the-way; the word 'pirated' adds to the aura of illegality. Only when you scrutinize the titles do you realize that pirated books are no alternative to the bookshop chain. The selection represents the most conservative bourgeois taste; popular fiction, horoscopes, best-selling non-fiction (*Mein Kampf* is perennially available), and Booker Prize winners are arrayed side by side.

★

'Literary activism' positions itself not against the market, but the sense of continuity it creates. For instance, literary activism needs to proclaim its solidarity with, as well as distance itself from, the old processes of 'championing' and reassessment. Distance itself because, in the age of the market, publishers and marketing institutions such as the Booker Prize themselves became champions. Their aim was to enlist notional 'readers' in greater numbers. In one of the many semantic convergences of the period, the language of championing, so fundamental to criticism and its influence, flowed, with the Booker Prize and publishing houses in the 1990s, into the market's upbeat terminology of 'bullishness'. (It would be worth knowing when betting was introduced in the run-up to the Booker results. Ladbrokes seems to have been operating in the Booker arena from 2004.)

The Booker Prize morphed from a prize judged by distinguished novelists into a device for 'market activism' in the 1990s, with juries made up of politicians and comedians. The agitation it caused was, even by the late 1980s, not so much related to the excitement of the literary, which has to do with the strangeness of poetic language (or as

Housman put it, 'If a line of poetry strays into my memory, my skin bristles so that the razor ceases to act'[3]), as it was an effect of a hyper-excited environment. The way in which the Booker achieved this was by confirming, and allowing itself to be informed by, the market's value-generating characteristics: volatility and random rewards. The market never promised equitable gain; what it said was: 'Anyone can get rich.' The distance between equitable gain (the idea that everyone can be reasonably well-off) and the guarantee, 'anyone can get rich', seems at first a matter of semantics; but it is very real and is reproduced exactly by the distance between the reader in the 1970s and the 'reader' in the time of market activism. In the age of full-blown capitalism, anyone *can* get rich through the market, and, also, anyone can get poor; these occurrences are disconnected from anachronistic ideas of merit and justice. In this disconnection lies the magic of the free market, its ebullience and emancipation. So the Booker Prize implicitly proclaims: 'Anyone can win.' As long as the work in contention is a novel and is in English, both qualifications embedded in, and representing, the globalized world, we can peel away the superfluous dermatological layers of literariness by agreeing that the essay, the story, poetry, and novels outside the two nominated by publishers are ineligible and superfluous. 'Anyone can win' suggests a revolutionary opening-up typical of the language of market activism. As the Booker's constituency—for some time now, a worldwide one—accepts the fact that anyone can win, there is, ritually, a degree of volatility about the construction, announcement, and reception of the shortlist—of late, even the longlist—which captures the agitation that propels market activism. Famous writers and critically acclaimed books are often ignored; at least one unknown novelist is thrown into the limelight; one putatively mediocre novel is chosen. The book is severed from oeuvre and literary tradition, as if it existed only in the moment; the history and cross-referencing that creates a literary work is correctively dispensed with.

Since the history of so-called 'new literatures' such as the Indian novel in English is tied up (especially since *Midnight's Children*) with the Booker Prize and the manner in which it endorses novels, we subsist on a sense that the lineage of the Indian English novel is an exemplary anthology of single works, rather than a tradition of cross-referencing and interdependency. The random mix on the shortlist and the incursion of first-time novelists as shortlisted authors, often even as winners, might echo the sort of championing that drew attention to new or marginal writing; while it is actually enlivened by the volatility of market activism. Each year there's the ritual outcry from critics and journalists that the judges have missed out on some meritorious works. This outcry is not a critique of the Booker; it's germane to its workings and an integral component of its activism. The culminatory outcry comes when the winner is announced; the result is occasionally shocking. Again, this phase, of disbelief and outrage, is an indispensable part of the Booker's celebration—its confirmation—of the market's metamorphic capacities; the prize would be diminished without it. This randomness should be distinguished from the perversity of the Nobel, where a little-known committee crowns a body of work marked by the old-fashioned quality of 'greatness', or rewards a writer for what's construed to be political reasons. The Nobel's arbitrariness is bureaucratic, its randomness a function of bureaucracy. (Recent developments suggest that the Nobel may no longer be averse to a bit of market activism itself.)

Partly the Booker goes periodically to first novels because its form of activism dispenses with the body-of-work narratives that conventionally define literary histories and prizes such as the Nobel; it responds to the market's shrinking of time, its jettisoning of pedigree in favour of an open-ended moment: the 'now' of the market, in which anything can happen, and everything is changing. The fact that Indian writing in English since *Midnight's Children* has been handcuffed to the Booker means that it exists in this perpetual now, that its history is periodically obliterated and recreated each time an Indian gets the prize, leading Indian newspapers to proclaim every few years: 'Indian writing has come of age.' The first novel, since the early 1990s, came to embody this compressed timeframe in which speculation occurs, fortunes are lost and made, radical transformation effected. Publishers who contributed significantly to market activism appropriated this sub-genre and, by often calling books that were yet to be published 'masterpieces' (the publisher Philip Gwyn Jones's pre-publication statement about *The God of Small Things*, 'a masterpiece fallen out of the sky fully formed', comes to mind), made pronouncements in terms of the market's shrinking of time, its subtle reframing of context and linearity, its insistence on the miraculous. The word 'masterpiece' itself became a predictive category, connected to the market's bullishness and optimism, rather than a retrospective endorsement. When a publisher proclaims today: 'The new novel we're publishing in the autumn is a masterpiece', they mean: 'We think it will sell 50,000 copies.' No novel that's expected to sell 500 copies is deemed a 'masterpiece' by a mainstream publisher. Gwyn Jones's statement about Arundhati Roy's first novel needs, then, to be read as a prediction rather than an assessment, and a prediction made in a bullish marketplace. On the other hand, the Booker's retrospective accolades—'Which book would have won in 1939?'—again disrupt conventional histories and aim to bring past texts into the 'now' of the market's activism.

The most striking instance of a publishing house and author inhabiting this 'now' through a literary concept that once represented historical time is the publication of the musician Morrissey's first book, *Autobiography*, in 2013 as a Penguin Classic, the rubric evidently an authorial prerequisite. In 1992, Vikram Seth undertook a pioneering form of market activism by interviewing literary agents in order to decide who would be best equipped to auction *A Suitable Boy* to UK publishers. Notwithstanding Seth's commercial and critical success with *The Golden Gate*, he had only written his first (prose) novel. Meetings between authors and agents usually take place on fairly equal footing, with the weight of authority slightly on the side of the more powerful party. Seth's unprecedented style shifted the balance in the interests of the novel's commercial success and the sort of advance on royalties he thought it deserved. Morrissey's pre-publication mindset, two decades later, represents an evolution. No overt mention is made of figures or of the advance; it's the standard of the 'classic' that's at stake. It's as if Morrissey grasps the reification of literary concepts in the 'now' of the marketplace. Once, critics spoke ironically of the 'stocks and shares' in a writer's books being high or low with reference to their critical reputation; today, the same statement is made without irony and with a straightforward literalism. As part of this reification, however, certain words—such as 'classic'—become ironical, and come close to signifying a guarantee that needs to be fiercely bargained for. That Morrissey's hunch was right was proved by *Autobiography* climbing to number one on the bestsellers' chart upon publication. It would surely be the one Penguin 'classic' to have had such an entry.

★

This, then, is what the piazza began to look like by the mid-1990s. We may have been bemused by what was unfolding in the first two years, but by the third year we believed it had always been like this. We had no memory of the car park. This no doubt had to do with the way the mind converts the dead into a fact: the dead are incontrovertible, but we don't know who they are. But partly it was the effect of the compressed time and space of globalization, of inhabiting an epoch in which materiality was shrinking and our principal devices could be fitted into the palm of a hand, and periodically replaced. Personal memory, cultural institutions, and popular culture responded to this shrinkage, this ethos of recurring disposability, variously, for distinct but contiguous reasons. While literary language was acquired by publishers for the purposes of marketing, literary departments reneged, as I've said, on any discussion that connected value to the passage of time: they disavowed the 'masterpiece', 'canon', and 'classic'. Popular culture not only annexed these concepts, it produced its own terminology of eternity: for instance, the word 'all-time', as in 'all-time favourite guitarist' or 'all-time great movie director'. 'All-time', it soon became evident, covered a span of five, maybe ten, years; that is, the time of deregulated globalization—'all-time' was a means of managing the classic. In consonance with the eternity conjured up by 'all-time', popular culture—and even the so-called 'serious' media—abounds with lists: '10 favourite movies'; '100 great novels'; and so on. Lists both mimic and annihilate the historicity of the canon; they reduce time, making it seemingly comprehensible; they exude volatility and are meaningless because the market is energized by the meaningless. Given the pervasiveness of the 'all-time', it wasn't surprising that it was difficult to give credence to the car park.

But other things were happening in the 1990s that didn't quite fit in. I was rereading, and often discovering for the first time, the modernism of Indian literatures as I compiled the *Picador Book of Modern Indian Literature*. In 1992, I'd also turned my attention to Arvind Krishna Mehrotra, whose poetry I'd read on and off since the late 1970s and whose anthology, *The Oxford India Anthology of Twelve Modern Indian Poets*, published that year, made an intervention on behalf of a discredited tradition, contemporary Indian poetry in English, without having recourse to the new interpretative apparatus. His primary intervention was the making of the anthology itself, where he brought poets and their work together in a way that redefined their relationship to each other without either explicitly rejecting or taking for granted the notion of a pre-existing canon. This was a way of looking at literary history that neither fitted in entirely with the humanist procedures of valuation (Indian poetry in English had never anyway really been a legitimate subject of such authoritative procedures) nor subscribed to the prevalent methods connected to the postcolonial, the hybrid, or even to list-making. Mehrotra's juxtapositions seemed to be exploring a particular experience of the literary.

I recalled, as I was thinking of essays to include in the Picador anthology, a long, polemical critical article that Mehrotra had published in 1980 in a little magazine out of Cuttack called *Chandrabhaga*, edited by the poet Jayanta Mahapatra. The essay was 'The Emperor Has No Clothes', and I was 18 when it came out, but I still had a sense of its central tenet: simply put, the Indian poem in English has no obvious markers of 'Indianness'. Similarly, the poem produced by the multilingual imagination has no visible hierarchy in, or signs of, the manner in which a multiplicity of languages inhabits it. With hindsight (and upon rediscovery of that issue after a strenuous search), this argument read like a prescient rebuttal of one of the sacred dogmas that came into play from the 1980s onwards: that, in the case of the multicultural literary work, the admixture was immediately noticeable, and it was therefore possible to applaud and celebrate it, rather than necessarily the work, accordingly.

When the idea crystallized of getting Mehrotra nominated for the Oxford Professorship of Poetry, I can't recall, but it was obviously post-1989, with the Benjamin Zephaniah nomination pointing towards a course of action. Not that I was thinking of Mehrotra in terms of his potential comic disruptiveness; but *some* sort of unsettlement was going to be welcome. Besides, Mehrotra would make for a genuinely interesting lecturer, and his self-aware position as an Indian modern made him a far better choice for the Professorship than the sort of 'great' poet who'd lost his tenancy in the emptiness of evangelical liberal democracy during globalization.

The Picador anthology came out in 2001. The director of British Council India, in a moment of generosity, commissioned a poster exhibition as a response to it. I asked Naveen Kishore, publisher of Seagull Books, an imprint known for the beauty of its jacket designs, whether he'd take on the brief of producing the posters. Naveen created a series using black-and-white photographs he'd taken himself, playing with typeface and selecting one randomly chosen quotation from pieces in the anthology per poster. One poster bore a line from Michael Madhusudan Dutt; one a remark from a letter Tagore had written; another a quote from 'The Emperor Has No Clothes'; another simply displayed the title of an A. K. Ramanujan essay, 'Is there an Indian way of thinking?' Peter D. McDonald, who teaches English at Oxford and saw some of the posters I'd taken there with me, was struck especially by the Mehrotra quote that Naveen had used, a slightly edited version of this long sentence: 'Between Nabokov's English and Russian, between Borges's Spanish and English, between Ramanujan's English and Tamil-Kannada, between the pan-Indian Sanskritic tradition and folk material, and between the Bharhut Stupa and Gond carvings many cycles of give-and-take are set in motion.'[4]

The sentence is doing something that isn't obvious at first. The back and forth, or the 'give-and-take . . . motion', between 'Ramanujan's English and Tamil-Kannada, between the pan-Indian Sanskritic tradition and folk material' et cetera, isn't an unexpected sort of movement—between the 'high', and the 'low' or 'popular'. It's the transverse movement *across* the sentence, connecting Nabokov, Borges, Ramanujan, the pan-Indian Sanskritic tradition and the Bharhut Stupa to each other—characterizing another kind of 'give and take' that enables these very analogies—that constitutes its departure. It signals Mehrotra's unwillingness to be constrained by conventional histories of cultural interaction or influence across the 'East' and the 'West'—so that he slyly sidesteps them or appears inadvertently to ignore them. There's a transaction between the high, the sacred, with the vernacular and the profane, the sentence claims; this much is conventional wisdom. But the sentence also claims that such a transaction characterizes every culture, in ways that put cultures in conversation with each other. These conversations between cultures aren't to do with 'difference' (in which, say, the East might play the role of the irrational, the West of Enlightenment humanism); nor do they represent a conciliatory humanism, in which East and West seek versions of themselves in each other. Instead, Mehrotra behaves as if each pairing represents comparable literary trajectories that echo and illuminate each other; one of the things that the sentence declares is that the colonial encounter is hardly the only way of interpreting the contiguity between the West and the East, or even the 'high' to the 'vernacular'. The echoes that comprise the conversation ('Borges's Spanish and English . . . Ramanujan's English and Tamil-Kannada . . . the pan-Indian Sanskritic tradition and folk material') exist independently of each other, but their overlaps aren't entirely coincidental. They can only be noticed and connected in a head such as Mehrotra's, in whom, in some way not entirely explained by colonialism and Empire, with their restrictive itineraries, these histories (catalogued in the sentence) come together. The echoes, overheard by Mehrotra, signal a liberation from those clearly demarcated histories of cultural interchange.

It was around that time that I asked Peter to read 'The Emperor Has No Clothes' in the Picador anthology, and also to consider the thought that Mehrotra be nominated for the Oxford Poetry Professorship. I hoped that Peter would be drawn to Mehrotra's larger statement, indeed to his work. This did become the case; so I'm not surprised to find an email query in my 'sent' inbox, addressed to Peter on 23 January 2009, when the opportune moment had clearly arisen:

> 'Dear Peter,
> I notice they're looking for a new Professor of Poetry to dawdle beneath the dreaming spires. Should we conspire to get Arvind Krishna Mehrotra nominated?'[5]

Peter replied an hour later, saying he was going to try to enlist colleagues in the department and then proceed with the nomination, for which ten 'members of congregation and convocation', or fully paid-up Oxford University employees and/or degree-holders, were required. I alerted the Irish poet-critic Tom Paulin, who was out of sorts but still teaching at Hertford. Peter photocopied 'The Emperor Has No Clothes' from the Picador anthology, I poems from *Middle Earth: New and Selected Poems* and *The Transfiguring Places* (the books, like those of most Indian English poets, were out of print) at a shop in Gariahat in Calcutta, and scanned and sent them to Peter, for circulation, and also to Tom, who said he would decide after he had investigated further.

Who is Arvind Krishna Mehrotra? No full account could be given to people—and I include, here, some of the nominators—who knew little of him and his work. All that could be done was to put samples, the essay, and a short biography out there and hope that this would open up a conversation that would introduce, in the lead-up to the elections, a new set of terms. Some might have noticed that Mehrotra, born in 1947, was a 'midnight's child', but that neither his work nor life carried any news of the nation as we'd come to understand it. The middle-class suburb figured in the most characteristic poems—but not the state. He was born in Lahore. He grew up in a small town, Allahabad, and was educated there and in another one, Bhilai, and was later a graduate student in Bombay. Still later, he'd spend two years in Iowa, homesick for India, but there was no whiff, until the 2009 campaign, of Oxbridge about him. Allahabad was an intellectual centre that was moving unobtrusively, by the time Mehrotra was 17 and already entertaining ambitions of being a poet, towards decline. And yet Allahabad is where he discovered Ezra Pound and the Beat poets, and, with a friend, brought into existence a short-lived little magazine, *damn you/a magazine of the arts*, echoing Ed Sanders's New York periodical from the early 1960s, *Fuck You: A Magazine of the Arts*. The publication's name, it seems to me, is intent on turning Sanders's challenge into a Poundian imprecation, from one who clearly shared with the narrator of 'Hugh Selwyn Mauberley' a combative impatience about being 'born / In a half savage country, out of date; / Bent resolutely on wringing lilies from the acorn'.[6] What sorts of lilies? At 19, he was a youthful and exasperated satirist in *vers libre*, in a declamatory mode borrowed from Ginsberg, opening his long poem to the nation, *Bharatmata: A Prayer*, with: 'india / my beloved country, ah my motherland / you are, in the world's slum / the lavatory'.[7] It was 1966, two years after Nehru's death, a time in which the late prime minister's projects of industrialization and austerity continued doggedly to be pursued. Then, around 1969–70, something magical happens, and, in rhythms and imagery that glance knowingly both at French surrealism and American poetry, Mehrotra begins to produce his first mature poems, which are often parables of Allahabad's neighbourhoods:

> This is about the green miraculous trees,
> And old clocks on stone towers,
> And playgrounds full of light
> And dark blue uniforms.
> At eight I'm a Boy Scout and make a tent
> By stretching a bed-sheet over parallel bars...
> ('Continuities')[8]

At least two things strike us as we acquaint ourselves with Mehrotra's life and oeuvre. The first has to do with movement. How does a person who has moved relatively little encounter and even anticipate the contemporary world of ideas and letters—in an age without the fax and internet, in which the speediest epistolary communication is the telegram? It's a mystery that has no adequate explanation. Yet scratch the surface of the life and the history that produced it, and you find that Mehrotra exemplifies not an aberration but a pattern. It's a pattern that defines both India and much of literary modernity, and Mehrotra embodies it in the singular way in which he traverses the provincial and the cosmopolitan. This would have always made it difficult to present him in the campaign as a postcolonial who—like Derek Walcott, according to his supporters—had somehow transcended his identity into the realm of universality. ('With Walcott, you need only to remember the name,' an English professor had said dreamily to students.) Mehrotra, like Allahabad, was an anomaly, and modernity was local and anomalous. The second thing that becomes clear quickly is Mehrotra's indifference to creating an authentic 'Indian' idiom in English. Instead, like the speaker of a later poem, 'Borges', he seems content to let 'the borrowed voice / [set] the true one free'.[9] In an email to me he once admitted that, as a young man, he'd turned to French surrealism because he wanted to escape 'the language of nightingales and skylarks'.[10] The same could presumably be said of his lifelong preoccupation, as both a poet and translator, with Pound, William Carlos Williams, and the emphatic dialogue of American cartoons. What's notable is the historical and creative intelligence latent in this statement: the notion that neither the English language nor Western culture is a continuous and unbroken entity, that each is heterogeneous and will contain within itself breaks and departures (such as French surrealism and the diction of Pound). No break need be made from it, because that's probably impossible; instead, a break might be effected through it by deliberately choosing one register or history over another. Modernism and Pound's poetry, then, aren't absolutes for Mehrotra; they comprise, instead, a breakdown in 'the language of skylarks and nightingales'. This breakdown will resonate very differently for an Indian—for whom 'Western culture' is an ambivalent but real inheritance—from the way it will for a European to whom that inheritance is a given. It also means that the Indian poet in English will be less of a creator busy originating an authentic tongue, and more like a jazz musician, listening acutely to the conflicting tonality—nightingales, skylarks, the Beat poets, Pound—of what surrounds and precedes him. Out of this curious tradition (which in no way precludes Indian writing: Mehrotra's translations include versions of Prakrit love poetry, of Kabir, and of the contemporary Hindi poet Vinod Kumar Shukla, and it's often at the moment of translation that the registers I've mentioned are counterintuitively adopted), he must make something of his 'own'.

The enervating, bewildering, and thrilling elements of the Mehrotra campaign are too many to enumerate here. Let me recount a few points, some of which are already familiar to those who kept track of the event. We ended up recruiting a mix of well-wishers and personal contacts, all of them distinguished in their fields, as supporters, some of them already admirers of Mehrotra. Among the latter were the novelists Geoff Dyer and Toby Litt and the Romanticist Jon Mee. Tariq Ali was made to reacquaint himself with the work and became one of the most vocal supporters of the candidacy; Tom Paulin joined the campaign once his investigations confirmed the value of the candidate; Wendy Doniger and the philosopher Charles Taylor discovered Mehrotra for the first time and came on board; Homi Bhabha pledged support and mysteriously vanished; old friends and recent acquaintances including the writer-scientists Sunetra Gupta and Rohit Manchanda, the historians Shahid Amin and Ananya Vajpeyi, the political thinker Pratap Bhanu Mehta and the literary scholars Rajeswari Sunder Rajan, Swapan Chakravorty, Uttara Natarajan, Rosinka Chaudhuri, and Subha Mukherjee—all 'members of convocation'—put in their signatures. A lot of leg-work was put in by Dr Sally Bayley, then a part-time lecturer at Balliol College, and she didn't seem to mind offending the faculty's inner circle, comprising, among others, Hermione Lee and my excellent former supervisor Jon Stallworthy. I was thinking of approaching another friend, the poet Ruth Padel, for a signature, when, curiously, she announced her candidacy and approached me for mine. Ruth is charming, and a good poet and speaker, but her hands-on approach to her own nomination *was* unprecedented; nominees are historically aloof from electioneering. Whether her style was an appropriation of the methods of market activism, to which the author's cooperation in, and production of, PR is oxygen, I can't decide; some form of activism it certainly was. Later, after the whole abortive 2009 elections were over, Tariq Ali, in a fit of anger, would, in an email to me, call Padel's a 'New Labour-style campaign',[11] a style manufactured in the 1990s and discomfiting to the old Left.

Still in the early days of the lead-up to the elections, I wrote a sonorous paragraph that was only slightly tweaked by Peter: 'Arvind Krishna Mehrotra is one of the leading Indian poets in the English language, and one of the finest poets working in any language.

Influential anthologist, translator, and commentator, he is a poet-critic of an exceptionally high order. Mehrotra has much to say of value—of urgency—on the matter of multilingualism, creative practice, and translation (in both its literal and figurative sense), issues that are pressingly important in today's world. He is not an easy "postcolonial" choice, for he emerges from a rich and occasionally fraught world history of cosmopolitanism; but he is proof—as critic and artist—that cosmopolitanism is not only about European eclecticism, but about a wider, more complex network of languages and histories. For these reasons he would make an excellent, and timely, Professor of Poetry at Oxford.' This was circulated widely and put in the flyer; Peter sent it out along with the poems and the essay into the English faculty. By now, the official candidate, Derek Walcott, was in place. Poems by the three contenders appeared in the *Oxford Magazine*, chosen by Bernard O'Donoghue of the 'official' camp, but enough of a devotee of poetry (and a gentleman) to convey his admiration for Mehrotra's verse to Peter.

One thing Mehrotra had on his side as a writer was age—he was 62. In the time of Romanticism and in the Modernist twentieth century, early death or suicide was the writer's sole means of unfettering themselves of conventional valuation and breaking through instantaneously. In the shrunken time of globalization, in the eternity of the piazza, when the constant cycles of boom and bust that governed the market ensured that many economic and cultural lifetimes could occur in a decade, the writer needed to simply survive, to grow old, so that he might outlive those cycles, the piazza's eternity, into a mini-epoch (maybe a period of bust) when the literary is again visible. This crucial task, of growing old, Mehrotra had performed perfectly. Just as the market had triumphantly annexed and put to use the language of literary valuation disposed of by literature departments, the literary activist after the 1990s must ideally study the patterns of the free market, its repetition of boom and bust, its unravelling, to employ those rhythms on behalf of the literary. In the (often self-destructive) unpredictability of globalization, the literary writer's function is to wait; and not die.

The story of the 2009 elections threatened to become sordid when the *Independent*,[12] and consequently the *Sunday Times*[13] and other papers, carried a report about how a dossier had begun to be circulated about Walcott's past misdemeanours: in particular, his alleged sexual harassment of two students, one at Harvard University and the other at Boston, in 1982 and 1996 respectively. Before very long, Walcott withdrew from the race, with Padel earning great resentment from the 'official' camp as she was accused of first alerting the press to Walcott's undeniable history—a charge she strenuously denied. Many in the 'inner circle' pointed out that the only honourable course of action for the two remaining candidates now was to withdraw. Among those who advocated this course of action was *a different* Peter McDonald: the Irish poet and Christ Church lecturer. All this time, another upheaval was taking place, unreported: various faculty members were discovering, via the emailed scans, a compelling poet and essayist in Mehrotra. So much so that Mehrotra became the first contender who, as a losing outsider, gained as many as 129 votes. Padel won handsomely with 297 votes on 16 May and in so doing became the first woman to be elected to the post in 301 years. She resigned nine days later, admitting, after her involvement in the matter became undeniable: 'I did not engage in a smear campaign against [Walcott], but, as a result of student concern, I naively—and with hindsight unwisely—passed on to two journalists, whom I believed to be covering the whole election responsibly, information that was already in the public domain.'[14] Tariq Ali and others wondered why Mehrotra wasn't made Professor by default, as did a *New York Times* editorial on 26 May, which pointed out: 'The only person who comes out well in all of this is...Mehrotra...Oxford would do well to confirm him and allow everyone to move along until the next election, five years hence.'[15] But Oxford declared the elections invalid, so paving the way for Geoffrey Hill's uncontested appointment to the post the next year: another 'great' poet hobbled in some ways by the political order under liberal democracy, envious, occasionally, of the authoritative suffering caused by a now-historic totalitarianism.

What the 2009 elections are largely remembered for is Padel's radical, discredited, *sui generis* style, leading at first to success and then disgrace, but which widened the arcane sphere of the Professorship into the logic of the epoch: the activism of the marketplace, where volatility now takes on the incarnation of literary value, now of justice, but remains otherwise irreducible. It is remembered for those regal, glacial categories or objects, such as Walcott's reputation, and, on closer examination, the undemocratic 'inner circle', that transcended the workings of the market, but were vulnerable for precisely this reason and in a way appropriated. As for the Mehrotra campaign, which approached the press only on behalf of a poetic and critical practice and not ethnicity or identity, and which fell on neither side of the dichotomy, its fate, despite its impact, was to be not properly noticed. Perhaps it's integral to literary activism that it not be properly remembered or noticed, but experienced, uncovered, excavated, and read?

I should mention, before I conclude by reflecting on our adventure, that there was an attempt to push Mehrotra's candidacy into a postcolonial rubric, and then also to claim that he threatened to split the valuable 'postcolonial' vote. That his candidacy was deliberately distanced from such a positioning—echoing Mehrotra's own description of the Indian multilingual poem as something that possesses no reliable signs of identity—should be something we consider when we account for what the aims of literary activism are. The official Oxford dispensation didn't know what to make of Mehrotra, as he didn't come with mainstream markers of literary pedigree; nor was he a hero of the new peripheries; nor did he embody market style. His behaviour as a candidate was impeccable, but the nature of his candidacy was on more than one level resistant. If resistance, or difficulty, enlarges our notion of literature, then the inner circle was, in turn, resistant to such an enlargement. After Walcott's withdrawal, it instructed its members and students—despite the fact that many of them were increasingly aware and appreciative of Mehrotra's merits—to abstain from voting: otherwise, there was every chance that Mehrotra would have won.

Our intention—the pronoun includes Peter D. McDonald, myself, and Mehrotra, who had graciously accepted our proposal in the first place—was, I venture, never to win. This doesn't mean that the campaign pursued a romantic courtship of failure; not at all. Rather, our marshalling of people and resources was worldly and political but being liberated from the thought of victory meant our activities could take on dimensions that would otherwise have been proscribed to it; it allowed Mehrotra to plot and devise his lectures in the way we had plotted the campaign, as a deliberate long shot that *should* succeed. To the literary pages of the *Hindu* Mehrotra proclaimed that he would 'broaden the scope' of what had been a 'Eurocentric' (an unusual word-choice for Mehrotra) job, and that he wasn't losing sleep over the imminent results. As it happens, Mehrotra and I had a long-distance phone conversation not long before the voting, and he said to me that he'd had a sleepless night at the not-wholly-improbable prospect of winning. It would have been a disaster—for him. In his way, Mehrotra was miming the elusiveness and difficulty of the literary as Padel had the methods of the market. This threw a kind of light, for me, on the event.

2014–16

* * *

3

Poetry as polemic

Whatever the unborn and the dead may know, they cannot know the beauty, the marvel of being alive in the flesh.

—D. H. Lawrence, *Apocalypse*[1]

I began to feel put off by Tagore in my late teens, around the time I discovered Indian classical music, the devotional songs of Meerabai, Tulsidas, and Kabir, not to speak of the work of the modernists. I was also—to place the moment further in context—reading contemporary European poetry in translation, in the tremendous series edited by Al Alvarez, the *Penguin Modern European Poets*. My father knew of my promiscuous adventurousness when it came to poetry, and, in tender deference to this, he (a corporate man) would buy these books from bookshops in the five-star hotels he frequented, such as the mythic Nalanda at the Taj. Among the poets I discovered through this route of privilege was the Israeli Dan Pagis, of whom the blurb stated: 'A survivor of a concentration camp, Dan Pagis possesses a vision which is essentially tragic.' I don't recall how my seventeen-year-old self responded to Pagis, but I do remember the poem he is most famous for, 'Written in Pencil in the Sealed Railway-Car'. Here it is in its entirety:

here in this carload
i am eve
with abel my son
if you see my other son
cain son of man
tell him i[2]

The resonance of the poem escaped me at the time: this history was not mine. What struck me were the qualities I found most attractive when I was seventeen—metaphysical despair; deliberate irresolution. I mention the poem because I think it figured as a subtext to a difference of opinion I had with my uncle when my parents and I visited him in London in 1979. My uncle, a bachelor and an executive in shipping, was the most shameless propagandist for Tagore I have ever met, and his enthusiasm only furthered my dislike for the Bengali poet. Walking around Belsize Park, he would tell me that Tagore was the greatest poet the world had ever seen, surpassing everybody, including 'the poets of the *Bhagavad Gita*'. (Homer and Shakespeare didn't even merit a mention.) I countered with the name of my favourite poet, T. S. Eliot, flag-bearer of a certain kind of twentieth-century despondency especially attractive to teenagers, and spoke too of Meera's devotionals, saying I preferred the latter to Tagore's lyrics. 'You somehow feel,' I said, 'that there's a real urgency and immediacy about her songs. They could have been scribbled upon a prison wall.' I was probably invoking Pagis here, and also having a go at Tagore's premeditated and loving craftsmanship. Many poets—besides, of course, philosophers—have insisted that there are things that are more important than poetry, especially in the face of trauma; for poets, this disavowal is, in fact, a respectable literary strategy. Even an adolescent detractor could tell that, to Tagore, nothing was as important as poetry.

My uncle attempted to indoctrinate me each time I went to London in the 1970s. In his eyes, Tagore was an amazingly contradictory agglomeration of virtues and characteristics. 'If Tolstoy was a sage whose heart bled for mankind,' said my uncle, 'then Rabi Thakur was a greater sage. No one has felt more pity for man's sorrows.' He spoke of him in the semi-familiar, affectionate way of the Bengali *bhadralok*, as if Tagore were a cherished acquaintance—'Rabi Thakur'—and not hieratically, as 'Gurudev', the appellation Gandhi had conferred on him (as, in turn, Tagore had reportedly conferred 'Mahatma' on Gandhi). He sometimes hummed Tagore's more popular and plangent lines ('My days wouldn't remain in the golden cage / those many-coloured days of mine' and 'I know, I know that the prayers that went / unanswered in life haven't been lost'[3]) mainly to express his sadness: for he was a man who loved company, and family, but had oddly chosen to be alone, and an expatriate. Then, the mood would change abruptly. Tagore, according to my uncle, was a 'tennis player'—this odd metaphor was deployed to suggest, I think, a series of departures: the breaking away of Tagore's family, starting with his great-grandfather Nilmoni Tagore, from its conservative Brahminical roots; Tagore's own breaking out from his 'aristocratic', landed past into modernity, art, individualism, and, of course, glamorous mystique. The latter, presumably, is what Tagore, the celebrity poet, and the tennis player had in common—besides finesse and control.

My uncle was as much in awe of Tagore's looks as he was of his work—both were, in fact, impossible to disentangle from one another. Despite his immemorial, world-denying air from his forties onward, Tagore and everything associated with him—his handwriting; the interiors he inhabited, with their new 'ethnic' design; the habitations he constructed for himself in Santiniketan; the paintings created out of manuscript corrections—had an air of provisionality and experiment. They emanated from a man taking his cue from, or experiencing resonances with, a number of sources and excitements—tribal arts and crafts; the devotional-mystic music of Bengal; the dance traditions of neighbouring regions, like Manipur; Shelley; the Upanishads; Paul Klee. All this translated, in the public domain, into the personality and the appearance themselves—the commanding but ineffable, and somehow wholly contemporary, presence of the 'world poet'. It was this image that held my uncle in thrall. '"People who compare me with Shakespeare should realise that I had to make a leap of five hundred years to write as I do," said Rabindranath,' reported my uncle calmly. There was a remonstrative edge to his words, though, for his identification with Tagore was fierce. 'All men who repeat one line of Shakespeare are William Shakespeare,'[4] said Jorge Luis Borges; all Bengalis of a certain generation were, at one point or another, Tagore. And, of course, there are many Tagores, as anyone becoming acquainted with him will discover. The phrase 'Renaissance man' does not capture the restless energy and vitality with which he—a colonial subject—journeyed towards different genres in the manner of one learning, mastering, and finally altering new languages. He undertook each genre as an exploration: the revealing (in all kinds of ways) letter-writing of the young man; the shadowy microcosm contained in the plays; the great novels and stories; the often deeply original but underrated essays; the paintings that emerged almost by accident—from manuscript corrections—when he was a much older man. The act of journeying and the element of chance were (as I discovered later) both crucial to Tagore.

For the versatility I've just mentioned, Tagore is occasionally compared to Goethe. I see him as being closer to another German, Josef Beuys, as someone who wants not only to address or to influence the world around him, but to rearrange and reorder it—creatively, radically, sometimes physically. As a consequence, Tagore was interested not only in literature but in book design, apparel, and the decorative and cultural aspects of our drawing rooms. Indeed, Buddhadeva Bose, writing about a visit to the Tagore household, mentions how subtly innovative and experimental (and finely judged) both the food and the decor were. Tagore's urge to experiment was relentless; and we can't really pretend that what he did within the covers of a book and what he did outside it emerge from two wholly divergent impulses. Beuys refuses to distinguish between the text and the world that is his immediate material and, in many ways, dissolves the frame around the artwork; Tagore, too, frequently refuses to make the same distinction. No volume or compilation of Tagore's songs, poems, stories, extracts from his novels, reflections on literature and politics and on his frequent and exhausting travels, and even instances of his *sui generis* humour should be read as his 'writings' alone, but seen in conjunction with his larger interest—evident in almost all he did—in intervening in and reshaping his surroundings. His school, Santiniketan, served as a hothouse and a laboratory for this creative experiment. In important ways, Santiniketan—indeed, the many-pronged, all-embracing Tagorean project—was a precursor to Beuys's vision of 'total art' and 'social sculpture', and a successor to the Wagnerian *Gesamtkunstwerk*, the art performance in which every form of art is incorporated. Yet Tagore's impulse needs to be distinguished from Wagner's messianic vision. Tagore was absorbed in the everyday, the domestic, and his love of the momentary.

Naturally, my uncle had a view on Tagore's metamorphic effect: 'Let's say you were to set a murder mystery in the early twentieth century, and the murder had been committed by someone who grew up before Tagore became famous. Let's say a manuscript page was the single available clue. You'd catch the murderer just by looking at the handwriting, because Bengali handwriting changed forever after Tagore.' Moreover, 'Words like Keatsian and Wordsworthian describe a literary style associated with that particular poet,' he pointed out, for he had read a great deal. 'Only Rabindrik'—the Bengali adjective derived from Tagore's first name—'encompasses an entire generation, an outlook, that came into being with the poet's work.' For my uncle, this was a matter of intransigent pride. For the very original poets who followed Tagore in the Bengali language, the legacy was a mixed one. 'It was impossible to write like Rabindranath, and it was impossible not to write like Rabindranath,'[5] said Buddhadeva Bose. When, in fact, I quoted and cited the great post-Tagorean poets I particularly loved, like Jibanananda Das or Bose, to my uncle, he was completely immune to their music: 'I've heard it all before. Don't you see none of this would be possible without Rabindranath?' Thus my uncle, an idiosyncratic but sensitive reader, deliberately echoed a vulgar undertone of a particular form of Bengali romanticism—that Tagore was a historical pinnacle, after which everything was a kind of decline, and every writer a latecomer. This view precluded any further fruitful discussion between my uncle and myself, though that didn't stop either of us.

There was another dimension to these conversations in London. My uncle knew, as I think I must have, that the dismantling of Tagore's reputation as a serious poet had started early—soon after the Nobel Prize in 1913—and that, by the 1970s, very little survived of that reputation in the West, or, for that matter, anywhere outside the cocoon of Bengal. The rise itself had been at once astonishing and suspect, impossible without the interconnectedness of the world from the nineteenth century onward, and points to the dangers and benefits of the sort of global fame we've now become familiar with. In my introduction to the *Picador/Vintage Book of Modern Indian Literature*, I'd said that Tagore was probably the world's 'first international literary celebrity'; an Indian reviewer, who must have immediately concluded I was celebrating the fact, said my claim was 'risible'. An English poet who taught at Oxford said the dubious honour might belong to Byron. People have forgotten how startling Tagore's incursion was into the various languages of the twentieth century. Martin Kaempchen points out that he was Germany's first best-seller; Jiménez's translations made him a cult in the Spanish-speaking world; this is not to invoke his renown in China, Japan, Russia, Eastern Europe, and the United States. This fame was a product, largely, of Tagore's English-language, Nobel Prize-winning *Gitanjali*; the English *Gitanjali* is perhaps one of the earliest examples of how capitalism fetishizes the book. To use the word celebrity, then (rather than terms like 'high critical standing'), isn't inappropriate, as Tagore's presence was felt so predominantly outside the field of literature, as it still is—except in the forgotten sphere of Bengali literature. And to recover Tagore today as a poet and writer must entail some sense of the Bengali language becoming a realm of literary possibility.

★

Looking back today to the middle of the nineteenth century, we feel compelled to admit that something exceptional occurred with the emergence of Bengali as a literary language. Disturbingly, we still know very little of this moment, partly because an easeful way of looking at colonial history (according to which modernity comes from elsewhere, bringing with it certain genres and practices) has saved us from engaging too strenuously with the question of how and why things changed when they did. For instance, I don't think we still have a proper genealogy of the word *sahitya*, which we've been using for more than a century to mean 'literature' and 'literary tradition' in the modern, secular sense, and not to mean, as it once did in the Indian languages, 'literary content' or 'literary meaning'. Tagore's own etymological gloss on the word asks us to look at its root, *sahit* ('to be with'), thereby turning literature into a social, companionable thing. It is fairly certain, though, that *sahitya*, as we understand it, is not a timeless Indian verity (for that, we should perhaps look up the word *kavya*) but a contingent, humanist construct, just as 'Indianness' and the modern Bengali language are. It is also certain that the emergence of Bengali encompassed more than nationalism. It became—in lieu of English—a respectable vehicle for cosmopolitan self-expression by the 1860s. It is the latter development that failed in Ireland and Wales with regard to Gaelic and Welsh, and nationalism alone (of which there was no shortage in Ireland) didn't succeed in turning those languages into viable literatures or prevent them from becoming, essentially, curios. In Ireland, it is the English language that became the medium through which the modern formulated his or her ambivalence and self-division, so giving Irish literature and diction its shifting registers in English. Gaelic, largely associated with identity and nation, became, with a few striking exceptions, an unusable artefact. Something quite different and exceptional happened in Bengali colonial modernity. The Bengali language emerged from not only a conviction about identity but an intimation of distance, from not just the wellspring of race but disjunction and severance. These essentially cosmopolitan tensions always animate Tagore's language.

I used the word 'curio' deliberately, in order to recall Buddhadeva Bose's unfair but revealing attack on Indian poets writing in English in the 1960s, in which he accused them of producing, by choosing not to write in the mother tongue, not poems but 'curios'. In one sense, Bose is right. It is the English language that has risked becoming, over and over, a sort of Gaelic in India: not because, as Bose would have it, it was a foreign or colonial tongue, but because, like Gaelic, it bore too notionally the burden of identity and nationality. The relative and paradoxical freedom from this burden in the emergence of modern Bengali gave it its special air of play and potential. In other, fundamental ways, Bose was wrong. The poets he attacked had based their achievement on a cunning with which they had sabotaged and complicated the possibility of a pan-Indian tradition; they too were writing, in their way, in a vernacular. In fact, it was the long poem that Bose held up as the great exemplary Indian English poem, 'Savitri' by Sri Aurobindo, that the shrewd Nissim Ezekiel pointed out as the actual curio for, presumably, its faux high cultural atmosphere of the Orient as well as its emulation of the English canon (it was composed in iambs). It should be pointed out that Tagore's English translation of *Gitanjali* would be—for Indian poets writing in English like Ezekiel, A. K. Ramanujan, Arvind Krishna Mehrotra—yet another Gaelic artefact to bypass or circumvent. In his brief memoir 'Partial Recall', Mehrotra quotes, with little indulgence towards his youthful self, from the ambitious and sonorous pastiche of that *Gitanjali* which he produced as a teenager.

★

The fact that literature—specifically English literature—was a university discipline first invented for the colonies is fairly well known today. In the 1880s, English literature became an object of study leading to a degree at the University of Calcutta, well before any such development had taken place elsewhere, let alone Oxford or Cambridge. But the incursion of English and European literary texts into Bengal had begun a century earlier. The study of literature cannot be seen simply as an instrument of imperialist pedagogy from the 1820s onward (when it first surfaces as a taught discipline in Calcutta). By the early nineteenth century, Bengalis, especially when naming literary and cultural societies, were reflecting on what literature, or, in Bengali, *sahitya*, might be—great texts of all kinds, or a different way of approaching and valuing texts? A significant historical narrative is contained in the evolution of the word *sahitya* into its present-day meaning. What seems pretty sure is that it was not a word just lying around, ready to slip into its contemporary, secular role. Nor is it a simple translation of the word literature, though it means much the same thing from the middle of the nineteenth century onward. That is, it is neither a purely Indian (whatever that may be) nor colonial term, but one that keeps abreast of these dichotomies until they start to waver. Tagore, in his first essay on the subject in 1889, defines it in negatives: 'The essence of literature does not allow itself to be trapped within a definition. It is like the essence of life: we know what it cannot exist without, but what it is we do not know.'[6] These are the words of a poet who has come into his own at a cusp in history. Perhaps the specificity of Tagore's problem, and the duress of the historical moment he's speaking in and of, would become clearer if the key word were left untranslated: 'The essence of *sahitya* does not allow itself to be trapped', and so on. But the translator, Sukanta Chaudhuri, doesn't do so because he presumes Tagore has already leaped towards the sense in which that word operates today; and, in part, he's right. By 1889, Tagore's readers have definitely begun to recognize the literary, in spite of the strangeness of the sentences I have quoted. Yet one must keep in mind the strangeness of the time. Tagore's complex and difficult position as a modern Indian, a colonial subject, an elite cosmopolitan, an inheritor and inventor of Eastern civilizational values, and a progeny of the Enlightenment allows him to partake of the exclusive secular ethos of literature but also to view it from the outside, as a process. You feel more than once as you gaze back on that crucial period that you are over-familiar with its outlines, and also that you are only on the verge of understanding it.

★

Tagore has been such a fountainhead of nationalist pride, such a static emblem ever since one can remember that we forget that he was clearly aware, as a writer, of living in a unique and transformative time. There is, in Tagore, a constant acknowledgement of the power of the past, and of the canonical riches of Indian tradition, and constant inquiry about the terms in which these are available to us. In this, he is different from either the Hindu reformers or the Indian nationalists, for whom tradition has an integrity and wholeness, and is a given to be improved upon or invoked in the services of politics and identity. For Tagore, tradition is at once contemporary and immediate, and inaccessible and disjunctive. As a result, contrary emotions permeate his great essay on the fourth-century Kalidasa's poem on the rainy season, 'Meghadutam' ('The Cloud-Messenger'):

From Ramgiri to the Himalayas ran a long stretch of ancient India over which life used to flow to the slow, measured *mandrakanta* meter of the 'Meghadutam'.

> We are banished from that India, not just during the rains but for all time. Gone is Dasharna with its groves hedged with *ketaki* plants where, before the onset of the rains, the birds among the roadside trees fed on household scraps and busily built their nests, while in the *jaam* copse on the outskirts of the village, the fruit ripened to a colour dark as the clouds.[7]

The intimation of contemporaneity here is astonishingly suburban; it has to do with nature, yes, but nature viewed from the point of view of the town and the ebb and flow of domesticity: the 'household scraps' the birds feed on, the ripening *jaam* that will be collected and brought home to the family. Kalidasa is not a naïve poet; he is a court sophisticate, an urban sensibility, already viewing the natural at one remove. The loss experienced here, then—'We are banished from that India, not just during the rains but for all time'—is a double, even a multiple, one. From which India, exactly, are we banished? This paradox—to do with immediacy, recognizability, and absolute inaccessibility—is also the subject of Tagore's own poem, 'Meghdut', which records the experience of rereading Kalidasa's eponymous poem. Tagore's poem, filled with images of human activity and habitation, describes how the reader comes to inhabit Kalidasa's world as he reads and becomes an exile from it once the poem is over.

Tagore's fascination and absorption in heritage could have made him an elegist, or a poet who turned from the physical life of the present to contemplate the ruins of the past. This trajectory was, to a certain extent, T. S. Eliot's. But, oddly, this is not the case. Tagore's way of suggesting that he lives in a unique moment in history is to embrace change as a fundamental constituent of existence—indeed, as a crucial constituent of diction, imagination, and craft. 'In order to find you anew, I lose you every moment / O beloved treasure.'[8] In this line from a song and others like it, Tagore embraces accident. He weds contingency to the modernist's love of the moment, the here and now. The latter—as in the Joycean epiphany—heightens the quotidian: Tagore's welcoming of contingency introduces an element of risk to the epiphany and the image. He introduces the possibility of any imaginable consequence, including an intuition of the divine. Tagore's apotheosis of his historical moment, his here and now, is not a surreptitious celebration of the colonial history into which he was born, but a recognition of the fact that no historical period can be contained within its canonical definition. Accident and chance ensure that its outcomes are unpredictable and life-transforming.

This embrace of life, of chance, of play, makes Tagore stand out in the intellectual and moral ethos of late romanticism and modernism—an ethos with which Tagore shares several obsessions (time, memory, the moment, the nature of reality, poetic form), but whose metaphysics he constantly refutes. By *metaphysics* I mean a system whereby value and meaning have their source elsewhere, somewhere beyond the experienced world—whether it is European civilization, antiquity, the Celtic twilight, or some other lost world. The present, severed from its organic resources in that past, becomes degraded and splintered, and yet continues to be haunted, even burnished, by what it has lost. I think Tagore is deeply interested in this metaphysics in the context of Bengal, and it runs through his songs, with their momentary scenes, encounters, and revelations, where any hint of transcendence is qualified by the temporal and the fragmentary. This metaphysics is partly invoked as incantation in the refrain from the poem 'Balaka', or 'The Wild Geese': '*Hethha noi, hethha noi, onno konokhane!*' ('Not here, not here—elsewhere!')[9] But there is also—in the same oeuvre, often in the very same songs and poems—the Tagore of whom I have become more and more aware, the near-contemporary of Nietzsche's, who, like the latter, makes a break with that 'elsewhere' and constructs a sustained argument against it in song, and in the terms that life and desire give him: 'I've become infinite: / such is the consequence of your play. / Pouring me out, you fill me / with new life once again.'[10] This, in many ways, is an astonishing and audacious assertion, all the more striking for being entirely self-aware about its audacity (this is a tonal characteristic Tagore shares with Nietzsche). The oeuvre is full of such assertions, running counter to both romanticism's backward glance and his own 'Not here, not here' refrain. It marks him out, like D. H. Lawrence, as a writer embodying a radical historical break. The lines I have tried to reproduce in English are among the most difficult to translate from the work of this largely untranslatable poet. They (in Tagore's own English) are also among his most famous, being the opening lines of the first song in the English *Gitanjali*. In Tagore's English prose-poem version: 'Thou hast made me endless, such is thy pleasure.' All sorts of echoes adorn the next two lines in Tagore's English—'This frail vessel thou emptiest again and again . . . ' and 'This little flute of a reed thou hast carried over hills and dales'[11]—placing the song now in the context of a psalm-like, New Testament sweetness ('this frail vessel') and now in an English arcadia ('little flute of a reed . . . hills and dales'). The words are removed, in effect, from the radical moment they inhabit in the Bengali. The original—'*Amare tumi ashesh korechho / emoni leela taba*'—is remarkable, as I've said, on many levels. The word *leela* can be translated as divine play: Hindu philosophy sees divine play as childlike and solipsistic, and the creation and destruction of the universe, and of man, among its various corollaries. Tagore translates the word as 'pleasure', to denote the primacy of delight and desire, rather than moral design, in divine creation. Among the unintended, almost inadvertent, results of that play, the song has it, is man's immortality, or 'infinity' (my word), or 'endlessness' (Tagore's). And so the centrality of the human is bestowed upon her or him by divinity, certainly, but not by design or according to a legible purpose. In this way, Tagore introduces the notion of chance and coincidence into the story of man's emergence, and removes the human narrative from its familiar logical movement (an ascent or a decline) from the past to the present, from tradition to modernity.

Radical claims abound in the songs and poems. Also in the *Gitanjali* is the song beginning (in my translation): 'To the festival of creation I have had an invitation: / Blessed, blessed is human life!' In Tagore's English prose-poem, though, the song's declaration is more modest: 'I have had my invitation to this world's festival, and thus my life has been blessed.'[12] This is almost Christian, a muttering of grace. The Bengali is far more unsettling: it has 'human life' (*manab jiban*) instead of the prayerful 'my life'. It is more triumphal. Again, alongside the celebration of the occurrence of life and consciousness is the deliberate celebration of contingency. An invitation is always a bonus and a gift; you can't really expect it or plan for it or demand it. And, once more, the two lines, with their narrative of cause and effect, are structured at once to invoke logic and to mock it. In the earlier song, Tagore writes as if he knows that the self's infinity or endlessness should be a natural consequence of divine play, while also knowing very well there is absolutely no logical reason for the one to lead to the other. In the second song, the progression, from discovering the invitation to the festival of existence to the assertion that human life is 'blessed' (*dhanya*), is presented seamlessly, although we know there is actually no good reason why the second should follow from the first. (In the English version, which adds a 'thus' that is absent in the Bengali, the progression in the first line is far more acceptable.) But why should divine play lead to the speaker's belief in his own infinitude? Why should his being invited to earthly existence be a cause of joy for all human life? There's a logical structure to the way these statements develop, but it is a structure that conceals a deep arbitrariness. The second song strongly implies, in its movement from the first line to the second in Bengali, a 'thus' or 'therefore' or 'tai', without being able to quite justify or explain that powerful implication. The English translation, by adding a 'thus' and substituting 'human life' with 'my life', simply dispenses with that mysterious tension and diminishes the audacity of the opening. We, as listeners of the Bengali song, are moved and unsettled, but we ask, in the end, for no justification: it is almost as if we know that, in Tagore's world, anything is possible.

Much of Tagore's work, then, is preoccupied with—indeed, mesmerized by—coincidence and possibility. It is a preoccupation that seems to go against the closure and yearning of 'Not here, not here, elsewhere', because one can never predict when or where that moment of possibility will occur. One of the songs I have translated for *The Essential Tagore*, 'The sky full of the sun and stars, the world full of life, / in the midst of this, I find myself— / so, surprised, my song awakens',[13] is, again, a paean to coincidence. It is also a refutation of metaphysics, of a higher purpose (whatever that might be), according to whose design existence or consciousness might find its proper meaning and arrangement. I have translated Tagore's word *bismaye* as 'surprised', though it could plausibly be rendered as 'in wonder'. The role of the naïve or nature poet, or even a certain kind of romantic, is to wonder at the real, at the universe, but the speaker in the song is not just transfixed by the beauty of the universe but by the happenstance that's brought him to it: 'in the midst of this, I find myself'. This is what gives to the poet-mystic's *bismay* (his sense of wonder) the element of the unexpected, of surprise—the surprise of the time-traveller (expressed in the poem 'Meghdut') moving between worlds and phases of history. Tagore's peculiar lyric voice, with its curiously urgent apotheosis of the world, its constant note of arrival, can be partly understood through the trope of science fiction (one of whose recurrent themes is the sudden advent into new universes), or through the notion of rebirth and return, or both. This is an odd but powerful, and revealing, characteristic in the foremost artist to have emerged from a background of Brahmo reformism and the Bengali Enlightenment.

★

Tagore's recurrent metaphors of time travel, return, and arrival, and the fact that the great protagonist of his songs and poems is a figure determinedly committed to journeying towards life and birth, were picked up by two great Bengali artists who came after him: the poet Jibanananda Das and the filmmaker Ritwik Ghatak. Das (1899–1954), who, after his untimely death in an accident with a tram, has come to be seen as the outstanding Bengali poet after Tagore, and whose personality—solitary, disturbed—is the antithesis of the older poet's, sensed that Tagore was the principal writer of his time of the will to, and desire for, life. Without remarking upon this in so many words, he took on this mantle himself, but expressed himself far more equivocally, if no less forcefully. Das's time traveller, in his poem 'Banalata Sen', moves through epochs and civilizations, arriving at last in a modern drawing room in Bengal, in a journey during which both mythic and ordinary place-names are made strange:

> For thousands of years I roamed the paths of this earth,
> From waters round Ceylon in dead of night to Malayan seas.
> Much have I wandered. I was there in the gray world of Asoka
> And Bimbisara, pressed on through darkness to the city of Vidarbha.
>
> I am a weary heart surrounded by life's frothy ocean.
> To me she gave a moment's peace—Banalata Sen from Natore.
>
> (trans. Clinton B. Seely)[14]

The irrepressible Tagorean energy, the irresistible will to arrive—'in the midst of this, I find myself— / so, surprised, my song awakens'—has faded here but not vanished. Das gets his habit of repeating ancient place-names from Tagore as one of the ways in which the traveller orders his journey while commemorating past arrivals; here is Tagore in his eponymous essay on Kalidasa's poem, 'The Meghadutam': 'Avanti, Vidisha, Ujjayini, Vindhya, Kailas, Devagiri, the Reva, the Shipra, the Vetravati.'[15] But Das's speaker experiences a fatigue that the radical Tagorean protagonist didn't know. Das's hero, or antihero, must press on, despite his 'weary heart': he has inherited, perplexingly, the same life-urge. Das too is a great poet of the will to live—precisely because his view of it is darker, and far more qualified. His protagonist desires to be born despite being conscious that birth is not an unmixed blessing. This is Das's troubling modulation upon the Tagorean idea of the 'invitation' to earthly existence, as a result of which 'human life' is 'blessed':

Drawn to the Earth's ground, to the house of human birth
I have come, and I feel, better not to have been born—
yet having come all this I see as a deeper gain
when I touch a body of dew in an incandescent dawn.
('Suchetana', trans. Joe Winter)[16]

In the first two lines of this famous stanza, Das has a familiar Sophoclean moment; but, in the third and fourth lines, he's come round to the Tagorean belief that arrival and return create their own article of faith; the body becomes an incarnation of the will ('I touch a body of dew'); in Tagore's words, 'I've pressed upon each blade of grass on my way to the forest.' Again and again, Das will be of two minds about this matter, about withdrawing from the cycle of life or, taking his cue from his great precursor, returning to it:

When once I leave this body
Shall I come back to the world?
If only I might return
On a winter's evening
Taking on the compassionate flesh of a cold tangerine
At the bedside of some dying acquaintance.
('Tangerine', trans. Clinton B. Seely)[17]

For Tagore, withdrawal was out of the question. 'In the midst of this, I find myself', he'd said in the song. In the poem 'Liberation' ('Mukti'), he put it elegantly but with directness: 'Liberation through renunciation—that's not for me'; and, later, 'To shut / in penance, the senses' doorway—that's not for me.' We can connect this to the Buddhist thought that deeply attracted Tagore; but if we place it in the context of his oeuvre, of the modernity he lived in, and the modernism he was always ambivalent about, we must put him in the lineage of Nietzsche, Whitman, Lawrence, and others who made a similar rebuttal of negation. Actually, looking again at the poem 'Balaka' ('The Wild Geese'), in which the admonitory refrain 'Not here, not here, elsewhere' occurs, I find it lit not so much by a desire for 'elsewhere' (the foundational desire of metaphysics) but, again, by the subversive urge for life itself. The poet is standing after sunset before a landscape of hills and deodar trees, near the river Jhelum, when, unexpectedly, the sudden transit of a flock of geese flying transmogrifies the observer and his vision of nature. The Tagorean landscape is often orchestral, participatory, musical, synchronic, but not Wordsworthian, with the 'still, sad music of humanity'; it is alive, but not in an anthropomorphic sense.

In another, early poem, '*Jete nahi dibo*' ('I Won't Let You Go!'), all of nature, as the speaker departs from home and family on a long absence involving work, echoes his daughter's final words to him in an actively participatory way, in what can only be called an orchestral threnody:

> What immense sadness has engulfed
> The entire sky and the whole world!
> The farther I go the more clearly I hear
> Those poignant words, 'Won't let you go!'
> From world's end to the blue dome of the sky
> Echoes the eternal cry: 'Won't let you go!'
> Everything cries, 'I won't let you go!'
> Mother Earth too cries out to the tiny grass
> It hugs on its bosom, 'I won't let you go!'
> (trans. Fakrul Alam)[18]

This is not anthropomorphism; it is the landscape agitated by the life urge, and making a vocal, direct intervention. In 'The Wild Geese', Tagore revisits and revises his vision:

> It seemed that those wings
> Bore away tidings
> Of stillness thrilled in its innermost being
> By the intensity of motion...

And again:

> ...The grass fluttering its wings
> On the earth that is its air—
> Underneath the darkness of the soil
> Millions of seeds sprouting wings
> I see today (trans. Fakrul Alam)[19]

From Tagore, the filmmaker Ritwik Ghatak (1925–76) got his sense of the landscape being not just a serene, indifferent, permanent background to human endeavour, as in the Brueghel painting of Icarus's fall described wryly by W. H. Auden in his 'Musée des Beaux Arts', but as a multivocal, orchestral entity actively involved in the desire for existence. So, at different points of time in Ghatak's films, the landscape appears to move and listen; it is aware of the protagonist, just as the protagonist is partly conscious of it being conscious of him. Ghatak's great modulation upon 'The Wild Geese' and its cry—as well as the cry 'I won't let you go'—occurs towards the end of *Meghe Dhaka Tara* ('The Cloud-Covered Star'), his most fraught and painful film. Nita, once the breadwinner of a family of East Bengali refugees displaced by migration, is now terminally ill with tuberculosis. She has been transferred by her brother, Shankar, from their house in Calcutta to a sanatorium in the hill-station, Shillong. Anil, now a successful singer, comes to visit her; the two figures are surrounded by an astonishing panorama. As she listens to him talk about their younger sister's mischievous child, Nita bursts out without warning, 'Dada, I *did* want to live!' Crushed, attempting to placate and silence her, Anil responds with 'Idiot!' (Indeed, there is something comic, even imbecilic, about the life-urge and its insistent simplicity; which is why we, on occasion, shake our heads in consternation at Tagore and Whitman and Lawrence and Ghatak—all very different kinds of artists, admittedly.) In a series of rapid frames, we witness the landscape congregating from various angles and echoing her words, 'I so love life, dada! I *will* live!' This is the primordial Tagorean 'message' ('I felt the message of those beating wings'[20]) of a near-heretical faith; ironicized by Ghatak, seen unflinchingly for its heresy, but not made meaningless. This faith contains an acknowledgement of death and 'elsewhere', but also an answer and a refutation.

*

Death and life share the quality of being contingent, accidental: we don't know when and how they will happen, or even, really, why they do. (This would have been pretty clear to Tagore, who lost his muse and sister-in-law Kadambari Devi when he was twenty-two—she had died by her own hand—and then, over the years, his wife and two of his children.) Tagore's work is less about universals, absolutes, and unities (though it is also about these) than about the role of chance governing the shape of the universe and of the work itself, taking the form of a sustained meditation: 'In order to find you anew, I lose you every moment / O beloved treasure.' Contingency preoccupied him all his life. In 1930, when he had a couple of meetings with Albert Einstein, he opened the dialogue enthusiastically with, 'I was discussing with Dr. Mendel today the new mathematical discoveries which tell us that in the realm of infinitesimal atoms chance has its play; the drama of existence is not absolutely predestined in character.' Einstein replies with a dampener: 'The facts that make science tend toward this view do not say goodbye to causality.'[21] This famous, over-publicized conversation can be read in a number of ways. Einstein clearly sees Tagore as a 'poet' in the 'high' cultural Western sense, but still more as an Eastern sage, and is dry and cautious as a result. He—not Tagore—keeps bringing up the word *religion* in a mildly defensive, mildly accusatory manner. Einstein, responsible for a shatteringly disorienting theory that would forever change philosophy and the humanities, not to speak of the sciences, forecloses, in response to Tagore, that strand of insight, and becomes a conventional scientist-empiricist: for 'that', he says, 'is my religion'. Tagore, in the course of the two slightly anxious, circular conversations, appears in various fluid incarnations: as a romantic poet, talking about beauty and truth; as a transcendentalist; a believer in the absolute; a propagandist for universal man. We have dealt with him in these guises in the last one hundred years of discussions about Tagore; no doubt we will again, 150 years after his birth. But Tagore's secret concern with life, play, and contingency keeps resurfacing in his part of the dialogue; he might well have believed that this powerful undercurrent would provide common ground with the German. Einstein, though, pushes the interaction towards a more conservative dichotomy: that of the romantic, the man of religion, or the metaphysician with his purely subjective response to the universe, on the one hand, and the scientist with his empirical and objective vantage-point, on the other.

⋆

For me, there are two great lineages in poetry from the upheavals of the nineteenth century onward: the metaphysical, or the poetry of the beautiful (sometimes anguished) fragment made radiant by the light of the vanished old world and of bygone value; and the polemical, sounding the note of constant, occasionally arbitrary, arrival and return, disrupting not just linearity, as the former does, but causality. I think Tagore belongs deeply, if only partially, to the first category, and I have written before of his songs in this light. But, increasingly, I believe his great power derives from being essentially in the second camp, from denying, like Whitman and Lawrence, that there is any need to apologize for life and its accidental provenance. One characteristic of the writers in the first camp is how they practise their art and their criticism in distinct domains, and, in a sense, detach themselves from the 'meaning' of their artistic work, like Joyce's fingernail-paring author-god, or James's evolving 'figure in the carpet', upon which the narrator will deliberately not elaborate. The polemicists, on the other hand, not only immerse themselves in the thrust of their work with every fibre of their being—'a man in his wholeness wholly attending', as Lawrence said of poetry—but in every sphere of activity they undertake, as Tagore did. This is why they seem open to deciphering and are more vulnerable to misunderstanding.

I had begun by mentioning my adolescent impatience with Tagore and my enthusiasm for Dan Pagis's poem about the Holocaust. I still admire that poem—in fact, more than I did when I was seventeen—for its craft, tragic exactness, and its shrinking shape informed by Adorno's stark dictum that poetry is no longer tenable after Auschwitz. Adorno's admonition, however, has a history older than the horrors of the twentieth century: it comes from a metaphysical belief that, on many levels, life (and, as a result, its chief expression, language) is too fragile to wholly justify itself. Tagore is still the great poet in our age of life's inherent and inexhaustible justification—this is what he is actually conveying to Einstein—but his argument is plainest in the songs and poems. Accustomed as we are to the luminosity of elsewhere, to the backward glance, to action and outcome with a cause, and less accustomed to the joy of unforeseen arrival (which, after all, rapidly wanes into alienation), encountering Tagore has to be an unsettling experience—but one through which we also come to recognize our deepest unspoken urges and beliefs incarnated in the most surprising and incomparable language.

2009

* * *

4

What we do

Deprofessionalization and legitimacy

I first heard the word 'deprofessionalized' from Ashis Nandy, about a decade ago. In the course of conversation, he had said, 'Gustavo Esteva calls me a "deprofessionalized intellectual".' With quiet satisfaction, he added that he couldn't have maintained his singular status without the support of the CSDS, the institution at which he was a Fellow. I immediately took to the word and to the idea. The negative prefix 'de', as in 'demobbed', suggests a certain lack of volition (one doesn't choose to be but one *is* 'demobbed') in relation to occupying this category, while hinting at a quality of belatedness, of following an epochal shift (soldiers are demobbed after a war). These echoes made the state of deprofessionalization eccentrically attractive. That Nandy should have found an institution to pay him for undertaking this project of calculated unemployment, and unemployability, was fortunate.

This is not about Nandy. What I hope to put together is a series of moments. But I wish to stay with Nandy a bit longer, since the episode I've referred to comprises one of those moments. What's odd about Nandy, and what has made him resistant to our latent notions of professionalization, is that he doesn't have a clear disciplinary denomination. Nandy is a psychologist (psychology accounts for his training and inflects his interpretative apparatus) and a cultural commentator (given his wide-ranging inclinations and also taking into account how he's read). But he's clearly no public intellectual in the American sense. His language is too arcane and pedagogical to fully inhabit the public sphere. Nor is he an exemplary post-Independence academic, as his output isn't pedagogical or disciplinary enough. To a certain extent, Nandy has had to make up his own pedagogy as he's gone along.

Maybe the best definition for him would be the open-ended category of the 'writer'. The fact that we never actually speak of him as a writer probably addresses our steadfast attempts to professionalize him and others like him.

*

Let me say a few words about my own relationship to that word. Being a 'writer' involves the pursuit of a species of accomplishment that no one wants to easily own up to. There was a time when I understood V. S. Naipaul's sense of fraudulence about committing it to his passport in the blank space next to 'Profession'. It took him six novels to finally shake off that anxiety to do with being identified with what is possibly—despite the undeniable fact of publication (a word that, of course, contains 'public' within it)—a covert ambition. Today, I'm still unsure about using the term of myself. What has pushed me towards it is, paradoxically, an institutional position I have held since 2006. The position comprises a title that is itself a generic description: Professor of Contemporary Literature. Apparently to be a professor means, first of all, to profess who you are; only on the basis of this disclosure can you then profess to others. If anything, the invocation of the word 'professor' creates a sense of unease in me that exceeds the sleight of hand I feel I'm involved in when I call myself a 'writer'. This is partly because I never entered academia, as a student, for any other reason but to further my project of becoming a published novelist. I played around with the thought of dropping my doctorate but completed it to keep up appearances. I was successful in my agenda: my second novel was published a week before my viva in June 1993. Since then, I held a two-year research fellowship but no regular job until I took up the post at the University of East Anglia in 2006. About that institution, I feel as I had about England when I was a student: that I happened to be in it at a certain point of time, and that I have been there for longer than I thought I would be. I always expected—and expect—to go back one day to where I came from. One thing I've noticed about myself in this period is that I've made it a point, semi-consciously, to hold on to my personal email address, and to use the institutional email address sparingly. The latter is an area of domicile; I inhabit it in name only. My personal email address, on the other hand, isn't 'home'; it's an anywhere; it has no actual identity. That I often use it for institutional work isn't inconsistent with this fact. It's in this period, especially in the last six years, when I've been increasingly trying to escape being called an academic, that I find myself admitting, with less prevarication than before, to being a 'writer'.

★

The period I've mentioned—between 1993 and 2006, the time when I was more or less unemployed, engaged in the experiment of being a full-time writer—was remarkable for the changes it consolidated in connection with 'professionalization'.

Developments in America in the sphere of what might loosely be called the 'literary' were at once self-perpetuating and polarizing, bringing another dimension to the relationship between the worlds of 'creative writing' and 'literary studies'. 'Creative writing' would become a self-contained economy in the US; it's an economy that has been taxonomized more recently by the novelist Chad Harbach as, simply, 'MFA'. It comprises students of creative writing who, upon attaining doctorates in creative writing, then become teachers of creative writing; in contrast, say, to an earlier lot of teachers, who would be appointed to those posts on the basis of novels they'd published. MFA teachers publish novels, too, but there's a growing number of such professors who, according to Harbach, are read and known only in the ecology of MFA.[1] Harbach compares and contrasts 'MFA' with what he calls 'NYC', or writers published and disseminated by mainstream New York publishing houses. What's also striking is how the self-sustaining specialization of MFA finds an unmistakable echo in American literary studies. On the one hand, MFA is, of course, the 'other' of literary studies. It pursues an ethic of craft, the sentence, the appropriate adjective, and the placement of the comma, deriving its advocacy of the value of writing from Flaubert and from US editors, such as Gordon Lish, who reiterate Flaubertian directives. Literary studies' eschewal of literary value is also an eschewal of the seemingly fragile world enshrined in MFA; on the other hand, though, it mirrors it perfectly. The true subject of the scholarship and discussion within American 'literary studies' since the 1990s has neither been literature nor the critical theory that problematizes literature, but the works produced by scholars of literary studies. The auto-nourishing ecological model that has, according to Harbach, characterized 'MFA' is also one that almost entirely shapes American literary studies. The animosity and distance between the two is very real; but so is the particular mode of professionalization that defines these competing pedagogical domains.

★

For me, 'creative writing' was a rumour till I taught literature to MFA students for a few months at Columbia University at the end of 2002: there, I confronted it as a discipline for the first time. But the kind of professionalization it represented was, to me, a distant threat or problem. Even the term 'writer', about which, as I've said, I had a Naipaulean hesitation, was less troublesome, less of an immediate concern to be grappled with, than the word 'novelist'. It had begun to speak for me. Yet both it, and the genre it derived from, the 'novel', were uneasy constructs, and my fidelity to them was, by the end of the 1990s, wavering. The 'novel', as much as the 'novelist', seemed to involve a set of guidelines that might be of no interest to those who are practising or exploring that form, or who inhabit that role. The word 'novelist', as a proprietary definition, underestimates the ambivalence practitioners sometimes feel towards their practice, or the genre or form they're using. It is, then, salutary to be reminded by the writer Kirsty Gunn of Virginia Woolf's disavowal of these terms in a diary entry on Saturday 27 June 1925, when she's composing one of her greatest pieces of writing: 'I am making up "To the Lighthouse"—the sea is to be heard all through it. I have an idea that I will invent a new name for my books to supplant "novel". A new ____ by Virginia Woolf. But what? Elegy?'[2]

In 1999, I returned to India, having published three novels, and about to publish the fourth in 2000; then I began to deprofessionalize myself. On the face of it, this might refer to the process by which I left the next nine years open-ended, publishing my fifth novel only in 2009, using the interim to bring to light a book of stories, another of poems, a critical study, a collection of critical essays, edit two anthologies, and record and perform music. All this was certainly integral to my deprofessionalization. But I wasn't only attempting to part ways with the 'professionalized', however one wishes to interpret that term. Increasingly, I wished to break with mimesis, and the mimetic tendencies of both the novel and the novelist in the last twenty-five years.

The novel, unlike other literary forms—the poem, the story, the essay, the novella—is primarily identified with completeness. Whatever other traits it may have that make the genre heterogeneous, its formal rejection of synecdoche makes its capacity for accommodating, representing, engendering, and reflecting a world, or *the* world, its most characteristic feature. In some ways, it not only reflects the world, but is continuous with what we understand the world should be. To abjure this characteristic, as a novelist, is to say, contrarily, that you are ill-at-ease with the mimesis deep within the form. Neither mimesis nor completeness in fiction can, however, be wholly reduced to the practice of realism. Novels might be fantastic or hyperbolic, but those very traits of the fantastical or hyperbolic might be mimetic, as in the case of Latin American fiction, or a particular kind of Indian novel in English. Think of Marquez's apparently provocative remark, that the bizarre transmogrifications of his fictional terrain are actually not bizarre at all, but a record of the reality of Latin America, and you begin to understand the particular modulation of the mimetic compulsion—the project of creating a narrative language adequate to representing a culture—in the 'magic realist' novel. Formal mimesis—whereby pastiche, allegory, or fairy tale come to somehow be related to how we represent the globalized or multicultural world—was far more pervasive in the 1990s than a mimesis to do simply with how characters speak or how settings are described.

If the novel today is mimetic of how we understand the 'global', the cultural, the novelist too has as much a representative role to play as the genre of his or her choice. The novelist must be as complete in his or her identity as the novel is in its. The primary way of doing this is to produce novels, and to do so with regularity, every two or three years. The market has reified this pattern of productivity: it dictates that the novelist abide by it in order to adhere to a fundamentally mimetic principle. *You must produce a novel every few years*, it suggests. *How can you be a novelist if you stop writing novels?* It's a chain: the novel gives us the world; the novelist gives us novels. This is the market's parody of romantic organicism: 'as naturally as leaves to a tree, or not at all', Keats had said of how poetry should come to poets; and the market ensures that the novelist will need to write novels in the same way (periodically) that trees come into leaf or cows produce milk. Ian McEwan has, since the late 1980s, been the exemplar of this mimetic function. To break away is to depart the parameters that govern the representational.

Let me, here, introduce two brief variations on this theme. In a literary ethos in which a reliable means of identifying who a novelist is is essential, and the recurrent production of novels the most reliable mode of identification, the example of the author of the successful first novel is, paradoxically, central to how we now construct or conceive of this identity. In the shrunken time, the 'now', of globalization, the first novel is not a beginning: it's a culmination, a triumphant declaration. For the market, the author of the successful first novel is forever a 'novelist', whether or not they ever write a novel again; the novels to come are, in a sense, irrelevant. Here, the Naipaulean hesitation is incongruous and anachronistic, as are the niggles of fraudulence.

The second variation has to do with an actor I haven't mentioned so far: the reader. The main question regarding deprofessionalized time has to do, I suppose, with what one is doing with it. This is pertinent not only to the writer, or to the matter of what writers do all day, but also to the person who's absorbed in reading. In the interview in which Kirsty Gunn makes that pointed reference to Woolf, interviewer and interviewee spend a short while discussing the inexplicable time we spend reading books. Reading literature is hard work, notes the interviewer; it entails learning how to read. 'People often see me and they'll say: what have you done all day? If I tell them I've been reading they're often confused.' Gunn responds: 'There's a great Bill Hicks joke about that. A waitress comes over to him and says: what ya readin' for?'[3] The same could be said of the time spent listening to music. It no longer possesses that bewildering exclusivity. Living memory tells us that there was an age when we would buy a record and listen to it on a music system for about an hour. What were we doing in that duration, seated on a sofa and staring ahead of us?

*

I'd like to bring in a more conventional and sociological meaning of the word 'deprofessionalization' at this point, to do with how globalization and the market, which create a function for the writer, a function defined by a rate and type of productivity, also create contexts that take away the writer's metaphoric and literal functions. One of the most acute spokespersons for the writer's loss of function is the Croatian novelist Dubravka Ugrešić.

Ugrešić experiences a loss of function on several levels: of one who was a Yugoslav writer who had to 'wake up one day as a Croatian writer'[4] (notice the studied echo of Kafka); of one who believed that writing and freedom of expression were all on the 'other side', in the democratic West, only to discover, after the collapse of the Berlin Wall and the subsequent disintegration of various nations, that the market in the 'free world' chose producers of books over writers of books; of one who might have served a function in the 'free world' as a writer from a socialist state, except socialism had vanished. All this Ugrešić realized, like Gregor Samsa, upon waking up one morning: the abnegation from definition that would now dominate her work and life.

Ugrešić then went on to become a precise analyst of not just the writer's irrelevance, but the irrelevance of their compulsion—their malady or gift, whatever you wish to call it—in the new age. As Kafka knew, the malady—the deviation from normalcy—was both a curse and a claim to uniqueness because it only occurred in a few. So his 'hunger artist' confesses before he dies: 'I always wanted you to admire my starving', to which the overseer replies, 'We do admire it.' 'But you're not to admire it', protests the hunger artist, and utters, by way of explanation, his last words: 'Because . . . I couldn't find any food I liked. If I had found any, believe me, I wouldn't have made any fuss, and I would have eaten to my heart's content, just like you or anyone else.'[5]

The reason the hunger artist died was because he was no longer needed; the crowd 'got used to the oddity . . . people walked past him. Try and explain the art of starving! It needs to be felt, it's not something that can be explained.' But what if starving could be pursued and 'felt' by everybody: what then would be the hunger artist's fate? It's such a moment Ugrešić confronts in the recently globalized world as she sits in a New York hotel, reading the *New York Times Book Review*, struck in particular by a 'lengthy' review of a novel by Ivana Trump, a Czech beauty queen, a champion swimmer and skier, and ex-wife of Donald Trump. In her latest branching out, Ivana Trump has written a novel: the *Times* reviews it favourably. 'I wouldn't have noticed it,' says Ugrešić of the review, 'if Joseph Brodsky hadn't received in the very same issue an unjustly malicious review of his latest book *Watermark*. One reviewer vilified Brodsky for his language "jammed with metaphors," and the other praised Ivana for her analytical intelligence.'[6]

Brodsky is now the hunger artist, but not because his malady is no longer intriguing to others, or because it's found a cure, but because there's apparently nothing peculiar any more about the DNA that would have meant he was doomed to the malady. The writer is robbed of his 'condition' and sense of predestination, of being for some reason unable to escape his compulsion—the compulsion which he disguised as his craft, and which came to characterize him to others. In the new age, it's not the singularity of the malady that loses significance; it's the singularity of the genetic make-up that made it inevitable. This makes the artist pointless. As Ugrešić puts it, '[H]aving become a writer of world renown, it would have been difficult for Brodsky to become a brilliant skier, while it was easy for Ivana Trump to go from being a skier to a writer, even a brilliant analyst of political conditions in her former communist homeland.'[7]

★

The hunger artist's life revolves round two axes: the craft or art of starving, and an entity called the 'crowd'. Walter Benjamin, attentive to Kafka, introduces the 'crowd' as a key player as he constructs, in his essay, 'On Some Motifs in Baudelaire', a history of the rise of the nineteenth-century realist novel. This ascendancy he connects not to the author's wish to reflect society, but society's—or the 'crowd's'—new and unprecedented desire to see itself reflected in this burgeoning genre. 'It became a customer; it wished to find itself portrayed in the contemporary novel, as the patrons did in the paintings of the Middle Ages.'[8] So there's a remarkable process of democratization at work here, supplanting both an exclusive aristocratic clientele and the services of elite portrait painters, energizing, through mass readership, narrative portrayal. We live in the shadow of that moment in which the transition from the portrait painted in an opulent room to the public domain of widely disseminated fiction took place. The aftermath of the transition lasted for more than a century, but, in the 1980s, another comparable transition occurred. From now on, the crowd no longer wanted to 'see' itself in a work of art or in a novel; more and more, it wished to *be*—for a limited duration, even—the artist or novelist. At the heart of this was the emergence of karaoke, and a space for amateur, tuneless, and infectious music performances. Today, needless to add, we have the cell phone as the most significant facilitator of this second moment to do with the 'crowd'. In the interim have been released the variegated performers of amateurism, deprofessionalization, and reprofessionalization, rendering obsolete the old, non-technological figure of the amateur: the fascinating everyday photographers and makers of short films on mobile phones and YouTube on the one hand; on the other, the celebrity chefs and comedians whose memoirs and children's books are now the mainstay of reputed literary publishers. We must add to this an influential school of karaoke politics whose very lack of professionalism is alluring in an era in which the professional politician is contemptible; thus, the viability of the ragbag Aam Admi

Party and of the rebarbative Donald Trump. Here, an ontological predisposition, or affliction, or talent, like an artistic temperament, or a mastery of prose style, or the hunger artist's mysterious disaffection with food, must seem out of place. It's in this context that we must place Ugrešić's parable on Joseph Brodsky and Ivana Trump.

Let me refer in passing here also to the writer and critic Marina Warner's testament to 'quitting' (her word) the university—Essex—where she'd had a position for some years both as a professor and a writer (much as I do at East Anglia). The thoughts she put on record in the *London Review of Books*[9] after resigning are now well known. They trace the arc of how a writer who was trying to do something different within the department increasingly found herself unable to proceed, given the new, largely commercial, criteria related to measuring the importance of academic activities of departments (such as 'impact'), leaving her with no choice but to 'quit' and return to being a full-time writer. The untold story proximate to this narrative—as I put it to Warner later—has surely to do with how, in Britain, much the same sort of transformation has characterized publishing in the last two decades. To mimic Ugrešić's tone, it was easy for a respected professor to give up her job and go back to being a well-known writer; but what happens when the well-known writer ceases to be publishable? I reproduce my words from an email: 'I was struck by the similarities [between recent changes in British universities and] ... what has been happening in the world of publishing for two decades now: the solemnity of terms like "impact" is foreshadowed by the often theological nobility attributed to commercial ambitions in the name of "great writing". The matter is little spoken of, though. Editors are "quitting" all the time, but can't, apparently, go public about why they change or lose jobs, because they have to stay in the industry in one incarnation or the other: as publisher or, increasingly, as agent. Meanwhile, writers, alas, can be dropped, but they can't quit.'[10] We come back to Ugrešić's dilemma, whether it's crystallized via the *New York Times*, Joseph Brodsky, and Ivana Trump, through Kafka, or through a decision taken by a publisher to stop publishing you. You may become unviable as a writer; but how do you stop being a writer if you can't rid yourself of the habit and the act of writing?

*

I'll end with a brief coda on the words I referred to when I began—Gustavo Esteva's term for Ashis Nandy (and, apparently, himself), 'deprofessionalized intellectual'—and address the question they implicitly raise, to do with legitimacy. Legitimacy is especially pertinent to the intellectual's position in contemporary India.

I admit that my thoughts come partly as a response to an engaging essay by Ramachandra Guha, on the paucity of right-wing intellectuals in this country. Why are there so few, he asks, of any real note or merit; isn't the absence of such figures the reason why our presently dominant right wing is driven conceptually by shamanism, demagoguery, and magic? It's a good question, though it sidesteps the matter of how the extreme right has, in the past, been adept at appropriating the inheritance of the most angular of philosophers—like, say, Nietzsche. There's also the curious business of writers on the left occasionally making a philosopher with dodgy political affinities their intellectual mentor—Heidegger comes to mind as precisely such a mentor. There's a befuddling blurring of lines, then, not only to do with the intellectual history of the 'right' and the 'left', but with how discrete and competing lineages are invented.

What exactly does Guha *mean* by the term 'intellectual'? The outline of who this person might be occurs very early in the essay, when Guha contrasts the intellectual to the ideologue.

> One must distinguish here between the work done by intellectuals and that done by ideologues. Each academic discipline has its own protocols on what constitutes serious scholarship. Historians dig deeply into primary material, whether letters or manuscripts or state documents or court records or temple inscriptions; and sociologists and anthropologists do extended fieldwork in the locations they study. Their first-hand, original research is then written up and analysed, and presented in scholarly papers in academic journals or in books brought out by established publishers. The judgment on one's scholarly work comes principally from one's colleagues—first, before it is published, as part of the peer-review process practiced by professional journals and book publishers, and then, once it is in print, by how often the work is cited.
>
> There is a distinction to be drawn between intellectuals and ideologues, who are more interested in promoting their political or religious beliefs than in contributing to the growth of knowledge. The writings of ideologues are rarely based on serious or extended research.[11]

What we're being inadvertently introduced to here is a familiar habit of thinking, to do with legitimizing the intellectual. The term 'deprofessionalized intellectual', really a tautology—for you don't choose or desire to be an intellectual any more than you elect to think—must, in the context being set up by Guha, appear a contradiction in terms. But surely the difference between the intellectual and the ideologue can't be ascertained by comparing the marks of legitimacy to the ideologue's apparently illegitimate air; or contrasting the rational and verifiable (as shored up by archival research) with the unproven and the speciously dogmatic? Do thought and insight necessarily have to subsist on evidence? Surely what's important here is the significance ascribed, or not ascribed, to process. The ideologue is invested in fixity; since thinking is a process, the one who thinks finds themselves situated in, and as a result often reflecting on, the nature and value of process, which brought them to intellectual life in the first place. But if the one who thinks—the intellectual—is, without much reflection, conflated with an idea of the social scientist or the historian, only parts of whose practice are mentioned inasmuch as these legitimize the practice—'primary material'; 'first-hand, original research'; 'peer-review'—then we're confronted with a gesture that's over-familiar to us in India, and which itself represents a kind of fixity. What's been notable where Guha is concerned is how the more wayward aspects of his work and sensibility—his affinities with Verrier Elwin and C. L. R. James, his enthusiasm for cricket, and his beginnings as an anthropologist—have, as his reputation has gone mainstream, been downplayed for a more generic role: that of the historian. In fact, Guha, unusually for a historian, often prefaces his remarks with the words, 'Speaking as a historian', as if to be one depended on a Cartesian declaration. This is what sometimes happens in India: being a 'thinker' culminates in becoming a spokesperson for a discipline. One speaks as, and for, this or that; it's the discipline that needs confirming and upholding, as it upholds one's work. What we end up opposing the ideologue with is not thought, but legitimacy.

A word on 'research'. Since the rise of the historical novel in India and in Britain, 'research' is meant to professionalize the time of writing fiction, to take it out of the inexplicable domain that reading a book or listening to a record on the hi fi once belonged to, so that one might have an adequate—a respectable—answer to the question, 'What do you do?' The questioner is going to be less anxious if the reply, 'I'm a novelist', automatically implies, 'I engage in serious research'. Of late, in India—where the notion of research is deeply embedded in our regard for the plausible, the verifiable, and the professionalized—I'm often told, 'You must do a lot of research', when I say I write novels.

To which I reply, 'Yes, but not for particular books. I'm doing research all the time.' If one is engaged in uninterrupted research—as any writer or artist is—the question of the writer's use of time, of activity and productivity, once more becomes unsatisfyingly open-ended, and other questions—to do with how we think, work, prepare to and speak of work—must take the place of the recurrent one about what we do.

January 2016

* * *

5

The other Green

I bought a compendious volume in the late 1980s, when I was a graduate student in Oxford. I don't like long or big books, but this volume included three novels. They were by an author I hadn't heard of, Henry Green. The Green people were still talking about had an e at the end of his surname, and his first name was Graham. He was almost an exact contemporary of Henry's: born in 1904, a year before Green, he lived much longer. Both belonged to well-to-do families, but Green was particularly affluent. His father was an industrialist. I'd tried reading Graham Greene, because I liked the titles of his novels and because everyone who read novels seemed to have read him, but had never—presumably because of my inability to focus on narrative fiction—made much headway beyond three pages of any of his books. Then Henry Green came along, and Graham swiftly became, for me, the 'other Green', and then not even that. Although relatively few people had, or have, read Henry Green, there's an irreducible, long-standing excitement about him among those who have, an excitement that makes him periodically palpable to us, while other English novelists who were famous at the time—Angus Wilson, Iris Murdoch, Graham Greene—are now either largely forgotten or have turned into minor literary-historical facts. Time is nonchalant in its workings, but Green is exceptionally stubborn, and is still among us.

I must have bought the three-novel volume of *Loving, Living*, and *Party Going* because John Updike had, in his introduction, not only given Green centrality as a precursor, but called him a 'saint of the mundane'. The religious analogy was excessive and pseudo-Joycean, but what had made me admire Updike in the first place in *Rabbit, Run* and some of the stories about the town of Tarbox and the fractious, self-indulgent couple called the Maples was the way in which he'd deliberately made room for the mundane, for the banality that constantly populates our lives and makes them truly interesting. For all Updike's invocation of Green as a patron and father-figure, I found him to be a different kind of writer, with almost none of the chronicler's impulse that from time to time directed Updike's decade-long projects, with no abiding interest, despite his extraordinary eye and ear and his gift for capturing character, in realism. Replying to a question put to him by Terry Southern for the *Paris Review* in 1958—'You've described your novels as "nonrepresentational." I wonder if you'd mind defining that term?'—Green said:

> 'Nonrepresentational' was meant to represent a picture which was not a photograph, nor a painting on a photograph, nor, in dialogue, a tape recording. For instance, the very deaf, as I am, hear the most astounding things all round them which have not in fact been said. This enlivens my replies until, through mishearing, a new level of communication is reached. My characters misunderstand each other more than people do in real life, yet they do so less than I. Thus, when writing, I 'represent' very closely what I see (and I'm not seeing so well now) and what I hear (which is little) but I say it is 'nonrepresentational' because it is not necessarily what others see and hear.[1]

Green in fact stands somewhere between Joyce, in his tendency to be intolerant of 'normal' English syntax and punctuation, and Virginia Woolf, in his sense of how narrative can be shaped by things outside of event. But, as is clear from the comment he makes to Southern, he's also conflating his aesthetic with disability and eccentricity (right at the start of the interview, he refuses to field an inconvenient question on the grounds that he can't hear the interviewer, though it quickly becomes evident that the deafness is opportunistic). More than Joyce and Woolf or any other writer I can think of, Green's contribution to the modern novel is the imprimatur of eccentricity, of unforgettable oddity.

I have seen that Picador omnibus edition in the hands of readers and teachers, creased, carried with a degree of protectiveness; but, by all accounts, it didn't do well and soon went out of print. Since then, the books have had spasmodic resurrections, come and gone and come back again. What will it take for Green to penetrate the general consciousness? His writing went out of view after he died in 1973, and since the late 1980s he's been known as a cause among a handful of influential literary champions. But maybe it's to do with what Ezra Pound called 'the age'. Maybe the decades in which certain writers have been arguing Greene's case haven't been receptive to a novelist whose sole purpose seems to be to fashion a language with which to communicate delight and joy. Woolf was shockingly neglected; her return and present status owe not so much to literary critics as they do to feminism. Jean Rhys's last work, *Wide Sargasso Sea* (she was utterly forgotten till it was published), allowed her to be annexed later by postcolonialists, who focused on the Creole rewriting of Charlotte Brontë. Joyce's mythic scaffolding and verbal play identified him to academia as being essential to both modernism and to the project of hermeneutics. I mention these writers because of their capacity to transform and delight, but also because some aspect of their writing has been translated advantageously into a set of terms important to particular literary-historical moments. With Green, we're presented with a singular kind of artist who, like the poets of ancient India and Greece, has nothing to offer us but delight. We don't know what to do with such a writer.

I hesitate to call *Party Going* a modernist work, because it stands on its own, and has not lent itself out to the modernism industry. But it shares with standard modernist texts certain commonalities, by which I mean not only what Frank Kermode called its mythic structure, or its mythic punctuation of dead pigeons and bathing women, or its purgatorial fog-bound environment, or its diction, but the fact that it's interested not in the journey but the waiting, not the event but the interruption. Dense fog in London causes all trains to be cancelled. Traffic on the roads is at a standstill; some of the people on their way to the station have to abandon their cars and walk—a moment of both liberation from, and loss of, class privilege. Among throngs of frustrated but jubilant commuters is a group of rich people, hosted by the rich and intoxicatingly eligible Max Adey, which was to be off for a holiday to the south of France. Two women especially are in pursuit of Max: Julia Wray and Amabel. Max wanted to escape Amabel and make his trip with his friends and acquaintances, whose every cost he's bearing. But Amabel tracks him down. In the meanwhile, the group has been shifted, through the good offices of Julia's uncle, a very important person in the railways, to the station hotel and given rooms with baths. An old aunt has fallen ill after picking up and washing a dead pigeon, and seems to be on her deathbed in a hotel room. The shutters to the station have been brought down to keep more people from getting in. Amabel somehow finds her way inside despite these impediments, and Max is at once ashamed, caught out, and temporarily disarmed by her immense beauty. It seems to Julia, whom Max had been courting in a room not long ago, that her romantic holiday with Max—though she would disdain to think of it in those terms—is not to be.

The simultaneity of the narrative makes it less like a text overseen by an omniscient narrator than like a particular kind of cinema, a cinema not so much invested in a single protagonist as in what's happening at once in several rooms and the spaces around them. Not Christopher Isherwood's camera, then, which records in Berlin the dissolution of ways of life with faux objectivity and a doomed helplessness, but multiple cameras at work. The material has been organized by an auteur akin, in his method, to a film editor, creating a montage of swiftly juxtaposed scenes and creating the illusion of unity and continuity. The film I have in mind is Jean Renoir's *The Rules of the Game* (*La Règle du jeu*), which is about a group of upper-class people with conflicting love interests who find themselves along with their servants in a manor house on a country estate during the weekend. The restricted but unique locale and the limited duration of the action allow Renoir to explore how people, animals, and objects might inadvertently *make* a narrative out of nothing. The director observes not so much the characters and their surroundings (he does this, of course) as the patterns out of which this narrative is produced. It's arguable as to whether these patterns would have formed in the unprecedented manner they do in the film if the characters had stayed at home, or if their displacement had been long-term. *The Rules of the Game* is neither about belonging somewhere nor being in exile, but inhabiting a transient, busy state of unfinishedness. It was released in the same year as *Party Going*, 1939. The aesthetic of both works is remarkably congruent, as is the timing of their appearance, just prior to the destruction of the worlds contained within them. Both possess an odd indestructibility. Renoir's film was trashed by both the right and the left for its pointless portrayal of the wasteful rich. It was taken off screens prematurely and then banned, only to be recognized in later decades as a landmark of cinema.

Another film comes to mind, by Renoir's most gifted student, Satyajit Ray. It's from 1962, Ray's first film in colour, and the first he scripted himself. It's called *Kanchenjungha*, named after the mountain peak which the upper-class holiday-makers in the film are from time to time reminded of as they wander a limited ambit in the hill-station of Darjeeling, a glimpse of which they believe would make their excursion worthwhile. The holiday-makers are absorbed in themselves.

The Kanchenjungha is an opening into a world beyond that won't present itself, though these people themselves are already in the open, constantly exploring, or loitering in, a narrow maze of lanes and inclines. 'Can you believe this place was nothing but a Lepcha village before the British turned it into this town?' says the insufferable patriarch Sir Indranath towards the film's end. Empire! It was insubstantial by then, like the mist. It's becoming intangible in *Party Going* too, but it's there, in the global allusions, in the great railways.

The film is in real time—that is, the hundred minutes or so of its duration is also the time it takes the itinerants to do what they're doing, to say and think what they're saying and thinking. The experience of reading the book approximates this—the sense of having entered, via the sentence, a specific continuum and time-span. The four or five hours it takes us to finish the novel is also the period in which the fog rolls in and then starts to lift. The spell, too, lifts, and, like Tagore after he finishes reading Kalidasa's *Meghdut*, we realize we'd entered a world we can't possess. This conflation of the characters' time with the reader's (embedded in which is the nine years it took for Green to write the book) points to the author's preoccupation with, and mastery of, form, which is another kind of reality from the one the novel is depicting—the consequence of his abstract 'nonrepresentational' method.

One looks to other genres and art-forms for analogies because *Party Going* isn't a novel in the usual sense of the term. It gives us a wonderfully comic account of its characters; but it is also an assemblage—of moments, and of different kinds of awareness of the world and even of writing. Green is nothing if not self-conscious of his literary context: when Julia gets off the car to walk to the station and registers the procession of headlights in the dark, the narrator points sideways to the novel's antecedents: 'these lights would come like thoughts in darkness, in a stream'.[2] Then there are the epic similes, more reminiscent of Kalidasa and classical Sanskrit poetry and Indian iconography than Homer and even Milton, and signalling to us that Green lived in a time when the English writer's inheritance went far beyond European modernism. Here the narrator describes two people in Max's party waiting in the station to spot their host:

> Like two lilies in a pond, romantically part of it but infinitely remote, surrounded, supported, floating in it if you will, but projected by being different

on to another plane, though there was so much water you could not see these flowers or were liable to miss them, stood Miss Crevy and her young man, apparently serene, envied for their obviously easy circumstances and Angela coveted for her looks by all those water beetles if you like, by those people standing round.[3]

This is almost outrageous, except that Green makes these semi-ironical, vivid comparisons repeatedly. On the next page, the simile concerns the station master's view of crowds of smokers: 'every third person smoking it might all have looked to Mr. Roberts, ensconced in his office away above, like November sun striking through mist rising off water'.[4] As Max and Amabel talk to each other on the phone (he is going to go eventually to the station, and is lying to her about his intentions), the latter's observation that 'here we are like a couple of old washerwomen slanging away at each other' sounds more striking than it should, as if Amabel were unwittingly situating the story in a world-history of the epic. Two pages on, as Alex proceeds down the dark, fogbound street in a taxi, it seems that the

[s]treets he went through were wet as though that fog twenty foot up had deposited water, and reflections which lights slapped over the roadways suggested to him he might be a Zulu, in the Zulu's hell of ice, seated in his taxi in the part of Umslopogaas with his axe, skin beating over the hole in his temple...[5]

And Robert Hignam, as he presses through the crowd in the station, remembers that

[w]hen small he had found patches of bamboo in his parents' garden and it was his romance at that time to force through them; they grew so thick you could not see what temple might lie in ruins just beyond. It was so now, these bodies so thick they might have been a store of tailors' dummies, water heated. They were so stiff they might as well have been soft, swollen bamboos in groves only because he had once pushed through these, damp and warm...[6]

The shutters are soon going to come down in the station, keeping new commuters out; Max's group are going to be at once nervously and luxuriously ensconced in the station hotel. Despite the sense of enclosure and imprisonment ('we are simply in a state of siege you know, yes, no one's allowed in or out. Yes, nanny and her friend are with us, they have been angels'), the narrative has already ramified and been placed in the 'world': *Party Going* is both a comedy and a cosmology. It's not about being hemmed in or trapped, or about being English. It enacts a fluidity of perception where it's also about being Zulu, about people being compared to branches, to 'household servants in a prince's service', where Amabel is known not only in London but in 'Northern England' and Hyderabad, where the 'thousands of Smiths, thousands of Alberts, hundreds of Marys' seen gathered below from a hotel window seem 'woven tight as any office carpet or, more elegantly made, the holy Kaaba soon to set out for Mecca'. *Party Going* is partly art-house movie, with a singular soundtrack, and partly one of those extraordinary British texts, like *Briggflatts* or *The Anathemata*, in which locality, eccentricity, and even class flow in and out of other cultures. It's this flow that is envisaged here in terms of the din, the murmurs, the silences, the laughter, and the courtships that occur while the trains have stopped, so that any moment things might open up in an unlikely way, as in this passage about Max falling asleep briefly in a room in the station hotel with Amabel in his arms, whom he will unexpectedly lose interest in upon waking up:

> It was so luxurious he nodded, perhaps it was also what she had put on her hair, very likely it may have been her sleep reaching out over him, but anyway he felt so right he slipped into it too and dropped off on those outspread wings into her sleep with his, like two soft evenings meeting.[7]

2016

★ ★ ★

6

On the *Gita*

Krishna as poetic language

The Bhagavad Gita begins at a moment of crisis—not just a crisis of the community and the nation, as it certainly is, but one of a personal and (to use a relatively contemporary term) existential nature. When the influential Kannada novelist U. R. Ananthamurthy published his first novel, *Samskara*, about a Brahmin who deliberately chooses to estrange and isolate himself from other Brahmin priests, it invited the thought, even from its translator A. K. Ramanujan, that Ananthamurthy might have made his protagonist more of an existentialist than his Brahminical identity could credibly allow for. But Arjuna, in the *Gita* (of course, he's a Kshatriya, a warrior, not a Brahmin), reveals that anguished choice-making in relation to the world—the characteristic preoccupation and mood of existentialism—is hardly new to India; that, at least in cultural antecedents, Ananthamurthy's Praneshacharya is not alone.

What kind of crisis, exactly? The *Gita* is an episode—a slightly anomalous, somewhat unassimilable episode, but an episode nevertheless—in the epic the *Mahabharata*. The epic (composed roughly between 400 BCE and 400 CE) is the story of two warring clans of cousins, the Pandavas and the Kauravas. The Pandavas, the family to which the great warrior Arjuna and his four brothers belong, are the 'good guys'. In other words, Vyasa, the author of the epic, means us to see the action through the Pandavas' eyes, from (to use an ugly piece of creative writing school jargon) their 'point of view'. The Kauravas are treacherous; they inveigle the Pandavas into a game of dice and rob them of their kingdom, even attempting to disrobe Draupadi, the

Pandava brothers' wife (how Draupadi came simultaneously to marry five men is another story).

The Pandavas go into exile for the mandatory mythic period of thirteen years or thereabouts (the *Ramayana* has Rama banished for fourteen). The deal at the close of the game of dice was that they would resume their reign once that period was over. Returning, they discover the Kauravas have no intention of letting that happen. The two clans are now formally at war. There's a crucial scene before the actual conflict begins on the battlefield of Kurukshetra (which, in the course of the rest of the epic, will become a site that, in scale and destruction, out-Guernicas any imaginable Guernica). Both clans have gathered before Krishna, like bidders at a Premier League auction, to petition him for his support and also for his powerful army. Krishna says that each clan can have one or the other; that he will provide advice to the clan that chooses him over his army, but will abstain from fighting himself. The Kauravas decide they want Krishna's army; Arjuna elects to have Krishna as his charioteer.

Krishna is God incarnate; charming, beautiful, he is in other respects inexplicably volatile, unpredictable, and transmogrifying. In other words, being divine, in Krishna's case, is to be surprising to the point of being alienating: not burdened by a human code of conduct, Krishna can resort, occasionally, to all kinds of duplicity to further his team's interests. His amorality is quite different from the Kauravas' tragic treacherousness or the sleights-of-hand that the Pandavas indulge in; it leads us towards the abyss of meaning, or meaninglessness, from which the *Mahabharata*'s great power emerges. As a consequence, what's destroyed in the *Mahabharata* is not just a great deal of human life, but a stable 'point of view' that might give rise to a clear sense of good and bad characters, of virtuous and evil action. The great and perennial casualty of the *Mahabharata* is the stability of value; its excitement and animation lies in its constant shifting of the centre.

★

The *Bhagavad Gita* is a conversation between Arjuna and his charioteer Krishna which takes place just before the Battle of Kurukshetra is to begin. Both armies are on the battlefield: in the opposing camp, Arjuna can see kinsmen he's known since childhood, 'teachers, fathers and sons; grandsons, grandfathers, wives' brothers; mothers' brothers and fathers of wives'. On the eve of battle, then, he's agonized, full of doubt: 'These I do not wish to slay, even if I myself am slain.'[1] It's now up to Krishna to exhort and rouse him to action. This exhortation, briefly, is the gist of the *Gita*.

By the time we arrive at this point in the *Mahabharata*, we already know Arjuna as flamboyant and heroic, possessed of unsurpassed skills in the art of war, and, most importantly, as one of the privileged (despite his travails, and in contrast to his gifted but unfortunate half-brother Karna)—that is, as someone whom both the narrator and the gods smile upon. To see him now changed into an overwrought, Hamlet-like ditherer is intriguing. But Hamlet is no existentialist; he's disturbed, and part of the source of his disturbance is derived from his new-found disgust at his mother's sexual availability. Although, vacillating between 'being' and 'not being', Hamlet asks some of the same questions as Arjuna, Shakespeare allows us to view him from the outside, enmeshed in his own moment of theatre. A small but stubborn question mark hangs over him, both in our minds and inside the play, as to whether he's making too much of nothing (as T. S. Eliot accused Shakespeare of doing with the play itself). This distance opens up the character and his agonies to a latent comedy, which spoof-makers have tapped into in various parodies of the tortured prince. No such distance qualifies Arjuna, and, as a result, it's more difficult to parody his anguish. We don't, here, view Arjuna as a dramatic character with motives and a psychology, although we don't necessarily think he lacks these things. Nor is he a cipher, a mouthpiece, for a set of questions. In the *Gita*, Arjuna is inseparable from human language, a language alive with disquiet, prescience, and yearning.

Krishna, too, is a different Krishna in the *Gita*. In the rest of the epic, and even outside it, in songs and in folklore, Krishna is Ovidian. I use the word to hint at Krishna's self-transforming and metamorphic nature—an errant and greedy child in the *Bhagavata Purana* and in folklore; a lover of numberless women; in the epic, too, a politician, an inscrutable trickster and strategist; and, all the while, in various manifestations, divine. He is Ovidian because his transformations, or personalities, are, in a sense, material: a dazzling array of registers in the world we experience. Like the metamorphoses that Ovid ebulliently records, Krishna is a reminder that play and creation are synonymous and inexhaustible. Of all the gods, it's Krishna who's identified with *leela*, or the infinitely tantalizing play, chicanery, and light and shade of the created universe. This uncontainable Ovidian mood is particularly true of the folksy cowherd Krishna of the *Bhagavata Purana*, beloved of the devotional Bhakti poets; but we also encounter it in the *Mahabharata*, where Krishna, at once Machiavellian, merciful and estranging, engages in war as a very serious kind of game, or play.

In the *Gita*, we encounter a Krishna we can find absolutely nowhere else. This Krishna tells Arjuna that it's he who is the source of everything; and yet he's 'invisible'. This paradox demands a different response, a different order of recognition, a different sort of suspended disbelief, from the Krishna who performs astounding feats and multiplies through stories. What could run through the visible universe, but not be seen itself? We're not being asked to believe in the sort of astonishing event that epic, myth, or fiction often offer us, but in a paradox that's peculiar to the poetic: 'I am not bound by this vast work of creation,'[2] says Krishna. 'I am and I watch the drama of works.' What *is* he, then? Clearly something even more difficult to understand by a concatenation of logical thinking than the Krishna of the *Mahabharata* or the *Bhagavata* tradition is. Not only does Krishna at once situate himself in creation and distance himself from it ('I am not bound by this vast work of creation'); he appears to be distancing himself from the epic mode that the *Gita* and he are presently embedded in: 'I watch the drama of works.' On one revolutionary level, then, the *Gita* is a critique of the epic narrative that it finds itself in, of its outwardly endless range and its momentary way of making meaning: 'When one sees Eternity in things that pass away and Infinity in finite things, then one has pure knowledge. / But if one merely sees the diversity of things, with their divisions and limitations, then one has impure knowledge.'[3] Instead, the *Gita* signals its own radical shift in register by suggesting the power of something that's contradictory, something that inheres at once in the visible universe and in darkness, in abstraction and in language:

> a sense sublime
> . . . Whose dwelling is the light of setting suns,
> And the round ocean, and the living air,
> And the blue sky, and in the mind of man:
> A motion and a spirit, that impels
> All thinking things, all objects of all thought . . .[4]

Of course, this is not from the *Gita*, but from Wordsworth's 'Tintern Abbey'. But the lines (Wordsworth would have known the *Gita* in

Charles Wilkins's translation, and probably through August Wilhelm Schlegel) gesture towards the oddness of poetic meaning as a special meaning: something simultaneously animate and still, impelling and concealed. This note of eloquent, visionary special pleading for a meaning that contradicts itself constantly in order to generate itself, and which has no discernible justification, rationale, manifestation, or cause, comes from the *Gita*'s Krishna: 'That splendour of light that comes from the sun and which illumines the whole universe, the soft light of the moon, the brightness of fire—know that they all come from me.'[5] Again and again, in Krishna's most famous maxims concerning 'action' to Arjuna, it's the strange, contradictory nature of true meaning that's being explored and fortified. 'Arise and fight!' he exhorts the warrior, but asks him to do so without thought of the 'fruit of one's actions'. Meaning comes into being, then, only when there's no thought of, or desire for, the outcome. This difficult concept is what Arjuna gets, instead of a clear and practical manual of dos and don'ts, or an exhortation to selfless love and compassion, as in the Gospels. Where does that idiosyncratic idea of meaning, and the power of meaning, operate but in poetry itself? In the *Gita*, Krishna becomes poetic language.

★

This is not to say that there is a complete discontinuity between the *Mahabharata*'s analysis of the world as a place of politics, of actions governed by power, and the moment the *Gita* inhabits.

There are instances when Krishna's role in the *Gita* is at once historical, admonitory, and cathartic: 'When righteousness is weak and faints and unrighteousness exults in pride, then my Spirit arises on earth.'[6] At such points in the *Gita*, the world already seems very old, its conventions and pieties tested and turned inside out, as it does often in the rest of the *Mahabharata*, whose author manages the astonishing feat of being simultaneously disabused and wonderstruck. Certainly, neither the epic nor the song (for that's what *gita* means) has the auspicious, inaugural air of the early *Upanishads*, or the pastoral freshness of the *Bhagavata* tradition. Instead they possess (in the case of the epic, almost completely) a quality of lateness and intransigence ('I am time, destroyer of men') that's combined, in the epic narrative, with an amazing sense of fecundity. It's the *Gita*'s belated, backward look, glancing at the residues of texts and ages it's emerged from, that prompted J. Robert Oppenheimer to quote it when witnessing the first atomic explosion in New Mexico: 'I am become death'.

And although the *Gita* isn't, in a strict sense, mythopoeic, its central image—of Arjuna, unable to act in a battlefield full of kinsmen, turning to Krishna—is mythic. It is where, in India, history and myth, reality and the ideal, rulers and the notion of Man, converge repeatedly, in the series of tragic episodes and subsequent attempts at self-renewal of which this civilization is composed. The emperor Ashoka's massacre of innocents at Kalinga, and his later passionate turn towards non-violence and Buddhism; Gandhi and Nehru's terrible dilemma upon Partition—these, after the fact, set up a surreptitious confluence, in the Indian experience, between history and theatre, civilization and allegory.

★

The earliest mention of the *Gita* in an extant text occurs in the work of the philosopher Shankaracharya (*c.*788–820 CE), the first and most important theorist of *advaita vedanta*, or non-dualism. (For some of the facts in this section, I'm indebted to Professor Sibaji Bandyopadhyay.) Shankaracharya chooses three canonical texts to advance his argument: the *Bhramasutra* (a work whose centrality has receded entirely), the *Upanishads*, and the *Gita*. In relation to the first two, the *Gita* occupies, in Shankaracharya's argument and scheme, a relatively minor, supplementary position. It isn't known if prior commentaries on the *Gita* existed and are now lost. Shankaracharya's text is structured as a dialogue, where an interlocutor states a position regarding the *Gita*, and the author answers or refutes him. This could point to earlier positions, earlier commentaries; on the other hand, it might not, for, as Professor Bandyopadhyay tells me, this form of dialogue, at the time, was an accepted convention for presenting an argument.

The *Gita*'s next significant appearance in the chain of Indian thinking is when the anti-Shankaracharya philosopher, the dualist Ramanuj (traditionally *c.*1017–1137 CE), uses the same three works to advance *his* cause. That texts may yield a multiplicity of meaning to readers and commentators of different ages is clear when we glance at the *Gita*'s history; but the idea of multiple interpretations is a New Critical, literary one, and it's rarely an advertisement for the *Gita*, though it embodies it well.

What's striking about the *Gita*, and what's been noted about it more than once, is the constant cautionary note it sounds about the principal precursor scriptures, the *Vedas*. It's not enough to follow the word of the scriptures, and to undertake the various sacrifices and rituals they enjoin you to do: the *Vedas* provide no guarantee against darkness and unknowing, the *Gita* reminds us. Moreover, that kind of religious literalism is anathema to the man seeking knowledge and a detached, 'impersonal' (I use Eliot's now dated buzzword) state of illumination. Bankimchandra Chatterjee, the first major Bengali novelist, writing the earliest modern commentary on the *Gita* (published posthumously as a book in 1902), remarks on this rebuttal of the *Vedas* as evidence of the *Gita*'s subversiveness. But Professor Bandyopadhyay believes that, if the *Gita* was composed after the advent of Buddhism (as he thinks it was), it simply represents Brahminical thought's robust ability to appropriate critiques directed at it: for an antagonism towards the *Vedas*, emanating from Buddhist sources, was then very much in the air.

Whatever the truth, it's clear that the rejection of mere Vedic or scriptural observance is not just a strategic interpolation or an add-on that belongs to the time, but is contributory to the *Gita*'s peculiar tenor, and its oddly 'timeless' polemic. The study of the *Vedas*, we're made to understand, is instrumental; because it involves ritual and instruction, it belongs to the domain of the visible. The *Gita* distrusts the visible, and conflates it with instrumentality. Most interestingly, in criticizing the *Vedas*, the *Gita* is also criticizing the primacy of the textual, the verbal; in other words, the *Gita* is not only in a state of tension with the epic, narrative material it's inserted into (the *Mahabharata*), it's also, being a text, at odds with itself. It views the word suspiciously, as if the word were always in danger of becoming institutional. It's a pronouncement that's implicitly, and sometimes explicitly, against pronouncement. In this, it represents a Protestant moment (albeit several centuries before the European Reformation) that exceeds and complicates Protestantism. For the latter refuted the Church in the interests of the possibility of grace—but not the Bible. The *Gita*, in rebutting mere textuality, is rejecting the form in which it's available to us. In this capacity to be, in a sense, at war with itself, it constitutes a certain definition of poetry.

★

Charles Wilkins, a servant of the East India Company, was introduced to the *Mahabharata* by Brahmins, and undertook a translation into English. The *Gita* especially caught his and other Englishmen's attention, among them, Warren Hastings (then Governor-General of British India). It was published on the latter's encouragement and with the letter of support he'd written for it serving as a kind of foreword. In it,

Hastings predicted that the *Gita* would outlast the British Empire. His enthusiasm, like that of other English readers, derived from the echoes he caught in this Hindu text of certain strands of Christian theology, particularly Unitarianism. Wilkins's translation was published in 1785, and was probably read by most of the Romantic poets. They would also have possibly been acquainted, later, with August Wilhelm Schlegel's edition of the Latin translation of the *Gita* in 1823, and the excitement with which this was received in Europe. Indian antiquity was, by the late eighteenth and early nineteenth centuries, directly informing the European idea of humanism. By the late nineteenth century, the *Gita* had become not only a property of Indian nationalists, but a resource for secular modernity in India. That is, it was being approached by Indian moderns not just as a sacred text, but as a literary one—in other words, the type of chosen work that modernity deems, for a number of reasons, quasi-sacred. Gandhi, for instance, reads the *Gita* as 'allegory'—by which he means, I suppose, a work whose meaning must be created by the reader, a work that belongs neither to the old, exclusive world of Hindu conventions, nor to the realm of literal veracity in which history, the sciences, and even the Semitic religions exist (Christ *was* crucified; He *was* resurrected—these are not figurative events). By gradually turning the *Gita* into allegory and poetry, secular modernity in India responds in its own way to its call that veracity and truth are never visible or obvious. The *Gita*'s contribution to secular modernity in Europe too is, I think, immense, particularly the role it plays in the formation of the 'literary' in England. The reason this remains largely unacknowledged may have partly to do with the negative reception the *Gita*'s philosophy received in 1827 from Hegel, after which it slowly slipped from the canonical shelf of high 'Western' culture.

★

How does the *Gita* signal to us that it's a poetic text, which asks to be read differently from the way either the epic is, or a sacred text of practical and moral dos and don'ts, or a *sruti* text like the *Vedas*, whose message comes from high above, or indeed a purely philosophical work?

Firstly, the epic or fictional narrative may begin *in medias res*; but the poem or poetic text is an interruption. It's a hiatus, a diversion, in some sort of meaning-producing business or activity—a larger narrative or story, say, or even life itself. Within the space of that interruption, it either offers a different order or scheme of imagined events, as is the case when Dante momentarily finds himself lost in 'life's dark wood', or a different order of meaning, as with a Romantic or modernist poem. With the *Gita*, we're moving into the second kind of terrain, partly because some of us have been trained by the Romantic poem to read in a particular way, and partly because the Romantic poem, early in its career, might itself have received the *Gita*'s training. At any rate, the *Gita* constitutes not just an interpolation in the *Mahabharata*, an insertion by a later writer, but, on a more complex and generic level, a discontinuity in the narrative, a hiatus that's paradoxical, because it's surprisingly full.

The second difference concerns what happens to us, as readers, in the course of a poem. A narrative might unfold in a linear fashion, or in a manifold and multi-pronged way, as the *Mahabharata* does. It involves and engages us. It satisfies a particular appetite—to do with our curiosity regarding its characters and the world they live in—and, once it's done, that appetite is sated; we don't need to return to the narrative for a while. The poetic text transforms us; that is, we know something has been changed by the time we finish it, though we aren't sure what new piece of information we've *learnt* that we didn't have before we began reading the poem. The effect is very different from finishing a narrative, or coming to the end of a story. Once we've read a poem, we can reread it immediately, and, as it were, relive that transformation. Our repeated experience of this transformation takes place regardless of whether we've 'understood' the text completely; in this, too, the poem's impact differs from that of the narrative. We don't necessarily seem to have moved greatly from one point to another by the time we come to the end of a poem; but the poem *has* moved, achieving its transformative intention by a mixture of inner shifts and repetitions. This is how the *Gita* works: there are no plot developments, but there are movements—from Arjuna's despair to Krishna's advice on the nature of action, to the sections in which Krishna begins to divulge his own divinity, to where he 'appears' in his true form to Arjuna, to the mysterious verses on the Asvattha tree, to the closing section about the 'surrender of the reward of all work'. This final section is, in a sense, a rehearsal of the beginning; there is, in the *Gita*, constant repetition and cross-referencing. By the time we finish reading it, we are changed without necessarily having progressed a great deal. Arjuna is now convinced and ready to take up arms; not only will the battle begin, but we're about to witness the resumption of the epic mode. When Sanjaya, the reporter of this conversation, says, 'Thus I heard these words of glory between Arjuna and the God of all, and they fill my soul with awe and wonder',[7] we know we're bidding farewell to the domain of the poem.

★

A curious stasis, then, lies at the heart of poetry, and this contradictory stillness also defines the *Gita*. Krishna articulates it in various ways. In the second chapter, he tells Arjuna, 'Even as all waters flow into the ocean, but the ocean never overflows, even so the sage feels desires, but he is ever one in his infinite peace.' In the third chapter: 'I have no work to do in all the worlds, Arjuna—for these are mine. I have nothing to obtain, because I have all. And yet I work.' In the fourth: 'Although I am unborn, everlasting . . . through my wondrous power I am born.'[8] Here, whether we're conscious of it or not, we're awestruck by the *Gita*'s self-reflexivity. In giving such insistent value to the surplus, the superfluous ('I have no work to do . . . and yet I work'), the *Gita* defines an expression that's *sui generis* and ahistorical. It's related to the *Mahabharata*, too, as a text that's in surplus, that has no clear function. And it's precisely because it represents a break in the action that its effect and role are epiphanic rather than didactic; like the true knowledge and action described in it, it has no quantifiable outcome. The *Gita* is embedded in the *itihasa* (the historical narrative) of the *Mahabharata* more or less as the universal is putatively embedded, in literature, in the particular: as a superfluous emanation that, for some reason, we cherish. The *Gita* proposes an aesthetic rather than just a tenet: to live your life by it would be exceedingly difficult—'Let thy actions then be pure, free from the bonds of desire'—except in the special, fictitious realm of the literary.

★

What the contribution of the *Gita* is to the category of the 'literary' that emerged in the nineteenth and twentieth centuries—a category attacked and almost rendered defunct in the second half of the twentieth century—is a matter of speculation. A non-authoritative glance tells me that the *Gita*'s notion of the surplus—the idea that meaning lies not in consequence or outcome but elsewhere, in a simultaneous investment in and detachment from action—circulated in Europe in the nineteenth century, and informed certain people's view of the creative and critical act; indeed, of culture itself. The domain of culture is a superfluous domain; the creative act is a surplus without outcome. This is a familiar position; so is the interpretative move through which things once outside that domain are annexed to it—thus, Matthew Arnold's proclamation that the Bible is 'literature'. No doubt Arnold was making that judgement from the vantage-point of what he called 'disinterestedness', a critical mood that's akin not so much to tolerance or even objectivity, but to what Arnold's successor and rival T. S. Eliot called 'impersonality', or, an 'escape from personality'[9]—the upsurge of the surplus that has no worldly consequence. Eliot is proposing a paradigm for the creative act, Arnold for the critical one; the notion of the surplus runs like a thread through both, and fashions a definitive reciprocity between creative and critical actions. Arnold, who read Wilkins's translation of the *Gita* in 1845, makes a case for criticism nineteen years later, in 1864: 'It will be said that it is a very subtle and indirect action which I am thus prescribing for criticism, and that, by embracing in this manner the Indian virtue of detachment and abandoning the sphere of practical life, it condemns itself to a slow and obscure work. Slow and obscure it may be, but it is the only proper work of criticism.' 'Slowness' is stasis: Arnold is, via the *Gita*, blurring the boundary between criticism and poetry, and setting up, again, a reciprocity between the two that's crucial to secular modernity. For the poem, by having no clear outcome, by being 'a very subtle and indirect action', is also a critical act; and criticism, in being neither story nor history, is a narrative without an outcome. This takes us back to why the *Gita* itself is a critical work; why its 'slow and obscure' quality, its stasis, its lack of 'determinateness', its 'stupefaction', its *Insichsein* or quality of 'nothingness' (all Hegel's words), would so annoy the German historicist. And the *Gita*'s blurring of boundaries, such as Arnold implicitly encourages while defining the function of criticism, also unsettles Hegel: 'There is no distinction [in it] between religion and philosophy.'[10]

'Slow and obscure', says Arnold[11] of the work of criticism: 'slow' invoking stasis, and 'obscure' the near-invisible. 'Beyond my visible nature is my invisible Spirit,' says Krishna. 'This is the fountain of life whereby this universe has its being.' Further, 'I am the taste of living waters and the light of the sun and the moon.'[12] Wordsworth picks up on this when writing his 'Tintern Abbey'; and Coleridge converts the notion of invisibility, of a hidden surplus, into an immanent trope for both reading and writing: 'Our genuine admiration of a great poet is a continuous *under-current* of feeling: it is everywhere present, but seldom anywhere as a separate excitement.'[13] This echo of the *Gita* is itself echoed by Flaubert, who was deeply immersed in Indian texts, and who was trying to push prose towards a region where it would be read not for narrative consequence, but with the same sort of attention devoted to poetry: 'The author, like God in the universe, is everywhere present but nowhere visible in his work.'[14] Here's the irritating, contradictory 'remoteness' of temperament that provokes Hegel's disdain for the *Gita*; James Joyce, Flaubert's disciple, presents and parodies it in Stephen Dedalus's words at the end of *A Portrait of the Artist as a Young Man*: 'The artist, like the God of creation, remains within or behind or beyond or above his handiwork, invisible, refined out of existence, indifferent, paring his fingernails.'[15] This is the *Gita* again, resurfacing. But Stephen is double-edged ('refined out of existence') and may also be alluding to Hegel, who, in his 'On the Episode of the Mahabharata Known as the Bhagavad Gita by Wilhelm von Humboldt', describes sardonically the 'Yogi sitting there mentally and physically unmoved, staring at the tip of his nose'.[16]

By the middle of the twentieth century, the legacy of Coleridge, Arnold, Flaubert, Eliot, and Joyce had complicated the 'literary' to the point that it defied easy generic categorization. It became an act whose outcome might be argued over, but never entirely known. Flaubert, and the modernists who were indebted to him, pushed prose into an area that lay beyond the rewards of narrative, into a domain that Roland Barthes calls, retrospectively, in *Writing Degree Zero* in 1953, 'poetry'. In the classical period, says Barthes, poetry was simply prose dressed up with outward signs of difference: metre, ornament, rhyme. In modernity, he says, those visible signs vanish, and poetry becomes an ethos: 'It is a quality *sui generis* and without antecedents. It is no longer an attribute but a substance, and therefore it can very well renounce signs, since it carries its own nature within itself, and does not need to signal its identity outwardly . . .'[17]

How did this change take place? The query is similar to the question we ask ourselves upon being transformed after reading a poem. It's a singular way of viewing writing that lasted roughly two hundred years, and began to end about fifteen years after Barthes wrote those words. How is the *Gita* woven into that relatively brief history? My intention is not to prove its influence, but to review our experience of reading in the receding, but not yet vanished, secular world. Clearly, it's not just tolerance and multiplicity that define the secular, but some acknowledgement of the importance of the surplus: that which is valuable beyond the approbation of authority, whether of the *Vedas*, of an ideology, or even of 'literature'. It's the realm of the aesthetic that responds strongly to the *Gita*'s strange exhortation to ignore the visible. Secularism is a religion like any other, and its sacred texts are literary works. At some crucial point in history, in the late eighteenth century (around the time of the *Gita*'s worldwide dissemination), some sacred texts also began to *become* its literary works. The reason you hold the *Gita* in your hand today is the outcome of that legacy.

2011

★ ★ ★

7

The alien face of cosmopolitanism

An Indian reading of Cynthia Ozick on the Woolfs

Let me begin with a series of recent conversations. In fact, these are snatches of conversation from larger discussions, in almost all of which the subjects of cosmopolitanism and modernity—in their locations both in and out of Europe—were broached, explored, and argued over. In one of them (the venue was a bookshop), I was trying to articulate my unease with the term 'postcolonial writer'; not only as a description of myself, but as a description of a generic figure. Both the affiliations and the oppositionality of the 'postcolonial writer' seemed too clearly defined; while, for most of the more interesting canonical writers of twentieth-century India, the complexity and unexpectedness of their oppositionality took their affiliations to unexpected territory—for the Urdu writer, Qurratulain Hyder, therefore, there was Elizabeth Bowen; for the Bengali poet, novelist, and critic Buddhadeva Bose, who adored Tagore and also adored Eliot, there were the compensatory, contrary figures of the poet Jibanananda Das, a contemporary he did much to champion, and of D. H. Lawrence and Whitman. The richness of the various power struggles to define the literary within India in the time of modernity, and the robust, often contradictory creative opportunism that took place in the interests of that struggle, is, alas, considerably reduced and simplified by the terms 'colonial' or 'postcolonial'. If one were to map the strategic affinities of these writers, those terms would gradually lose their mythic integrity; what would begin to appear (almost accidentally, as not every point of the map would be known to the other) is a sort of trade route of vernacular experimentation, a patois of the concrete, an effervescent cherishing of the idiosyncratic. If we were to trace the lines radiating from one writer or location to another on this map, we might, for instance, find that, often, a high degree of attention and erudition had been brought to bear upon the commonplace.

Of course, no such map exists. But the fact that these forms of 'commerce' (Pound's word for his curious relationship with Whitman) did characterize literary activity in the late nineteenth and in the twentieth centuries comes back to us even today, in, as I've just suggested, unpremeditated instants. One of them occurred at the end of the discussion I just referred to, when, in that bookshop in Oxford, a young Bangladeshi graduate student said to me: 'I've spoken to Indian writers who write in Bengali'—and, here, he mentioned Sunil Ganguly, the leading poet, novelist, and ageing *enfant terrible* who lives in Calcutta, and Ketaki Kushari Dyson, poet, translator of Tagore, erstwhile star student, who lives in the Oxford she was an undergraduate at, and who was in that audience—'I've spoken to these people, and they aren't happy with the term "postcolonial".' He suggested this might be because of the sort of transverse mappings and affiliations I'd mentioned, and which these writers had pursued in the interests of arriving at the recognizable tone and métier of their enterprise, lines of contact that couldn't be contained by the orthodox demarcations of the 'postcolonial'. But it was, still, chastening and something of a salutary shock to be reminded of actual, specific individuals, and to become conscious of them in a new way, as I began to become aware of Ketaki Kushari Dyson that evening, sitting not a great distance away from me, in her seventies now. In constructing my argument, I'd thought about myself, about history and the great canonical writers of the Indian past, and even, in general terms, of writers like Ketaki Dyson; but I hadn't thought of her in particular, and, for whatever reason, it had never occurred to me to speak to her, or to query her, about the subject. I knew her opinions on a range of things; but, on this, there had been an inadvertent silence. Now, to hear from another source, during a public conversation (she, wordless, as if she had some of the sphinx-like instructiveness of history or the archive), that she was unhappy at being termed a 'postcolonial' was at once vindicating and, as I've just confessed, disconcerting.

In attempting to think about the alien face of cosmopolitanism, I've had to have recourse to moments such as this one, to impressions rather than hard historical fact. Something not spoken of, a question not asked, something you thought you'd forgotten, and remembered later in a different way: these are almost all that are left of the residual cosmopolitanisms of the world—an odd sense of discomfiture, and, in lieu of a definitive language, personal reminiscences that appear to have implications, but remain isolated and arbitrary. I'm interested in exploring whether these moments—essentially afterthoughts from itineraries that have almost been erased—can mark the beginnings of an admittedly desultory enquiry, as much as the assignation of an actual historical date might: a date such as the Indian art historian Partha Mitter fixes, for instance, when he argues that the Bauhaus exhibition in Calcutta in 1922 led to the formation of an artistic avant-garde in India.[1] The exchange that evening in Oxford, and my failure to follow up with Ketaki Dyson, who disappeared quickly after the event, have made me alert to the conversations I've had since with writers in, for the want of a better term, the Indian vernaculars—they being, often without quite knowing it, the sole remnants in our country of those vanished cosmopolitanisms. But there are remnants adrift everywhere—and, so, overheard remarks and incomplete confessions from people, especially writers and academics, from various parts of the world also shape my interpretation. I'm not, in doing this, hinting that the rumours of the death of the cosmopolitan are exaggerated; nor am I simply arguing for his or her survival. I am registering the persistence of a world-view as an angularity, resurfacing constantly, at a time when the old dichotomies that defined and animated it (for instance, the 'cosmopolitan' in relation to the 'provincial') have become largely irrelevant. How does one think of the cosmopolitan in the global world?

Let me cite three conversations, beginning with the most recent one. Not long ago, I had dinner with C. S. Lakshmi, who was visiting Calcutta from Bombay, where she lives; Lakshmi is better known by her pseudonym 'Ambai', and is one of the most sensuous and experimental short-story writers in the Tamil language. My wife had begun to talk about a little, comical altercation Salman Rushdie had initiated with me recently in print, while I, without irony, protested my admiration for *Midnight's Children*. 'But you can't just bring in these forms by force,' said Lakshmi, scolding an invisible third party. 'Firstly, you have to see if there's any such thing as "magic realism" in your tradition or not.' She'd clearly decided this was doubtful. She confided, perturbed, scandalized: 'Do you know, it's begun in the languages as well.'

By 'languages' she meant the Indian ones. 'Even Tamil and Kannada writers are now trying to be "magic realist".'

Before I reflect on these statements, let me quickly move on to the second conversation. This took place over the telephone, again in Calcutta; my interlocutor was Utpal Kumar Basu, probably the most accomplished and—if I might use that word—interesting living poet in the Bengali language. We were discussing, in passing, the nature of the achievement of Subimal Misra, one of the fiction-writing avant garde in 1960s Bengal. 'He set aside the conventional Western short story with its idea of time; he was more true to our Indian sensibilities; he set aside narrative,' said Basu. 'That's interesting,' I observed. 'You know, of course, that, in the last twenty years or so, it's we Indians and postcolonials who are supposed to be the storytellers, emerging as we do from our oral traditions and our millennial fairy tales.' 'Our fairy tales are very different from theirs,' said Utpal Basu, unmoved. 'We don't start with, "Once upon a time . . . ".'

In both cases, Basu's and Lakshmi's, a cultural politics to do with a more or less unexamined category, 'Indianness', was being used to advance a politics of the modernist avant-garde; both writers, in effect, were offering a throwaway polemic against what the postmodern and the postcolonial had largely rehabilitated—narrative and the fairy tale. A second glance at their remarks, and the suggestive way the word 'our' is used in them—'our tradition', 'our stories', 'our sensibilities'—tells us that it's not the essential and changeless that's being gestured towards, but the contingent and historical; a cosmopolitanism of the avant-garde that had been located in an India which, since the late nineteenth century, had been making those transverse mappings across territories in the pursuit of certain objectives: the fragmentary, the concrete, and a certain quality of the aleatory that narrative couldn't accommodate. If the didacticism of the postmodern and the postcolonial had taught us that narrative—especially in its guise as epic—was liberating, that storytelling was 'empowering' in its expression of identity, the cosmopolitan avant-garde all over the world in the twentieth century had repeatedly drawn our attention to the tyranny, the enforcements, of narrative: it was to the latter that C. S. Lakshmi and Utpal Basu were referring when using that pronoun, 'our'.

Using the rhetoric of cultural nationalism in the service of the interests of the avant-garde has a long history in the non-West, almost as long a history there as that of modernity itself, and I've written about this elsewhere. There is, for example, Tagore's strategic celebration of the fourth-century Sanskrit poet Kalidasa, as a great, possibly the supreme, describer of the 'real' (Tagore's word for the 'real' is 'nature'), a celebration undertaken while demonstrating that Western poetic language—especially Shakespeare's language—repeatedly falls short of the Flaubertian task of description. This praise is formulated in the first decade of the twentieth century; but even earlier, in 1895, to be precise, Tagore is already attacking rationality and teleology, and enshrining the aleatory, in his essay on Bengali nursery rhymes. Here, drawing the reader's attention to the presence of random associations that so-called 'grown up' writing often lacks, he borrows from, or echoes remarkably, William James's famous essay in *Psychology*, which had been published just three years earlier. The rubric of Tagore's meditation is shored up by forms of cultural nationalism (the invention of a literary tradition with regard to Kalidasa; the construction of a Bengali childhood in connection with the nursery rhymes), but the interests are the interests of the avant-garde (through Kalidasa, a privileging of the image and the 'here and now'; through the nursery rhymes, a celebration of the disruption of linear time, and of the mysterious importance of the 'superfluous'). And these interests, intriguingly, are being articulated right at the inception, worldwide, of the avant-garde, and, coincidentally, at the crossroads, or confluence, at which both political nationalisms and cosmopolitanisms are everywhere coming into being. The nationalism makes possible Tagore's cultural politics as a colonized subject, and the cosmopolitanism a certain kind of journey and mapping (for instance, the crucial and unprecedented borrowing of the notion of the 'stream of consciousness', 'nityaprabahita chetanar majhe', the first known literary transposition of the idea, in fact). Against what the nationalisms of the colonies are being fashioned we are certain, but to what end, and against exactly what, the anarchic play, the space for the superfluous, promoted by the various cosmopolitanisms are being posited we are still not entirely clear about; but it's clear that the urgency of the mission leads to an intricate and intense reciprocity over and across the values imposed by colonialism.

Here, I should also mention the Japanese writer Junichiro Tanizaki's brief, dream-like manifesto, *In Praise of Shadows*, where a civilized cultural politics carries forward an essentially modernist programme. Tanizaki is speaking of Japanese, even, occasionally, Eastern, architecture, habitation, allocation of domestic space, and domestic appurtenances in opposition to Western conceptions and traditions of the same things; in doing so, he's positioning shadows, indefiniteness, a desire for decrepitude and recycling, against the definiteness, the clarity, the newness treasured by the West. It's really a modernist dichotomy, a modernist polemic; in speaking of the East and the West, Tanizaki is subtly, richly, delicately, conflating the Japanese with the modernist. We should remember that, from the late nineteenth to the early twentieth century—when neither modernism nor the avant-garde had been ascribed the denominations, the locations, the histories and epiphanic moments by which we know them today—the West, for both European radicals and non-Western artists and thinkers, was identified with linearity, rationality, and naturalism. The Bauhaus painters' works—Klee, Kandinsky, and others—were brought to Calcutta at Tagore's behest; the latter had, Partha Mitter tells us, seen these paintings on a visit to Austria, and recognized a concordance, a convergence, of temperament and intention with his own; Mitter also reminds us of Klee's secret but deep absorption in Indian philosophy. Once the paintings were exhibited, they were reviewed in Calcutta's major English-language daily, the *Statesman*, by Stella Kramrisch, an art historian of Austrian-Jewish descent, who was also spending time in India at Tagore's invitation. In her review, Kramrisch told her readers that these paintings might reveal to them 'that European art does not mean naturalism and that the transposition of forms of nature in the work of an artist is common to ancient and modern India'.[2] The attack on linearity and naturalism cannot be characterized as a Western development alone, with occasional epiphanic and opportunistic uses of 'other' cultural resources by Western artists: Picasso with his African mask, Gauguin and Van Gogh with their Japanese prints.

A history of cosmopolitanism and modernism has to take into account both the incursion of the Japanese print into Van Gogh's painting and the peculiar mixture of identity-making, cultural politics, and modernist rhetoric in people like Tanizaki and Tagore: that both were happening at the same time, and, importantly, that the modernism we're aware of in different ways today was being fashioned in the same world. What is common to Picasso, Gauguin, Kramrisch, Klee, Tagore, Tanizaki, and others is an impatience with a certain kind of hard and finished object, a cosmopolitan profligacy and curiosity, a renewed, all-consuming attention directed to the contingent, the 'here and now', the particular, and a stated or secret flirtation with 'otherness' or 'difference', at a time when no language exists to do with 'difference', except the one dealing in terms like 'East', 'West', 'progress', 'materialism', and the 'primitive'. It is no historical coincidence that the avant-garde and the modernist was created everywhere in the time of colonialism. One exists in the other, in hidden ways—but not interred simply, as, in Edward Said's reading, the West Indian plantation is hidden in Jane Austen's work; a suppressed, indubitable truth that, once brought to light, would clarify and redress at once.

★

I had mentioned a third conversation. More enigmatic comment than conversation, I remember it dislocated me because of its suggestive rather than categorical nature, and because it gave me an intimation of lines of contact I should have known more about. It also hinted at a problem of language which is always with us, and prohibits a discussion of modernity without the use of certain catch-words and oppositions: 'Western', 'derived', 'mimicry', 'elitism'. The context here is my visit to the Wissenschaftskolleg in Berlin for lunch almost three years ago, as a preamble to a talk I would deliver in early 2006. My very generous hosts that afternoon all happened to be, fortuitously, Egyptian academics: probably because, given my own interests, all three—two women and a man—were from cultural studies or postcolonial studies or literary departments. Predictably, at some point, the conversation hovered around and then moved gently, but headlong, towards Indian literature, Salman Rushdie, and 'magic realism'; as predictably, my contribution introduced a note of uncertainty in relation to the question of unacknowledged modernisms. The women nodded; I sensed that their own trajectories and career choices would have ordinarily distanced them from my preoccupations, but that erstwhile literary investments, perhaps (who knows) buried family histories, and, more noticeably, Rushdie's recent pro-American politics in relation to Iraq had also alienated them from the project of epic fantasy. The man, however, was slightly different; unlike the women, at least one of whom seemed to have spent a lot of time in America, he taught in a department of literature in Egypt; his dilemmas, his biography, would have been somewhat unlike theirs, which is probably why it was in private that he told me: 'We have the same problem in Egypt. We find it difficult to talk about the cosmopolitanisms and modernisms in our tradition.' As I revisit the scene now, I become aware of distinctions and contrasts that my mind had suppressed at the time. The women were globalized individuals, and spoke English fluently: one of them, I think, was a naturalized American. The man, on the other hand, with all his unprepossessing sophistication, evidently spoke and wrote English as a second language. This reminded me of certain parallels in India, and the way the English language inflected histories there: the women, with their possible elite and global backgrounds, their command of English and their smattering or more of Arabic, echoed the contexts in India in which postcoloniality and notions of hybridity had been consolidated; the man, comfortable in Arabic, with more than a cursory knowledge of English, deeply engaged, in fact, with European literature, reminded me of an earlier, superannuated context in my country, in which, largely, our cosmopolitan modernity had been formed, and from which, with cultural inflections very similar to the Egyptian man's, writers like the poet Utpal Basu and the short-story writer C. S. Lakshmi had emerged.

★

What do I mean, or, for that matter, understand by the word 'cosmopolitan'? The primary sense that's operational in India is, as I've pointed out elsewhere, a constitutional one: it's related to a governmental guarantee that heterogeneous faiths, communities, and cultures might cohabit peacefully, even vibrantly, within a visible space—usually, the city—in the nation. In this, it's not unlike 'multiculturalism', or the special Indian post-Independence version of the 'secular': a domain not outside of religion, but a constitutionally protected space of interreligious, intercommunal co-existence. Perhaps the word 'cosmopolitan' also makes a gesture towards the urban middle classes; and, as a result, it's often Bombay (where I grew up), and whose educated middle class encompasses a multifariousness of faiths and provincial identities—Gujarati, Maharashtrian, Parsi, Tamil, Bengali, Bohri Muslims, 'East Indian' Christians, to name some of them—that's called the most 'cosmopolitan' of Indian cities.

I, however, for the purposes of this piece, have an idea of the word somewhat different from the constitutional one; it has to do with the notion of inner exile at the core of the 'high' cultures of the twentieth century. If one were to keep this notion in mind, the city of Calcutta would come powerfully into the frame; and a history of Bombay cosmopolitanism begs to be written that is more than, or distinct from, an account of variegated urban co-existence. I will return to these two cities later. But the theme of 'inner exile' reminds us that the bourgeois cosmopolitan (most profoundly, in our imagination, the European cosmopolitan)—whether artist or intellectual or writer—was never entirely at one with himself or herself. Let's stay with the European cosmopolitan for a moment, as an apparently founding, fundamental type. He or she presents a characteristic twentieth-century embodiment of Europeanness, but also an intriguing modulation upon it; in fact, a testing of the very limits and recognizable features of Europeanness, because the cosmopolitan, by his or her very nature, is constantly telling us they belong nowhere. In what way? One of the main reasons for this, as we know, is that at the heart of the hegemonic 'high' cultures of modernity is the Jewish artist or intellectual; simply put, the Jew, the Other. With the crucial involvement of the figure of the Jew—and I use that term metaphorically as well as literally, introducing all its specific physical dimensions—in the shaping of cosmopolitanism, European modernity becomes, at once, characteristically itself, with its unmistakable eclectic tenor, as we know it today, and deeply alienated from itself. All that is canonically strange about the European twentieth century—its avant-garde, its artistic disruptiveness, its experimentation—opens up, if we linger with the figure of the Jew for a while, into the strange that is not canonical, that is not European, that always carries within it the unrecognizable texture of the minority. But this pursuit can't be an exercise where we eventually rip off the mask to reveal the true face underneath, fair or dark; because we have to reconcile ourselves, in a new way, to the fact that cosmopolitanism does not, and never had, a true face; its characteristic domain, and achievement, is the defamiliarized.

⋆

Before I go any further, I should quickly distinguish what I'm doing here from the many excellent scholarly studies available on the role of Jewishness in modernity. My attempt is less rigorous and more impressionistic, and has, inescapably, to do with facets of who I am: raised in Bombay, a middle-class Bengali, located, as both a writer and a reader, in the histories of modernism in a putatively postmodern age. Chancing upon an old essay by Cynthia Ozick, 'Mrs Virginia Woolf: A Madwoman and her Nurse', from her 1983 collection, *Art and Ardor*, set into motion a train of thoughts that had been with me for a while, to do with Jewishness as well as the India I'd grown up in. It also made me think further into what, in the context of the conversations I've reported, I'd already been thinking about: who is the non-Western cosmopolitan? Did he or she, as it were, vanish thirty years ago into postcolonial identity and ethnicity? Or does the dichotomy of the Western and the non-Western, as we understand it today, actually fall apart in the cosmopolitan?

Ozick's essay is a review of Quentin Bell's biography of his aunt Virginia; and it is, as the title implies, an account of a difficult marriage held together by significant companionship. But it also contains a surprisingly large digression on Leonard Woolf's Jewish identity in particular, and Jewishness in general, the compulsive reflections of a commentator who, a privileged insider in American letters (and, increasingly, a passionate proponent of Zionism), must, at this moment of all moments, confront the spectre of non-Europeanness. Ozick, however, doesn't speak of herself directly; instead, she dwells on the ministering husband in the very heart of Bloomsbury, and, specifically, on faces and appearances. She introduces the theme, the hiccup, the rupture, after briefly sketching the educational background of the Bloomsbury set, and then narrowing upon Leonard: 'Cambridge was not natural to him, Bloomsbury was not natural to him, even England was not natural to him—not as an inheritance; he was a Jew.'[3] And then these comments, on the biographer's failure to properly imagine Leonard Woolf, leading to an unexpected consequence, an opening up; for, Ozick would have it, Bell's inability to 'get' Leonard makes him present to us, while aunt Virginia, whom Bell might understand intuitively, becomes distant: 'Quentin Bell has no "authority" over Leonard Woolf, as he has over his aunt; Leonard is nowhere in the biographer's grip . . . The effect is unexpected. It is as if Virginia Woolf escapes—possessing her too selectively, the biographer lets her slip—but Leonard Woolf somehow stays to become himself.'[4]

And in what way, in Ozick's essay, does he 'become himself'? She describes the strange courtship, the really very distinct worlds, domestic parameters, and lineages the husband-and-wife-to-be belonged to, Virginia's trademark enervating uncertainties, the careful and polite abstention, in their set, from any remark being passed either on Leonard's religion or his agnosticism, and, in spite of this, Virginia's bewildered admission: 'You seem so foreign'. Now, Ozick begins to discuss the inescapable marks of Jewishness, and, in doing so, almost accidentally touches upon an element in the fashioning of the cosmopolitan in the twentieth century that is rarely acknowledged; the way the cosmopolitan could, poetically, 'belong nowhere', be in a state of inner exile, while the subconscious responded to a register, an actual mark, in her or him, which it could never express itself about with the candour that Virginia Woolf, from her position of agitated intimacy, could: 'You seem so foreign'. This is the mark of alterity or difference: not antithetical to cosmopolitanism's homelessness, its internationalism, but, I hope to suggest, fundamental to it. Ozick brings us to the incontrovertible piece of evidence, the face, tracing its passage and vicissitudes from Woolf's paternal grandfather's time to his own. In connection, again, with his contemporaries, Ozick points out that 'if his own origins were almost never mentioned to his face, his face was nevertheless there, and so, in those striking old photographs, were the faces of his grandparents'.[5] Ozick quotes Leonard Woolf's own words, from his autobiography, on his paternal grandfather: 'a large, stern, black-haired, and black-whiskered, rabbinical Jew in a frock coat' with a 'look of stern rabbinical orthodoxy'. According to Ozick, he preferred his Dutch-born maternal grandmother's face, 'the round, pink face of an incredibly old Dutch doll', and he also wondered if this grandmother might have had 'a good deal of non-Jewish blood in her ancestry. Some of her children and grandchildren were fair-haired and facially very unlike the "typical" Jew.' About his grandfather, though, he was resolutely without illusions: 'No one could have mistaken him for anything but a Jew. Although he wore coats and trousers, hats and umbrellas, just like those of all the other gentlemen in Addison Gardens, he looked to me as if he might have stepped straight out of one of those old pictures of caftaned, bearded Jews in a ghetto . . . .'[6] And so, in his unconvincing 'coats and trousers, hats and umbrellas', Leonard's grandfather is already working his way towards that secular modernity that his grandson will come to inhabit, almost naturally, but whose neutral 'Englishness', in turn, even in the temporary persona of the colonial officer, a figure of authority, does not deceive Ozick. She is, again inadvertently I think, gesturing towards a history of the secular from the nineteenth century onwards that is as characteristic of the non-West as it is, as we see, of the heart of Empire itself; the fusing of ethnic identity, as in the case of the grandfather, with a European paradigm, an almost proud fusing, one can't help feeling, in spite of the grandson's misgivings; and then, two generations later, with the fashioning of the cosmopolitan, the modern, and the modernist, we have the grandson's invisibility, which, as Ozick shrewdly points out (without unfolding any of its consequences), is also a form of visibility. The process was taking place, let's say, in Bengal as much as in London; it is often called 'Westernization', which is an almost meaningless term, not only because the process meant very different things to, say, to Leonard Woolf's grandfather and to Woolf himself, but because it does not catch the intricacy, the cultural and emotional complexity, of the way 'difference' directs the process. It's something that could equally, and as validly, be called 'non-Westernization', without any of the assertiveness of the postcolonial discourses.

Ozick now turns to a photograph, part of what she calls a 'pictorial history of Bloomsbury'. Before she offers her reading, she offers her caveat: 'One is drawn to Leonard's face much as he was drawn to his grandfather's face, and the conclusion is the same. What Leonard's eyes saw [that is, when they confronted his grandfather] was what the eyes of the educated English classes saw [that is, when regarding Woolf]'.[7] Ozick is right to alert us to this; but there is also the question of what her eyes see, and what ours do. Ozick studies the 'arresting snapshot' of Leonard Woolf and Adrian Stephen, brother of Virginia Woolf. 'They are,' says Ozick, 'both young men in their prime; the date is 1914 . . . They are dressed identically (vests, coats, ties) and positioned identically—feet apart, hands in pocket, shut lips gripping pipe or cigarette holder . . . Both faces are serene, holding back amusement, indulgent of the photographer.'[8] At this point, we come to the anticipated turn in the portrayal: 'And still it is not a picture of two cultivated Englishmen, or not only that. Adrian is incredibly tall and Vikinglike, with a forehead as broad and flat as a chimney tile; he looks like some blueblood American banker not long out of Princeton; his hair grows straight up like thick pale straw. Leonard's forehead is an attenuated wafer under a tender black forelock, his nose is nervous and frail. . . .'[9] After a moment's reflection on what the correct analogy might be, Ozick decides to be, as she puts it, 'blunt': 'he looks like a student at the yeshiva. Leonard has the unmistakable face of a Jew.'[10]

Ozick is absolutely right, I think, in her preternatural and prickly sensitivity, to exhume the Jewish identity of the 'cultivated Englishman'; but she is perhaps wrong to give it such fixity. There is another kind of movement taking place in this image, this picture, which Ozick says nothing about, and which would consign Adrian Stephen's type—blonde, tall, 'Vikinglike'—into history just as Woolf's grandfather had been consigned to history; it involves, in the unwitting figure of Woolf, the emergence of the cosmopolitan—the person who belongs nowhere, the person whose alterity and state of exile are hidden but unmistakable. The old distinction between the 'student at the yeshiva' and the 'cultivated Englishman' may have been true of Woolf's grandfather's time, but it is, already, no longer of Woolf's: to be modern, increasingly, will be to be impure, to both conceal and exhibit that impurity. The great project of 'high' modernity, defamiliarization, and the principal discourse of postcoloniality, alterity, had always, we'd presumed, been distinct from each other, belonging to distinct phases of twentieth-century history, and even embedded in world-views at war with one another. A second glance at the cosmopolitan—especially at the Jewish writers and artists who lived in Europe, many of them transplanted to America from around the time of the Second World War, or who died shortly before (Walter Benjamin, Kracauer, Adorno, Schoenberg, Bloch, Hannah Arendt, to name a few)—reminds us that alterity is an indispensable and intimate constituent of the 'high' modern, that it is the hidden twin of what is already hidden but powerfully definitive of 'high' modernity—the defamiliarized. To be modern, Ozick accidentally reminds us, is to be foreign, to be 'different': not only figuratively, but, in significant ways, literally; and it is of course the literal, for obvious reasons of her own, that Ozick is here fiercely concentrated on. As far as appearances are concerned, the misfit in the picture, the one who is already beginning to date, is Adrian Stephen, not Leonard Woolf.

Let me, here, address my own recollections of cosmopolitanism; for Ozick's essay is of interest to me because, primarily, it makes me realign what I already know. I wish to refer to faces and styles of appearance in Bombay that gradually decided for me, as I was growing up in the 1960s and 1970s, what the lineaments of cosmopolitanism and bohemianism might be. In the light of Ozick's essay, I am led to wonder what made me take those decisions: for no clear or definitive catalogue of features had been put down. Of course, one identified an artist or writer of the avant-garde through their work, but there was clearly another realm involved, or else I wouldn't have registered the adolescent shock I did at the discrepancy between T. S. Eliot's appearance and his poetry, the canonical unfamiliarity and experimental nature of the latter, and the unfamiliar or unexpected conventionality of the former. We are aware, certainly, that Eliot made deliberate comic use of this discrepancy, in 'Prufrock', of course, but pointedly in 'Lines for Cuscuscaraway and Mirza Murad Ali Beg': 'How unpleasant to meet Mr Eliot! / With his features of clerical cut, / And his brow so grim / And his mouth so prim...'.[11] Here is the American exile, in middle age, a man who has, for long, deliberately emptied his appearance of signs of exile, and who seems to be mocking the visible features of cosmopolitanism (not in his poetry, but in his personal style), who seems to be refuting (and I'm making no easy connection with his publicized anti-Semitism) the subterranean ethos of alterity.

The realm of the visible, then, is an important one in recognizing the cosmopolitan, because it comprises both carefully orchestrated markers and intrinsic lapses. Visible signs also help us to distinguish between cosmopolitanism as inner exile, and the other, constitutional form of cosmopolitanism I mentioned earlier, a state-sponsored multiculturalism. As the decades after Independence went past, this second form became the authoritative one in India, and especially definitive, in a clichéd way, of society in Bombay; what the history of cosmopolitanism as a state of inner exile might be in that city has become increasingly difficult to remember or articulate. The visible markers of constitutional cosmopolitanism were symbolic and straightforward, as in a Hindi film set in the 1970s, signifying sub-nationalisms that added up to the nation: there was the Sikh in his turban, there was the Muslim in his skull cap, there was the Christian crossing herself, and there was the hero, at once Hindu and everyman, embodying the secular space—the film, the story, the nation—in which, despite tribulations and challenges, these particular elements unite. With the cosmopolitan as exile, the visible elements—the blue jeans, the handspun khadi kurta, the sandals, the filterless cigarette between the fingers, the copy of Lorca in one hand—did not add up; they did not cohere, as the constitution had foretold the heterogeneous fragments of the nation would; they were casual signs of belonging nowhere. I will elaborate on this in a moment.

I realize that, as I was growing up, I began to identify the cosmopolitan avant-garde and the bohemian artistic fraternity in 1970s Bombay not only by their practice, but also as a consequence of what they looked like. That tutoring had come to me from desultorily studying members of this sub-class from a distance, as well as both the works and faces of the American, especially, the New York, artists and poets; in fact, a certain kind of American person who happened to be quite distinct from the 'tall, Vikinglike' American banker prototype Ozick compares Adrian Stephen to. In this latter group, whose features I'd been subconsciously absorbing, I'd include a whole range of practitioners, whose work, at the time, I didn't necessarily admire: Allen Ginsberg (who'd visited India in the 1960s and hung out with the Bombay and especially the Calcutta poets, including Sunil Ganguly, whom I earlier described as an 'ageing *enfant terrible*'), as well as figures from pop culture and entertainment, like Bob Dylan, Woody Allen, Groucho Marx, and, with his diverse racial background and his benign belligerence, a sort of honorary Jew, Frank Zappa. There seemed to be an air of the outsider, of difference, about these people: I ascribed this to their practice, and to the persona being an extension of that practice. To be an outsider, in the twentieth century, was also to often have a curious combination of, on the one hand, the awkward, the pedagogical, the pedantic, and, on the other, the anarchic and comic, and, often, the two were interchangeable: thus, the anxious academic air of Woody Allen and Groucho Marx, and the quietly comic appearance of Albert Einstein. These were signs of the fine balancing act through which alterity was shaping modernity: a seriousness that was out of place and therefore foreign, mirroring a foreignness that was altogether too serious. The result could be comic, as is evident from Ozick's pitying, acerbic: 'he looks like a student from the yeshiva'.[12] The modern, marked and pursued by difference, also makes a mess of things: 'under the sign of Saturn'[13] is how Susan Sontag describes the condition in connection with Walter Benjamin, who is less than adept at the technology of everyday life ('my inability even today to make a cup of coffee'[14]), botching up too, with the yeshiva-student's seriousness, his final, attempted escape to the United States. In India, this serio-comic figure of the modern, singled out at once by modernity and difference, emerges in the nineteenth century with the Bengali babu, and is parodied by Bengalis and Englishmen alike—most savagely, for the Anglophone reader, by Kipling in *Kim* at the beginning of the new century.

As for myself, I didn't dwell on the fact that many of the faces I was studying, by some coincidence, belonged to Jews, though this was often a part of their self-advertisement; Jewishness, hidden or anxious, if ineluctable, in the Europeans, seemed to have become, with these Americans, a more acknowledged secular component, sometimes a subversive one, of defamiliarization. Many of the poets who lived or studied in Bombay, and wrote in English in the 1960s and 1970s—set apart in those relatively early decades after Independence, therefore,

Figure 7.1 The poet Arvind Krishna Mehrotra and his wife Vandana on a terrace in Allahabad circa 1974.

Photo by Herwig Palme.

Figure 7.2 Arun Kolatkar with a guitar.

Figure 7.3 Arvind Krishna Mehrotra and his wife Vandana leaning against the parapet on a terrace in Allahabad circa 1974.

Photo by Herwig Palme.

by the curious double prestige and disgrace of writing in a colonial language and an international one—this strange microcosmic minority (comprising, among others, Arun Kolatkar, Arvind Krishna Mehrotra, Nissim Ezekiel) were unmistakably cosmopolitans. They reminded me in some ways of the Americans, but this I might have taken to be a

Figure 7.4 Adil Jussawala.

Figure 7.5 Buddhadeva Bose and Amiya Chakraborty in the Boses' house in Calcutta.

Figure 7.6 Poet, critic, and modernist Buddhadeva Bose and others. Buddhadeva Bose is standing on the extreme left and the poet Premendra Mitra on the extreme right. Next to Buddhadeva Bose is the novelist and short-story writer Tarashankar, next to Premendra Mitra is Amalendu Bose, and next to Amalendu is Ashok K. Sarkar of *Ananda Bazar Patrika*, the leading Bengali daily in Calcutta, and a leading publishing house. Other figures not known.

family resemblance, integral to the texture of the time. I may have also assumed that there were elements in their visible and intellectual make-up that they'd fashioned after the Americans; certainly, Kolatkar and Mehrotra had studied, respectively, William Carlos Williams and Pound in order to create a vernacular that would allow them to move away from both Orientalist poetry and King's English, a language of defamiliarization, of finding the uncanny in the Indian mundane. Something in them also very powerfully echoed the Jewishness of American artists; but I was not conscious of this fact—nor do I think were they—except subliminally. The Jewish artist created a space that many non-Western cosmopolitans, especially in Bombay in the 1960s, came to rework seamlessly in their own milieu, without anyone either clearly noticing it, or being able to remark on it except in inadequate terms such as 'Westernization'. I say 'inadequate', because the Jew had almost unknowingly introduced a dimension of racial and physical alterity to the modern, which, almost unknowingly, the 1960s Indian English poets and bohemia presented their modulation upon. It was not simply towards the European or the Western that poets like Kolatkar and Mehrotra were aspiring, but a condition of twentieth-century modernity that crucially brought together what are seen to be incompatibles: defamiliarization and difference, modernist experiment and ethnicity, Europeanness and non-Europeanness. It also occurs to me here that the modernities and cosmopolitanisms that I am familiar with were all shaped by disenfranchised elites; that is, by groups of people who, in the contexts they found themselves in, had no natural—or had a somewhat ambivalent and subterranean—access to political power. This was true of the Jews in Europe and even America; it was true of the Bengali in the time of colonialism; it was true of the odd minority position of the Indian poets who wrote in English in the 1960s, at a time well before English was the 'boom' Indian language it would become twenty-five years later, being reproached by the canonical writers in the Indian vernaculars and Ginsberg alike for employing a foreign tongue. It was in these contexts of disenfranchised elitism that other, cultural modes of power were fashioned by these cosmopolitans. The question of legitimacy raised by each of the elites I've mentioned finds its odd, and possibly logical, counterpart in the constant question of the legitimacy of the artwork itself in modernism—is this art?—a challenge which has, of course, been domesticated in the triumphal narrative of European modernity.

Among the Bombay poets were a number of people who belonged to liminal religions: for instance, the founder poet of the group, the late Nissim Ezekiel, was Jewish, a descendant of the Bene Israel sect that had sought refuge in Gujarat in the second century BC; and there was Adil Jussawala, one of the most intellectual of that set, a Zoroastrian and a Parsi. I'll only point out here that their minority status played itself out in two ways: firstly, in a semi-visible relationship to the secular, largely Hindu nation, and, secondly, in connection to the prism of cosmopolitanism, where it also merged into their roles as sometimes derided deracinated writers in the English language. Occasionally, and this is only a hunch, being part of a minority seems to have given them, particularly Ezekiel, privileged access to international cosmopolitanisms; at least, this is what these lines from Ezekiel's autobiographical poem, 'Background, Casually', seem to indicate: 'The Indian landscape sears my eyes. / I have become a part of it / To be observed by foreigners. /

They say that I am singular, / Their letters overstate the case.'[15] 'Singular' is a word Ezekiel uses more than once; it encompasses both the resonance of the minority and of the privileged cosmopolitan. Living in India, being Indian, you almost feel that Ezekiel is aware of Jewish cosmopolitanism, but has forgotten the problem of Jewish alterity.

Interestingly, all these artists and poets—whether they were Hindus, Muslims, Parsis, Jews, Christians—made cosmopolitanism visible in a new way in the 1960s and 1970s, in that brief period when the old disenfranchised vernacular elites began to lose their intellectual hegemony in India, and before a new empowered post-Nehruvian ruling class emerged in the 1980s with Rajiv Gandhi; they fashioned a style called the 'ethnic', and, in doing so, complicated the relationship between the Indian and the deracinated, between authenticity and foreignness. 'Ethnic', at the time, used to indicate, generally, non-Christian, non-European identity; with the bohemian set in India, it denoted the condition of belonging nowhere. Among the visible symbols of the ethnic were handspun khadi kurtas, sometimes worn in conjunction with long churidar pyjamas, sometimes blue jeans, cotton Bengali tangail saris, and, on the foreheads of bohemian women, large vermilion Fauvist bindis or dots, the feet of both men and women in Kolhapuri chappals or sandals. The conventional Western clothes of the Indian middle class—shirts, trousers, suits, shoes—were set aside, not in the interests of nationalism, but for a combination of clothing which, individually, could be overdeterminedly 'Indian', but were now suddenly transformed into a signature of deracination. The 'ethnic', then, is a peculiarly 1960s Indian modulation of alterity's delicate relationship to the cosmopolitan and the defamiliarized.

On this matter of the visibility of the cosmopolitan, and its surprising allocations of the recognizable and the unrecognizable, I wish to end with a tiny coda on the city of Calcutta, and on the Bengali bhadralok or bourgeois—the descendant of the babu. The Bengali bhadralok emerges more or less parallel to the Jewish cosmopolitan in Europe; in him, once again, as in the Jew, we find the 'high' cultural defamiliarized merging with the irreducibly non-European. Unlike, for instance, the Japanese modern, the bhadralok eschews the Western suit; the suited Bengali, in fact, is often seen to be a government official, or a functionary of the Raj. The bhadralok's visible mark of deracination, of defamiliarization, is the once-feudal costume, the white dhuti and panjabi or kurta; at what point the transition took place from the feudal to the cosmopolitan is difficult to pinpoint, but once it had, it became increasingly difficult to mistake, from a distance, the wearer of that costume as anyone except a person belonging to a particular history that was, indeed, unfolding worldwide. The fact that—unlike the flowing Persian or Oriental robes worn by Rammohun Roy or the Tagores, or, for that matter, the club-goer's suit—the dhuti and panjabi was the attire of the Bengali everyman was important; for, like the 'cultivated Englishman', Leonard Woolf, it made the bhadralok at once invisible and newly visible. The worldwide history this person belonged to was a history of the modern, certainly, but it was also a history of the different; it was a narrative of 'high' culture as well as being a narrative of otherness. That narrative, as was to be expected, had a limited life; the figure in the dhuti and panjabi has all but disappeared. This makes it possible to consider afresh the contraries that were visible but never fully declared in its appearance.

2007

* * *

8

Qatrina and the books

Nadeem Aslam and others

What is Pakistani writing? Whatever it might be, it seems to have taken up newsprint lately. Things have been changing quickly and irrevocably over the last seven or eight years: a great symbol of American capitalism was destroyed by two aeroplanes; this was followed, some years later, by a crash in the market no less resounding and sudden; in South Asia, Pakistan (marginalized and nearly abandoned by post-Cold War politics) has been veering between being a frail democracy and becoming a basket case. In no obvious way connected to all this, a handful of Anglophone writers has recently been emerging from that country. Most of them are young, and have written one or two or three books; some, like Mohsin Hamid and Mohammed Hanif, have successful careers and lives elsewhere. Their work is not part of the long twentieth century; they are not a necessary component of a post-colonial efflorescence, as Indian Anglophone writing appeared to be in the 1980s; they are not in any clear way a part of a national literature; they do not bring with them the promise of offering to the reader the 'sights and sounds' of what used to be, in Kipling's time, North-West India. They are a twenty-first-century phenomenon, appearing at a time when the new supposed fundamentals of this century—free-market dominance, the end of history, the clash of civilizations—suddenly seem frayed and ephemeral. Pakistani writers are interestingly poised: implicated in both the unfolding and the unravelling of our age.

Who, or what, are the antecedents of this present lot: Nadeem Aslam, Mohsin Hamid, Mohammed Hanif, Moni Mohsin, Daniyal Mueenuddin, Kamila Shamsie? The answer—given the multilingualism of South Asia, its histories and enmities, its experiences of modernity and colonization—has to be a complex one. The riches and idiosyncrasies of Urdu writing must be one antecedent, as an Ur-literature which is seldom invoked but which must inform the work. Urdu's fastidious formalism, the predominance of the short form in its twentieth-century fiction, could help explain, for example, Hamid's choice in *The Reluctant Fundamentalist* of a form that's unpopular in Anglophone writing: what Henry James called 'the dear, the blessed *nouvelle*'.[1] But the French term reminds us of the currency the novella has had in Europe, and that Hamid has said he was drawn to the genre by way of Camus's *The Fall*. This makes things more complicated, not least because we can't set up an easy opposition between Anglophone diasporic Pakistani writing and Urdu-language literature—between the native and the foreign—because Hamid's response to Camus must have a deep and long lineage in Urdu cosmopolitanism and its engagement with Europe.

If we were to make a case for a Pakistani aesthetic, in the way that a case for an Indian aesthetic was once made by people like the art historian Ananda Coomaraswamy, and then reformulated in postcolonial terms after *Midnight's Children*, we'd have to use different rhetoric from the sort that has haunted a certain view of the Indian arts for a century. Salman Rushdie has been an iconic figure to at least some of the writers I've mentioned (and some have been blurbed by him), but they treat their cultural inheritance in a different way. For one thing, they're largely, and enigmatically, silent about that inheritance and aesthetic; for another, their work—heterogeneous though it is—doesn't send out the message, as Rushdie's did (through markers in the writing that sought to establish continuities with carefully chosen texts like the *Ramayana* and *The Thousand and One Nights*), that the impulse towards the epic dominates South Asian storytelling. If anything, the miniaturist's impulse, with its attendant craftsmanship—which has as valid a lineage (some would argue a richer one) in Indian aesthetics as the epic—determines the texture of many of these new works. But even to begin to make a case based on cultural characteristics would be disingenuous, partly because the works themselves resist such an argument, as does the culture itself, with its own tradition of eclecticism and contradictory borrowings.

Two precursors to these new writers should be mentioned; both are still productive. The older of them is Bapsi Sidhwa, who is roughly a contemporary of Rushdie's and shares some of his preoccupations: to construct an imaginative (in Rushdie's case, mock-serious) investigation into the conditions of Partition and Independence; to record the everyday lives of a minority within the new nation (in Rushdie, the secular Muslim bourgeoisie; in Sidhwa, the Parsi community); the urge to find, in English, something like an authentic South Asian vernacular. Although she is Pakistani, Sidhwa could be seen to fit in with the general project of Indian English writing from the 1980s onwards. The other precursor, Aamer Hussein, who moved to London from Pakistan when he was fifteen, and has lived here for forty years, is something of an anomaly. An obsessive and dextrous practitioner of the short story, he emerges from the earlier tradition of Urdu cosmopolitanism—he has translated some of these stories—and reinvents it in an English context. It isn't only that he might occasionally write about Maida Vale and Little Venice, because at least one of the writers he admires, Qurratulain Hyder, wrote about London too. His take on the tradition is informed by his longing to be embedded in a textual culture, a culture of allusions and references such as the Urdu avant-garde worked within, while at the same time having to negotiate a literary environment in which very different sorts of enterprise were underway: the English novel post-Amis, the Indian novel in English, traditions in which narrative supersedes allusion. It's in accommodating his own incongruity that Hussein has been particularly gifted.

Hussein was formed by a world where the Twin Towers had still not been brought down. The duress that he and his stories seem to be under has other sources: the displacement brought about by migration; the old legacies of class, of the wars with India; the struggle of writing, in what feels like a vacuum; the anxieties and achievements of multiculturalism. Hussein's fiction presents a fresh but melancholy interpretation of what those achievements are. However, a great deal—including much of what formed Hussein's cultural context—came crashing down with the Twin Towers. It's not as if the younger Pakistani writers habitually produce 9/11 novels, in the sense of the American and British sub-genre; it's as if 9/11 has simply made a certain rehearsal of South Asian identity and history impossible, or even irrelevant.

And so, although Nadeem Aslam's third novel, *The Wasted Vigil*, addresses recent and not-so-recent history—the withdrawal of the Soviets from Afghanistan; the fall of the Taliban and the ongoing war there—it is, implicitly, about revisiting the past and recording the present without having easy access, any more, to the liberal or novelistic solutions that were available until so recently: realist reportage and analysis, fantasy, the epic, the fairy tale. Aslam has a reputation for lush, ornate writing—it is supposed to go with his brand of 'magic realism'—which makes him appear to fit into a familiar and successful tradition, in which style and aesthetics comply with, and display, national characteristics, where 'national' is primarily defined by being non-Western. Butterflies and visions inhabit his fiction.

The brief first section of the new novel, in which we encounter the Englishman Marcus and his Afghan wife, Qatrina, seems to confirm this impression: they live in an Afghani village near the Tora Bora mountains, in a house whose ceiling is covered by the books Qatrina once nailed to it (books that had been banned and, as a result, transformed into symbolic objects under the Taliban regime). Lara, a Russian woman staying with Marcus while she searches for her lost brother, Benedikt (who was in the Soviet army), notices at night that the books are 'each held in place by an iron nail hammered through it. A spike driven through the pages of history, a spike through the pages of love, a spike through the sacred.'[2] That second sentence appears to place the narrative and its imagery and intent squarely in the line of what Fredric Jameson once called 'national allegory'.[3] 'National', here, doesn't refer to a country demarcated by borders: it denotes the political and the postcolonial, since if the West is disreputably 'universal', the non-West is, or at least was, nicely encompassed by 'national', in Benedict Anderson's sense of the word. The 'book' has been a crucial element in the unfolding of that history; after the banning of *The Satanic Verses*, and the book-burnings and desecrations that followed, at the hands of fundamentalists of all persuasions, including Hindu ones, the book, especially the novel, became a talisman. It became a fetish of humanism, an incarnation of history, not only a receptacle for human wisdom, but a living thing with its own precarious career in the contemporary world. This incarnate quality is hinted at: 'The books are all up there, the large ones as well as those that are no thicker than the walls of the human heart.'[4] Later, we learn that Qatrina is dead (she is mentioned in the first chapter in a flashback), and that, at the time she fixed the books to the ceiling, she was mad.

This may or may not be plausible, but it absolves the symbolism from too comfortable a resting place in liberal piety. Qatrina had lost her sanity because of what she'd had to do and suffer under the Taliban: accused of 'living in sin' with her husband, she'd had to chop off one of his hands as a punishment to them both. The Taliban are mad, but they represent a utopian idea of order; Qatrina's madness was a protest against utopia. But it was also a melancholy surrender of herself. The mad attack books; but the urge to fix books, to sacralize them by making them static, or to make them static by rendering them physically or metaphorically immovable, is also mad. It's an instance of the kind of liberal utopianism about culture that sounded very loudly after the fatwa. Aslam's novel, and the little fable in it about Qatrina and the books, reminds us that the liberal romanticism that appeared in the 1990s was, in its own way, problematic, one of the reasons being its soaring transcendentalism (it's logical that books should take refuge on a ceiling).

An example was Rushdie's letter to Rajiv Gandhi,[5] then prime minister of India, protesting at the government's feckless and opportunistic banning of *The Satanic Verses* (a ban that, extraordinarily, still stands). Rushdie excoriated Gandhi for forgetting, in effect, that writers were the unacknowledged legislators of the world: this was Rushdie speaking in a voice we hadn't heard him speak in before, that of the Shelleyan didact; but as rhetoric it remains unconvincing, largely because of its ingenuousness and lack of self-reflexivity. Much water has passed under the bridge since then. Aslam, in this unusually poised and illuminating novel, is rarely ingenuous. He decisively escapes the romanticism—despite, at first glance, seeming to edge close to it in his early pages—that has informed the liberal riposte to fundamentalism; Qatrina's madness is only one instance of the openness, and the difficulty, of Aslam's engagement.

Almost everyone in the novel is pursuing a mission of some sort, either a political mission or one that has to do with recovering the missing or the dead. The object of pursuit, in either case, is hallucinatory and tantalizing. Among the characters are two Americans: David Town, who, we hear much later, used to work for the CIA, and was also, once, the secret lover of Qatrina and Marcus's daughter, the murdered Zameen; and James Palantine, who's in the US army. Then there's Dunia, an Afghani schoolteacher harried by the remnants of the Taliban (who don't like women or education), and Casa, a radicalized young Afghan, who could loosely be described, in the official idiom, as a 'terrorist'. I don't remember Aslam using the word in the book, though—or not in relation to Casa. This abstention is one of Aslam's many strategies of defamiliarization; another is the mark of complicity on almost every character. The plot is hard to summarize, because the novel depends on discursive movement rather than plot; it circles round, as national allegory doesn't, the ancient epic themes of bereavement and search. All the characters are drawn to and repelled from each other by the varying forces of attraction and suspicion, as in the mixture of doubting curiosity and empathy that Casa and Dunia feel for each other, a curiosity leading, in Casa, to self-loathing. Often, the defamiliarization takes place at the level of description, as in the following passage, after Marcus has witnessed a truck exploding:

> For the next fraction of a second it is as though the truck is in fact the picture of a truck, a photograph printed on flimsy paper, and that the rays of the sun have been concentrated onto it with a magnifying glass. And then the ground falls away from his feet and a light as hard as the sun in a mirror fills his vision. The tar on a part of the road below him has caught fire. *Soon they will feed you the entire world.* The explosion has created static and a spark leaps from his thumb towards a smoking fragment of metal flying past him. Then he is on the ground. Beside him has landed a child's wooden leg, in flames, the leather straps burning with a different intensity than the wood, than the bright blood-seeping flesh of the severed thigh that is still attached. A woman in a burka on fire crosses his vision.[6]

Violence and refulgence, the religious and the political, cruelty and vision are compressed in a series of images seen in shattered, out of the ordinary, discontinuous contexts. These glimpses don't generally take place where the 'epiphanies' of modernism occurred, in the midst of the banal and the everyday, in cities and neighbourhoods that are half-familiar to us. Aslam handles his fragments distinctively, even theatrically, whether the image in question is the 'child's wooden leg, in flames, the leather straps burning with a different intensity than the wood' in the passage above, or the hidden stump of Marcus's arm, or the giant head of the Buddha in Marcus's disused perfume factory, or the semi-visible paintings of animals on the walls of his house, or the recurrent motif of the pomegranate, or the Soviet soldier's head (probably the missing Benedikt's) discovered by Casa towards the end of the novel: 'that parchment-like face pasted onto the skull, the lips pulled back to reveal blackened teeth'.[7]

These are not instances of the particular or the concrete as these things would have been understood by Ezra Pound or William Carlos Williams; they have an occluded quality, or the opacity of calligraphy or inscription ('that parchment-like face'). Civilization, history, and culture—the Buddha's head; Benedikt's severed head—are breakable, degradable, and literally (as with the pomegranate) or figuratively (as with television images of war) consumable: we have an appetite, for civilization and for its destruction. Aslam's extraordinary, complex style attempts to encompass these oscillations: it makes his language at once voluptuous and eloquent and scathing and melancholy. This language occasionally confuses his readers, critics, and even his admirers. It's what made James Buchan describe the novel's terrain, in the *Guardian*, as 'a Persian miniature under some terrible curse';[8] and provoked Adam Mars-Jones, in the opening sentence of his admiring review in the *Observer*, to tackle this question: 'There isn't enough beauty in the world, but isn't it true that a work of art can be too beautiful?'[9] It's also what causes the *New York Times* reviewer, Lorraine Adams, to caution Aslam about his tendency towards 'operatic effusion',[10] and to quote admonishingly, among other passages and sentences, this discomfiting, almost exhibitionistic, convergence of culture, wounding, appetite, and life: 'The pomegranate was on a table close to the fireplace. She slit it open now. The outer layer of scarlet seeds had been warmed by the flames. The temperature of menstrual blood, of semen just emerged from a man's body.'[11]

In a recent issue of the Indian newspaper *Mint*, Salil Tripathi, speaking of the new Pakistani writing in English, offers a thesis for what is still a small, though undeniable, flowering: 'With the state withdrawing from exercising even a semblance of authority, several authors of Pakistani origin or heritage have seized that space, writing seminal works that provide clarity in our absurd times. Maybe exceptional strife spurs imagination—think of the Samizdat writers during the Cold War—although responding to the crisis is not the overt intention of any of Pakistan's fine novelists.'[12] This may well be true, but it is also contentious. It's a version of the old adage about suffering making for good art, an adage whose political, rather than metaphysical, implications were embraced enthusiastically in Western, especially Anglophone, Europe in the 1980s, in relation to the poetry that was emerging from the totalitarian regimes of Eastern Europe and the Soviet Union. The poetry, for instance, of Holub, Milosz, and Brodsky led poets born to happier countries to register their envy, almost, of the former poets' histories. The 1980s also represent the dawning of the era we live in now, of deregulated markets, a framework which, in no small way, makes these particular Pakistani writers available to us, and which surely contributes to the absurdity of the 'absurd times' Tripathi says we live in.

Rather than a tragic but noble history of oppression, I would say that it's the burden of a conflicted and ambiguous relationship to national history that marks the imaginative world of the Pakistani bourgeoisie from which these writers have emerged. It's difficult to say if—outside its growing pan-Islamism in the last four decades—there ever was a national myth of Pakistan which supplied metaphors for its writing, as was the case for America and, just as strongly, and sometimes perniciously, for India. In India, the national myth developed in two phases: the first made a diffuse, amorphous, all-embracing version of Hinduism, as well as its later encounter with a tolerant Islam, a source for its secular humanism, where 'India' became a shorthand for a certain way of understanding the past and civilization. The second phase is the postmodern one, where 'India' becomes a means of appropriating and expressing some of the fundamental energies of globalization, to do with enterprise, aggression, prolixity, and interconnectedness. 'Hindutva', the BJP's special spin on Hinduism, was consolidated in this second phase, and a particular kind of national pride was formulated at the same time, summed up in the BJP slogan 'Garv se kaho ham Hindu hain' ('Say proudly: "I'm a Hindu"') and in a legend that appeared on the backs of buses, 'Mera Bharat Mahan' ('My India Is Great'), which led, later, to the BJP's disastrous election slogan for a free-market Hindu nationalism in 2004, 'India Shining'. All this put paid to the Nehruvian phase (itself a continuation of nineteenth-century humanism) of an austere, patrician, liberal, left-leaning nationalism, in which a multilingual, secular middle class whose status was not necessarily connected to inherited property and lineage came to exercise moral and intellectual power.

The one great difference between independent India and independent Pakistan is that Pakistan never had anything like a Nehruvian phase. What it had, besides the domination of the army and fitful, unconvinced attempts at democracy, was a decade—1978–88—under General Zia-ul-Haq (a decade that felt much longer than it was) when a military dictator shored up his regime in the name of Islam. This was a time when most of the arts, especially the classical arts, such as music and dance, which had evolved in the subcontinent through the interpellation of Hindu and Muslim sources, went underground, were silenced, or were purged of Hindu content (some of that content was the contribution of Muslim emperor-composers such as Wajid Ali Shah). It was in this period, too, that Nadeem Aslam's father, a Marxist, left Pakistan for Huddersfield. And it was in the same decade that India moved into the second, triumphal phase of its nationalism: the phase of Hindutva; of the professionalized diaspora in Silicon Valley and New Jersey; of the politics of postcolonialism in academic departments. All these developments made inevitable, in one way or another, India's journey towards the free market that Nehruvian socialism had viewed warily. The free market, fortuitously, gave to the 'idea of India' a new, contemporary, symbolic currency, just at the moment when its old humanistic weight began to become anachronistic. Zia's mixture of militarism and Islam made Pakistan an important player in the final years of the Cold War, but also isolated it; and it alienated Pakistan's intelligentsia and its artistic fraternity from their own heritage, and made impossible the transformation of Pakistani nationalism—unlike the Indian brand—into a commodity that would have a market everywhere.

In this context, the example of music is instructive. After independence, the Indian state became a patron of Indian classical music, and encouraged many maestros who had been born in what became Pakistan to settle in India to practise their art 'freely'. The Pakistani state was always assumed to be stepmotherly about classical music, which had Hindu ancestry, because of Islam's supposedly puritan disdain for music's sensuous qualities (a belief refuted by those who have studied Muhammad's life closely). This ambivalence deepened into hostility under Zia; Indian classical music, meanwhile, established itself as a pan-Indian art-form (some time before Bollywood and the Indian novel in English assumed that mantle) in the 1960s and 1970s and, in a significant sense, became an embodiment of the nation. By the 1990s, however, it had ossified into a series of gestures and genuflections, and the sitar, sarod, and the singer—even the kurta he wore—had become part of a cult of nationality rather than of a persuasive and self-renewing practice. Raza Karim, a Pakistani musicologist and musician, was surely right to point out that, although the suppression of North Indian classical music in Pakistan was tragic, its appropriation by the state, by an idea of the nation, had equally distressing consequences for Indian creativity. He'd noticed the emptiness that enters an art-form once it becomes an adjunct to a national project. The Indian novel in English has constantly run the same risk.

I had a Pakistani friend when I was at Oxford, with whom I was having an unpredictable but absorbing relationship. She put up a large sticker on the wall of my room one day, meaning to educate and embarrass me; it read: i love pakistan. It was a secular message, but there was no real market for it; Pakistan had floundered and blundered when it came to becoming part of the feel-good narrative that nationalism and the free market are both adept at creating. America had perfected it once; and India—with its democracy, its growth rate, its cavorting film industry, its fragrant cuisine, its IT experts, its call centres servicing remote American towns, its novels on the Booker Prize shortlist—was demonstrating, again, the possibilities of a celebratory nationalism. The problem is that such a nationalism, when it becomes a way of experiencing the world—in the arts, in the institutions that are involved in intellectual and critical life—tends to become immune to self-doubt and guilt and shame. The Pakistani Urdu-language writer Fahmida Riaz shrewdly portrays its proponents, with their curious mixture of ingenuousness and complicity, in 'Some Misaddressed Letters', an autobiographical short story (it appears in Aamer Hussein's 1999 anthology, *Hoops of Fire*) in which the protagonist, in exile from her homeland, finds herself addressing a group of attentive Indian intellectuals in Delhi:

> Amina wrote a number of passionate poems, exposing the gaping flaws in a democratic system that still allowed for horrifying poverty. She read them to a select gathering of Indian writers. The Indian intelligentsia, which has rarely known poverty since the last half-century, which is free to choose between the right and the left, between east and west, or north and south, is always thrilled by chastisement. They smiled warmly at her.
>
> One of them remarked: 'It is a very sincere attempt.'
>
> These words at once revealed to Amina that she had just posted another misaddressed letter.[13]

Riaz, in this passage, describes the predicament of the Pakistani writer, as well as the liberties and opportunities that predicament gives her; she suggests, too, that the freedoms available to the Indian writer bring with them paradoxical forms of imprisonment. The dichotomy may be too neat always to hold true, but it reminds us that what is at stake here is more than just one country's suffering and another's success. The contexts at work have to do with national shame and writing as a form of self-awareness ('misaddressed letters'), on the one hand, and a curious mixture of an upbeat openness and a certain suspension of critical faculties, on the other: a curious kind of self-absorption. Riaz's story is an example of fiction skirting, and engaging with, the boundaries of criticism. Aslam's considerable novel emerges from a related history and probably from some of the same pressures: it too describes the journey from the sensuous to the critical, from its lavish propensity for the poetic image to its exploratory, persistent, questioning intelligence.

2009

* * *

9

Ray and Ghatak and other filmmaking pairs

The structure of Asian modernity

It seems that there are all kinds of unresolved problems to do with Satyajit Ray—to do with thinking about him, with finding a language to speak about him that doesn't repeat the indubitable truisms about his humanism and lyricism. How does he fit into history, and into which history—the history of India; the history of filmmaking; some other—do we place him first? We don't ordinarily talk about Ray 'fitting in', because he is an icon and a figurehead, and figureheads don't generally have to fit in; traditions, schools, and oeuvres emanate from them. Glancing towards Ray, we see, indeed, the precious oeuvre, but it's more difficult to trace the tradition—either leading up to Ray or emerging from him. People closer to home will mention something called the 'Bengal Renaissance', and Tagore, when thinking of lineage; and even those who aren't students of film know who some of the precursors are: Jean Renoir, Vittoria de Sica, John Ford. As to inheritors of the style, you could, with some hesitation and prudence, point to Adoor Gopalakrishnan, and, a bit further away, to Abbas Kiarostami. But what does this constellation of names and categories add up to? For, in the end, we're reduced to looking at Ray as if he were alone, as someone who possessed, as Ray said of *Rashomon*, 'just the right degree of universality'.[1]

To me, it's increasingly clear—especially in the light of the changes in politics and culture in the last quarter of a century—that Ray is the only embodiment of an Indian 'high' modernity, specifically a vernacular 'high' modernity, that the world has had to deal with.

The 'world', in this instance, refers to places in Europe and America where film festivals were hosted, the great metropolitan centres in which debates to do with 'culture' were decided, and even sections of the Indian intelligentsia: Ray's humanism was noted in his heyday, but the encounter with Indian modernity that watching his films constituted was hardly mentioned, or only inadvertently experienced by the viewer. And yet Ray's work did occupy the consciousness of the second half of the twentieth century, and, to be understood, must have required a different set of rules from those applying to the paradigmatic, 'authentic' India of either the Orient or, later, of postcoloniality—the India of chaos, crowds, empire, resistance, voices, irresistible self-generation, and colour. Ray's India, or Bengal, was not, in this sense, paradigmatic—but, as with Apu's room overlooking a terrace and railway tracks in *Apur Sansar*, it was strangely recognizable and true. Were we being shown, then, that, it was, after all, 'recognizability', rather than cultural 'authenticity', that was a feature of modernity? And how aware was the audience, as they discovered Apu's world, of that distinction?

Let's go back at this point to Ray's own record of his encounter with Japanese cinema in the form of Kurosawa's *Rashomon*. Ray is writing about this in 1963, probably a little more than twelve years after its release—for Kurosawa's film went to the Venice Film Festival in 1951, winning the Golden Lion there, and Ray says, 'I saw *Rashomon* in Calcutta soon after its triumph in Venice.' He adds—for Japan seems as far away from Bengal as it is from Venice, and Venice probably closer to his Calcutta—'This is the point where I should confess that my knowledge of the Far East is derived largely from Waley and Lafcadio Hearn; and that while I know my Shakespeare and Schopenhauer, I have yet to know Murasaki and the precepts of Lao-tzu.'[2] This is not just the prototype of the colonized subject airily declaiming his allegiances; it's the modern as revisionist, impatiently estranging himself from a fundamental constituent of his identity: that is, the Orient as a point of origin. For Ray, I think, the prism of this revisionism is his particular understanding of 'Bengaliness': Ray once offended readers of the *Illustrated Weekly of India*—and I speak from living memory—by saying that he didn't think of himself as a Hindu, but as a Bengali. This revisionist view of Bengaliness is not so much a sub-nationalism, or even just a residue of his father's Brahmoism, as an opposition to cultural identity as we understand it today. It's an opening out onto a secular, local, even regional sense of the everyday, cohabiting, at once, with a constant premonition of the international, which defines the 'Bengaliness' of the first half of the twentieth century.

In the same essay on Japanese cinema from which I've just quoted, 'Calm Without, Fire Within', Ray, still discussing *Rashomon*, makes a shrewd observation, to do with the culture of filmmaking certainly, but also the sort of questions that the sudden appearance of a compelling cultural artefact raises. 'It was also the kind of film that immediately suggests,' says Ray, 'a culmination, a fruition, rather than a beginning. You could not—as a film making nation—have a *Rashomon* and nothing to show before it. A high order of imagination may be met with in a beginner, but the virtuoso use of cutting and camera was a sort that came only with experience.'[3] Those first two statements are among the cleverest statements I've read on the reception of the product of one culture into another, a cautionary reminder of how the critical language of reception simplifies and caricatures, even while occasionally applauding, the encounter with the foreign artwork or phenomenon, and ignores certain blindingly obvious problems. Remember that Ray is not speaking here of the classic encounter with 'otherness', with the savage or the peasant, the staple archetypes of postcoloniality, but of something—in this case, *Rashomon*—that only occurs in the economy and theatre of modernity, of a moment of dislocation, of revaluation, taking place within that terrain of film festivals, film societies, and educated—maybe even cinematically educated—middle-class audiences. Why is it that, when a clearly modern non-Western phenomenon emerges globally—say, Mandela, or Ray himself, or Arundhati Roy's environmental activism, or a liberation movement—he or she or it is seen as a 'beginning' rather than a 'fruition' or 'culmination', as if they belonged to an intellectual environment without texture or entanglements or process, a history composed, astonishingly, of supermen or women who rise without explanation from the anonymity around them? Even more than Western history after Carlyle, non-Western history still seems, at least in the popular imagination, condemned to be an account of exceptional men and women and events springing out of an undifferentiated, homogeneous landscape: the site of development. In coining the wonderful rubric, 'film making nation', with its conflation of a specialist activity with a political entity, Ray is not so much being a cinema geek as he's reminding us of the nitty gritty, the materiality, the processes, of history, and of crafting history.

The opening sentences of Ray's next paragraph give us an important key to understanding the sort of encounter he's talking about, but end in a somewhat conventional formulation: 'Later revelation of Kurosawa's past work and the work of other Japanese directors has confirmed what *Rashomon* hinted at: the existence of an art form, western in origin, but transplanted and taking root in a new soil. The tools are the same, but the methods and attitudes in the best and most characteristic are distinct and indigenous.'[4] Is that all, however, that the encounter with *Rashomon* hints at—a transplantation of an art-form, and its subsequent indigenization? Is the history of the modern artwork simply a history of its production in the West, and its indigenization elsewhere? (These are questions, of course, that have been raised by historians such as Dipesh Chakrabarty and others in other contexts, to do with the nature of the 'modern' itself, but not, I think, in connection to the specific business of genre.) We must remember that, crucially, Ray's own response to *Rashomon* could not have come out of nowhere; we couldn't, to paraphrase his words on Kurosawa's film, have had that response and 'nothing to show before it'. It—that response to *Rashomon* in 1963 in Calcutta—is not so much a beginning as a 'fruition, a culmination' of something; and the history from which it emerged at that moment, in the context of *Rashomon*, cannot be summed up as a history of Western origination, colonial dissemination, and, finally, indigenization; of import and export. Yes, it's a history that involves travel, but travel as a means of unravelling meaning rather than just moving forward in a landscape; modernity, in the realm of culture, appears to consist of a series of interchanges and encounters in which the putatively initiating meeting—such as the one between Ray and Kurosawa's film—is also a 'culmination, a fruition', of interchanges that have already taken place.

One is reminded of this if one thinks back to the emergence of Iranian cinema in the late 1980s. There was that initial moment of surprise when, in London and other cities, audiences viewed the films of Abbas Kiarostami and Mohsin Makhmalbaf and, in the 1990s, Jafar Panahi and others, for the first time. There was fairly widespread acknowledgement that a form of art-house cinema that was at once deeply humane and innovative was coming out of a country about which the secular middle classes around the world knew relatively little, and about which they knew already whatever they needed to know. Into this frame, the frame of preconceptions, entered, for instance, the engineers, film directors, and drifting professionals who drove through Kiarostami's tranquil but earthquake-stricken landscapes, with middle-class children sitting, often, beside them in the car, journeying towards families in houses in remote villages; also in that frame appeared Makhmalbaf's weavers, village primary schoolteachers, Afghan daily wage-earners, carnival bicyclists. Objects came into the frame as well—apples; fabrics; the blue tile on the wall of a village house; shoes in a shop window in Tehran. The audiences noted these people and things with a mixture of delight, surprise, and recognition, seeing them as elements of what they hadn't known before, as well as of the already known. The quality of the already known gave to these details their recognizability, their authenticity; viewers knew almost straightaway that what they were watching was indisputably 'real' cinema, with cinematic values of a high order; the details possessed not just universality, but the pacing and aura of the modern, particularly modernism, with certain modulations on that sensibility that these very gifted film-makers' works introduced. So, 'foreignness' wasn't the crux and core of Iranian cinema; the crux was its enlivening and dislocating recognizability. The fact that this cinema had its impact at a time when the infrastructure and *raison d'être* of the art-house cinema movement was, worldwide, being dismantled was an irony that was either not noticed, or not considered worth commenting on. Yet the most important question regarding these films still remains unaddressed. Here was a kind of cinema that 'immediately suggested', as Ray had said of *Rashomon*, 'a culmination, a fruition, rather than a beginning'.[5] What was it a fruition of? What had happened, or was happening, in Iran, and, for that matter, elsewhere, that these films were powerfully hinting at—not through their subject-matter, but through the culmination of a certain practice, and all the more powerfully for that? Not knowing leaves a gap in our understanding, and dependent on that model of transplantation and indigenization. And what happens when something that's purportedly been indigenized is carried back to the land it was transplanted from—an occurrence such as the first showing, say, of Iranian films in New York? Whatever the answer to that might be, it cannot approximate the frisson that the actual event—the New York audience watching the Iranian film—would have involved. The emergence of Iranian cinema represented not just a culmination of certain filmic styles and values, but a convergence of links, hitherto unnoticed, that came together to create a new-minted but unexpected, even unlikely, experience of the 'modern', in that decade when modernity, apparently, had finally begun to wane. 'Modernity' was the unlooked-for culmination through which New York and Iran momentarily came together.

And yet this experience of the 'modern', which arises not from a canonical history of modernity written solely by and in the West, but through a series of interchanges and tensions (such as Ray's encounter with *Rashomon* embodies)—this continual experience of the 'modern' is almost always, if it involves a non-Western artist, subsumed under the categories of 'East' and 'West', and within issues of cultural authenticity. Everyone collaborates in this emotive and persistent haziness to do with cultural characteristics, including the commentators and the artists themselves. That is, they fit their thoughts and justifications into one of two compartments: that either the artwork, if it was produced in the East, bears the unmistakable and ancient imprint of its cultural lineage; or that it transcends all those marks into the convenient domain of the universal. Only the artwork itself refuses to collaborate in this formula, insisting that the intersection between cultural lineage, foreignness, and recognizability must, in the time of modernity, be arrived at as, in Ray's word, a 'fruition', that is, as a radical moment of awareness of underlying histories, and, at once, as an unpremeditated but considered acknowledgement of that 'fruition'. By 'fruition' Ray means, as we have seen, not something static, not a pinnacle of development, but a sudden intimation of intelligibility, and modernity as a language dependent on, and constantly illuminated by, such intimations. But then Ray himself, in his essay, goes on to speak in the terms of the same dichotomy that I just described. 'Of all the Japanese directors, Kurosawa has been the most accessible to the outside world,' he says. 'There are obvious reasons for this. He seems, for instance, to have a preference for simple, universal situations over narrowly regional ones . . . But most importantly, I think, it is his penchant for movement, for physical action, which has won him so many admirers in the West.'[6] Ray then clarifies that he isn't overly bothered by whether the 'penchant' for action is a consequence of a 'strong Occidental streak' in Kurosawa, or whether it springs from something 'within the Japanese artistic tradition'; for he is still 'able to derive keen aesthetic pleasure' from Kurosawa's work. However, he points out that 'there is no doubt that he is a man of vastly different temperament from Ozu and Mizoguchi, both of whom come nearer to my preconception of the true Japanese film maker. Here, too, I may be wrong, but a phrase of my dear old professor sticks in my mind: "Consider the Fujiyama," he would say; "fire within and calm without. There is the symbol of the true Oriental artist." '

Ozu and Mizoguchi are actually, as far as filmmaking temperament and subject-matter go, quite different from each other: in contrast to Ozu's subtle suburban idylls, Mizoguchi's work, in fact, shares with Kurosawa a fascination with premodern Japan and its distinctive artistic resources. I suppose what Ray is talking about—and the basis of the comparison he's making—has more to do with pacing: the 'movement' and 'action' of Kurosawa's kind of cinema, the slowness of Mizoguchi's and especially of Ozu's universe. Slowness, who knows, may well be an Oriental characteristic; it may also be part of the colonialist construction of the Orient, as well as of the response of Western critics to directors like Ozu. Ray points out, bringing his own métier, at this point, into the picture, that the 'complaint is frequently heard that some Japanese films—even some very good ones—are "nevertheless very slow". Some of my own films, too, have drawn this comment from Western critics.'[7] (Chandak Sengoopta, in an issue of *Outlook* magazine,[8] reminds us of the sort of early criticism that Ray is talking about here.) Ray points out that 'a slow pace is, I believe, as legitimate to films as it is to music. But as a director I know that a slow pace is terribly hard to sustain. When the failure is the director's fault, he should be prepared to take the blame for it. But it is important to remember that slowness is a relative thing, depending on the degree of involvement of the viewer.' With the phrase 'a relative thing', Ray is, I think, gently refuting the 'universal' cultural situation presumed by Western critics, and arguing, somewhat diffidently, for his Easternness. But he doesn't remind us that slowness is also a principal, even sacred, feature of modernism, which privileges the image over narrative, the individual moment over the overarching time-span, thus holding up the way a story ordinarily unfolds. It's possible, of course, that Ray's pacing is the result of an Oriental identity that he's usually at pains to distance himself from. For instance, the sequence in Ray's first film *Pather Panchali* (based on Bibhutibhushan Banerjee's 1928 novel of the same name) in which the camera spends a noticeably large amount of time observing the movement of water insects upon a pond during the monsoons might be, as Max Lerner said of the Apu trilogy in the *New York Post* in 1961 (and this kind of opinion is obviously still fresh in Ray's mind in 1963), 'faithful to the Indian sense of time, which is actually a sense of timelessness'.[9] Or it could, more plausibly, be at once a sideways reference to the long descriptions of Apu reading by a pond in Banerjee's novel (which Ray makes no attempt to invoke directly), as well as a homage to and a reworking of the forty seconds or so (a considerable amount of time in a film, even more considerable when the film is about half an hour long) in Renoir's *Une Partie de Campagne*, given to the swirls and eddies of river-water as the holiday-makers paddle downstream. The eddies of water in Renoir's river and the agitated pool in Ray on which the narcissistic water insects jump, absorbed, not to mention the mysteriously alluring pool by which Apu keeps his vigil, are part of the gluey, non-linear substance of modernism, its flow and pattern of consciousness. We don't need to decide, for now, whether or not the pond sequence in Ray's *Pather Panchali* is 'faithful to the Indian sense of time', or is another instance of 'transplantation and indigenization'. I see it as a 'fruition' of something, giving way to a moment of recognition that undermines these polarities, and ramifying into an awareness of other moments and histories available to us in modernity, which we didn't necessarily think of until that moment. Renoir's own shots of the river, too (in a film based on a Maupassant story that comes from a different impulse: to narrate the arc of a lifetime without abandoning economy and compression), I'm sure, must have appeared to Ray a 'culmination, a fruition, rather than a beginning'.

It's interesting, though, that, when Ray worries briefly about whether Kurosawa's predilection for 'action' comes out of a 'strong Occidental streak' in the filmmaker, or whether it arises from 'within the Japanese artistic tradition', he doesn't mean by the latter the work of Ozu and Mizoguchi, or the constituents of a 'film making nation', but an older, perhaps a purer, tradition. Yet, barely a paragraph ago, when speaking of the 'culmination' that *Rashomon* is, he'd appeared to be locating that film (and, by implication, his encounter with it), in a context more complex, more impinging, and less pastoral than a Japan seen through the eyes of Lafcadio Hearn. In fact, it was *Rashomon* that had led Ray to the idea of a modern Japanese cinema, and to discover and uncover the different perspectives and convergences that Ozu and Mizoguchi represented. If we take stock today, we see that Kurosawa is still the best-known Japanese filmmaker outside of Japan; and, almost as well-known in the West, but certainly a slightly larger presence in Japan than outside it, is Yasujiro Ozu. What's noticeable about this confluence—between Ozu and Kurosawa—is how it brings into play two very distinct styles of seeing, two different approaches to time and movement, with the flow of the confluence weighted more in one direction—Kurosawa's—than the other. And, because of this difference of temperament (Kurosawa's polyphonic, sometimes mythopoeic; Ozu's urbane, quiet, and still), and also because, for a long time, we'd come to identify Kurosawa with Japanese cinema—for these reasons, Ozu must, for us, even now retain the air and freshness of a secret, of a personal discovery: almost as much as, in fact, he would have for Ray. He is the hidden coordinate in that 'fruition' and 'culmination', the one that lies behind the revaluation and opening that *Rashomon* involves, implicating us in a sense of the modern that is deceptively simple and immediate but far-reaching. To contain this pairing by saying that Kurosawa is less Japanese than Ozu is to miss the many-sided way in which we receive and interpret modernity. If we look at the countries I've cited in the course of this talk—Iran and India—we see how this pattern, in the context of film, repeats itself strangely but tellingly, and even, sometimes—challenging our preconceptions about cultural authenticity—inverts itself. In India, for instance, Ray himself is part of a pair, and the other half of the pair is the prodigiously gifted, but self-destructive, Ritwik Ghatak, who died in 1976 probably as a result of his alcoholism. There are many ways in which this pairing could be described and contrasted; one could call Ray a classicist, and Ghatak the possessor of an operatic sensibility. One could also describe Ray as a progeny of the Enlightenment and its flowering in Bengal, and Ghatak as an errant son, someone who turned the Enlightenment inside out in his movies. More characteristically, however, Ray's temperament has been called 'Western' by some Indian critics, and Ghatak the more genuinely 'Indian' of the two, and for reasons completely opposite to those pertaining to Ozu and Kurosawa. I think that, in this formulation, Ray's slowness, which in Ozu is a mark of recondite 'Oriental' stillness, his air of 'calm without, fire within', is seen as a kind of European reserve, and associated, in particular, with Western-derived realism; while Ghatak's narrative energy, his melodrama, his fascination with mythic grandeur (all of which in Kurosawa can be seen to be driven by a 'strong Occidental streak' that prefers declamation to suggestion, 'action' to stillness), is, in the Bengali filmmaker, often supposed to emanate from authentically Indian, and oral, modes of storytelling. One can imagine a parallel planetary configuration in which Ghatak is more famous in the West than Ray, and Ozu than Kurosawa, and sense that, in that universe, the terms would be adjusted, and mirror each other, accordingly, and essentially remain unchanged.

Similarly, Iran: the two major filmmakers from that country, Abbas Kiarostami and Mohsin Makhmalbaf, have strikingly contrasting sensibilities, the former presenting a very interesting development on neo-realism, where nuance, bourgeois ordinariness, and leisureliness, along with odd but rich self-reflexivity, create the lens through which Iran appears; the latter, Makhmalbaf, making use of folklore, bright colours, and fairy tales. This sort of dichotomy rehearses one that's been familiar to us for more than twenty years now: the one that identifies suggestiveness, compression, and realism with canonical Western traditions, and storytelling, fantasy, orality, and passion with postcolonial ones. When we are viewing Ray or Kurosawa or Kiarostami, however, we are really witnessing a 'fruition' which always suggests more, which, at that moment, we are capable of sensing but not grasping. Not necessarily more of the same—other Kiarostamis and Rays and Kurosawas, confirming, thereby, these filmmakers' traditions and cultural identities—but of their opposites and others: Ozu and Makhmalbaf and Ghatak. All these form the hidden coordinates of what that moment of 'fruition' gestures towards: tensions and contestations that form the fabric around, and of, the artwork, and of which we too are a part. They make, in a sense, the old opposing categories of 'East' and 'West' seem cumbersome—even, in the limited but pervasive roles ascribed to them, redundant.

2009

★ ★ ★

10

The photographer as onlooker

On Raghubir Singh

People will have their overviews of Raghubir Singh, with a consciousness both of the remarkable range of the work and of its continuities. There is the extraordinary exploration of colour, for example: a putatively dull medium at the time Singh began to use it, and always a treacherous one when the subject is 'India'. How to stay open to the accidental proximity of things—including colours—in a photograph, and take the focus away from colour itself? Then there's the agglomeration of people, animals, and objects in the pictures: heterogeneous, unrepetitive, and recognizable. How not to reduce these images to 'India'; to keep their discrete identities in small towns, streets, suburbs, rooms, bungalows, and promenades alive and revelatory? These questions must come to us when we try to discuss Singh's photos.

My concern here, though, isn't with the overview, but with the movement between two books—*Calcutta* (1988) and *Bombay* (1994)—and my own relationship with them over time. In their titles and within their covers are two cities that I have formative ties with. I was born in Calcutta and grew up in Bombay. Growing up in Bombay, I would become a student of the modern city whenever I visited Calcutta. Living now in Calcutta, I become a student of the past on my infrequent visits to Bombay. The personal may be the political—but it is also the aesthetic.

My view of the two books I've mentioned is, then, informed by—and, inevitably, also informs—my experience of the cities that Singh photographs in them. But, as experience is never static, my assessment of those books and the development they represent is susceptible to change.

Let me first dwell briefly on what I mean by 'movement'. Since the Calcutta of the first seven decades of the twentieth century embodies, for me, a kind of 'modernity', and I see this 'modernity' as synonymous not with progress but with a state of unfinishedness, of contemporaneous flux, I used to place Singh's Calcutta photographs in the lineage of those whose work responds to and exemplifies that unfinishedness. I'm thinking of Satyajit Ray, whose approach to cinema makes a case for provisionality, and who also pointedly conflated his location, Calcutta (which he said he preferred to, say, Geneva), with the provisional. That Singh admired Ray is well-known. ('I became a regular visitor to the Ray home,' Singh says in 'River of Colour: An Indian View', an essay in the book of the same name.[1]) I used to instinctively place Singh's *Calcutta* within this artistic and visual history. I saw his response to Bombay in the late 1980s and early 1990s—the time leading up to, during, and after economic deregulation, when Bombay came into its own—as a striking departure. Singh had moved from his home in modernity to—what? It was certainly not to the postmodern he'd migrated. In *Bombay*, at a time when novelists and academics seemed to believe postmodernism (whether they adhered to it or not) was a playful exposure of the constructedness of reality, Singh gathered moments that were marked by a personal and poignant relationship to the constructed. The construct, here, was Bombay, and the remaking of its identity by the free market. While postmodernism had made the notion of 'home' obsolete, Singh, in *Bombay*, showed us how one might desire to surreptitiously linger in and inhabit the places we visit in the time of globalization. He uncovered, in this book, a vital link between the modern and whatever it was that came after it. In this, his Bombay photographs point not so much to an idea of the postmodern prevalent twenty years ago, but to the form of the essay as it's being recuperated today: something that's at once knowing and personal, imaginative and historical. The successor of the 'modern' isn't something quite as easy to pin down as the 'postmodern'—it's a space whose relationship to modernity is only gradually becoming clear. The emergence of the non-academic essay in the last fifteen years—exploring, and essaying into, the mental and visible worlds of globalization—marks a development in the ethos in which we live in a way that's at once subtler, more indeterminate, and more significant than 'postmodernism'. Photography is a precursor of the contemporary essay. Raghubir Singh's *Bombay* was the one of the first instances I encountered—before the delineations of either globalization or the essay had fully emerged—of another way of looking at the postmodern world.

★

I thought *Calcutta* belonged to the avant-garde traditions of modernity, but I now see it occupies a cusp. I want to dwell on the various streams of Calcutta's history that flow in and out of these pictures. Among these streams is the one we associate with the word 'renaissance'. In relation to that word, I wish to think a bit about the portrayal of power in these photos—the power of the classical, of 'finished' representations, of landowners' mansions, and, finally, of the bourgeoisie (the Bengali *bhadralok*) that (even before 1947) replaced both the colonial rulers and the landowners. And I also wish to place that portrayal of power in the context of the decline of the city, as Singh's images do.

Why not start with the cover image of *Calcutta*? It's picture number 20 in the book (Figure 10.1). By now, as we turn the pages, we have seen a succession of images of nineteenth-century landowners' mansions

Figure 10.1 Raghubir Singh, Kaḷi Puja in the Marble Palace, built in 1840 by Raja Rajendra Mullick. Kali and Durga, the warrior goddesses, are personifications of the mother goddess, the premier deity of Bengal. Calcutta, West Bengal, 1971–2.

in North Calcutta. We have become familiar with the grandiose elements—the monumental air of the building, the Corinthian pillars, the neoclassical features, the furniture and opulent collections from two centuries ago, the dereliction, the parodic context: of clothes drying on the street from which the shot is taken, or cows roaming the quadrangle. The cover image too could be seen to be parodic. There's a Kali Puja taking place in the Marble Palace, a palatial mansion built in 1835 by Raja Rajendra Mullick, a merchant who made his money in gold and was a collector of art. Today, part of the mansion is inhabited by the family; but it's open to the public. In the photo, if we look from left to right, we discover an uneven band of figures. First, there's the clay likeness of Kali on the dalaan, the raised platform which hosts deities on festive days. A young priest is half hidden by a slim Doric column. An older one is bowing at the right of the dalaan (which is made of marble). Both men are in white dhotis, their upper bodies bare. The older man's back and legs are concealed by a huge classical urn. To the right of the urn is Artemis, or her Roman incarnation, Diana, with her bow and arrows and a deer. She is roughly parallel to Kali on the left. The goddesses—one black, one white—create the bold margins of the picture.

One is tempted to interpret this picture (from 1972) on familiar lines: to do with the way different cultures co-exist unselfconsciously in India, or how the ancient permeates the new. Or one could treat it as a visual incarnation of a comparativist method that originated in the late eighteenth century with William Jones, a Welshman whose discovery of the similarities and echoes between, say, Sanskrit and Latin words, or Hindu and Greek gods (like Kama and Cupid, both of whom shot arrows at the unsuspecting), fashioned the crucible of the Indo-European languages in which we now place many of the civilizations of the world. Jones arrived at his insights in Calcutta, and Singh's frayed but serene scene could be placed in that lineage even as it quietly mocks it for what it's become.

Both readings are too neat, though. The photograph's power derives not from the fact that the juxtapositions—old and new, Indian and European, mortal and immortal—add up to what we theoretically believe is 'India', but from how the elements possess, at once, an implacable fixity and randomness. There's a strangeness to the photograph that has nothing to do with the strangeness of India. There's a blurring of lines here between stillness, composure, the reverential hiatus, and indifferent languor. As in many of his pictures, Singh is absorbed in impediments to viewing, which restructure what we're looking at—for instance, the pillars that keep us from clearly seeing the priests and the entirety of the Kali icon.

★

For me, the tension underlying the photo doesn't have to do with Kali and Artemis. It's related to Artemis and the aesthetic that Singh's photograph represents. Artemis refers me to the European Renaissance; the photo, and Singh's sensibility, to the disputed Renaissance that took place in Bengal.

What does one mean by 'Renaissance'? The European one may have existed in the fifteenth and sixteenth centuries, but the myth of that Renaissance is a little more than a hundred and fifty years old, going back to Jules Michelet's *Histoire de France* (1855) and Jacob Burckhardt's *The Civilisation of the Renaissance in Italy* (1860). Michelet and Burckhardt both had their intellectual formation in the time of the neoclassical turn (against the rococo and the baroque, and, in England, against the gothic), and, while neoclassicism might be a product of the Renaissance, the Renaissance too, since it was formulated retrospectively in the mid-nineteenth century, could be classified as a neoclassical myth. Neoclassicism coincided with the 'Grand Tours' taken in Italy by the European upper classes, with excursions into classical buildings and accompanied by the collection of antiquities. The presence of Artemis is a reminder of those excursions and of the ambitions of the European aspirational classes, ambitions that also belonged to figures further afield, like Raja Rajendra Mullick.

If you view London from, say, the topmost level of the Tate Modern, you will see a multiplicity of styles, buildings, and objects, but you will also notice that what you had once taken to be a given in certain Western cities—history, the imperial past, and their attendant grand features—is also a consequence of neoclassical aspiration, a determination to be Rome. You see it in the gilded figures; in the columns; the dome of St Paul's Cathedral, rebuilt from the gothic structure it once was into a classical building in the late seventeenth century, in the age of the Grand Tour. Paris was even more aspirational: its Roman delusion shapes the city you confront across and by the river from St Michel. In Calcutta, the colonial institutions and to some extent the mansions in the North—the bit that was both the 'black town' and the 'city of palaces'—are inheritors of that Renaissance, that Roman grandeur. In England, one of the fiercest and most persuasive critiques of neoclassical pretension, John Ruskin's *The Stones of Venice* (1853), preceded only by a few years Burckhardt's and Michelet's theories of the Renaissance.

★

When you go to North Calcutta and turn left while going up Central Avenue into the dingy lanes between it and Chitpur Road, you have the choice of visiting two remarkable buildings, both of them once residences, each a ten-minute walk from the other. The first is the Marble Palace, a part of whose interior you see in Singh's photograph. The other is the Tagores' house in Jorasanko, from whose aesthetic preferences Singh's own creative choices, and the texture of the Bengal Renaissance, are partly derived.

'I have borrowed a lot from the West, as well as from independent-minded Bengal, the same Bengal which was the first place in the subcontinent to attempt a fusion of the modern arts with the centrifugal force of India,'[2] said Singh in 'River of Colour: An Indian View'. We needn't agree with Singh's assessment of Bengal here. We have to understand the process of self-analysis the sentence contains, and what it means by the word 'fusion'. Singh is important not only because of his gifts, but because he's an artist who won't take for granted where he's coming from. In his essay, Singh embraces Western modernism while distancing himself from its dominant tone, its 'angst'. To grasp Singh's position, we must, at his prompting, engage with what he means by 'Bengal'.

First, let's acknowledge the confusion over the word 'Renaissance', specifically in its conjunction with 'Bengal'. The scholar Sivanath Shastri (1847–1919) used the term *nabajagaran*—'new awakening'—in the nineteenth century to encompass the wave of reforms and the 'enlightenment' that transformed Bengal at the time. (One should recall in passing that the neoclassical turn in Europe occurred in the age of the Enlightenment, from the eighteenth century onward.) I'm not sure if *nabajagaran* is a version of 'renaissance'. But in 1946, the Marxist historian Susobhan Sarkar formally adopted the term in his booklet, *Notes on the Bengal Renaissance*, to describe a period in the nineteenth century marked not just by the emergence of nationalism, but by a fundamental humanistic break with the past. Since then, the designation—'Bengal Renaissance'—has been used often, and frequently derided. The reason for mockery is the presumptuousness of the term, the implied comparison between the European and Bengal Renaissances.

To walk in the environs of the Marble Palace and Jorasanko presents us with the trajectory of the two renaissances in Bengal, especially in the domain of the arts. The Marble Palace is inhabited by the legacy of the Grand Tour—in it are not only Artemis and other classical gods and goddesses, but painters like Rubens. Beside mythic presences are historic ones: statues of Victoria; a figurine of Napoleon. The style that predominates is the muscular, frozen, magnificent hyper-realism of the European Renaissance. Everywhere, you encounter the impulse towards the monumental. What could count, today, as having descended from the world in the Marble Palace? There is Raja Ravi Varma's art, with its verisimilitude and perfect reproduction of perspective in its portrayals. The Marble Palace has at least a couple of unusual family portraits by Varma. As with the European Renaissance, the medium of this realism is oil. Its concern, in sculpture or painting, is completeness. Its inheritance defined popular culture and the quasi-religious: the Hindu 'mythologicals' of Indian cinema (the target of the young Satyajit Ray's polemics when he began to write on film in 1940); calendar art; comic books about historical episodes and Hindu legends. Renaissance representation energized popular culture in India. You can revisit its origins in the social aspirations contained within the Marble Palace.

A ten-minute walk away is Tagore's house in Jorasanko. Though it's built on the same lines as landowners' mansions in North Calcutta, there's no neoclassical paraphernalia within. What you have an abundance of—in the rooms, the verandahs, and the quadrangle—is that Tagorean contribution to Bengali modernity: space. In space begins Tagore's—and the Bengal Renaissance's—riposte to the essentially representational nature of the European Renaissance. Rosinka Chaudhuri, in her essay, 'Modernity at Home: A Genealogy of the Indian Drawing Room', remarks on this widening, this making room, which comprised a style of habitation even outside the Tagore family. She quotes from the poet Nabinchandra Sen's account in his autobiography *Amaar Jiban* (*My Life*) of his impression of the novelist Bankimchandra Chatterjee's drawing room in his house in Naihati in 1877:

He [Sanjibchandra Chatterjee, Bankimchandra's older brother] put his left hand affectionately around me and, taking me to a room, seated me on a thick rug [*phorash bichhana*] and sent word to Bankimbabu. I heard that this was Bankimbabu's drawing room [*baithak khana*]. There was a Shiva temple alongside a *hall*, and on the other side, two rooms. All around the *hall*, near the walls, there were two or three *couches* and *cushioned chairs* upon the rug. The walls had a few paintings hanging on them, and in one corner, there was a harmonium. I was looking at the way in which the room was decorated and talking to Sanjibbabu . . .[3]

That observation—'I was looking at the way in which the room was decorated'—registers surprise; in the neoclassical age into which Calcutta too has been inserted, this simplicity of arrangement is deliberate and new. Chaudhuri quotes from Bankimchandra Chatterjee's own 1872 essay, 'Confessions of a Young Bengal', as an instance of a 'satirical description of the sitting room of a Europeanized babu':

Chairs, tables, punkahs (fans)—seldom meant to be pulled, American clocks, glassware of variegated hues, pictures for which the *Illustrated London News* is liberally laid under contribution, kerosene lamps, book-shelves filled with Reynolds' Mysteries, Tom Paine's Age of Reason and the Complete Poetical Works of Lord Byron, English musical-boxes, compose the fashionable furniture of the sitting-rooms of Young Bengal . . .[4]

Chaudhuri says: 'The bareness of Bankimchandra's own drawing room may now perhaps be read as deliberately arranged in stark contrast to the European clutter that he finds so distasteful in the imitative Derozian's room, keeping in mind all the while, however, his own not inconsiderable investment in the cultural appurtenances of European civilization.'[5]

In other words, Bankimchandra's cultural antecedents—like that of many of his middle-class contemporaries—imply that we can't see his drawing room simply as an attempt to arrive at an authentically Indian ethos. Everything about it emerges from a complex intellectual history. It's worth recalling that the 'authentically Indian' was, by the time Nabinchandra visited Chatterjee's house in Naihati, making a decisive journey towards neoclassicism (Varma's paintings had burst onto the scene in 1873). Chatterjee seems to be arguing in his drawing room for a non-representational modernity, in which space and even texture (the '*phorash bichhana*') marginalize the representational, neoclassical tendencies of the European Renaissance (which had been embraced by a large section of the Calcutta landed aristocracy). In 'Modernity at Home', Rosinka Chaudhuri also quotes—from Tagore's 1916 novel *Ghare Baire* (*The Home and the World*)—'a significant passage in [which] Bimala comments on the politics of her husband Nikhilesh's aesthetic sense':

He used to use an ordinary brass pot on his desk as a vase. On many occasions, when I knew that a sahib would be visiting, I would secretly remove that pot and replace it with an English coloured-glass vase, in which I would arrange some flowers. My husband would say, 'Look Bimal, the brass pot is as unselfconscious as these flowers. But that English vase of yours proclaims too loudly that it is a vase—instead of keeping real flowers in it, you should fill it with artificial flowers.'[6]

This is not, I think, a nationalistic gesture. Nikhilesh is as sceptical of, and ill-at-ease with, the nationalist *swadeshi* movement (promoting homemade rather than foreign goods) as his creator was. The key to the passage lies not in the opposition between 'real' and 'artificial', but in words like 'unselfconscious'—the emphasis on the fluidity of texture over solid representation—and in the statement arguing directly with the representational: 'that English vase of yours proclaims too loudly that it is a vase'. In order to view the brass pot as an element in modernity, Tagore needed, as Chaudhuri remarks, the 'new eyes' given to him as a result of being situated in the confluence of Asia and Europe. But the Mullicks had 'new eyes' too. They led them to the muscular and the hyper-real—the neoclassical emphases of the European Renaissance first making inroads into the Calcutta aristocracy before shaping popular culture (of which Hindutva is a curious offshoot).

The nineteenth-century artistic aristocracy in Bengal (which included Bankimchandra and the Tagores) ran counter to these emphases in its preoccupation with incompletion, impediments to the clarity of perspective, and its preference for tempera and water-colour over oil. If this comprises the imaginative life of the Bengal Renaissance, then it represents not an attempt to be the European Renaissance at all, but to fashion a non-representational modernity in its place.

Although I had no idea of Nabinchandra's essay on Bankimchandra's drawing room until I read about it in 'Modernity at Home', I would have, as a child visiting Calcutta from Bombay, encountered the spatial dimensions of a certain kind of Bengali home in the 1960s, and tried to make sense of its impact on me. This is what I was attempting to describe in my first novel, *A Strange and Sublime Address*, when the ten-year-old Sandeep (like me, a visitor from Bombay) goes with his cousins and uncle to a relative's house on the outskirts of Calcutta:

He glanced around him. A single blue, fluorescent tube was burning on the wall. It was not a big room. Despite its bareness, the impression it gave was of austerity rather than poverty. It made one remember that poverty meant displacement as well as lack, while austerity meant poor in a rooted way, within a tradition and culture of sparseness, which transformed even the lack, the paucity, into a kind of being. There was a wooden table in the centre of the room and a divan on one side; there was a series of shelves, carved into the wall, that had a picture of Ramakrishna and a statuette of Shiv next to incense sticks on a stand... there was a harmonium, and a tanpura laid horizontally. On the floor, two cane shatranjis were rolled out to sit on. The objects in the room were numerous enough to be noticed and few enough to be counted and remembered... Space gave the little room its strange composure...[7]

The 'tradition and culture of sparseness' the narrator mentions above is, I now see, a Bengal Renaissance invention, a response to, and departure from, the realism of the European drawing room. Its 'composure' meant a lot to me, as it did, I think, to Singh. *This* is where the photographer viewing, at a slight remove, the interior of the Marble Palace is coming from. And informing him is a perspective that's not so much interested in supplanting Artemis on Kali's behalf as it is in the version of the modern incarnated in the priests half-hidden by the pillar and urn.

⋆

Neoclassicism in India is propelled by, and propels, aspiration. It informs a certain view of the past: full-bodied and iconic. The nineteenth- and twentieth-century artistic aristocracy turned to the past, however, as something that's synecdochic and textural. An example of this can be found in Mani Kaul's film *Duvidha* (1973). Kaul's movie presents us with a version of a Rajasthani folk tale. Rajasthan, with its turbans, forts, and colours, is the home-grown alternative to neoclassical Europe, and generates its own 'grand tour'. But Kaul, in *Duvidha*, looks at colour as abstraction, and village life primarily as pattern and form. *Duvidha* is a reminder that Indian artists saw the past not as a unitary presence, but as a resource for the nonrepresentational. 'I also owe a debt to that spirit of my native Rajasthan,'[8] says Singh in his essay. When he mentions the 'vibrant colours' of his home state and the 'painted scrolls' that precede Alexander's invasion, I think he's referring to the formalist elements of folk art in Rajasthan. For an example of tradition as pattern and abstraction in *Calcutta*, look at the white, red-bordered cotton saris worn by the women of the Sen family during worship or festivities, or the *dhakai* sari in which Aparna Sen poses in her drawing room. Notice the rug she's sitting on, an echo of the *phorash bichhana* (see Figures 10.2 and 10.3).

Figure 10.2 Raghubir Singh, Actress and filmmaker Aparna Sen. Calcutta, West Bengal, 1987.

Succession Raghubir Singh, Paris. Reproduced by permission.

Figure 10.3 Raghubir Singh, Women of the Sen family worship the tulsi (basil) plant, sacred to Krishna and Laxmi. Calcutta, West Bengal, 1986.

Succession Raghubir Singh, Paris. Reproduced by permission.

If we go further back to the origins of art-house cinema in India, we'll find, prefiguring Kaul's eccentric formalism, a love of the provisional. The provisional is a feature both of life and tradition for Satyajit Ray, and this must have come to him when he was an art student in Santiniketan, where he was taught by Benode Behari Mukherjee. For Mukherjee, the main revelation of Indian art was the frescoes of Ajanta, which—Buddhist pictures inside the caves—were badly illumined as well as deliberately never completed. How could Ray, given this pedagogical background, *not* have turned to Italian neo-realism when he became a filmmaker? He was prepared for it by Santiniketan. Singh's photo too, with its balance of the monumental (Artemis) and the incompletely represented (the priests semi-visible behind the columns) must be placed within a project that includes both Ray and Kaul. One should also study his picture of the decrepit-looking mansion of Raja Ram Mohan Roy (1772–1833), reformer and founder of the Brahmo Samaj, taken from an adjoining terrace with a clothes-line obscuring the view (Figure 10.4). It isn't irony that makes this

Figure 10.4 Raghubir Singh, The crumbling house of Raja Rammohun Roy, the reformer and pioneer of the Bengal Renaissance. Calcutta, West Bengal, 1986.

Succession Raghubir Singh, Paris. Reproduced by permission.

photo worth pausing over. What's interesting is the way it's distracted by texture, and its acceptance of obfuscation over unimpeded clarity of vision.

*

The Bengali middle class's relationship with tradition as synecdoche used to be evident during Durga Puja. For instance, 'cultured' people who'd visit the pandals or marquees and discover a goddess Durga made along Hellenistic or Renaissance lines would remark that they wanted the traditional images. This was not because they were traditionalists or religious; as part of the twentieth-century middle-class aristocracy, they were secular, as was their relationship to the goddess and the harvest festival. Bengal Renaissance modernity had inculcated a love of synecdoche (and the 'traditional' image lends itself naturally to Bengali modernity because it's non-realistic, the eyes and mouth comprising a few lines) and a prejudice against neoclassical completeness. In their turning away from the Greek-style Durga images, one noticed this class's intolerance for the representational and their quest for the modernist in the traditional. By contrast, one is reminded again, by the popularity of the Hellenistic idols among the more devout working class, of the influence of neoclassical realism in the shaping of Hinduism *outside* of the reign of bourgeois taste.

The artistic aristocracy—propagating sparseness over, say, the hyperrealism of the Mullicks—might have originated in Jorasanko, but it soon, by the end of the nineteenth century, was dominated by this class I described in the last paragraph: a bourgeoisie of limited means, which sometimes owned no property. In Singh's photo of the Mullicks' house that captures a group of animated bhadralok in leisurely conversation, faced by a large statue of possibly Socrates, you see the last moments—the picture is taken in 1985—of this civil, often rent-paying, aristocracy (Figure 10.5). They sit in the room—they don't own the house—with the ease of usurpers, since their modernity has made the neoclassical so irrelevant that it may as well not exist even if it stares them in the face. That these middle-class people had become, in their articulation of the modern, a sort of quasi-princely set in cultural history is wonderfully captured in Singh's photo of an event celebrating Calcutta's birthday, in which the historian Nisith Ranjan Ray, the antiquarian and art collector R. P. Gupta, and their companion Jiban Tara Haldar lean languorously against bolsters like rajas (Figure 10.6).

Figure 10.5 Raghubir Singh, In his dining room, Ramendranath Mullick, and friends engaged in an Adda, the Bengali institution of discussion and storytelling. Calcutta, West Bengal, 1985.

Succession Raghubir Singh, Paris. Reproduced by permission.

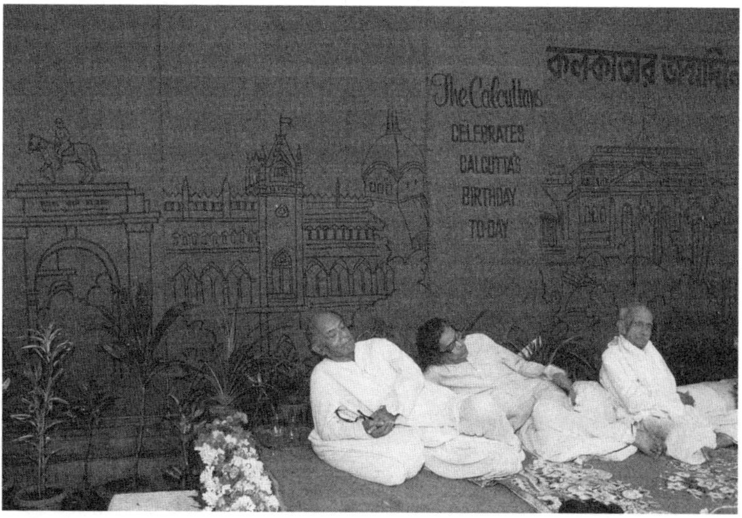

Figure 10.6 Raghubir Singh, Three Bengalis, Nishit Ranjan Ray, R. P. Gupta, and Jihan Tara Haldar at a gathering to celebrate the founding of Calcutta in 1690 by Job Charnock, an English trader. Calcutta, West Bengal, 1985.

Succession Raghubir Singh, Paris. Reproduced by permission.

★

'If photography had been an Indian invention,' says Singh in his essay, 'I believe that seeing in colour would never have posed the theoretical or artistic problems perceived by Western photographers.'[9] There are several cultural reasons for the prejudice against colour. Singh outlines them, but they can be summed up under a single charge: colour lacks seriousness. Singh loves modernism, but can't do business with its putative preference for solemnity over delight: 'Much of Western vision in this century has been a depiction of angst, alienation and guilt.'[10] In photography, Singh had to part ways with a man he admired, Lee Friedlander, whom he called 'the master modernist of our time'.[11] 'In India, Lee was looking for the abject as subject.' However, the 'truly Indian colour photographer... cannot escape... enchantment... My subject is never beauty seen as abjection, but... the high range of the colouratura [the word is coined by Singh] of everyday India.'[12] Singh's task is to find a way of accommodating the joy that his cultural formation in Rajasthan gave him within modernism's fragmentariness, its openness to texture and sensation.

Since Western modernism isn't a monolith, he could have turned to *it* for a cue: to James Joyce, say, whose name and writing both had 'joy' inscribed in it. Instead, Bengal came of use. In it, Singh found that convergence—of delight with the modernist scepticism of Renaissance realism—which he identifies by the word 'fusion': 'Bengal... was the first place in the subcontinent to attempt a fusion of the modern arts with the centrifugal force of India.'[13] This could well be a reference to the import, by Debendranath Tagore, of the Upanishadic notion of *ananda* (bliss or joy) into contemporary Bengal. His son Rabindranath would make *ananda*—rather than, say, the 'angst' Singh believes directs the Western sense of value—a key word for understanding the impetus of art.

My investment in Raghubir Singh comes from my admiration of his art and the courage with which he grapples with the position in which finds himself. He rejects middlebrow realism and conventional storytelling. This leads him logically to modernism. On the other hand, he rejects angst and abjection. I found myself in a similar place when I embarked on my first novel. I was a teenager in a decade—the 1970s—in which the Holocaust was deemed to be the central human experience of the twentieth century. It led modernism and what everyone called 'existentialism' to be interpreted as an allegory 'of angst, alienation and guilt'. But my approach to fiction, when I began writing my novel in 1986, took me away from plot and protagonist on the one hand and 'alienation' on the other. I even turned to Tagore's *ananda*, and brought it together with what Singh calls 'the colouratura of [the] everyday', by having the principal character, the uncle whom Sandeep calls Chhotomama, singing Tagore's *bahe nirantar ananta anandadhara* ('endless and unbroken flows the stream of joy') as he bathes under 'an old, ineffectual shower'. *A Strange and Sublime Address* was to be a narrative about joy.

This returns us to the problem of representation. 'Narrative' and 'joy' comprise an antinomy. How do you *narrate* or represent joy? Tragedy, calamity, conflict, loss—these constitute a story or 'theme'. Joy, or its small-scale, secular cousin, happiness, are not, according to parameters set by Western aesthetics, *subjects*. 'It's very difficult to write about being happy. Very easy to write about being miserable,'[14] Philip Larkin had said to the *Observer* in 1965. Colm Toibin echoed Larkin when he wrote a foreword to the 25th-anniversary of *A Strange and Sublime Address*: 'What distinguishes Chaudhuri's book is his concern with happiness, the hardest subject of all for the writer of fiction.'[15] I bring this up because I think that the problem of *ananda* was Singh's problem too, as it was his subject; what joy was to me, colour and the rejection of abjection were to him. This—*ananda*—is where modernism and Bengal's preoccupation with what *can't* be represented, with what *isn't* event, converge.

⋆

However, I discovered two things when I looked at Singh's pictures in *Calcutta* after many years. The first is that they're not only the record of neo-realist quirkiness as I'd presumed they were. I'd believed that Singh had had to come to terms in the early 1990s with the passing of the non-representational modernity that was important to his sensibility, and which had formed artists crucial to him, like Ray. India deregulated in 1991 and 'opened up' to the free market; this was also the time that Singh was taking his Bombay photographs. Bombay's post-deregulation metamorphosis was remarkable, as was Calcutta's marginalization by the same development. I saw *Bombay* as Singh's artistic response to this momentous change: the transformation of the modern into something else, with the modernist or neo-realist photographer as onlooker. But I see the acknowledgement is already there in *Calcutta*; a consciousness of no longer inhabiting a living modernity. The book is a disjunctive chronicle of decline. Not the decline of Empire—that is a long-gone episode which in the 1980s would become the engine of the Raj industry. Not the decline of the old rajbaris and mansions like the Marble Palace. Not even the decline of the aristocracy of the bhadralok, though this brings us closer to the moment Singh is confronted with.

Most of the photos have been taken in the late 1980s. The Left, by now, has been in power for about a decade, with over two more decades to go. Bhadralok modernity is illegitimate—if it is the *Statesman*'s theatre critic Dharani Ghosh, as it appears to be, who sits talking with R. P. Gupta and others in the Marble Palace in 1972, he was, by the early 1990s, when I first met him, less an actual force than a historical curiosity. Calcutta—by 1987–8, the years in which many of these pictures were taken—was in a time warp. Consider the photograph of the extraordinary poet Shakti Chattopadhyay reciting poetry at a dinner party, earnest and clown-like, ignored by those around him (Figure 10.7).

Figure 10.7 Raghubir Singh, Poet Shakti Chattopadhyay recites at a dinner party. Calcutta, West Bengal, 1987.

It's a scene from the 1970s, though the photo was taken in 1987. And then you see it's a parody of the recent past, a dead past—time has not moved on—because, actually, the early 1970s were far more interesting than this mimicry suggests. Singh is conscious something has happened; that's why Chattopadhyay, arms extended, mouth open, is at once central, and tragicomically peripheral, to the frame—neither we nor the people in the room can hear him. He's as invisible and redundant to that gathering as Socrates and the neoclassical figures were fifteen years earlier to the modernity he emerged from. Singh is the onlooker; he sees, as in many of the photographs in the book, that the history that created his own predilections has passed; what's left is mimicry and parody. This gives the photo a self-reflexivity prescient of *Bombay*.

★

The study, and the framing, of power and affluence in the world in the years leading up to and just after deregulation: this is the preoccupation evolving through, and connecting, *Calcutta* and *Bombay*. Oncoming globalization pushes the artist—Chattopadhyay and Singh—and the city itself (Calcutta) to the sidelines; occasionally, in *Bombay*, it offers the artist a tiny foothold. Singh's response is, often, to contain and frame power by neo-realist means—to create impediment, to not give us a clear view of the great and the monumental. He does this in both books. Look in photograph 3 in *Calcutta*, for instance, at the shining dome and neoclassical structure of the Governor's House as seen between the concrete balustrades of a neighbouring building, where the colourless grid of the concrete imposes its own form and abstraction on the view (Figure 10.8). This deliberate containment is repeated a few years later when the breathtaking view from a flat in Malabar Hill (Bombay's richest residential area) is portioned out between scaffolding and pipes in the foreground—the Doric columns of earlier pictures replaced by the scaffolding's functional lines (Figure 10.9). Here, in both photos, is Singh's neo-realist emphasis on the provisional, his dissension from the kind of gilded frame created by landscape architecture in Europe in the time of neoclassicism.

From impediment, Singh moves, in *Bombay*, to the reflected, or the reflexive—the glass shop windows that partly obscure what's within, and partly throw back light, a spectral echo of the photographer's flash, while containing his own blurred outline. Singh had already begun taking pictures of reflections in *Calcutta*. Here is the artist just before,

Figure 10.8 Raghubir Singh, Raj Bhavan, residence of the governors of West Bengal, formerly of the governors-general and viceroys. Built for the Marquess of Wellesley in 1803. Calcutta, West Bengal, 1988.

Succession Raghubir Singh, Paris. Reproduced by permission.

Figure 10.9 Raghubir Singh, Bombay from Malabar Hill, Bombay, Maharashtra, circa 1990.

Succession Raghubir Singh, Paris. Reproduced by permission.

and at the time of, globalization: an observer, someone who's not wholly visible in an age in which 'visibility' is everything, yet who's also complicit. Glass is impediment too—it's partly opaque in Singh's work—and therefore represents a neo-realist memory. But its reflecting shine, and the self-reflexivity it brings to the photograph, translates impediment into the new age. Singh, in his pictures—like the essayist today—is trying to find a way of describing how the modern flows into what comes after it. Looking back at the *Calcutta* photos in the light of *Bombay*, we see now that the neo-realist also had a hint of knowingness about him; that the clothes drying in front of a decrepit landmark are also a kind of mirror recording the artist's presence; and that within the mansions and apartments are glass surfaces and coverings telling us that nothing—not even the photograph's own aesthetic—was readily available in the age we'd already begun to inhabit thirty years ago.

2017

* * *

II

The sideways movement

I can't remember when I first read Arvind Krishna Mehrotra's poetry—it must have been in the late 1970s—but I do know that the book in which I found his poems was an anthology, R. Parthasarathy's *Ten Twentieth Century Indian Poets* (1976). I was immediately intrigued by Mehrotra. Just as Nissim Ezekiel had rejected, in his own work, the sentimental, the vague, and the bombastic (seen to be Indian tendencies, but only by those who have never read an Indian literature in the original), Mehrotra seemed to have rejected Ezekiel's ironical and careful approach for the weirdness, the essential foreignness, of Surrealism. This was too good to be true. Precociously, I myself had discovered at the age of sixteen a selection of Surrealist verse in an anthology, *English and American Surrealist Poetry*, edited by Edward B. Germain (anthologies were a lifeline then) and taken to writing in that mode. Being a Surrealist seemed easy; it required a devotion to what Louis Aragon called the 'immoderate drug', the image, but, more than that, to making incredible juxtapositions (as in Magritte's paintings). In the staid world of Indian poetry in English, its propriety defined not only by England or America but also by Ezekiel, Mehrotra appeared to be what is today called 'cool'. At the time, I had only a remote idea of what he was up to, what his compulsions were, and that the bizarre surface texture of Surrealism comprised the least of his departures. Nor was Parthasarathy's little headnote—which made it clear that he'd taken Mehrotra to be an 'Indian Surrealist', just as I had—much help in reading what was really a new kind of practice or even thinking about poetry, reflected in Mehrotra's and others' work in that slim volume. What was most startling about Mehrotra, in retrospect, was not so much the procession of his images but the range of cultural milieus and impulses that had made him a poet. Parthasarathy's emollient manner—common to

Indian commentators when they claim a particular author or tradition is of interest—made the juxtapositions and fusions in the book (as in Arun Kolatkar's testing, in his collection of poems *Jejuri* [1976], of William Carlos Williams's idiom) seem so natural so as not to be noticeable at all, while never quite addressing the fact that these poets represented an experiment, a process, whose workings and outcome were uncertain.

The pages of the magazine *Kavi*, with its advertisements for Clearing House books, and the books that appeared intermittently in Bombay's Thackers Bookshop from that publishing house (set up by Mehrotra, Kolatkar, Adil Jussawalla, and Gieve Patel primarily to publish themselves), kept me apprised of his peculiar universe. But I encountered his writing properly again in Jayanta Mahapatra's magazine *Chandrabhaga* in 1980. Coincidentally, this meeting too involved the earlier trinity: Mehrotra, Parthasarathy, and myself, the bystander. The piece of writing in question was a long essay, 'The Emperor Has No Clothes'. It had already become famous—or notorious—in certain circles for its demolition of Parthasarathy; so I must have read it with some prior knowledge. I call myself a bystander because my poems (written when I was 17; I had turned 18 that year) were in the same issue, and the reason I had, in fact, two copies with me: one from Mahapatra, the other purchased from Strand Bookshop.

When he'd accepted my poems (apprentice stuff, really), Mahapatra had taken the trouble to send me a detailed letter, which I long treasured for its generosity, and then lost. The world of Indian poetry in English was an enigmatic one at the time—at once inchoate and purposive, perceived to be elite (because it was synonymous with the English language), and quite uniquely non-hierarchical. I got a sense of this last quality from my brief interactions with the poetry scene, and from Mahapatra's letter, which, with its candour and warmth towards an unknown would, I think, have few equivalents today. But I was planning to leave that world behind and go to England, where, a part of me probably secretly believed, 'real' poetry was written. Still, Mehrotra's long essay must have struck me as being significant; something about it stayed with me for about twenty years, so that when, at the end of the millennium, I began to put together the *Picador Book of Modern Indian Literature*, I knew I'd have to retrieve that issue of *Chandrabhaga*, with its distinctive maroon cover, from my scattered books.

I think one of the things I retained from that essay was its unusual confidence, besides its rage. I don't mean confidence in the sense in which that word has been brandished in India in the last two or three decades: the confidence of the economy (suddenly, now, a thing of the past); of the nation-state; of the way we've turned English into an Indian language; of 'being Indian'. I mean a critical confidence. This enabled Mehrotra to jettison particular truisms and givens—however precious they might have been to the Indian English writer's self-image at the time, however comfortable they would have been to fall back on—and, having done so, to arrive at a judgement: in this case, about the poetry of A. K. Ramanujan and what it represented. The ability to make a judgement, or a case for someone, without the shoring up of national pride or a worthwhile cause is what I mean by critical confidence: a quality rare in any culture, but especially so in India, and one that to some extent defines what's important about Mehrotra's work. In 'The Emperor Has No Clothes', that confidence exceeded, in impact, the other kinds of confidence the essay exuded—an impatience with high-handed decisions about what was good or bad, and foreign or native, literature (thus the attack on Parthasarathy); the impressive array of references (making up the arsenal for the demolition).

In the essay, included in his new prose collection *Partial Recall* (Permanent Black, 2012), Mehrotra discusses some passages written by Parthasarathy to Mahapatra, which the latter subsequently shared with Mehrotra. 'The letters of Indian writers in English may never be published, but in case they are they will open up new areas of the literary terrain,'[1] notes Mehrotra. The fatalistic, pessimistic note—'may never be published'—is clearer and more direct today; in his Introduction to *Partial Recall*, he reminds us that the 'great betrayal of our literature has been primarily by those who teach in the country's English departments, the academic community whose job it was to green the hillsides by planting them with biographies, scholarly editions, selections . . . '.[2] Writing to Mahapatra, Parthasarathy had protested about the temerity of a Sambhalpur academic who'd taken Ramanujan mildly to task in *Chandrabhaga* in the summer of 1979: 'I have serious doubts if you should encourage dillentantish writing of the sort displayed by Rabi S Mishra . . . This kind of irresponsible writing must not go unanswered . . . Mishra's is an irresponsible and unfortunate exercise in debunking a poet who is generally considered significant . . . Mishra, the English teacher, chastises him for not writing like Pope, Yeats, Eliot or Neruda.'[3]

Mehrotra clearly doesn't disagree with the fact that Ramanujan is, for good reason, 'generally considered significant'; nor would he have disputed, I think, the remark that there's no point in going to the work of a contemporary Indian poet expecting them to be Yeats or Eliot. Mehrotra was exercised, rather, by Parthasarathy's tone, and his assumption that Ramanujan's work was beyond discussion ('Are [the poems] going to be... worshipped like a village deity?'); but he was perhaps more profoundly troubled by the terms in which Parthasarathy expressed his high estimation of the poet: 'Ramanujan's repossession, through his poetry, of the past of his family and of his sense of himself as a distillation of that past is to me a signal achievement...'. Moreover, and importantly, Parthasarathy had continued:

> Ramanujan's work offers the first indispensable evidence of the *validity* of Indian English verse. Both *The Striders* (1966) and *Relations* (1971) are the heir of an anterior tradition, a tradition very much of the subcontinent, the deposits of which are in Kannada and Tamil, and which have been assimilated into English. Ramanujan's deepest roots are in the Tamil and Kannada past, and he has repossessed that past, in fact made it available, in the English language. I consider this a *significant* achievement.... He has conveyed in English what, at its subtlest and most incantational, is locked up in another linguistic tradition... 'Prayers to Lord Murugan', overlooked by Mishra, is... embedded in, and arises from, a specific tradition. It is... the first step towards establishing an indigenous tradition of Indian English verse.[4]

Mehrotra finds much in these remarks that is 'vacuous, tautological, and ipse dixitish'. In pinpointing a particular tone in Indian criticism and commentary, he retrieves a Coleridgean adjective, 'ipse dixitish', indicating, through it, a form of declaration that privileges assertion and sonority to argument. Mehrotra, in his essay, makes assertions and insights that are embedded in his thinking, reading, and creative practice; it's from these that they derive their authority. In disagreeing with Parthasarathy's remarks, then, Mehrotra also critiques a certain notion of what a critical essay should be, giving us something else: not an *ad hominem* attack or a put-down, but a way of thinking about, and around, a problem. In large measure, that problem (which still hasn't gone away) is 'Indianness', and what counts for 'an indigenous tradition of Indian English verse'.

Neither Parthasarathy nor Mehrotra could have guessed how durable the banal utopianism to do with 'an indigenous tradition of Indian English' writing would be. Only a year after the first, substantial instalment of 'The Emperor Has No Clothes' appeared in *Chandrabhaga* (the essay came out in two parts), *Midnight's Children* was published to a neglectful silence in Britain, and then, after winning the Booker Prize, was almost immediately reassessed as having given, in the words of the *New York Times* reviewer, a 'voice' to a 'continent'.[5] Rushdie's novel should have been placed in the unique line of Indian cross-cultural works that Mehrotra was arguing for in his essay. Instead, *Midnight's Children* was appropriated by a powerful new discourse, postcolonialism; applauded for its 'difference' from 'well-made' English novels; congratulated for 'writing back' to the Empire and making English an Indian language—while Rushdie cooperated with this large-scale makeover. In this way, the idea of 'an indigenous tradition of Indian English' took root through a novel, and not through Ramanujan's poetry, as Parthasarathy had hoped. Parthasarathy had spoken of the 'anteriority' of Indian languages and traditions leaving their residues in Ramanujan's English; he mentioned 'deep roots'; but now, after *Midnight's Children*, food metaphors abounded to suggest a development on the notion of Indian English being a mix or melange: to do with not residues, but chutney, and 'chutnification', and even masala. Yet the homogenizing power of either condiment—chutney or masala—was underestimated. Masala might be made of a heterogeneity of elements, but whatever you put it in—Coca Cola, puffed rice, potato chips, chick peas—ends up tasting more or less the same. The Indian mix, too, as an artistic genre or critical idea, is most recognizable by its sameness.

Mehrotra arrives at some of his most important insights as he tackles Parthasarathy's reflections on how Indian traditions and languages shape the composition of the modern Indian poem in English. Mehrotra takes his cue from the George Steiner of *After Babel*, the Steiner who still hadn't quite mounted the high horse of 'high' European culture, and was trying to figure out a model with which to discuss the astonishingly varied multilingual contexts of European modernism and American writing—of the imaginations and literary languages of Kafka and Nabokov, for example (both writers who didn't compose in their mother tongues). For Mehrotra, a geological model such as Parthasarathy put his faith in when advocating Ramanujan's poetry—with Kannada and Tamil forming the deep reserves at the bottom, and English the relatively recent topsoil—won't do. Steiner points out the way Mehrotra will take by rejecting this model as being entirely inadequate: 'Layers is, of course, a piece of crass shorthand. It may mean nothing. The spatial organisation, contiguities, synaptic branching between, which account for the arrangement of different languages in the brain of a polyglot... must be of an order of topological intricacy beyond any we can picture.'[6] The mention of the brain and 'synaptic branching' draws our attention away from interiority (and anteriority) to the physical, biological, and corporeal: a refutation that T. S. Eliot (whom, given his anti-Semitism, Steiner wouldn't have liked to keep company with) had made earlier in his riposte to Philip Sidney for his advice to poets ('Look into thy heart, and write!'[7]): 'One must look into the cerebral cortex, the nervous system, and the digestive tracts.'[8] Eliot too, after all, had 'the brain of a polyglot', something we tend to forget because of the scandalous force of his infamous remarks later about 'free-thinking Jews' being 'undesirable'.[9] But, as a bewilderingly diverse polyglot artist susceptible to 'contiguities' and 'synaptic branching', Eliot started out thinking of poetry as a sensory tissue ('as if a magic lantern threw the nerves in patterns on a skin')[10] and was suspicious of depths, of the Hegelian 'abyss'—as he is, for instance, in his imperious dismissal of Matthew Arnold's claim that 'poetry is, at bottom, a criticism of life':[11] 'At bottom: that is a great way down; the bottom is the bottom. At the bottom of the abyss is what few ever see . . . '.[12]

Mehrotra is unmistakably in this tradition, which he extends unexpectedly in the connections he throws up between multilingualism and English poetry. In contrast to Parthasarathy, Mehrotra simply will not presume that the Indian poem in English becomes truly Indian only when the topsoil where it subsists in the world begins to exhibit marks of the ancient subsoil and bedrock below. For Mehrotra, there may be such a thing as an 'Indian poem' (as another essay in *Partial Recall* shows), but he's wary about determining what its symptoms are, or what makes an Indian poet using an Indian motif or form different from an American poet using an Indian motif or form:

> When Parthasarathy says the poem is embedded in another tradition which Ramanujan makes available to us, he is already reducing languages which are tissued in the multilingual sensibility to pictural shreds . . . The other does not enter the Indian English tradition in the guise of a god, a river, a place, a cow named Gopi, or a Tipu Sultan; nor as a poetic shell: a *rubai*, a *doha*, a *vacana*, or an *abhanga*. Their presence alone does not reflect the inlay of, for instance, Tamil or Kannada in Ramanujan, and their absence will not mean that no inlaying has taken place. Ramanujan writes in the manner of Tamil heroic poetry, Adrienne Rich writes seventeen poems based on the ghazal . . . Is there any difference in the way non-English traditions operate in Ramanujan and Rich? . . . Ramanujan's multilingualism . . . is so inlaid in his work that in order to trace it we will have to look outside the obvious signs.[13]

To these caveats and statements Mehrotra later adds a question: 'Am I also to believe that had Parthasarathy and Shiv K Kumar written in their mother tongues, Tamil and Punjabi respectively, their contributions to those literatures would have been any more remarkable?'[14] Through such counterfactual queries, that go to the heart of the dystopian anxieties of the postcolonial, and through negation in particular ('The other does not enter... Their presence does not reflect... their absence will not mean'[15]), Mehrotra brings into existence a way of thinking about those absurd problems, 'Indianness' and 'indigenous traditions'. The question as he asked it in 1980 and the negation as he formulated it then have a fresh bearing on the inexhaustible and largely pointless *bhasha*/English-language debate today.

For Mehrotra, following Steiner and Ramanujan, the way different languages and traditions inform each other in a poet's head is through 'osmosis', by seeping through the porous membrane that separates them, and with consequences that make it difficult to say in which direction the seepage took place, and where, in this model, the original location of one or the other language was. Mehrotra demonstrates this through a close-reading, performed with great skill and delicacy, of two clarificatory sentences by Ramanujan:

> English and my disciplines (linguistics, anthropology) give me my 'outer' forms—linguistic, metrical, logical and other such ways of shaping experience; and my first thirty years in India, my frequent visits and fieldtrips, my personal and professional preoccupations with Kannada, Tamil, the classics and folklore give me my substance, my 'inner' forms, images and symbols. They are continuous with each other, and I can no longer tell what comes from where.[16]

Ramanujan privileges Kannada and Tamil by making them 'inner', by identifying them as the resources that give him his 'substance'. English is 'outer', comparatively superficial, socialized, and recent (though Ramanujan doesn't say this explicitly). The statement is preparing itself for auto-destruction, as it's written in English, and is probably being ventriloquized by the Anglophone nationalist superego, which invariably says one thing (celebrates native languages) and does another (speaks in English). By its own definition, it's a statement that has to be 'outer', public, social, and 'ipse dixitish', coming, according to its speaker, from a place different from the one from which the 'images and symbols' come—so can we trust it? Immediately, though, the second sentence, 'They are continuous with each other...' undoes the previous one, and forgoes a definite conclusion, as if the undecided poet had made an interjection while the superego was speaking. It's Mehrotra who points out the tiny detail of punctuation in the first statement through which its binary is eroded: 'The semicolon in the first sentence is the osmotic membrane' through which 'inner' and 'outer' are made to seep into each other, until it becomes impossible to 'tell what comes from where'.[17] We wouldn't have noticed this point of seepage without Mehrotra's eye.

Rereading this essay yet again in *Partial Recall*, I realize these passages had stayed with me in some hinterland in my consciousness for twenty years, until I encountered them at the end of the last millennium when putting together the anthology for Picador. They'd survived the alarming burgeoning of the Indian novel in English; survived critical theory, with which they shared, fascinatingly, a suspicion of 'deep roots' and origins, though not what Tom Paulin called its 'punitive attitude to author, artistic form, style';[18] survived postcolonial theory, which, thoroughly dependent on 'hybridity' and 'Orientalism', gave an account very different from Mehrotra's as to how cultures inform each other. Deconstruction was extant when it appeared, but still hadn't penetrated the Anglophone consciousness; nor had Edward Said's *Orientalism*, the sacred text of postcolonial studies, published in 1978, two years before 'The Emperor Has No Clothes'. So the world I first read it in was a different one—but certainly no longer the old socialist-Nehruvian universe which was soon due anyway for a complete overhaul.

Knowing more about Mehrotra's work now than I did when I was 18 (there is also, now, more of it to know), I see how his sensibility, ill at ease with the linear—that is, with seeing a tradition purely as something that forms our historical identity and past—embraces the spatial, and especially the sideways movement. This is expressed in the arrangement of this essay and other critical pieces in the book (like the epitaph for Kolatkar, 'Death of a Poet', with its patterns of quotations from Kolatkar and blues songs); the array of quotes used in 'The Emperor Has No Clothes' to further Mehrotra's analysis are juxtaposed against each other to suggest a sense of the space that comprises Mehrotra's world. It's a world marked by overlaps, and it abides primarily in a moment in the present, in which the Gond carvings, the Bharhut stupa, Rimbaud, Richard Wilbur, Ezra Pound, Confucius, and Steiner exist transversely, in a constellation-like simultaneity in which convergences become possible with an immediacy that would be difficult if they were located in linear traditions, or anterior to, or behind, each other. Mehrotra's spatial critical temperament is also evident from the unique way in which he puts together his anthologies, particularly the *Oxford India Anthology of Twelve Modern Indian Poets* (1992), and the books he edits. In the former, he's concerned not so much with beginning at the beginning of this tertiary tradition, Indian poetry in English, but with unearthing relationships and establishing meeting-points, so that the anthology becomes less a retrospective historical document than something that captures the feel and texture of Mehrotra's intellectual world.

For Mehrotra and some of his contemporaries, the spatial perspective on modernity and the appetite for moving sideways explains much—for instance, why Kolatkar could choose to speak in Williams's diction in *Jejuri*; why Ramanujan could reach for Marianne Moore when translating from the ancient Tamil; why Mehrotra, as both a poet and translator, could fashion affinities with the Surrealists, with Pound (in his translations of Prakrit love poetry), and with the idiom of the American comic book (the recent Kabir translations). In his penchant for making the canonical uncanonical, in his inversions of linear progression, and in his assumption that literature is a space rather than an inheritance, Mehrotra is akin to Borges. 'A borrowed voice sets the true one / free', he'd said in his distilled eponymous poem on the Argentine writer; but even 'true voice' is overstating the case. In 'The Argentine Writer and Tradition', Borges remarks, 'I believe our tradition is all of Western culture, and I also believe we have a right to this tradition, greater than that which the inhabitants of one or another Western nation might have.'[19] Borges uses words like 'our', 'tradition', 'all', and 'nation' in a way that entirely controverts the manner in which these words usually come together, in the process conjuring up a space that can't be conflated with national identity, but which can't be—given the unequivocal 'our'—made to speak for an anodyne internationalism either. It is, in fact, a new formulation of what the Argentine literary text might be, without having recourse to the usual signs: 'Gibbon observes that in the Arabian book *par excellence*, in the Koran, there are no camels; I believe if there were any doubt as to the authenticity of the Koran, this absence of camels would be sufficient to prove it is an Arabian work.'[20] It is beside the point here that the Koran *does* have camels in it. Those with a conception of tradition as space have a proprietary access to it in a way that those who experience tradition as inheritance, time, and nationality don't: 'we have a right to this tradition, greater than that which the inhabitants of one or another Western nation might have'.[21]

A passage from the historian Haraprasad Shastri, cited in Swapan Chakravarty's *Bangalir Ingreji Sahitya Charcha* (*The Bengali Pursuit of English Literary Studies*, 2006), and quoted in Rosinka Chaudhuri's book, *The Literary Thing*, uncannily anticipates, in its configuration of the Bengali's cultural universe in 1880, Borges's Argentine writer:

> At that time [in Europe], it was only classical Greek literature that was disseminated. But look at what has happened today in Bengal! All of the hidden storehouses of Eastern and Western knowledge have revealed their treasures in front of the Bengali. . . . The dissemination of one country's literature in another country causes a tremendous revolution. English literature travelled to France in the last century and achieved so much, and today, the literature of England, France, Germany, Italy, and that of the ancient Hindus and Buddhists has arrived in our country . . . and Young Bengal is better equipped than the people of any other country have ever been to take advantage of this variety of literatures from many countries for new creations. [trans. Rosinka Chaudhuri][22]

It's as a record of a moment of simultaneity in late nineteenth-century Bengal—'the literature of England, France, Germany, Italy, and that of the ancient Hindus and Buddhists'—and in its firm rebuttal of the notion of national rights and inheritances—'Young Bengal is better equipped than the people of any other country have ever been to take advantage of this variety of literatures from many countries for new creations'—that Shastri is provocative in a Borgesian manner (albeit, in a Borgesian inversion, he predates the Argentine). Almost a century later, Kolatkar made a statement (quoted in 'Death of a Poet') to Eunice de Souza that belongs to the same category of provocation: 'I want to reclaim everything I consider my tradition.'[23] 'Everything I consider' is the Borgesian modulation here: without those three words, 'I want to reclaim my tradition' would have been extremely close to the claim Parthasarathy was making on behalf of Ramanujan. In inventing 'my tradition', Kolatkar bypasses the linear, given that linear time constitutes not just proper beginnings, but proper endings: 'It's a browser's approach, not a scholarly one; it's one big supermarket situation. I read across disciplines and don't necessarily read a book from beginning to end.'[24] Here again is the sideways movement—'I read across'—that characterizes Mehrotra. The 'supermarket' analogy is inappropriate inasmuch as the browser, or the collector (such as both Mehrotra and Kolatkar are: collectors of texts, sayings, poems, and artefacts), is not a passive consumer of a predetermined set of objects, but a person who creates a pattern or motif from whatever they read or collect, however randomly they appear to do it; but appropriate too, in that it evokes movement from point to point. Even when this movement doesn't go sideways, it refuses to advance conventionally; here's Kolatkar speaking with de Souza again: 'I jump back and forth from one subject to another.'[25]

Borges's prejudice against linear time is well known; his ironical view of literary inheritances is evident in the essay 'Kafka and his Precursors': 'In the critic's vocabulary, the word "precursor" is indispensable, but it should be cleansed of all connotations of polemic or rivalry. The fact is that every writer *creates* his own precursors. His work modifies our conception of the past, as it will the future.'[26] Note the mocking reworking here of T. S. Eliot's reflection, in 1921, on the word 'tradition': 'Tradition... cannot be inherited, and if you want it you must obtain it by great labour... No poet, no artist of any art, has his complete meaning alone... what happens when a new work of art is created is something that happens simultaneously to all the works of art which preceded it.'[27] This is a throat-clearing for the publication of *The Wasteland* the following year. But it shows us the relatively young Eliot's attempts to describe tradition as a montage (as his poem too would be), something that inhabits not just time and history, but space, to be regarded not only for its anteriority, but—with all the styles, genres, and languages that comprise his present moment in 1921 (as it did James Joyce's just leading up to *Ulysses*)—its capacity to 'happen simultaneously'.

Eliot, of course, is being juridical, and making a critical intervention; but Borges is playful. The scholarly tone he assumes in 'Kafka and his Precursors' is no different from the fusty mock-scholarly air of many of his fictions, such as 'Tlön, Uqbar, Orbis Tertius' and 'Pierre Menard, Author of the Quixote'. So, when Borges sets out an argument, the note of irony and play and the texture of the pastiche also signal to us that the *opposite* of what the scholarly voice is telling us might be true. Oddly, this doesn't subvert the argument, but only amplifies its attack on linearity and the canonical, gesturing to the fact that Borges lives in a world of juxtapositions and ramifications unavailable to the 'proper' scholar, or 'proper' scholarly discourse. Such a world is also Mehrotra's, although he adopts the pastiche mainly in his poems. When he remarks, in an interview to a newspaper, that Prakrit love poetry has the economy and concreteness of Ezra Pound, he's playfully reversing the historical direction of the canon, and also telling us that modernity, and modernism, not only engenders legacies but precursors too—and that these precursors are scattered further afield than we'd thought. It's a new perspective on that bogey, 'world literature', on the international networks of modernism, and on the notion of influence itself. Just as the appearance of Kafka gives rise to the 'Kafkaesque', and enables us to discover that quality and tone in writers preceding and quite unrelated to him, Kolatkar and Ramanujan's poetry must one day make us consider—though we're still unused to this form of traffic—Williams and Marianne Moore yet again, and find in the second pair some of the first's preoccupations.

For Borges, the advent of Kafka in European literature is akin to a critical intervention, in that it's only after we grow familiar with Kafka's unmistakable vision that we realize that there are other writers (including those who never read Kafka) who have 'Kafkaesque' qualities. A tradition is uncovered in this manner. For Octavio Paz (whom Mehrotra quotes at length in 'The Emperor Has No Clothes'), this is the job that criticism performs—of inventing the cartography, or the cosmology, of literatures:

> the space created by critical action, the place where works meet and confront each other, is a no man's land in our countries. The mission of criticism is not to invent works but to establish relations between them... In this sense, criticism has a creative function: it creates a literature (a perspective, an order) out of individual works. This is precisely what our criticism has failed to do. And that is why there is no Hispano-American literature, even though there exists a whole body of important works.[28]

This spatial arrangement, this cosmology, is what Mehrotra mimics in a paragraph from the eponymous essay 'Partial Recall', his account of the artist as a boy and a young man, when he catalogues his childhood reading in Bhilai, while also slyly, humorously (Mehrotra can be very funny), satirizing the critic's task of creating 'a perspective, an order':

> Neither of my parents was fond of reading, and except for those condensed by the *Reader's Digest* I had not known many books in Bhilai. Afterwards, when my father became interested in Hindu religion and philosophy, commentaries on the Gita and the paperback lives of sundry saints, mystics, yogis, and gurus were added to the memoirs of field marshals and the accounts of World War II naval battles. We also possessed some books on shikar, a three-volume set of Somerset Maugham's stories, a biography of Napoleon Bonaparte printed in double columns, and *Gray's Anatomy*. As a boy, the only book I consulted was the

Anatomy. It was always open on the page containing an illustration of the female pudendum, and I dipped into it whenever my parents were out of the house.[29]

'Tradition . . . cannot be inherited', said Eliot, and must be 'obtained . . . by great labour.'[30] Yet 'labour', for Borges, Mehrotra, and Kolatkar, becomes, largely, play. In his early poem, 'The Sale', Mehrotra, in his faux-Surrealist mode, reminds us, with the critic's experience, how feeling for the outline of a space can be full of false starts and surprises:

I wish you had asked me earlier.
The paintings have been bought
by a broken mirror
but I think I can lead you
to a crack in the wall.[31]

In the lines that then follow, Mehrotra's many selves (critic, memoirist, collector) come together in their concern with how, within that particular space—part library, part habitation, part recollection—'works meet and confront each other':

I've also a wheelchair to show you;
it belonged to my uncle
and one day the hook
that hangs from the sky
touched him. If you open the cupboard
you'll see his memory
on the upper shelf and two books
now yours:
Ruskin's *Lectures on Art*
and *A Short History of English Literature* by Legouis.[32]

If there is no anterior lineage to fall back on, if our tradition has no reliable markers when it manifests itself—'The other does not enter the Indian English tradition in the guise of a god, a river, a place'[33]—how do we achieve an 'order' or 'perspective' out of the bewilderingly disparate elements that form it? Both Kolatkar and Mehrotra seem to want the relationships to emerge from an enumeration of elements, rather than it being imposed from outside. So, when Kolatkar speaks about the way he 'reads across' subjects while reclaiming 'everything I consider my tradition', he allows the movement from one kind of enthusiasm to another to establish a relationship where none previously existed: 'I am particularly interested in history of all kinds, the beginning of man, archaeology, histories of everything from religion to objects, bread-making, paper, clothes... The history of man's trying to make sense of the universe and his place in it might take me to Sumerian writing.'[34] As can be seen from the first sentence, Kolatkar is fond of lists. So is Mehrotra—as a list-maker, he's once again the anthologist and collector, bringing together things which you wouldn't have ordinarily united under a single rubric; here he is in his essay, 'The Bradman Class', quoting a list of taboos compiled by Pythagoras:

> To abstain from beans.
> Not to pick up what has fallen from the table.
> Not to stir the fire with a knife.
> To rub out the mark of a pot in the ashes.
> Not sit on a bushel-measure.
> Not to wear a narrow ring.[35]

And so on. In his poem 'Bhojpuri Descant', he records, imitates, and parodies folk aphorisms: 'Piss after dinner, / Sleep on your left side: / You'll never fall sick'; and 'If landlords are saints / Pestles are bowstrings'; and 'A servant who knows / The secrets of the house, / A pretty wife, / Spetched clothes, / A wicked king: / They need careful handling';[36] and so on. Mehrotra, through such contiguities, both mocks and hints to us the method of creating a critical tradition.

Of course, part of the reason why Mehrotra sought an idiom borrowed from, at different points in his oeuvre, the French Surrealists, Pound, and American slang is because of his desire to write in a language unburdened by the overtones of Aurobindo's *Savitri*, the English *Gitanjali*, and King's or Queen's English. Like the young R. K. Narayan, the young Mehrotra was seduced by the triumphant, oracular sweep of Tagore's prose poem, producing lines like 'Let not the cloud remain and dirty the sky, let it not shade the sun, let it not be tossed about by the wind or be pecked by birds',[37] before widening his reading and moving on to the *Penguin Modern Poets* series, and to the American Beats, whose punctuation and typographical style would inspire Mehrotra at 19 to compose his poem 'Bharatmata', and start, in Allahabad, *damn you/a magazine of the arts*. With his first book of poems, *Nine Enclosures*, it was as if he were starting from scratch—in his introduction to *Twelve Modern Indian Poets*, he'd said that the poetic tradition he belonged to went back 'no further than the poets in this volume',[38] of whom the oldest was Ezekiel. And, like his contemporaries, he had to create a vernacular by *not* doing certain things, by *not* looking towards Indian poetry, Indian English, or his Indian forebears; after all, as he recently said in an interview, Indian English 'has no demotic'. Like many Indian poets in English, Mehrotra would have engaged with his 'inheritance' and history principally when serving his apprenticeship as a teenager, and speaking in the voice of dead poets; as a mature poet, he would have to become a scavenger, hoarder, and curator of the demotic registers of other Anglophone literatures, and still speak in other poets' voices, but in a way that now converged with his own voice, the 'borrowed' one 'setting the true one free'. Later on, he would have the courage to make adjustments and corrections to his own mappings. Toru Dutt, whom he'd rejected with Poundian finality in his anthology as one he couldn't 'do business with', he has now reclaimed as both ancestor and fellow-traveller, as another poet who, in the 1870s, had to start from scratch and work towards an Indian vernacular in a handful of English poems out of her readings in French and other European languages, and from her memory of Bengali, her mother tongue. By 'vernacular' I mean not so much a language of the people, but, in a meaning crucial for poets, a language not official.

Unlike Creole, types of pidgin, or Scots dialects, indigenous varieties of English in India are a form of officialese or bureaucratese, even when they appear on shop signs and menu cards. This is especially true when it's spoken as a second or third language; the syntactical disruptions, unlike those in Creole, don't constitute a liberation from the rules of English grammar, but a straining for, at once, sincerity and pomposity—the tone Mehrotra had called 'ipse dixitish'. Pomposity is not the prerogative of the powerful and erudite alone, but of anyone reaching for sonority and power. The upper class in this country speaks in a unique mongrel tongue, of course, but it isn't, strictly speaking, a 'demotic'; that is, the language of the street. It is, in fact—whatever its colourfulness, charm, and energy—largely a bearer of privilege. The petit bourgeois' indigenized English can be a mixture of the heartfelt and the bureaucratic, as the neighbourliness of 'sweetness' with the ugly, technical (but typical) 'external' and 'internal' in these lines from Nissim Ezekiel's 'Goodbye Party to Miss Pushpa TS' show:

> You are knowing, friends,
> what sweetness is in Miss Pushpa,
> I don't mean only external sweetness
> but internal sweetness.[39]

Technical, arcane, archaic (for example, 'dastardly'), ponderous, difficult words can be particularly effective as a component of literary style when they're used with deadpan irony; Ezekiel realizes that it's the lack of irony to do with such words in Indian English that makes it, when transformed into a dramatic monologue (or farewell speech), naturally funny. In most cultures, pomposity—unlike the joke—is funny to everyone except its repository. In India, pomposity forms a legitimate style of interaction, and denotes a patrician sense of responsibility; it also denotes a high-minded nationalism that finds a perfect home in indigenous English, and makes it very unlike a demotic or pidgin; here's Ezekiel again, from 'Some Very Indian Poems in Indian English':

> I am standing for peace and non-violence.
> Why world is fighting fighting,
> Why all people of world
> Are not following Mahatma Gandhi,
> I am simply not understanding.[40]

In comparison to this, Ezekiel finds syntax, precision, economy, and grammar incongruously liberating—features of a non-official diction. We see this in the first four lines of the poem, 'Guru', which is right next to 'Goodbye Party to Miss Pushpa TS' in the *Collected Poems*:

> The saint, we are told,
> once lived a life of sin—
> nothing spectacular, of course,
> just the usual things.[41]

The commas are in the right places, and yet the lines are closer to the rhythms of speech, and show what speech can achieve in literature, in contrast to the Indian English declamations. They, rather than the Indian English parodies, are an example of the strategies for fashioning an English vernacular by Indian poets.

Precision, wit, and elegance, on the one hand; a vernacular, agile diction on the other—these sets of qualities might seem to form a binary, but Indian poets would have known how they were indispensable to each other. They would have known, too, how critical language in India is very often oblivious to this, and is at once high-minded, imprecise, and bureaucratic; as a result, some of them would have elected to write criticism themselves, thus contributing to what is, Mehrotra reminds us, a remarkable tradition of English prose written by Indian poets (for instance, Ezekiel, Dom Moraes, Adil Jussawalla). In 1974, Ezekiel, writing a strikingly perceptive essay about an artist—Bhupen Khakhar—who had a sensibility quite unlike his own, recorded the way the abstract tone of Indian English (whose true source may lie in the gibberish of the national discourse: 'I am standing for peace and non-violence') inflects Indian criticism in English, and responded peremptorily:

> The pedantic, the literary and the rhetorical should dissolve in the presence of this gifted humourist [*sic*]. Instead we have this, from the art critic of *Link Magazine*: 'Bhupen Khakhar's pictures by and large, give the feeling of a wandering soul in the void. The soul is empty. It does not know what it is eternally seeking on earth. In the air and in the sky. It knows that it has lost something valuable.' The critic does not know that he has lost something valuable: his common sense.'[42]

In the next sentence, Ezekiel reports to us exactly what the critic from *Link Magazine* had missed: 'Far from wandering in the void, seeking obscurely in the air and in the sky, Bhupen's "empty" soul sports in *paan* shops and Irani restaurants, in tailor and watch repair shops, in the offices of branch managers and assistant accountants.'[43] In other words, while speaking indulgently of the 'void' and the 'soul', the critic hadn't actually looked at or *seen* the world depicted in Khakhar's paintings—which is worrying, since painting is a visual medium. How much worse would he or she have been with a non-visual art, like writing? Although other words have replaced 'soul' and 'void' today, we find the same abnegation from the sensory, the same indifference to the habit of noticing or looking. The language shifts from the opaque to the political—with the reflexive accusations of elitism and the passionate invocations of the 'real' India—to the bureaucratic, but it's generally written by one who has no use for the eye, or the ear, or the other senses. Mehrotra, in his introduction, tells us that his favourite example of this pervasive discourse is a sentence from a review of a book by V. S. Naipaul in *India Today*: 'The heart of darkness beats on the pacemaker of history.'[44] Long ago, clarifying that *Jejuri* is not a religious poem in his headnote to Kolatkar in *Twelve Modern Indian Poets*, Mehrotra had declared firmly: 'The presiding deity of *Jejuri* is not Khandoba, but the human eye.'[45] In saying this, he was articulating his own credo, not only as a poet, but as a critic who notices things. He was also unwittingly—but fortuitously—echoing Satyajit Ray, when the latter (still an enthusiast, in 1948, and not a director) had exhorted Indian filmmakers in a piece called 'What is Wrong with Indian Films?' that 'The raw material of cinema is life itself. It is incredible that a country which has inspired so much painting and music and poetry should fail to move the film maker. *He has only to keep his eyes open, and his ears* [my emphasis].'[46]

Partial Recall is divided into two sections. The second gives the reader the critical essays—'The Emperor Has No Clothes'; 'Street Music: A Brief History', where Mehrotra yet again reveals his delight in the everyday and in the literature of the everyday, which was what joined him to Kolatkar in the first place; essays on the enigma and achievement of Ramanujan, on translating Kabir, on what an Indian poem and a history of Indian literature might be; and 'The Bradman Class', a small meditation on the mathematician G. H. Hardy, where, once more, Mehrotra's view of the artist (and mathematician) as a person with a capacity for delight, 'engaged in the ... task ... of creating beauty',[47] is very much in evidence. Among the sentences he quotes from Hardy, one—'A mathematical proof should resemble a simple and clear-cut constellation, not a scattered cluster in the Milky Way'[48]—most describes the spare, crystalline, formal designs of his poems, but not so much his critical and editorial interventions, whose importance lies in how they have made sense of those 'scattered clusters'. Yet that sentence, with its advocacy of the beautiful, reminds us why Mehrotra had chosen as an epigraph to *The Absent Traveller* (1991)—his translations from the Prakrit—a declaration from Pound's *Confucian Analects* that had made a Nabokovian (Nabokov the lecturer, not Nabokov the novelist) distinction: 'Those who know aren't up to those who love; nor those who love, to those who delight in.'[49] Nabokov's way of expressing this hierarchy is less exact and succinct, but worth looking at: a writer 'may be considered as a storyteller, as a teacher, and as an enchanter'. We turn, says Nabokov, to the storyteller for 'entertainment, for mental excitement of the simplest kind, for emotional participation', while a 'slightly different though not necessarily higher mind looks for the teacher in the writer', manifested as 'propagandist, moralist, prophet'. Still, 'above all, a great writer is always a great enchanter, and it is here that we come to the really exciting part when we try to grasp the individual magic of his genius and to study the style, the imagery, the pattern of his novels or poems'.[50] Different people will find different things 'really exciting', but Mehrotra will agree with Nabokov about the compulsions of the 'individual magic' and the 'pattern'.

Mehrotra probably also knows that he lives in a country where 'knowing' is deeply prized; where, as a result, the social sciences form the predominant stream in the humanities, and, for all their postcolonial, anti-Enlightenment rhetoric, are heavily dependent for their validity on the word 'sciences'—that is, on the rational and verifiable. 'Knowing' is shored up in India by the Hegelian distaste for ambiguity on the part of our academics and intellectuals; by the talismanic value given to archives, research, fieldwork, and information in our history-writing and fiction-writing; by the newspaper reports and issues that comprise our Manichean national life, where we're constantly aware of being on one side or the other. Here, Mehrotra sounds a discordant, occasionally polemical, note, reminding us, especially in the book's second section, of other matters: of the sensory, of the realms we 'delight in', and of the need for a language—an unofficial language, Indian (because Mehrotra is Indian), but without any overdetermined signs of Indianness—that would be adequate to recording these experiences and embodying them, and to voicing the dilemma it itself represents with urgency. In the first section, comprising marvellous autobiographical essays (including the one after which the book is named), and the part-autobiographical, part-critical 'Death of a Poet', on Kolatkar's final hours, he shows us what such a language or vernacular might be—barely noticeable at first, since it refuses to strain for the status or appearance of a special language, but wholly plausible, relevant, and absorbing: the writing not only of one our most considerable prose stylists, but a self-effacing and single-minded exemplar.

2012

* * *

12

Unconstitutional spaces

The mathematical sublime

As a malingerer in school, doing poorly in studies and skipping PE classes by citing health reasons, I was naturally drawn to poetry. I began my apprenticeship early, under Dr Seuss, and, by the time I was fifteen, was soaring with Walt Whitman, Neruda, Khalil Gibran, and, of course, Tagore. One thing I recall from that time is how excited I was, not only by my discovery of these poets, but my ability to write just like them.

By the time I was sixteen, I also wanted to be a philosopher. This was not going to be a profession on the side. Each time I took on a persona through which to view the world—poet, philosopher, singer-songwriter ('novelist' was too dull to figure in that list)—I did so exclusively, making other vocations dispensable. My handbook was Will Durant's *The Story of Philosophy*.

Despite my eagerness to inhabit all intellectual and cultural history through my appropriation of a succession of poetic voices, and by moving swiftly from one chapter in Durant to another, my only philosophical breakthrough, which happened that very year, veered towards eventlessness. I'd always been poor in maths, but my theory involved numbers, albeit in the most basic way. One and minus one was a series that went on without cessation, went the first part of my theorem: it comprised an idea of infinity comprehensible to Reason depended on, given that Reason can't cope with the non-linear. And yet Reason, in the end, couldn't possibly imagine what an idea of space and time that was premised on their going on and on, in an endless progression that Kant had called the 'mathematical sublime', could be. In relation to this conception of space and time, the great childish questions were still pertinent: where did space end?—and when did time begin? In this context, what—my adolescent mind wanted to know—was emptiness? Was it the space surrounding solid objects, extending further and further away, as more and more space, until it reached the next object—say, a star—and then the galaxies beyond? Was reality a three-dimensional realm of objects and emptiness extending endlessly? Where did it stop? The same question pertained to the series of numbers, one and minus one, two and minus two, etc., echoing the binary of thing and non-thing, subject and object (a pairing I'd recently heard about) going on and on forever.

Here, my intervention took the form of a question: what, then, was zero? Was it not, too, infinity? Was it a different kind of infinity from the on-and-on progression starting with one and minus one? And was zero nothing, or something? If it was nothing, wasn't it a different kind of nothing from the one represented by minus one? I preferred—now being a philosopher who had to coin his own terminology—to call minus one 'absence', since it was always defined by the presence of one. Zero was emptiness, but not absence; it was also a kind of fullness, but a different kind of fullness from that which objects comprised, or the numbers one, two, three ad infinitum. Unlike these, it didn't occupy the world in the same way. The little I remembered of maths instructed me that one and minus one added up to zero. Was zero a kind of transcendence, then, into which reality, in its infinitude, dissolved? One and minus one coming together sounded like the reunion between the two bereft creatures described by Aristophanes. Moreover, I'd been lately exposed to the songs of the bhakti poets: could it be that the transcendence of the dreary infinitude of the world could only be achieved through love? I wasn't content with these conclusions.

After that illumination, I put both Will Durant and the transcendental to one side. But numbers, and the whole business of adding things up, came back to haunt me, even after I was a published novelist. Firstly, there was the problem of the reality contained in the novel itself: was it the sum total of character and setting? Was setting itself the sum total of detail and of physical and historical information? And character—was it something you came up with when you added together traits, thoughts, and physical characteristics?

There was also the fact that I'm an Indian. Did this mean that I was the sum total of my Indian heritage and Western influences, following some Nehruvian model? Being Indian meant I had to deal with the notion of the secular, and its Indian spin-off, 'secularism': because the India I belonged to was a secular nation-state, pursuing, in the public sphere, policies informed by the secularism its constitution vouchsafed for and protected. Secularism meant that the nation-state was, in theory, a liberal space, which allowed for the peaceful cohabitation of a multiplicity of world-views, religions, and communities. If you added up these communities, religions, and world-views, you arrived at the 'secular', whose best-known guarantor lay in the Indian Constitution. The secularist nation-state was a transcendental space, like the liberal consciousness, in that it could entertain or host two different points of view, or two antithetical religions, without itself being tainted by either opinion or religion. In other words, it was more akin to contemporary British multiculturalism than to the French idea of the secular, in that it was even-handedly tolerant towards all religions instead of being determinedly purged of the religious. But it *was*, in its way, purged of the religious, because (again, in theory) its neutrality and lack of investment in the religious it made space for was indispensable to its nature. The word 'secular' has variants in India—like 'cosmopolitan', for instance. In India, this usually indicates a space (a neighbourhood, a city) that is hospitable to a range of creeds and communities, which is why it has been frequently used of Bombay. It shares, with the constitutional secular, a cumulative character: it is the sum total of its parts, as secularism is, as India and the Indian identity are. The constitutional secular is a mutation of the mathematical sublime, in that you can only arrive at an understanding of its liberal inclusiveness through addition.

As a novelist, as a reader, as one who listened to music and watched movies, as a possessor of memory, I had developed a sense of the secular too. For me it had to do with the assignation of value to aspects of the world and of perception that couldn't be accounted for by religious dictates or prescription. The immediate environment I live in, the rhythms of my day, aren't religious. Yet I assign value to things in that world, to particular streets, walls, facades, and objects, to certain times of the day and certain sounds, to light and space. Most of what I have enumerated in the previous sentence can be encompassed by terms like the 'ordinary', the 'commonplace'. When I decide I'm drawn to one object or street more than to another one, I might be making a decision that's aesthetic and experiential, but it's also one that's secular. When I look at the arts in India—cinema, literature, painting—in the last two hundred years, I see that my responses and assignations have a history. But they seem to have no place—indeed, they're unheard of—in the history of secularism in my country. If the arts do enter that narrative, its only inasmuch as they are recruited to reflect secularism's constitutional interpretation, as a cumulative coming-together of diverse identities, as an example of the cohabiting, or the lack of cohabitation, of communities and world-views. For this reason, certain aspects of the experiential and the secular in modern India, aspects which we all, as moderns, in some way embody and are governed by, remain unaddressed or as good as non-existent; because they're extra- or un-constitutional. The experience of the secular that doesn't fit into a constitutional definition remains a rumour.

At what point this experience of the secular—the pre-constitutional, unconstitutional experience—emerges I can't be altogether sure. But emerge it does. If I were coerced to date that emergence, I'd opt for 1894, given it's the year that Tagore's essay on children's nursery rhymes, '*Chhelebhulano chhara*', is published. This is how it begins: 'For some time now, I have been collecting the rhymes current in Bengali by which women divert children. These rhymes may have a special value in determining the history of our language and our society; but to me, their simple natural poetic strain seems more worthy of regard' (Sukanta Chaudhuri's translation).[1] 'Collecting the rhymes'; 'determining the history of our language and our society': these formulations gesture towards the organizational, the business of adding up and putting together, the incremental task of arriving at and establishing that history—'of our language and our society'. Tagore is referring to the kind of labours of love undertaken by Reverend Lal Behari Day, who produced his magnificent anthology in English, *Folk Tales of Bengal*, in 1883; to the historian Dineshchandra Sen, whose magisterial *Banga Bhasha o Sahitya* (*The Language and Literature of Bengal*) would come out a year after Tagore's essay, and whose selfless excursions into the countryside to collect medieval manuscripts would have already been famous by the time Tagore was reflecting on nursery rhymes. Add to these the indefatigable archival labours of amateur historians and the recently formed historical societies, the field trips taken to villages by writers such as Abdul Kareem to recover and collect *puthis* or old manuscripts, and the discovery of the *Charyapad*, which set back the date of written Bengali to the twelfth century, and you have an idea of the ethos within which Tagore is making his, at first strategically tentative, then increasingly intricate, intervention.[2] Of course, he's deeply beholden, like every other modern Bengali of that age, to these researches and acts of recovery, saying of Dineshchandra Sen's book upon its publication: 'Before the appearance of this work, we hadn't known such a thing as old Bengali literature existed.'[3] Some of his responses to the new collations had been unexpected and deeply creative, like his pastiche, as a fifteen-year-old, of Vidyapati and Chandidas, whom he'd discovered in the then recently compiled *Vaishnav Padabali*, and his simultaneously lyrical and nationalistic preface to Dakkhinaranjan Majumdar's anthology of nursery rhymes in 1907, *Thhakurmar Jhuli* (*Grandmother's Bag*). Although about thirty years separate these last two instances, the nature of Tagore's response to these collations reveal how the material in them was transforming, remaking, and in transaction with, the Bengali's—in this case, Tagore's—imagination. But for all that, in 1894, it seems that Tagore senses that Lal Behari Day and Dinesh Chandra Sen's exemplary work is a model for history-writing and for arriving at an account of an Indian, and Bengali, history that was hitherto missing; crucially, Day's and Sen's undertaking also reminds us that the moment, the impulse, and the emergence of that history, are all secular in tone. Whether it's a Christian or a Hindu doing the job of the collating, there are no ostensible religious impulses informing their task; the mathematical labour of putting together the shards that comprise a tradition presages the undertaking of making a nation, a history, an identity, and of making, in this context, the secular.

Tagore intuits the validity of this mission, but in the second half of the sentence quoted above, making a case for the importance of Bengali nursery rhymes, he distances himself from it with an anodyne disclaimer: 'but to me, their simple natural poetic strain seems more worthy of regard'.[4] Taking refuge in the persona of a mere poet, he then goes on to complicate the notion of the 'simple'. (It's worth noting how the creative writer or poet, in contrast to, say, the historian, has the privilege of beginning his argument with the confession of not knowing enough about his chosen subject. This move makes the poet-critic akin to a particular sort of phenomenologist.) Tagore continues by admitting to an intimation of the significance of the rhymes, as well as a confession of inadequacy and not-knowing in relation to that intimation: 'It is impossible for me to dissociate my delight in savouring children's rhyme from my memories of childhood. The present author does not have the acumen to judge how much of the sweetness of these rhymes is owing to those memories and how much to the perennial principles of literature. I should admit this at the outset.'[5] Here, again, a new note is being sounded in Bengali literature, with this invocation of the persona of the 'mere poet'. The term is the historian Ramachandra Guha's, an unwitting rephrasing of Tagore's own self-definition as a 'mere Bengali poet'. Guha uses it while clarifying that Tagore *wasn't* a 'mere poet': there's much more to him than poetry. Yet Tagore's disavowal of an authoritative position here—despite, or because of, his writerly vagueness, indeterminacy, and lack of expertise and seriousness ('lack of acumen')—introduces an unprecedented tenor to the discussion. Tagore says:

> Nor can I otherwise explain why so many epics and lyrics, theories and precepts, so much human labour and sweating toil should be spent in vain and forgotten every day, while these inconsistent, meaningless, wilfully composed verses should flow for ever through popular memory.[6]

The key words here are 'inconsistent' and 'meaningless'. The first is Sukanta Chaudhuri's translation of *asangata*, which also carries the sense of 'inappropriate' or 'out of place'; while the Bengali original of 'meaningless' is *arthhahin*. What weight do these terms have? We know, after all, that the inappropriate, the out of place, the inconsistent, the meaningless can't inform any conventional definition of secularism, especially in its organizational, archival, political, and multicultural capacities. The out of place, according to the Constitution's guarantee, will find its equitable place in the nation-state; it can't *continue* to be innately strange, and alienated from the national secular framework. Besides, by *asangata*, I don't think Tagore is referring to politically marginalized identities that can be addressed or empowered, let's say, by postcolonialism. Which is why Sukanta Chaudhuri deliberately translates the word as 'inconsistent'; Tagore is invoking something disruptive, which, at both first and second glance, is *arthhahin* or 'meaningless'. Constitutional secularism gives meaning and value to every world-view, aspect, and religion, however peculiar or minor, that adds up to contemporary Indian life; is Tagore, then, hinting at something that's religious when he speaks of the *asangata*? It doesn't look like it. Instead, under the guise of being a 'mere poet' lacking in 'acumen' and judgement, he seems to be, while describing these nursery rhymes, giving them a value that's at once secular and apparently meaningless, or inappropriate. Is this value, then, a mutation of the 'literary' in modern Bengal? That is, is the 'inconsistent' a metaphor for literature? Even if it is, we need to acknowledge the rhymes won't even be wholly contained by that sphere, given Tagore's uncertainty about 'how much of the sweetness of these rhymes' owes 'to the perennial principles of literature';[7] at times, it seems, in the essay, that this value is intrinsically uncanonical, inasmuch as the literary canon is a mathematical formulation, a collection of chosen texts, adding up to a national heritage: 'Nor can I otherwise explain why so many epics and lyrics, theories and precepts, so much human labour and sweating toil should be spent in vain and forgotten every day, while these inconsistent, meaningless, wilfully composed verses should flow for ever . . .'.[8] 'Human toil' and 'sweating labour' are as much a reference to Dinesh Chandra Sen and the historian or expert as 'theories or precepts' is; whatever this thing that Tagore's talking about is, it resists being incorporated in the building of a secular, national heritage in the manner that was familiar at the time, and still is. Yet it is secular.

Two more passages from the essay are worth pausing over. Tagore speculates about the sort of mind that composed these rhymes, and made possible in them their startling and illogical transitions, their restless flitting from one image to another:

> In the normal way, echoes and reflections of the universe revolve in our minds in a scattered, disjointed manner . . . As in the atmosphere, roadside dust, flower-pollen, assorted sounds, fallen leaves, water droplets, the vapours of the earth—all the ejected, whirling fragments of this turning, agitated universe—float and roam meaninglessly, so it is in our minds. There too, in the ceaseless stream of our consciousness, so many colours, scents, and sounds; so many vapours of the imagination, traces of thoughts, broken fragments of language—hundreds of fallen, forgotten discarded components of our practical life—float about, unobserved and purposeless.[9]

Tagore is drawing our attention, here, to the way the rhymes are able to give a home to the fragments that 'float and roam meaninglessly' in the universe and in our minds; he's making a case for the inchoate, the chaotic, the residual, the fading. It is 1894, and the phrase translated by Chaudhuri as 'the ceaseless stream of our consciousness'[10] is striking; the original, '*nityaprabahita chetanar madhye*', or, 'in the midst of our daily flow of consciousness', makes us ask, immediately, if Tagore had been reading William James, whose *Principles of Psychology* (1890), in the chapter 'Stream of Thought', had begun to broach and explore these themes for the first time; or, for that matter, whether he'd come across the American's essay, 'Psychology' (1892), where James uses, inaugurally, the now-tired term, 'stream of consciousness'. Whatever the case, and however remarkable the coincidence or convergence, there's no doubt, again, that this *chetana* or 'consciousness' that Tagore mentions is, given its inconstant nature, uncontainable and irreducible, but also human and secular: it isn't shored up by religion. But in making the 'whirling fragments' of which it's composed so central to it—'*uddinakhandangsha-sakala*'—Tagore is telling us that this is a notion of the secular that resists being arrived at by addition, by collating, collecting, and bringing things together (though he too has been collecting these rhymes for years); it's not a version of the secular which comprises an equitable guarantee to each of its facets. Its incongruous significance lies in its being 'scattered and disjointed', 'unobserved and purposeless'. The word Chaudhuri translates as 'purposeless'—*anaavashyak*—could as plausibly be translated as 'superfluous'. And superfluous and unobserved this particular realm of the secular largely remains in India, partly because it embodies and contains the superfluous: you wonder if Tagore feels that it's from this superfluousness that it derives its tenacity.

Tagore then reveals to us what he believes is inimical to the superfluous:

> When one starts to think consciously with a specific objective in view, these shadowy mirages vanish in a moment: one's intellect and imagination take on an integrated purpose and begin to flow in a single direction. The substance one calls one's mind is so authoritarian that when it awakens and emerges into the light of day, the greater part of the world within and outside us is obscured under its influence: its own retinue of attendants fills all creation under its power, its law, and its bidding. Think about it: the call of birds in the sky, the sough of leaves, the babble of waters, the hubbub of human habitations—so many thousands of sounds, big and small, rising without end; so many waves and tremors, comings and goings...yet only a small fraction of all this impinges on one's consciousness. This is chiefly because one's mind, like a fisherman, casts a net of integration and accepts only what it can gather at a single haul: everything else eludes it...It has the power to move all irrelevancies far away from the path of its set purpose.[11]

'Thinking consciously', teleology ('flowing in a single direction')—these are Tagore's culprits, and they're all characteristics of the 'authoritarian' behaviour of the 'substance called one's mind', a substance that is endowed with a specific power: the 'power to move all irrelevancies far away from the path of its set purpose'.[12] It's worth stopping for a minute to think of what, or whom, Tagore might be attacking here. Tagore can't abide English society or imperialism, but he's not attacking colonialism, colonial institutions, or the English language; he's not holding up the nursery rhymes as an authentic homegrown alternative to the foreign. Tagore is a son of the co-founder of the Unitarian sect, the Brahmo Samaj; but he's neither attacking Hinduism nor religion. What he's arraigning, and referring to in slightly disdainful terminology—'*mana-namakpadyarthati*', or 'that thing called the mind'—is almost certainly secular, but so is what he pits against it: 'irrelevancies'. We are taken back to the Romantic quarrel, not with religion, but between Reason and the Imagination, both secular, historical antagonists, as when Shelley remonstrates in 'A Defence of Poetry': 'Reason is the enumeration of quantities already known; imagination is the perception of the value of those quantities, both separately and as a whole. Reason respects the differences, and imagination the similitude of things.'[13] The word 'enumeration' is striking, and points to Shelley's animosity to the mathematical sublime; but what we have here, in 'A Defence of Poetry', is a quarrel over what best represents, for him, the power of the secular. But for all his fondness for Shelley, the young Tagore parts ways with the Englishman over the question of 'similitude'; for, not 'the similitude of things', but the disjointed and the superfluous are what preoccupy Tagore at the end of the nineteenth century, and make his reinterpretation of the secular a modern rather than a romantic one. Yet the fact that both the Romantic and the modern, the Englishman and the Bengali, find a certain variant of the secular authoritarian is indisputable: it's a sentiment that's clearly expressed and, where Tagore's concerned, prefigured in Book XII of Wordsworth's *The Prelude*: 'The mind is lord and master—outward sense / The obedient servant of her will . . . '.[14] In modern India, it's clear that one version of the secular sought, and achieved, mastery, while the other—the everyday—necessarily became, in its own self-interest, superfluous.

The constitutional version of secularism, cosmopolitanism, and the nation-state in India implies, and ensures, that much of what comprises its modernity will be seen as a sum of its parts—like the modern Indian identity, for instance, which, as in A. K. Ramanujan's portrait of his mathematician-astrologer father, is a proportionate mixture of East and West, ancient and modern: 'He was a mathematician, an astronomer.

But he was also a Sanskrit scholar, an expert astrologer. He had two kinds of exotic visitors: American and English mathematicians who called on him when they were on a visit to India, and local astrologers, orthodox pundits who wore splendid gold-embroidered shawls dowered by the Maharaja.'[15] Parts of the mix might seem incompatible to the younger Ramanujan, but in the end he sets to one side the fact that he was 'troubled by his [father's] holding together in one brain both astronomy and astrology', and accepts his admonishment: 'Besides, don't you know, the brain has two lobes?'[16] At this point in his essay, 'Is There an Indian Way of Thinking?', Ramanujan is close to affirming—in spite of his tone of bemusement—a constitutional, secularist way of looking at the Indian self, where his father's brain, holding, simultaneously, like and unlike, modern and immemorial, foreign and native, religious and rational together, becomes a microcosm of constitutional space. What's crucial to this air of secularist wholeness is that Ramanujan Senior is perfectly aware of the incompatible facets of his personality, and is able to accommodate them without anxiety or disjunction or disconnect; it's as if over and above the brain's two lobes is a superego that's able to make these different parts cohere in a harmonious mixture. This view of the personality—which, elsewhere in his essay and his writing, and in his creative practice, Ramanujan questions and subverts—is located in the way Indians look at creativity, especially the many-sided creativity of a 'renaissance' figure such as Tagore. Tagore was a poet, composer, novelist, short-story writer, painter, and critic, and we look upon these facets and talents as if they were continuous with, and complementary to, each other, as the bass guitar and sitar might be in a piece of fusion music. Tagore is the sum of these parts, and in his brain there was evidently a control room that held them together and directed their development. This is why we regard Tagore with nationalist pride: not only because he was a genius, and won the Nobel Prize, but because his personality echoes our utopian, secular idea of constitutional wholeness. His impossible renaissance wide-rangingness is, in more senses than one, a symbol of the nation. It's in this way that he appeals to a commentator such as Ramachandra Guha and to many others, for whom the poetry is, in a sense, 'irrelevant', 'superfluous', or '*anaavshyak*', and the creative process of marginal importance.

Tagore's interest in pattern and flow (dwelt on at some length in his nursery rhymes essay) over the fixed or the unidirectional goes back to his early youth. In 1883, when he was twenty two, he wrote a short essay, '*Lekhaa Kumari o Chhapa Sundori*', roughly translatable as 'Handwriting, the Maiden, and Print, the Beautiful Lady', arguing for cursive handwriting over print, where he makes clear his preference for the fluidity of the first over the static quality of the second. This essay, as an exploration of what can only be called a dormant modernist predilection (which would gradually have an impact on various branches of Bengali culture, including design, typography, and architecture), is a precursor to the nursery rhyme essay, where the modernist agenda is at once articulated and presented in an unexpected manner. That is, nothing in world literature till now has prepared the reader for 'the current of daily consciousness' as a way of interpreting writing and reading. The art historian Partha Mitter, in an observation uncharacteristic of cultural historiography in India, identifies the hosting of the Bauhaus artists, alongside their Bengali contemporaries, in Calcutta in 1922, at the initiative of Tagore and Stella Kramrisch, as the originary moment of modernism in Bengal. (I call this an uncharacteristic observation because contemporary Indian historians, in art or otherwise, lay no claim to modernism—indeed, they'd profess a vague hostility to the 'modern' as an idea, and to the hubris of an Indian wanting to have anything to do with it. When discussing this date with Mitter, I was touched by his art historian's immersion in his fascination with that Bengali 'modernist' moment, an immersion unimpinged upon by the literary: he was unaware—until I pointed this out—that 1922 was the year in which *The Wasteland* and *Ulysses* were published.)

I like Mitter's gesture, while being sceptical about the use of such a calendar for modernism, and of the Western strategy of using dates to claim ownership. Yet if I were to assign an originary moment, or inaugural artistic statement, for modernism, I would go back to 1894 and that essay on nursery rhymes. Something has begun to happen in Tagore's head and in Bengal in the last two decades in the nineteenth century which is not just a straightforward consequence of an engagement with Western culture; it both presages movements yet to take shape in the West and is a precursor to Tagore's own particular engagements with Western movements. Bauhaus in 1922 in Calcutta is a case in point. Tagore's interest in flow and pattern thirty or forty years prior to the exhibition finds a kind of fruition in the new century in his invitation to the Bauhaus artists he found himself increasingly absorbed by.

The incompatible bits

Just as Tagore's poetry is largely forgotten today, he himself was forgetful; he also had spells when he put one identity in abeyance and took on others. This notion of forgetfulness, where we're unaware of our selves, or certain parts of our selves, is something I'd like to introduce here as a further modulation on the secular, as something that doesn't fit into the secularist mainstream, where all the selves within ourselves necessarily combine into our identity. In Tagore, the facets won't quite come together. His first slip comes when, at the age of fifteen, upon reading and being won over by the fifteenth-century devotional poets Chandidas and Vidyapati, newly collected in the anthology, the *Vaishnav Padavali*, Tagore decides to become, for a period of time, a devotional poet, Bhanusingha, writing not in modern Bengali but in *brajbhasha*. Admittedly, the pseudonym Bhanusingha makes sly reference to Tagore's first name, Rabindranath, in that both words have to do with the sun; admittedly, the catalyst for Tagore's short-lived loss of personality is Chatterton, who also revisited history through the pastiche. But the first line of the first song, *gahana kusama kunja maajhe*, apparently comes to him unbidden, out of nowhere, when he's sitting with a slate on his lap; and he begins to ventriloquize in a language that is, essentially, not his natural or his mother tongue: *brajbhasha*. As is the case sometimes with such experiments, this one is durational and fitful; Tagore doesn't revisit this personality later in life.

This experience of disjunction and alienation, in Tagore, was repetitive. At the time of his marriage in 1883, he sent his friend Priyanath Sen a curious handwritten invitation: 'Priyababu—on the auspicious day of the coming Sunday of 24th Aghrayan [Nov./ Dec.], my close relative Sriman Rabindranath Thakur will be married at an auspicious hour. We would be grateful if you could join us on that occasion in the evening at No 6 Jorasanko at Debendranath Thakur's house to participate in the wedding celebrations. Yours sincerely, Sri Rabindranath Thakur.'[17] The tone of estrangement—self-mocking in the wedding invitation—is apparent again, but in an awkward, unwieldy way, when, approaching the end of his life, the eighty-year-old Tagore describes, retrospectively, a heightened experience he had when he was a boy in Calcutta: 'But in the history of that day there was no one other than myself who saw those clouds in the quite the same way as

I did... Rabindranath happened to be all by himself in that instance'; and 'In the entire history of that day it was Rabindranath alone who witnessed the scene with enchanted eyes. This I know for certain.'[18] The language is grandiose but alienated; if Tagore is referring to himself in the third person, then whose voice are we hearing in this utterance made in 1941, or for that matter in the earlier one, from 1883? Whoever it belongs to, this voice—in its abrupt transitions between pronouns, between the first and third person—fails to provide the uniform, overarching perspective that would make the various selves cohere; it's a voice that needs to be distinguished from the voice that proclaims, 'Besides, the brain has two lobes, didn't you know?'

Tagore would continue to forget things, and also encroach upon new personalities and languages. In this way, he embarked upon his strangest excursion, the English version of the *Gitanjali*, a sequence whose aesthetic bears little resemblance to its Bengali namesake. The English *Gitanjali*, although it claims to be a translation of the Bengali book, is (for more than one reason, not least that it's a selection of songs from four of Tagore's collections) really a book without an original. The manuscript of the English translation itself he lost—perhaps deliberately—in the London Underground, and it was returned to him by the Lost and Found office. Then there are the paintings in later life, emerging from exceptional patterns created accidentally from his manuscript deletions. Among the paintings are remarkable self-portraits, of which the most compelling is a series, strangely prescient of Warhol's take on celebrity iconography, in which he scribbles on, and defaces, copies of a photograph of himself on a magazine cover, turning one into a woman, another into a clean-shaven youth, a third to a sea-captain, a fourth to a prophet; and so on. On re-examination, Tagore the multi-faceted genius, the 'myriad-minded man', turns out to be a Tagore of transitions and forays, of extant, old, and new personalities, some of which have no clear bearing on the others. The statist model of Tagore's mind begins to fall apart.

As a consequence of this 'falling apart', it's possible to connect Tagore to a man at the opposite end of the Bengali cultural spectrum, the semi-literate mystic Ramakrishna Paramhansa. Ramakrishna was, himself, a devotee of Kali; but he's been co-opted as a figurehead of Indian secularism. In large part, this has to do with his pronouncement, '*Jata mat tata path*', or, 'There are as many ways to God as there are religions', a message echoing the Constitution's. But Ramakrishna's testing the waters of world-views and faiths was fundamentally a volatile business; he periodically took on new personalities, and his religious experiments didn't cohere, or result in an equable endorsement of the validity of all religions. His forays were fraught with competitiveness. Ramakrishna wasn't just a worshipper of Kali; he claimed he could see her. When experimenting with Christianity, he reportedly saw Christ as a young English boy playing a flute. His temporary immersion in Islam is famous; he began to eat beef, and entered the Islamic personality so completely that he noticed he was developing a distaste for Kali. At this, he grew nervous, and, with an effort, rescued and returned himself to his customary Kali-devotee's consciousness. The manifestations of religious experiences in Ramakrishna are often antagonistic; one personality briefly annuls another; they don't comprise a tranquil whole of many selves cohabiting in, and merging to form, an identity. Unlike the constitutional nation-state, which encourages and protects a multiplicity of faiths without adhering to any of them, Ramakrishna is implicated in the religion he's exploring. Temporarily, he suffers from forgetfulness in relation to his 'real' faith, his 'real' deity, as another embrace takes precedence in its immediacy. Many faiths may lead to God, but, not, in Ramakrishna, with equal validity at every point of time.

It's possible to find yourself encroaching, in your own domain, upon Ramakrishna's terrain. During the 7 July bombings in London in 2005, my family and I were in Cambridge in England. I was shocked by the explosions. Some of them had occurred in areas—Russell Square, Tavistock Square—that I was familiar with from my undergraduate years, not to mention the fact that my wife was travelling weekly then to the British Library, taking the train to King's Cross, where a bomb had gone off. This, more than 9/11, was to be a test for multicultural Britain, I thought. Waiting for the bus to the city centre, I was, for the first time, anxious. Would the bus driver's appraisal be different? After all, where he and the commuters were concerned, I was indistinguishable from a Muslim. No one so much as glanced at us when we got on to the bus; but I, during that journey to Bridge Street, began to feel increasingly isolated, more and more Muslim, until I imagined I'd be relieved to see the Muslim Sylheti restaurant staff who hovered around the city centre. I also felt, suddenly, a sharp intolerance for vegetarian cuisine. This was different from simple identification or solidarity; I was beginning to experience the anxieties, pleasures, and prejudices of being Muslim. The spell didn't last long, but it was powerful while it lasted. It had neither to do with brainwashing nor with loyalties, but with the fragility of the sense of self; and the way that fragility, that unreliability, allows one to enter into incompatible cultural affiliations. There's a range of creativity in literary history, besides the example of the Renaissance man, Tagore, that isn't that remote from this unreliable fitfulness.

Modern Urdu literature's great novel is, arguably, *Aag ka dariya*, or *River of Fire*, by Qurratulain Hyder, the river being time, or history. Beginning in the Buddhist era and ending after Independence, the novel's linear flow is disrupted by an anomaly; four characters, Gautam, Champa (both Hindu), Kamal (a Muslim), and Cyril (an Englishman), recur through the epochs (though Cyril comes in much later)—these are characters that are born, die, and reappear in succeeding contexts and eras. They are not incarnations of their previous selves; nor are they, as a result of this repetition, 'characters' in the conventional sense. They represent, at each stage, a fresh fate, a new starting point and opportunity. I see that the website Goodreads takes a constitutional view of them in its summary of the novel, claiming that 'together the characters reflect the oneness of human nature: amidst the nationalist and religious upheavals of Indian history, Hyder argues for a culture that is inclusive'. Maybe; but I see the characters gesturing towards that forgetfulness, the sort of spasms and departures that punctuated Ramakrishna's life, when he moved between adoring Kali and detesting her, towards the disjunctions between Bhanusingha, Tagore, and Rabindranath, all poets related by a name and meaning but writing in different languages. Gautam, Champa, Kamal, and Cyril are unaware of their previous or future occurrences in Hyder's narrative. There's an illegitimacy to our forays into different selves that won't be addressed by the constitutional account.

That sense of illegitimacy, along with the forgetfulness, can be very real, as I experienced on that bus. The great modern bilingual artist is Arun Kolatkar, and about his creative practice in English and Marathi he had this to say in a posthumously published sequence called 'Making love to a poem': 'Translating a poem is like making love / having an affair'.[19] The translations he's referring to might be his versions of the medieval saint-poet Tukaram, in which Kolatkar sometimes adopted a language inflected by Beat Americanese—'We are the enduring bums'[20]—or, in his version of the mystic Janabai, an unsavoury gossip columnist's tone—'god my darling / do me a favour and kill my mother-in-law'.[21] This cartoon language, and a certain fecklessness, marks Kolatkar's recurrent crossings between English and Marathi, as does his insistence that some of his own English poems are translations from Marathi originals—originals that, unlike those in Beckett, don't exist, as Arvind Krishna Mehrotra has pointed out. We now see why translating a poem might be like 'having an affair', given Kolatkar's blithe disregard for fidelity, and all the lies involved: the aphorism fortuitously echoes Ramakrishna who, in one of his homilies, said, 'You must long for God as a woman longs for her paramour'—not husband, mind you, but paramour.

In English, Kolatkar was a follower of William Carlos Williams, an enshriner of the commonplace; in Marathi, he was surreal and mythopoeic. The two oeuvres aren't really continuous with each other, any more than two genres might be in an artist who both writes and paints. And so it's no surprise, then, that, in the same sequence, Kolatkar notes: 'I generally try not let my left hand know what my right is doing'. 'My pencil is sharpened at both ends,' he continues, 'I use one to write in Marathi / the other in English'.[22] Here, again, we've transgressed the constitutional, where the cultural mix that forms our identity exists in an equitable, in some ways self-congratulatory, balance. One must place Kolatkar's reflections within the curious tradition he belonged to, of Indian poetry in English, where practitioners and contemporaries sometimes seemed to choose a literary language to write in, or translate into—such as the Marianne Moore-inflected diction and stanzas that Ramanujan creates for his translations from ancient Tamil verse; such as Mehrotra's rich and provocative surrealist phase, the Poundian exactness of his translations of Prakrit love poetry, and, most recently, the zany comic-book Americanese of his translations of Kabir. Are any of these idioms or languages more their 'own' than certain others? What justification—given we have no Constitution to guide us here—do these Indian poets have for adopting these idioms and personae? How do we distinguish these creative selves and moments from colonial mimicry, disentangle them from the critical dead-end of 'influence', and distance them, once and for all, from the Goodreads variety of syncreticism? Whatever it is I'm trying to get at, it seems it can only be approached by a form of rebuttal. First, to recapitulate, there's my uneasiness with a definition of the secular that doesn't recognize the fact that, in its constitutional guise, it can be at once protective and authoritarian, legitimizing and minatory; it's against this notion that Tagore places the 'superfluous'. Secondly, that constitutional understanding doesn't, for me, bring adequately into the discussion how, when we pass from self to self, culture to culture, language to language, genre to genre in our actions and imaginings, we follow no prescriptions to do with the inclusive, the harmonious, the national, or the international.

2012

* * *

13
Un-machinelike

In the early 1980s, we—by which I mean our little nuclear family at the time; but, effectively, my father—owned a white Ambassador. In retrospect, it's clear that the last days, by then, of the Ambassador's long resented supremacy were upon us; but the last days have been with the Ambassador several times; it's a machine that has digested and out-waited extinction. Luck, in Auden's sense of 'divine grace', had a great deal to do with the workability of automobiles in the India I grew up in. The company my father worked in gave him an Austin in the 1970s, in a city—Bombay—where anything that smelled foreign was a way of according recognition. The trouble it brought! It had a habit of stopping anywhere without warning; on the Marine Drive; in Walkeshwar. Then came, after my father rose to the company's helm, a Mercedes Benz, about which I was, given my teenager's acute conscience, always mortified, and am still wary owning up to, except that I can probably do so now in the interests of hinting at the shape of a 'high' bourgeois biography from before the days of globalization.

In that pre-globalization age, to retire from the corporate world was to recede—some would say progress—from the superhuman to the human; in Heraclitus's words, 'The immortals become mortals'.[1] The Mercedes disappeared; and a fairly new, but second-hand, Ambassador, which my father bought from the company, materialized one day. Its beginnings in our lives were inauspicious, with infrequent and infuriating breakdowns; its engine was already in decline, exacerbated by the indulgence (so it seemed in those newly post-Nehruvian, but still mildly self-flagellating, days) of having an air-conditioner fitted into the car. The word I'd hear then was 'load'; when the car went on the blink at a traffic light, the driver would say, 'It can't take the load.' Yet the Ambassador stayed—just as cameras, fridges, and gramophones seemed to abide in a family, then, for well over a decade—and moved with my parents to Calcutta in 1989. Here, it passed unobtrusively from being migrant to native when its Maharashtrian number-plate, MRZ 117, was replaced with a Bengali one—WB O2 9993. It was sold in 1998; but, intermittently, we continue to be made aware of its existence, since some error in the transfer papers ensures that my father is notified by the police every time the present owners commit a traffic violation.

One of the morals of this small reminiscence has to do with the lives, and especially the afterlives, of machines. There are other reminders—besides the violation notices—of that Ambassador, and one of them comes annually in late November, when, towards the end of the autumn term at the University of East Anglia, I show my MA students Ritwik Ghatak's film, *Ajantrik* (which I translate tentatively for them as 'un-machinelike'). It's not just the nature of the theme that serves as a reminder; it's the fact that, by a coincidence, the number of the taxi in the film is also 117. Those numbers are, for me, associated with obduracy and failure, and stir within me—as they probably do in the taxi driver in the film—some unacknowledged spring of affection.

Many of us in this city[2] will be familiar with the film: the taxi driver, so enamoured of his steadfast but increasingly debilitated vehicle that he sees it as a companion; his refusal to sell it, despite all its signs of giving up the ghost, and despite the mockery of the other taxi drivers; the plaintive conversations he has with the car; the threats he hurls at it; the bitter denouement when it's sold as scrap to a Marwari businessman. Then there are the bare but grand vistas around the Bengal–Bihar border; the landscape of milestones, horizons, and level crossings through which the taxi moves; the long interruption when it and its owner encounter the Oraon tribals dancing—all these comprise, seemingly, a world far removed from the machine.

Yet one senses, somehow, that Ghatak isn't setting up contrasts and oppositions here—between man and nature, nature and machine—but hinting at a breakdown: not only of the machine, but of boundaries. 'The people at the Bengali Club say I've become a machine,'[3] says the driver Bimal (played by Kali Banerjee), woefully addressing the car by the name he's given it, 'Jaggadal', and as the familiar '*tui*'. 'What they don't realize is that you too are human.' What's extraordinary here is not only that the observation is uttered at all, but that the driver doesn't bother to refute the first half of the statement. In remaining silent on the matter (is the driver part machine?), Ghatak is working towards an alternative autobiography of filmmaking, one that takes the debate from whether 'we' use technology, or technology surreptitiously uses us. It's a line of inquiry that was later opened up—in no simple way, alas—by the philosopher Gilles Deleuze, whose challenging and radical use of the term 'machine' suggests—as in the driver's summation—a flow rather than an entity, a field of relations enmeshing man, nature, and technology.

Not long ago, a young political scientist, Rajarshi Dasgupta, used the term 'prosthesis' in the context of *Ajantrik*, to pinpoint its idiosyncratic portrayal of man and machine. Dasgupta, like me, is probably searching for a vocabulary that would accommodate the intuition that Ghatak is not so much interested in anthropomorphism—that is, attributing human impulses to non-human phenomena—as in redrawing the human itself, and in measuring, poetically, the material parameters of his craft. The 'prosthetic', at its most literal, suggests the artificial limb, a mechanical extension of the body. Let's take this thought a bit further. Neurologists have told us that the brain can make amputees sense appendages they no longer have; for instance, it's possible to feel like scratching an absent limb. If this is so, then the opposite must also be true: that the process by which we become part-mechanical—prosthesis; or becoming a cyborg—might well be one we aren't fully conscious of. At what point—with our romantic dualisms about man and technology still intact—we passed into this stage of evolution isn't clear; but it's indubitable that in the filmmaker the twentieth century had an entity that was both human artist and machine: part 'driver' or 'pilot' (the word used in our city buses of the driver) or 'director', part slow or hurtling movement, part affect, and part vision.

The cinematic consciousness 'is not us, the spectator, nor the hero, but the camera,' said Deleuze, 'now human, now inhuman, or superhuman'.[4] Both Ghatak and his contemporary Satyajit Ray were acutely aware of the camera, and its principal medium, light, but in different ways. This has to do with Ray's craft originating, at least partly, in Renoir and French cinema, whose use of light Deleuze calls 'Cartesian', a beam-like emanation from the subject, making things luminous; while Ghatak's debt to German expressionism—which uses light to create movement and conflict, and even to animate inanimate objects—is pretty clear. But there's also the happy convergence of that 'Cartesianism' with the inheritance of Bengal's 'enlightenment', its late nineteenth-century humanism, for Ray, and it constantly returns him, as an artist and theorist, to the importance of the gaze; the Indian filmmaker 'has only to keep his eyes open, and his ears'—thus Ray, in 1948. That 'only', one notices on a second reading, turns the assertion into an understatement: for what could be more difficult, really, than working towards a vision of the world?

★

It's no surprise that the camera, in Ray, is a synecdoche for—not a prosthetic appendage of—the human, especially of the eye and its magnificent capacity to receive the world: the eye itself embedded in the humanist wonder of 'seeing'—'*chokh melechhi*'. Metaphors for seeing populate the oeuvre, from the opening scene of *Pather Panchali*, where we look out on Durga's face from darkness—of the theatre, with its Cartesian beam of light illuminating the screen, as well as from the inside of the basket of kittens whose lid the little girl has just removed. The instant when Apu, pretending to be asleep, opens his eye is almost too famous to mention; that eye reappears as the rent in the curtain that lets daylight into Apu's rented room in *Aparajito*; the binoculars in Charulata's hand; the slats in the Venetian window she peers through urgently. Rents, tears, keyholes, the act of spying (think of Feluda in *Joy Baba Felunath*, hidden behind a string cot, looking out through a rent at the prime suspect): all these are pregnant, in Ray, with revelatory value. To give primacy to the eye, Ray must make the camera—the machine—not irrelevant but seamless: not an artificial but an organic element in filmmaking. Just as Ray's relationship, as an artist, with the visible world is Flaubertian—involving fashioning an exact cinematic language to show it *as it is*—the camera, in his hands, approximates the model of the Flaubertian author: self-effacing, transparent, 'nowhere visible but everywhere present'.

In *Ajantrik*—'a silly story,' Ghatak said with evident relish; 'Only silly people can identify themselves with a man who believes that that God-forsaken machine has life'[5]—there seem to be at least a couple of references to the Tagorean brief of 'looking', or '*dekha*', a brief passed on, for the purposes of Bengali cinema, from Tagore to Ray. (The small, rather pious poem Tagore wrote in Ray's notebook when the latter was seven, about having travelled the world and oceans without noticing the dewdrop upon a stalk of rice, not only unconsciously transfers the mantle and reiterates the morality of the gaze, but is prescient in its advice: it reminds the young recipient to narrow the vision, as in a cinematic frame—for the frame is about excluding unnecessary material.)

The roof of Bimal's taxi has a tear, which lets in the rain, embarrassing Bimal, making him defensive; it also offers fleeting glimpses of the sky and sun. The 'ramshackle' (Ghatak's word) vehicle makes the main feminine presence in the film, Kajal Gupta, collapse with laughter upon entering it, till she sees Bimal glowering. But the tear in the roof, and the promise of space it offers, entrances her momentarily. This tear is a rare figure, in Ghatak, for the Tagorean eye, opening out onto the luminous ('more space, more light', in Tagore's formulation); and, as in Ray, its context isn't grand, or grandiose, but comic, shabby, homely. The location of the human, in Ray, indeed, in much of modernism, is the finite and the commonplace; and it's also the commonplace the eye consistently transposes value to. It's this homeliness that makes camerawork in Ray organic, 'natural'.

Despite the rent, Ghatak's visual métier is (as I pointed out earlier) strikingly different from Ray's. It's not so much the eye that interests Ghatak, as bringing the camera—the machine—face to face both with nature and with the audience. Ray beholds the world but leaves it *as it is*; this is a mark of his Flaubertian temperament, but it's also, probably, his modulation (as a product of Shantiniketan) on Tagore's peculiar Oriental humanism—for Tagore argued that the Orient had a long lineage of the human co-existing with nature, in contrast to Western man's relentless compulsion to dominate it. Ghatak, however, wants technology—the camera—to interfere with, and transform, nature; but in a manner unlike, I think, the way in which the Romantic believes technology appropriates the natural. Ghatak's intention is not only to give the machine subjectivity—to anthropomorphize it, to commit the pathetic fallacy—but to allow it to occupy a subjective space—the space of feeling, of suffering and celebration, which only *we* are conscious of occupying. In *Ajantrik*, he's always playing around with both the pathetic fallacy—conferring subjectivity—and with, in a bustling, powerful way, reshaping the subject. How does he do this?

There are, of course, the delightful examples of anthropomorphism, of which the car, as Bimal pours water into its radiator, going 'Glug... glug... glug... aah!' is justly well known. There's also the moment when the boy who lives with Bimal tries his hand, without permission, at driving the car; it goes out of control, only to stop inches before the laughing Kajal Gupta, who's indifferent to her own danger. Is this a transference of subjectivity, or a creation of it ('They don't realize that you too are human')? The other half of the observation ('They say I've become a machine') is invoked in Ghatak's films, including *Ajantrik*, in relation to how the lens of the camera records panoramas, especially during crises, or during some apocalyptic intuition of joy. When Bimal begins to reconcile himself to the fact that the car has no future, the camera suddenly presents us with the range of the unexpectedly participatory landscape around Bimal, reminiscent of the way it behaved in *Meghe Dhaka Tara* when Nita cried out, '*Dada, ami kintu bachte cheye chhilam!*'[6]

Ghatak isn't instructing us, as Auden did, that the quotidian is essentially indifferent to, and outlasts, suffering; here, the quotidian is unnaturally alive to grief; it seems to be listening—another pathetic fallacy. But the machine, in this instance—the camera—is what's committing the fallacy, giving to the landscape a human sensitivity, while being complicit with, and inextricable from, the moment's brimming over with emotion; it's a witness, a creator, an actor, and one that's implicated, embarrassingly, in the longing for life.

When it comes to panoramas, Ghatak's lens is profligate in the possibilities it ascribes. The opening of *Titas Ekti Nadir Naam* comprises a remote aerial shot of a great delta; till we realize it's a close-up of a sandbank. Not only does this surprising view allegorize the literal ebb and flow of the narrative, the extinction and birth of communities and a river; it abnegates the eye for a vantage-point that belongs to the machine. In *Komal Gandhar*, as Rishi sings '*Akash bhara surja tara*', the camera keeps going in and out of focus as it reshapes the panorama of Kurseong, a device far more estranging than the tracking shots that mimic the movement of the body and the eye: first focusing on Rishi, then on the woods behind him, letting Rishi fade; later showing us another character, Shibu, against the backdrop of hills, then allowing him to evaporate while shifting focus to a waterfall behind, which shines like a molten thread. Unlike Ray's eye, or 'I', forever situated in the makeshift and commonplace, Ghatak's most dislocating transactions between technology and nature take place in vastness, and constitute his repeated, fitful attempts at the sublime.

Finally, the way in which Ray and Ghatak think of the child is intimately connected to the manner in which they perceive the natural on the one hand, and the mechanical on the other. Ray's child is organically whole, and, from the moment Apu opens his eye, an astonishing, magical, and transparent receptor of the universe. For Ghatak, though, the child is incomplete, and is in the process of *becoming human*; and, in this, it resembles Bimal's idea of the machine. Unsurprisingly, then, the child and the machine frequently converge in Ghatak's work; as in the marvellous scene in *Subarnarekha* in which the boy in the abandoned military outpost has been metamorphosed, as it were, into an aircraft, and is accompanied, on the soundtrack, by the engine's roar; or the tender sequence in *Komal Gandhar* in which a toddler pursues Supriya Choudhury, dragging a toy automobile by a string.

But remember, the difference between the organic and the mechanical is that the latter can be dismantled, and then even fused again. Thus, the cyborg (Arnold Schwarzenegger) in *Terminator*, sitting and repairing his own damaged arm; and Jaggadal, taken apart and sold in bits and pieces. The child, like the filmmaker, is more cyborg than human being: at the culmination of *Ajantrik*, he smiles and blows the abandoned horn, displaying to us how the imminent but not-quite human and the mechanical might be conjoined with one another.

2008

⋆ ⋆ ⋆

14

Nissim Ezekiel

Poet of a minor literature

It might be best to begin by explaining what I understand by the word 'minor'. The word is out of serious use, since the value-judgement implicit in the dichotomy, 'major' and 'minor', has long been out of favour, and awaits rehabilitation. Better, usually, to speak of 'minority', a term with political resonances that many can work with. And yet to approach the provenances of Nissim Ezekiel's work, we probably need to go back to those value-judgements and inquire into how they affected, and were even appropriated by, Ezekiel, and rewritten as a particular aesthetic.

How conventional literary history or criticism decides who is a major or a minor poet depends partly on subjective assessment and partly, as present-day wisdom would say, on culture-specific biases. But let's second-guess what the assumptions of 'being major' are. A major poet appears to be a practitioner who's crucially related to an epoch and to the zeitgeist, and our vocabulary formulates this relationship in a number of ways—that the major poet embodies the zeitgeist; that he or she actively contributes to shaping it; that he or she subverts or transgresses it; that the major poet occasionally remains unrecognized in the epoch they live in, and anticipates a zeitgeist that's to come. The minor poet performs none of these tasks; he's not to be confused with being a *bad* poet—instead, he's one who is, in a sense, solely an aesthetic or literary figure, a faithful, competent, even accomplished adherent of the literary rulebook of his age, a practitioner who's content to be a producer of good poems. The minor poet doesn't aim—it would seem—to question the literary (or the assumptions surrounding it in the time he lives in) or put it to test. As a result he doesn't engender an oeuvre but writes good poems—at most, her or his oeuvre might be an agglomeration of individual good poems. The minor poet's oeuvre is not—unlike the major poet's—a mini-tradition or a parody of a lineage, a competitor with or a version of literary history and tradition itself. The great poets in the English and American traditions explore a range of form and material as well as pursue unwieldy, risk-prone projects, like *The Prelude*, the *Cantos*, or *The Waste Land*, so that the oeuvre not only aims to be a sum of great works or comprise a significant legacy, but to mimic the shifts and unwieldiness of literary history. The excellent minor poets, like Housman, display no such hubris; they are remembered for individual offerings. These, at any rate, are some of the explicit or unspoken assumptions that underlie the distinction.

This is not to say that the minor poet might not embody an epoch. Conceivably, there are always going to be minor poets around when major poets are predominantly at work. But certain poets might also come into their own, or become productive, during a cusp—between one age of major practitioners and another. The exemplary group in relatively recent English literary history in this regard is the Georgians, including figures like Lascelles Abercombie, Rupert Brooke, G. K. Chesterton, Walter de la Mare, John Drinkwater, John Masefield—all contributors to the *Georgian Poetry* anthologies from 1912 and 1922, writing after the waning of the prominent Victorians and before the breakthroughs of modernism were properly recognized or absorbed. The Georgians epitomize—in fact, the name was shorthand in English literature for—'being minor'. Closer to our time, and still staying with the English, there is 'the Movement'. As with any grouping, certain figures were recruited into both these constellations that sooner or later broke away, or came to have an independent significance—like D. H. Lawrence, also a contributor to *Georgian Poetry*. Thom Gunn, similarly, was an escapee from the Movement. In fact, in the end, the Movement had very little to show except Philip Larkin; while the Georgians never had a poet of Larkin's significance in their group. If they did—like Isaac Rosenberg or Lawrence—those poets became far better-known for other reasons, events, and allegiances. Larkin is an exception, precisely because he's the one poet among the ones I've mentioned so far that openly and sustainably makes a case for 'being minor', turning it, subtly, into the *raison d'être* for an oeuvre. Studying him, we find how a poet who seems to self-consciously pursue a minor practice might come to articulate the zeitgeist in an age in which, apparently, ambition is suspect for specific political and aesthetic reasons.

Let's stay with Larkin for a while to deepen our contact with the importance and tone of the 'minor'. The poet-critic A. Alvarez, a champion of the poetry of extremity, of Sylvia Plath, and of the sub-mythopoeic poetry of Ted Hughes, made no secret of the fact that he thought Larkin circumscribed by his middle-Englishness, by being educated and 'less deceived': by inhabiting the median in every sense. Following the publication of his first book of verse, *The North Ship*, in 1945, Larkin positioned himself against romanticism and 'greatness' by excavating a minor tradition in English literature, by exchanging the music of W. B. Yeats, his first poetic mentor, for the 'tunefulness' of Thomas Hardy (a major novelist who was long held to be a good but minor poet): 'He's not a transcendental writer, he's not a Yeats, he's not an Eliot; his subjects are men, the life of men, time and the passing of time, love and the fading of love.'[1] By the close of his career, it was clear that the sort of fulfilment or 'happiness' that made Larkin uneasy was a 'happiness' jettisoning a humdrum (possibly Protestant) continuity in favour of absolute, epoch-changing rebellion and sex:

> When I see a couple of kids
> And guess he's fucking her and she's
> Taking pills or wearing a diaphragm,
> I know this is paradise
>
> Everyone old has dreamed of all their lives—
> Bonds and gestures pushed to one side
> Like an outdated combine harvester,
> And everyone young going down the long slide
>
> To happiness, endlessly. ('High Windows')[2]

Fulfilment, in keeping with Larkin's relationship to the zeitgeist, his attempts to fashion a poetry adequate to it, and his poker-faced revisionism, must have to do with a deliberate self-curbing, and an apparent sociability (the tension between the sociable and the unsociable, the humanistic and the misanthropic is constant in Larkin), as in this address to his friend Kingsley Amis's just-born daughter:

> May you be ordinary;
> Have, like other women,
> An average of talents:

Not ugly, not good-looking,
Nothing uncustomary
To pull you off your balance,
That, unworkable itself,
Stops all the rest from working.
In fact, may you be dull—
If that is what a skilled,
Vigilant, flexible,
Unemphasised, enthralled
Catching of happiness is called. ('Born Yesterday')[3]

Here, then, is a catalogue of characteristics for poetic diction in an age that's post-imperial, post-modernist (in the literal sense of following modernism), in a time of curtailed desire, rationing, and intelligent practicality before Margaret Thatcher would eventually transform Britain: 'skilled, / Vigilant, flexible, / Unemphasised, enthralled'. There is also the veiled rejection of modernism's hubris and aesthetic mode: '... unworkable itself, / Stops all the rest from working'.

Alvarez's anthology, *The New Poetry*, is a refutation, among other things, of the 'minor' as a poetic strategy in the aftermath of modernism—or, for that matter, of Empire and the Second World War. Auschwitz caused the idea of poetry to self-destruct; in response, Alvarez seems to want poets to self-destruct, either in a disciplined, ironic way, by rehearsing suicide (as Plath did), or by disappearing into nature (like Hughes), the subsequent transmutation paradoxically ensuring the continuance of poetry by making the poet iconic. Larkin's rebuttal of the 'major' begins with his decision not to die, to be obsessed with death but choose to live with boredom, to not travel, and situate himself neither in the metropolis nor in the countryside (in whose proximity Hughes lived in Hebden Bridge). Larkin locates himself, as a librarian, in Hull, a town neither important nor deprived, among the 'cut-price crowd' he describes in 'Here', not far from, but not too close to, 'unfenced existence, out of reach'.[4] His métier is boredom ('Life is first boredom, then fear...'[5]); not the cosmic boredom of Beckett, but a dogged, almost virtuous, cultivation of bourgeois dullness. Ezekiel's shrewd assertion in 'Background, Casually', 'My backward place is where I am',[6] could do equally for Larkin (who said in 1982 to an interviewer from the *Paris Review*: 'Hull is a place where I *have* stayed'[7]). Larkin's formulation, that Englishness is synonymous with the minor, and is cherishable precisely for this reason (see, for instance, 'The Whitsun Weddings', 'An Arundel Tomb', 'Going, Going', and 'MCMIV'), has had its activists, like Alan

Bennett and John Betjeman, and its historians, like E. M. Forster, who notes, in *Howards End*: 'Why has not England a great mythology? . . . It has stopped with the witches and the fairies'.

Larkin's manner is a deliberate low-level, petty cavilling against monstrosity, ambition, and foreignness—a cavilling, indeed, against modernism and the avant-garde which includes his hostility to 'the three P's', Ezra Pound, Charlie Parker, and Picasso, in the name of common sense, rationality, rationing, and a sort of decorum. Larkin's repeated attacks are made on behalf of the minor. They also entail a curious turn homewards: home, the familiar, the boring, and the minor are, in Larkin's reading, interchangeable—or should be. Confronting his origins on a train journey passing through Coventry, his birthplace, the speaker concludes the poem 'I Remember, I Remember' with an observation—'Nothing, like something, happens anywhere'[8]—that anticipates the stoic illumination upon which 'Background, Casually' ends.

*

I've discussed Larkin because he's almost an exact contemporary of Ezekiel's, who was born two years after Larkin, in 1924, but also because both poets emerge at a particular moment in literary history in which they have to grapple with and reshape, from within, the category of the minor. Larkin's first collection, *The North Ship*, hadn't come to terms with what it means to be a practitioner in an age succeeding modernism, but the title of his first mature collection, *The Less Deceived* (1955), announces the nature and tone of the new project. Ezekiel's first book, *A Time to Change* (1952), has a title that's quasi-revolutionary in its echo of Ecclesiastes 3:

> To every thing there is a season, and a time to every purpose under the heaven:
>
> A time to be born, and a time to die; a time to plant, and a time to pluck up that which is planted;
>
> A time to kill, and a time to heal; a time to break down, and a time to build up;
>
> A time to weep, and a time to laugh; a time to mourn, and a time to dance . . .

The title of Ezekiel's first book simply adds to the long list of antinomies: Ecclesiastes does not mention 'change', perhaps because it doesn't fit into its pairings—for what is the opposite of change but death? Five years after Independence, having returned to India after reading philosophy at Birkbeck College, London, Ezekiel knows change is at hand for those who, like him, fit in neither half of an antinomy—but change of what sort? He is, of course, also echoing T. S. Eliot's adaptation of Ecclesiastes 3 for the purposes of expressing, through the persona of J. Alfred Prufrock, the stirrings of belatedness, of being in the wrong place at the wrong time, of *not*, despite the repetition of the word, being on 'time': 'There will be time, there will be time / To prepare a face to meet the faces that you meet...'. Despite the assertive, quasi-revolutionary title, Ezekiel is closer to Prufrock's sense of having missed his calling—'Do I dare / Disturb the universe?' and 'I am no prophet—and here's no great matter: / I have seen the moment of my greatness flicker'. This is exactly the kind of tone Ezekiel will inhabit—comically self-questioning, urbane, seemingly underconfident, sly. To be minor is to be without a history; it is to possess, programmatically, a faux-seriousness and dignity that invites mockery:

> Politic, cautious, and meticulous;
> Full of high sentence, but a bit obtuse;
> At times, indeed, almost ridiculous—
> Almost, at times, the Fool. ('The Love Song of J. Alfred Prufrock'[9])

'Politic, cautious, and meticulous' could well be adjectives chosen by Ezekiel to define his distanced cultivation of a particular manner; but, in 'On Meeting a Pedant' (from *A Time to Change*), Ezekiel also alerts us to the fact that the 'politic' defence of cautiousness that will mark his work is also to be constantly challenged—in others and, secretly, in oneself: 'Words, looks, gestures, everything betrays / The unquiet mind, the emptiness within'. This leads to an invocation, in 'On Meeting a Pedant', of the social situation in *Prufrock*, reprised in the terms of 1950s Bombay:

> Give me touch of men and give me smell of
> Fornication, pregnancy and spices.
> But spare me words as cold as print, insidious
> Words, dressed in evening clothes for drawing rooms.[10]

To be minor is to be unsure, like Prufrock, whether the pedant is the person one meets at the party or oneself; it's to risk being too serious or not serious enough. The very means of survival and of singularity—being 'politic, cautious, and meticulous'—lead towards the 'ridiculous'. To be minor is to occupy yet another median, between serious and comic endeavour. It's to practise an irony of diction that's partly self-sabotaging.

★

Eliot's first major poem, *Prufrock*, is an enactment of what it means to 'be minor'. But Eliot, in the poem, as in his oeuvre, transcends minor writing by fashioning, and inventing, a relationship with European literary history—a relationship at once political and aesthetically productive, if often dubious. *Prufrock* gestures towards this project—which is Eliot's principal intellectual achievement—via the epigraph from Dante's *Divina Commedia*, situating London ('unreal city') both in purgatory and in the literary-theological European imagination. Part of Larkin's eschewal of the 'major' involves his rejection of what he contemptuously called the 'myth-kitty'.[11] But what kind of lineage, mythology, or precursor-text could Ezekiel have turned to as a route to composing major poetry? According to Arvind Krishna Mehrotra in his introduction to his anthology, *The Oxford India Anthology of Twelve Modern Indian Poets* (1992), 'The origins of modern Indian poetry in English go no further back than the poets in this anthology'[12]—Ezekiel being the oldest of, and the earliest to publish among, the poets he'd selected. Unless he chose to be a parody of a 'great' poet, either by invoking a utopian Indian past or by wishing to himself be a canonical 'English' poet (as Michael Madhusudan Dutt did before he turned to the Bengali language), it seemed that Ezekiel had no choice but to shrewdly embrace the minor. Of Ezekiel's location at the 'origins' of a tradition whose very existence was often in doubt, Mehrotra said:

> In the absence of a good literary history, it is difficult to say what sustained this heir to Sarojini Naidu's mellifluous drivel when he started out as a young poet in the mid-forties. The espousal of the self in his work is perhaps one consequence of the realization that he must create his own life-support system. There was nothing in the literature then, or even in the following decade, that could have sustained him.[13]

No 'myth-kitty', then, to fall back on. And, despite coming along consciously (thus, as Mehrotra says, the studied gesture of the title, *A Time to Change*) at the beginnings of a tradition, Ezekiel makes no attempt to present us with a creation-myth. For a creation-myth in English in India that's at once literary and political, we will have to wait for 1981 and *Midnight's Children*. For Rushdie to pull this off, he had to have recourse to arguably the most powerful mythology of Anglophone, independent India: the mythology of the nation. To be minor, for Ezekiel, is also to be politely distanced from the national.

There are important differences between what the 'minor' means to Larkin and to Ezekiel. But I suppose the significant difference has to do with Larkin positioning himself, self-consciously, as a minor poet within a major literature: this is what gives his work its peculiar distinction. Indeed, it isn't clear that *any* literature views itself as minor. There are literatures that are, for one reason or another (usually political ones) obscure; but few that see themselves as semi-legitimate and, as a result, congenitally minor. Even the more obscure literatures have their canon, their constellation of lesser and greater writers. Deleuze and Guattari recognize that the use of a second language—a language that one has, morally and politically, relatively little ownership of—constitutes a characteristic of a minor literature, and the example they provide us with is a Czech, Franz Kafka, using a language for his fiction, German, not by rights his.[14] Here, the idea of the minor overlaps with that of the political notion of minority, so that, for instance, in Deleuze's reading, Joyce's works should qualify as some of the greatest examples of a minor literature, especially the Joyce who, in *A Portrait of the Artist as a Young Man*, has Stephen Dedalus inwardly fulminate as he converses with an English priest: 'The language in which we are speaking is his before it is mine. How different are the words *home, ale, master*, on his lips and on mine!'[15] Yet there can't be much of a quarrel with the fact that Joyce—like Kafka—is primarily engaged in fashioning major works and a major oeuvre; those fictions may comprise instances of a 'minor literature', but Deleuze and Guattari don't argue with the fact that Kafka is a 'major' figure. It's only with Ezekiel that we find the convergence of a particular kind, a specific form, of creative opportunism, and an acknowledgement: that not only will minor writers generate a minor literature, but that a literature once recognized as minor can only be fully addressed and interpreted by a minor writer and by minor works.

★

What would have made Indian writing in English, at the moment at which Ezekiel embarked on his career as a published poet, 'minor'? Firstly, this 'tradition' or practice, which had been inaugurated in the early nineteenth century and then either gone underground or become incompatible with serious literary attention, stood at the crossroads of two 'major' lineages or ideas. The first of these was English literature, itself designed, of course, as a post-classicist pedagogy for the benefit of the colonies. Ezekiel would have considered this literature to be one of his principal inheritances, but would have known that the relationship of the 'Indian'—which was itself a relatively new category—to the language and the literature of the English was never a wholly legitimate one.

The other major idea that would have dwarfed the Indian poet in English in the 1950s and 1960s, when Ezekiel published his first four collections, would have been the idea of Indian literature, or literatures. One of the reasons that this lineage had become subterranean from the 1860s onwards had surely to do with the fact that some of its most dogged adherents and practitioners, from Kasiprasad Ghose to members of the Dutt family, lived in Calcutta, where, by 1861, a turn had taken place towards the mother-tongue: in this case, the Bengali language. This turn was enacted by a former Anglophone poet, Michael Madhusudan Dutt, in sonnets composed in the early 1860s in, and, sometimes, addressed to, the Bengali language. From being a failed English poet, Dutt went on to become the author of Bengali's first modern mock-epic. By the time Ezekiel began to write, it was a truism that 'major' literature must be culturally authentic, and that it was probably impossible to undertake major literary productions in another's tongue.

⋆

The difference between the 'major' and the 'minor' isn't that the former represents success and the latter tragic failure. In fact, the tragic note, the spectacle of the grand failure, is necessarily unavailable to the minor tradition and minor poet. The tragic failure captures the agonistic, Bloomian battles of the major literatures, causing the renewal or the creation of significant canons by greatly gifted and recalcitrant artists. So Dutt explores the tragic in two ways as a means of establishing the intensity of a major lineage and art: firstly, he writes a mock-epic based on the *Ramayana* in which he makes Meghnad, the son of Ravana (Rama's traditional adversary), the tragic, Miltonic protagonist. What we have in Dutt's mock-epic is an aestheticization of the struggle to create the 'major'. Secondly, Dutt leads a tragic life himself, and dies young. He is, as it were, consumed by the great lineage he helps create.

In the case of the minor poet writing in the minor tradition, there is no possibility of grand failure; there is only inconsequentiality and decorum. Even death must become an occasion for comedy; the only way to approach such themes, for the minor poet, is without afflatus, and with self-reflexivity, as Kasiprasad Ghose, one of the first Indian poets in English, does in 1830 in his 'To a Dead Crow'. (I should point out here that Ghose's poem and his work were brought to my attention years ago by Rosinka Chaudhuri.) Ghose deliberately argues for the crow as a peculiarly Indian bird, and its death becomes an occasion for elegy that must inevitably lapse, in the minor tradition, into the comic and the apologetic; the minor poet, then, must use platitude to fend off platitude, and throw light, at the same time, on the historical situation on which the 'minor' rests:

> Gay minstrel! ne'er had Death before
> Its dart destructive, sharpened more
> To pierce a gayer, mortal heart
> Than thine, which ah! hath felt the smart!
> Though life no more is warm in thee,
> Yet thou dost look as though't may be
> That life in thee is full and warm;
> Not cruel death could mar thy form;
> Thy features, one and all, possess
> Still, still their former ugliness.
> . . .
> Stretched at full length I lie like thee,
> On mother earth's cold lap, so ne'er
> To spin such verses out I'll dare.
> And please the public ear again
> With such discordant, silly strain.
> As thou didst once delight to pour
> At morn or noon, or evening hour.[16]

Compare, too, not just the death of protagonists in the major and the minor poem, but the death of the major poet to the minor one. Dutt dies of tuberculosis at the age of forty-nine in a way that at first seems wasteful, and later, in the sort of rereading the major tradition provides, appears exemplary and symbolic. On the other hand, the lives of Henry Vivian Louis Derozio, a predecessor of Dutt's who died when he was twenty-two, and Toru Dutt, who died when she was twenty-one, are seen to be abortive rather than tragic. Their deaths pose the question:

'Who knows what they would have written had they lived?' The great works were yet to happen. Their remarkable oeuvres lack the shape and the sense of culmination that's imparted by a major tradition even to those who die early. The question, 'Who knows what they would have written had they lived?' is a version of Mehrotra's speculation about Ezekiel's oeuvre: '[I]t is difficult to say what sustained this heir to Sarojini Naidu's mellifluous drivel when he started out as a young poet in the mid-forties'. It's a form of speculation pertinent to the practitioner within a minor literature, just as it is, in a slightly different formulation, to those who didn't survive long enough to produce their major work. Ezekiel lived till he was eighty years old. He died of Alzheimer's disease, thereby uniting himself again with the mysterious historical nullity ('There was nothing in the literature then') from which Mehrotra says he temporarily escaped. With the minor poet, it would seem there would be no clear explanation for the oeuvre that had occurred in the interim, between the absence of antecedents and the absence of memory. This, too, must not be confused with a tragic ending, for it is really a meandering, a drifting off.

★

No clear literary history precedes Ezekiel; but the self-reflexive gesture, to do with writing in the minor tradition, is sounded early on, and it recurs. More than one writer is fitfully aware of working in a space without forebears or history—or without readers, for that matter. There is Kasiprasad Ghose, in his poem to the dead crow, acknowledging the ontological absurdity of an Indian versifying in English: of producing a 'silly, discordant strain' (here, the elegist becomes one with his subject) that is a nuisance to the 'public ear'. There is Toru Dutt, who, at the conclusion of a narrative poem reminiscent of Christina Rossetti, 'Jogadhya Uma', apologizes on behalf of the triviality of the story, but also, in an energizing, self-conscious turn, on behalf of the provisional tradition she inhabits:

Absurd may be the tale I tell,
Ill-suited to the marching times,
I loved the lips from which it fell,
So let it stand among my rhymes.[17]

Mehrotra has alerted me to the title of a collection published by the poet Fredoon Kabraji in 1944—*A Minor Georgian's Swan Song*. There are fifty-one poems in the book, of which Kabraji says, in one of the short sections that make up the introduction:

> I have brought together in these pages a variety of poems forming a variety of experiments... The fact that the majority of the poems have been rejected during a number of years by a number of periodicals clearly establishes that they are 'unsuitable'—as judged by editors—for a large number of potential readers. Why then have I assembled, of deliberate intent, a small body of work that has found approval with a bigger body of work that has failed?
>
> I believe that this 'failure' by the same standards by which a few of my poems have been moderate 'successes' might be converted into the same moderate success if the work in these pages could be judged as a single contribution, in its entirety.[18]

It seems to me that the word 'Georgian'—combined tautologically with 'minor'—is being used not to periodize a body of work or to identify a lineage, but to suggest, figuratively, a twentieth-century Anglophone Indian's middle-class sense of being on the periphery. I say 'middle-class' because to be a 'Georgian', or to belong to a minor literature, is different from being a proponent of the low, the popular, and the folk (or even the postcolonial), wherein one would have been in a parodic or subversive relationship to 'high' culture; it is, in fact, to be outwardly timorous, seemingly unconfrontational, and at once 'politic, cautious, and obtuse'.

The desire to transcend individual 'moderate' (the word anticipates Ezekiel's strategic containing of ambition) successes by creating a body of work that constitutes a 'single contribution, in its entirety' is connected to a desire to temporarily abandon the impulse to compose single poems in favour of fashioning a literary history. This is possibly what Mehrotra is referring to when he says of Ezekiel: 'The espousal of the self in his work is perhaps one consequence of the realization that he must create his own life-support system.' The creation by the poet of his own 'life-support system' is akin to the nostalgia for the 'single contribution, in its entirety', a quasi-tradition brought into being perhaps by an intervention, a critical act of 'conversion'. Otherwise, the minor poet is doomed to a series of fresh starts, to writing, again and again, solitary Indian poems in English, the earlier poems never forming a 'background' to the current production, the oeuvre never tracing a 'development', the output remaining the sum total of individual 'successes' and 'failures'.

Ezekiel not only came to terms quite early in his career with what it meant to be writing at the crossroads of 'major' traditions: he decided to become a commentator on the minor, to constantly, through his poetry, illuminate its position and to declare its constraints. The position was a moral one: to fight against vanity, delusion, and excess, to commit oneself to a rationality and 'balance' that was a justification of the act of steering clear, deftly, of ambition:

> The image is created; try to change.
> Not to seek release but resolution,
> Not to hanker for a wide, god-like range
> Of thought, nor the matador's dexterity.
> I do not want the yogi's concentration,
> I do not want the perfect charity
> Of saints nor the tyrant's endless power.
> I want a human balance humanly
> Acquired, fruitful in the common hour. (A Poem of Dedication)[19]

This list of ideals that a minor poet who belongs to a minor literature—Indian writing in English—must *not* aim for appears in 'A Poem of Dedication', addressed to 'Elizabeth'—'This, Elizabeth, is my creation'—from *Sixty Poems* (1953). What exactly *is* Ezekiel's creation? It isn't clear. Can a desire for a 'human balance humanly / Acquired' be termed a creation—or is the 'creation' in question the catalogue itself: a guide to how *not* to create? Here, we see that Ezekiel's critical impulse—so important to subsequent generations of Indian English poets—is directly related to his self-appraisal and self-assessment to do with being a minor practitioner within a lineage that must, too, inevitably, be minor: an aesthetic of intelligent curtailment rather than explosive dissolution; a strategy, then, for low-key, long-term survival. The romantic or modernist epiphany or spot of time must be rejected ('not to seek release but resolution'); Renaissance auteurs like Tagore must be viewed with scepticism ('Not to hanker for a wide, god-like range'); so must any notion of a synthetic Indian heritage ('I do not want the yogi's concentration') and the hubris of being an acknowledged legislator ('the tyrant's endless power'). Not 'endless power', then, but power of a particular kind, which comes from knowing you must not ask for too much: for it is not your place to do so. In this way, Ezekiel begins to situate exactly the Indian poet in English, and also construct his or her biography.

Ezekiel's strongest account of the experience of the minor and of how one might inhabit its definition usefully as an Indian poet in English comes a decade later, in *The Unfinished Man* (again, a loaded self-definition), in the poem he called 'Enterprise'. The narrator who describes the sequence of events related to the 'enterprise' has been around from the beginning:

It started as a pilgrimage
Exalting minds and making all
The burdens light. The second stage
Explored but did not test the call.
The sun beat down to match our rage.[20]

The word 'pilgrimage' and the phrase 'exalting minds' might well refer to the ingenuous originary excitement of the Indian poet in English, to, for example, whatever it was that seized Ezekiel in 1948 and took him to London and to Birkbeck College to read philosophy, or would later drive Jussawalla to London and Oxford. Or it could be a way of mocking the faux romantic background of Indian writing in English, the 'mellifluous drivel' that Sarojini Naidu composed, Aurobindo Ghose's Miltonic long poem *Savitri*, all meant to 'exalt minds'. By the second stage, the group involved in the enterprise are in a less exalted location, somewhere where the 'sun beat down' (Ezekiel returned to Bombay in 1953). 'We stood it very well, I thought,' says the narrator of this second stage, 'Observed and put down copious notes / On things the peasants sold and bought'.[21] This phase, then, is not just to do with travel; it concerns being among the people of the land, the process of being re-assimilated. It's now that there's discord in the group, perhaps with the realization that assimilation is impossible; the group splinters:

We noticed nothing as we went,
A straggling crowd of little hope,
Ignoring what the thunder meant,
Deprived of common needs, like soap.[22]

The minor tradition in never entirely a finished tradition, in that its works seldom wholly cohere into a body: it is an agglomeration of works. Similarly, the poets of a minor literature always threaten to become dislodged from tradition and turn merely into individuals who write poems ('We noticed nothing as we went') rather than carriers of a history. The outcome of such an adventure is ambiguous:

When, finally, we reached the place,
We hardly knew why we were there.
The trip had darkened every face,
Our deeds were neither great nor rare.
Home is where we have to gather grace.[23]

It's unclear whether 'Our deeds were neither great nor rare' is an admission of failure or an utterance emerging from self-knowledge, and an awareness of limitations, which, in Ezekiel's writing, is seen to be a virtue: in the context of a minor tradition, the line has a double resonance. 'Home' is similarly ambiguous; 'away' might present the minor tradition with the possibility of excitement, but, in the end, it must be rejected on behalf of the familiar, which itself becomes an event: thus, Larkin of Coventry—'Nothing, like something, happens anywhere.'

Ezekiel's most explicit assertion after 'Enterprise' to do with being a practitioner of a minor literature comes five years later in the short poem 'Philosophy', which opens *The Exact Name* (1965). 'There is a place to which I often go,' says the speaker, 'Not by planning to, but by a flow / Away from all existence, to a cold / Lucidity . . . '.[24] 'Cold lucidity' recalls the hauteur of middle-period Yeats (the ambition of writing 'a poem as cold / And passionate as the dawn'[25]): the first half of the poem moves towards a dream of control, a 'final formula of light', and then it retracts and withdraws: 'I, too, reject that clarity of sight: / What cannot be explained, do not explain'.[26] Control and overview ('clarity of sight') are forfeited; inconsequentiality and the rejection of ambition are embraced deliberately in the final stanza, which states, in effect, that the principal vocation of the minor writer is not to be annihilated by the idea of the major—it is to seek survival:

The mundane language of the senses sings
Its own interpretations. Common things
Become, by virtue of their commonness,
An argument against the nakedness
That dies of cold to find the truth it brings.[27]

The word 'virtue' is important; its presence is neither simply idiomatic nor inadvertent—it's directly related to the minor poet's morality, his studied resistance to delusion, his persistent training in withdrawing from excess, or from the 'major'. The training, by the time this collection is published, is more in evidence than before: it expresses itself repeatedly. In 'Poet, Lover, Birdwatcher', a poem describing three types of pursuit of a desired object, we are told: 'The slow movement seems, somehow, to say much more.'[28] This, after another rebuttal of restiveness or ambition: 'To force the pace and never to be still / Is not the way of those who study birds / Or women. The best poets wait for words'.[29] In 'The Visitor', this training and self-discipline permit the speaker to set aside the mythic: 'Three times the crow has cawed / At the window', and this is at first taken to be a sign:

> All day I waited, as befits
> The folk belief that following
> The crow a visitor would come.
> An angel in disguise, perhaps,
> Or else temptation in unlikely shape...[30]

To belong to a minor tradition is to learn that one is often wrong about what is significant—'It was not like that at all', begins the next stanza—and that the minor poet is hardly ever privy to signs, prophecies, and portents: 'His hands were empty, his need: / Only to kill a little time'.[31] The minor poet's training, his or her self-discipline, transforms error and disappointment into a kind of knowledge: 'I see how wrong I was / Not to foresee precisely this: / ... The ordinariness of most events'.[32]

Ezekiel's poems continue, fundamentally, to be a record of a sort of education, a description of an unlearning which is also a form of learning, a relentless attempt to rectify wrongs—for the discipline of the poet of the minor literature involves a relentless reassessment of what one knows. Thus, in 'Lawn', written in 1965:

> My knowledge
> never looked
> beneath its nose
> to learn
> how lawns are made.
> I thought
> grass grows
> as Topsy grew.
>   Not so.[33]

The soil requires 'not only water / and the seed,' says the speaker, 'but patience at the root— / the gentle art / of leaving things alone'.[34] By now we have become familiar with this advice, its call for temperance, its distrust of signs and prognoses:

For weeks
this earth
is like a prophet
who will not give a sign.[35]

Not only the unlikelihood of a great outcome but the meagreness of output has been a problem for Indian poets in English (it wasn't one of Ezekiel's problems though). Or the lineage has had in its ranks poets who simply refuse to publish—like Arun Kolatkar, a prophet who often stubbornly gave no sign at all. Nevertheless, there's a 'stir of growth / an upward thrust / a transformation':

At last
a thin transparent green appears
and there you have the lawn.
  That is all.[36]

The two very short lines—'At last' and 'That is all'—remind us that epiphanies are unavailable within a minor literature; in lieu, you make do. Understanding this ('Not so') is key to Ezekiel's repeated invocation of his discipline, his continuing attempts to educate himself.

In 'Background, Casually' from *Hymns to Darkness* (1976), Ezekiel composed his most powerful statement about the types of education he'd had—as a Jewish boy of 'meagre bone' in a Roman Catholic school dominated by 'strong but undernourished' Hindu lads; reading Philosophy as a student in London; scrubbing decks on the ship as he returned to India; apprenticeship as a poet ('The later dreams were all of words'[37]); and, of course (here we move towards the minor poet's sense of what's moral), the recognition of error, and the consequent decision to reject a 'god-like range':

I did not know that word betray
But let the poems come, and lost
That grip on things the worldly prize.
I would not suffer that again.

I look about me now, and try
To formulate a plainer view:
The wise survive and serve—to play
The fool, to cash in on
The inner and the outer storms.[38]

'To play / the fool': this returns us to *Prufrock*, to the minor poet as comic player, the enjambment after 'play' instructing us that the role cannot be undertaken entirely seriously, or even without a kind of delight. 'The wise survive and serve': here are the two aims of the minor writer and his tradition—to not challenge, to not ask for independence or mastery, and thereby to continue to be able to write, to produce, to 'survive'. To know this is, in Ezekiel's lexicon, and in a manner that's informed much Indian poetry in English after him, to be 'wise'.

2016

* * *

15

The emergence of the everyday

Kipling, Tagore, and Indian regional writing

In 1857, eight years before Kipling was born, Indian soldiers in the north of the country rebelled against the representatives of the East India Company.[1] The uprising was known as the Sepoy Mutiny and, later, somewhat romantically, as the First War of Independence. Although its impact on the Indian and Anglo-Indian middle classes was probably not as immediate and direct as it has been made out to be in subsequent colonial and nationalist narratives, it brought to an end a period of cultural exchange between different races. The late eighteenth and the first half of the nineteenth century had seen the commercial and colonial expansion of the East India Company in Bengal and other parts of India, thanks to a series of military victories and not a few dishonourable transactions, but it was also a time of commingling, especially in Calcutta, between the new, post-feudal Indian middle class and members of the British scholarly and administrative classes. William Jones, whose researches at the Asiatic Society in Calcutta were largely responsible for inaugurating Orientalist scholarship and the reconstruction of Indian heritage, wore native clothes made of muslin in the heat—the sola hat and khaki uniform that Beerbohm has Kipling wear in one of his caricatures were not yet *de rigueur*. There are early portraits depicting Englishmen with their Indian wives, dressed in a mish-mash of Persian and Hindu styles. In the first half of the nineteenth century, the Hindu College saw teacher and student, Englishman, Indian, and Eurasian, engage in a colloquy at a crucial moment of modern history—people like the educationalist David Hare, the Anglo-Portuguese poet and teacher Henry Derozio, the Bengali poet Michael Madhusudan Dutt.[2] If Kipling had been born fifty years earlier, he might have hesitated before writing the cheerfully assonantal lines: 'O East is East, and West is West / And never the twain shall meet!'[3] It would have been equally difficult for the narrator of the story 'Beyond the Pale' to make his seemingly unequivocal statement without a residue of irony: 'A man should, whatever happens, keep to his own caste, race and breed.'[4]

In that time of commingling and displacement in India, a new literature in English was coming into place elsewhere, in America, which D. H. Lawrence, with the benefit of hindsight in 1923, in the middle of the glaring white heat of modernism, claimed was characterized by something he called 'spirit of place'. He had Fenimore Cooper, Poe, Melville, Hawthorne, and especially Whitman in mind, but he was thinking most pressingly of the first, Fenimore Cooper, when he said, 'We like to think of the old-fashioned American classics as children's books. Just childishness, on our part.'[5] About this putative 'spirit of place', Lawrence, after much invigorating scolding and hectoring, is largely vague: 'Every continent has its own great spirit of place. Every people is polarized in some particular locality, which is home, the homeland. Different places . . . have different vital effluence, different vibration, different chemical exhalation, different polarity with different stars: call it what you like. But the spirit of place is a great reality.'[6] For myself, what I find intriguing is the phrase 'polarized in some particular locality', for the use of those last two words, entailing a sudden and immense narrowing after the vastness of 'every continent'; also, the word 'polarized', which almost suggests that, in this new conception of place, people behave not like citizens at home, enfranchised, visible, but like members of a minority, concealed and engaged in creating together a microcosm. And that escape clause, 'call it what you like', is more eloquent than anything that's preceded it, as is the daring assertion made on the basis of no persuasive proof or evidence: 'But the spirit of place is a great reality.' It's as if Lawrence is acknowledging that place is beginning to be manufactured and made incontrovertible through utterance and incantation; that to bring a place into being, one first needs to say it exists. And, as a preamble to these claims, Lawrence asks a couple of questions that are pertinent to both Kipling and the Bengali writer in the second half of the nineteenth century: 'Let us look at this American artist first. How did he ever get to America, to start with? Why isn't he a European still, like his father before him?'[7] Similarly, the matter of why, say, Bankimchandra

Chatterjee or an English writer such as Kipling can't plausibly establish, in the moment they inhabit, anything but a fictitious or fictional continuity with their inherited identity or their ancestors, is crucial to a genealogy of the thing called 'place'.

★

With the Sepoy Mutiny in India, attitudes hardened, and the rule of the East India Company passed to the Crown. Psychological boundaries came into existence, to reinforce the physical ones—the 'White' and 'Black' town—that were already there. The social and racial structure of the India Kipling was born in and later returned to as a journalist was determined by the Mutiny and, later, by the defeat of the first version of the Ilbert Bill, which would have given Indian magistrates the right to try Englishmen. But by the time Kipling wrote *Kim* in 1900, he was dependent, in his vivid record, on the Mutiny having become an unthreatening, dreamlike memory.

★

During that period of commingling, well before the Mutiny, arrived a curious precursor and antidote to Kipling in Calcutta, Henry Meredith Parker—probably becoming a part of the city's intercultural world in 1824, and leaving it eighteen years later. During this time, besides working for the Bengal Civil Service and contributing to the *Calcutta Journal*, he wrote poetry, which he published in myriad ephemeral journals, magazines, and newspapers in the city—poems later collected in the oddly titled *Bole Ponjis* upon his return to England. Parker was a contemporary of the Orientalist scholars, whose work and researches would find their deepest, if seldom acknowledged, imaginative and intellectual response from Bengalis later in the nineteenth century. But he himself was a blithe anti-Orientalist—and here I use the word 'Orientalist' with the specific polemical meaning Edward Said gave it, as a person or act that exercises power over the Orient through representation, the 'exotic' being a particularly seductive and recurrent example of this construction. In this, Parker needs to be distinguished from Kipling, who, in effect, shrugs off and rebuffs not Orientalism in particular, but the Orientalist scholarship which formed his father John Lockwood Kipling's horizon; instead, the younger Kipling often seems to speak of the treasures of 'native' culture in the language of James Mill, calling the *Mahabharata* a 'monstrous midden'.

Parker's project was a different one, to replace the 'midden' of Indian antiquity with the 'scummy tank' of the present, and its contribution, through its impatience with the Orient, to our sense of place in writing about India, and about Calcutta specifically, is unprecedented. I discovered him through Rosinka Chaudhuri's researches into the archives of nineteenth-century Bengal, and I will quote from her essay, 'Young India: A Bengal Eclogue; Meat-Eating, Race and Reform in a Colonial Poem', in which Parker and his work figure prominently:

Writing from Calcutta in the early nineteenth century, eminent Anglo-Indian poet Henry Meredith Parker was provoked to sarcasm by the clamour of English critics for works produced in the East to exude an Indian air. Reacting to the comments of two English critics in the *Monthly Review* and the *Morning Herald*, who were demanding, respectively, "subjects entirely Indian, or at least Asiatic", and "[of] more . . . Eastern character", Parker wrote: "So the English critic complains that we are not Oriental enough, and your master begs that our lucubrations may henceforth be lighted by lamps filled with uttr; that we will compose in bowers of gul, growing green and thick under the shade of the tamarind and the pepul; that we will abstain from all food but kubaubs and pillaus; that our bread may be Bakhir Khana and our drink sherbet of rose apples, while we tinge the web of our story with all the henna and soormah of the East."[8]

Parker robustly disregards these requirements as well as the Orient itself. But, in his poem 'Chateaux en Espagne', he positions his narrator not only as one who's addicted to the notion of the Orient, but who's been long apprenticed to it in England:

As for myself, my fate was doomed,
  As soon as I could totter,
By tales of golden realms, perfumed
  With cinnamon tress and ottar:
And thus the sapling of my youth
  Was trained to point to India,
Where I'd an uncle, that's the truth,
  With Maha Rajah Scindiah.[9]

The poem itself takes its cue from 'Yarrow Unvisited', so that the wide-eyed protagonist arrives in the Orient, and finds, instead, Calcutta—not only a city, then, but modernity, in the sense that the modern is not mythopoeic, but urban, ungrandiose, and, indeed, disappointingly unmonumental. The narrator is devastated; but Parker, we sense, is addicted to the unlovely:

The Palace City which he sketch'd
Into vast splendor starting
Like one by Pirenini etch'd,
Or Babylonian Martin,
He finds half rubbish and half glare,
Whitewash, and green venetians,
Straw roofs, and orders which I swear
No Romans knew or Grecians.

Instead of fountains, scummy tanks
Emitting smells unsavoury;
For rich *Bazaars*, brick cells in ranks
Teeming with filth and knavery:
Mud huts in many a rotten row,
('Tis true those are the people's,)
But Asia's capital can show
Three brand new plaster'd steeples.[10]

Parker's narrator is mourning the unavailability of the mythic Orient; Parker is relishing taking it apart. Through the interstices of History and landmarks peer out 'scummy tanks' and the modern—real, though not natural and rational, as 'reality' is supposed to be, but strange, as reality and the everyday will be in this new conception of place, city, and neighbourhood. Parker made his position on this clear in his ferocious reply to what he called 'English critics' (as if he, like Lawrence's American settlers, had unexpectedly and inadvertently lost his cultural inheritance), and while doing so was being prescient, in his language and tone, of Walter Benjamin's genealogy of the 'modern' in relation to place and the city. Why is the flaneur 'the creation of Paris', Benjamin asks us in 'The Return of the Flaneur', and not Rome, despite the latter's various landmarks and monuments? Rome, he explains, is 'too full of temples, enclosed squares, and national shrines to be able to enter undivided into the dreams of the passer-by'.[11] He goes on to passionately describe an aesthetic that may have well germinated in the early nineteenth century in people like Parker, and their discomfited suspicion of the 'Orient':

The great reminiscences, the historical *frissons*—these are all so much junk to the *flaneur*, who is happy to leave them to the tourist. And he would be happy to trade all his knowledge of artists' quarters, birthplaces, and princely palaces for the scent of a single weathered threshold or the touch of a single tile—that which any old dog carries away.[12]

In a crucial sense, Benjamin's aesthetic of modernity—'that which any old dog carries away'—is a critique of the European Renaissance, with its grand vistas, monuments, historicism, and, in its oil paintings, its masterful hyper-realism. Benjamin situates the modern city, Paris, not as a successor of but counter to Rome, or to History or the Renaissance. (This was a radical move, going as it would have against Paris's official self-image.) Parker's rebuttal of the 'Indian air' or the Orient is reminiscent of the texture of this positioning; and it also suggests to us that the Orient, with its palaces and kingdoms, is at once the Renaissance's Other as well as one of the primary articles fashioned in its forge. The modes of representation that mastered and produced one kind of reality at the heart of the Renaissance—the array of still life, religious scenes, and the human figure—found its extension and further outcome in producing reality of another kind where the construction of the Orient was concerned. The Orient, if not the Renaissance's twin, is at least its progeny. Parker, in his poems, presages, unwittingly, the fact that the 'other' Renaissance, in Calcutta, would constitute, in its way—inasmuch as it would be located in the quotidian, the wayward, the indefinite, and premised on the exchanging of 'princely palaces' for the 'weathered threshold', of setting aside an idea of the 'East' for the here and now—an eccentric critique of that earlier, better-known Renaissance.

★

The defeat of the Ilbert Bill in 1883 increased the distance between the Indians and their rulers. As Harry Ricketts points out in his biography, *The Unforgiving Minute*, Kipling was, at the time, a very young journalist on the *Civil and Military Gazette* at Lahore. The newspaper was 'strongly against the Ilbert Bill', as most Englishmen were, but was pressured by its 'larger sister-paper, the *Pioneer*', to make more supportive noises. 'One evening after work,' according to Ricketts, 'Rud walked into the Punjab Club in Lahore to find himself "hissed" by all the other members, because that day's *CMG* carried a leader... voicing... approval of the bill.'[13] Kipling describes the scene in *Something of Myself*: rather than making him recoil, the 'hissing' leads him to 'see a great light', and come round, fully, to the point of view of the Bill's opponents. Ricketts explains this capitulation by pointing out that Kipling was, as he would be all his life, an outsider who 'desperately wanted to fit in'; and not a little of his racist posture stems from that desperation.

As the gap between 'native' and European worlds widened, crossing the boundaries had, for Kipling, an air of illegality about it, as, indeed, had the act of writing itself. Kipling's prose was erotic in its texture and effects, in its elisions and momentary absorption in small shocks of pleasure. He would always have to reconcile his devotion to the artistic, with its fluid, feminine, even 'Eastern' associations, with the grandiose overview of Empire. In *A Passage to India* Forster points out that the furthest Ronnie Heaslop, the City Magistrate in Chandrapore, was prepared to go in the direction of Art was to sing the national anthem—and Kipling was always prepared to launch into the national anthem as a counterpoint to the subtler melody of his prose. Writing became for him a matter of subterfuge and concealment: a nocturnal activity, distinct from the preoccupations of his daytime world. It would lead to the ulcer that tormented and, eventually, killed him, as if his more vituperative side had turned on him. Like his writing, his forays into the 'native' city were also largely undertaken at night. Of one excursion into Lahore, he observed:

> It was impossible to sit still in the dark, empty, echoing house and watch the *punkah* beat the dead air. So, at ten o'clock of the night, I set my walking-stick on end in the middle of the garden, and waited to see how it would fall. It pointed directly down the moonlit road that leads to the City of Dreadful Night.[14]

The ideas of poetic inspiration producing a physical restiveness that can be allayed only by perambulation and that of the illicit transgression of a boundary are conflated here. The native world, which is not quite possessed of legitimacy under the Crown, is perceived in fragments: 'There was a sharp clink of glass bracelets; a woman's arm showed for an instant above the parapet, twined itself around the neat little neck, and the child was dragged back, protesting, to the shelter of the bedstead.'[15] The word 'instant' links Kipling to the Modernist enterprise (Ricketts points out, as others have, that in his ellipses and his exploration of the shifts of narrative voice, Kipling is a precursor of the Modernists), to Joyce's 'epiphany' and Woolf's fleeting 'moment' of heightened perception and 'being'. But Kipling's 'instant' is also situated in colonial history, for, in the latter half of the nineteenth century, the subcontinent, for the resident colonial, was unweighted by history—it had become, at least in one sense, insubstantial. Whatever complexities of dialogue had existed in the early years of the colonial encounter, as the different races delved into each other's cultures, had largely vanished; the land, to the white man, had become the backdrop for a series of random perceptions, 'sights, smells and sounds', vivid but indirect, without substance or context, but, occasionally, oddly beautiful and compelling. It is this India, mysterious not because it withholds its secrets, but because the colonial enterprise demands that it withhold them, that constitutes Kipling's sound-inflected landscape.

What, then, was the principal secret? It was, first of all, the formation of modern India itself: of a hybrid but nationalistic middle class, created by history and the colonial encounter, and to which both the Indian intelligentsia and its administrative, clerical cadre belonged. From this class would emerge writers, social reformers, professionals, and, later, politicians like Nehru and Bose and Gandhi. Kipling, in fact, was born in 1865 during the first efflorescence of the Bengal, or Indian, Renaissance. Michael Madhusudan Dutt, after years of attempting to become a canonical 'English' poet, published in 1861 his epic, *Meghnadbadakabya*, a revisionist work based on an episode in the *Ramayan*, reworked through the lens of *Paradise Lost*, thereby bringing into existence modern Bengali and, in effect, Indian literature. In the year that Kipling was born, Bankimchandra Chatterjee, a magistrate who had already written one of the first Indian novels in English, *Rajmohan's Wife*, wrote the first significant modern Bengali, and Indian, novel, *Durgeshnandini*. These writers, and others, were, to paraphrase what Pound once wishfully said about Tagore, singing India into existence. The Bengal Renaissance, by obsessively reconfiguring the Western and the local, seemed to be providing, for Indians, a reinterpretation of what it meant to be Indian. What did this mean, and how was it achieved? Partly by making use of a resource and inheritance that was at once immemorially Indian and the invention of Orientalist scholars—the Sanskrit archive; Kalidasa; the *Upanishads, Vedas*, and the *Gita*—and partly by using this ancient resource and the fact of modernity to situate the Indian and his or her literature decisively outside of the 'Orient', as described irritably by Parker in his riposte to the 'English critics', to attempt to take the culture that was coming into existence out of the emanation called the East, and rethink its relationship to contemporaneity, to the West, and to the past. In this extrication of culture and literature and literary practice from the realm of abstraction, such as the East and the Orient represented, an idea of place, of region, was being articulated implicitly—and, by the twentieth century, it had become an explicit concern in Bengali writers like Bibhutibhushan, Tarashankar, and Manik Bandopadhyay, all writers of particular terrains. The task of creating a modern literature was not so much the task of creating national identity but of staking out place, region, and territory—and its context was the fact that the 'high' literatures of Bengal and other parts of India were being formulated in the time of the modern, contributing to and in transaction with the traits and quirks of an incipient but unmistakable modernism, quirks such as the antipathy to the overarching and the general, and a militant support for the particular. These would flow into the peculiarity of the Indian canon in modernity—that it comprised literatures in regional languages; that it would leave the task of the overarching narrative to English, to the lost worlds of Sanskrit and Persian, and to the 'East' and the 'Orient'. The idea of Bengali literature, for instance, uses the notion of contemporary literary practice as a subterranean argument against categories like both 'Indian' and 'Eastern', and places itself somewhere that's provisional, workaday, transient, and not even properly articulated: in Bengal, in place, in 'region' itself. So, in 1870, five years after writing his first great Bengali novel, *Durgeshnandini*, Bankimchandra Chatterjee, in his essay in English, 'A Popular Literature for Bengal', begins by explaining:

By a popular literature for Bengal I mean a Bengali literature. Bengali literature must for a long time to come be nothing more than merely the popular literature of Bengal. As long as the higher education continues to have English for its medium, as long as English literature and English science continue to maintain their present immeasurable superiority, these will form *the* sources of intellectual cultivation to the more educated classes. To Bengali literature must continue to be assigned the subordinate function of being the literature for the *people* of Bengal, and it is as yet hardly capable of occupying that subordinate, but extremely important, position.[16]

This is not, I think, a romantic *Lyrical Ballads*-type declaration, despite the emphatic reference to the 'people'. It's a description of the function of language and writing in modernity, as a concealed, makeshift, ongoing task, located in the specific—in detail and in place—leaving the overarching and the generalized project to either a 'high' or official version of itself, or to a 'high' antecedent tongue, or to a resource of 'immeasurable superiority', such as 'English literature and English science'. The 'subordinate task' is the task of the modern writer, working, whether they're writing in English, American, French, Urdu, or Bengali, at fashioning a vernacular—by which I mean not some magical postcolonial orality, but a realm of writing such as Barthes meant, containing unmistakable signs of its writerliness. When it comes to the writing of a region such as, say, early twentieth-century Bengal, that literature carries marks not of the characteristic identity of that region, but of a distinct imaginative and poetic signature. This peculiar signature, and not regional identity, was what Bankimchandra and others opened up Bengali literature to. That's not to say that there was no nostalgia, in Bankimchandra, for what he describes, in the same essay, as 'the singular harmony of character' between the 'popular culture of a nation and a national character', a 'harmony', he claims, which was in evidence in Bengal in the 'days of Vidyapati and Jayadeva'[17]—in other words, the unsullied, golden period between the twelfth and sixteenth centuries. Afterwards, apparently, 'the Bengali stood crushed and spiritless'; until, in the late nineteenth century, a different kind of moment presented itself, and the modern could begin to perform that 'subordinate function', that ambiguous task, of fashioning a literature that was specifically, narrowly, located. Of course, Bankimchandra knew very well that Bengali itself had its own Sanskritic, official, and 'immeasurably superior' registers: but the peculiar crucible of the regional in which modernity was largely fashioned in India meant that it would always be busy in its subterranean capacity, and partly at odds with the larger narrative. This being-at-odds, this resistance, would soon become a characteristic of Bengali 'high' culture itself. The modern Indian languages are often called, even today, the 'vernaculars', and they inhabit a paradox: of seeming to be authentic and ancient, of being in a position of power because they're supposed to be truly 'Indian', while being relatively new-minted, playful, and provisional, and curiously empowered and liberated by never being able to encompass 'India' in its entirety. They—like region itself—are where the local resides, as do, also (and unsurprisingly), all sorts of international and cosmopolitan preoccupations. The definition of the 'regional' in India, however, is entirely constitutional and state-related, and refers to the federal structures that arose in independent India after the passing away of the old Presidencies and the even older *rajyas* and kingdoms; it doesn't take into account these inconsistencies, paradoxes, and this deceptive doubleness. The vernaculars—the languages and literatures of these regions—have seemed to keep the outside out, while, more than any official tongue, and unburdened by the chore of national representation, they've always been letting the outside in. In performing their 'subordinate function', in being 'high' cultural and secretive at once, they've echoed, in their way, many of the avant-garde projects of Europe and America in modernity.

★

Tagore himself was born four years before Kipling; and if Kipling made a dazzlingly precocious debut with *Plain Tales from the Hills*, Tagore's first book of poems, *Prabhat Sangeet* ('Morning Songs'), published even more precociously when he was sixteen, made no less unsettling an impact. Decades later, well after winning the Nobel Prize and witnessing the decline of his literary reputation accompany his incremental celebrity in the West, Tagore had said to E. J. Thompson in 1921: 'My original vocation was as a mere Bengali poet. I know I am misrepresenting myself as a poet to western readers. Now I am becoming frightened of its enormity and am willing to make a confession of my misdeeds.'[18] The impact of that first book of poems had been unsettling because critics in Calcutta had quickly realized that the young Tagore was taking the Bengali poem and Bengali literature, neither by any means a readymade given, towards a practice that was unprecedented and unfamiliar. But, where the international public was concerned, Tagore situated himself in the 'East', the crime for which, in 1921, he sought absolution from Thompson. Tagore's 'Bengal'—his actual locus as a writer—was a specific place, but not in the sense the English mining town was for the early D. H. Lawrence, or the Parisian suburb was for Colette, or Jackson or New Orleans for Eudora Welty, or, for that matter, what Calcutta would be for Buddhadeva Bose or the remembered landscape of undivided North East Bengal for Jibanananda Das. For Tagore, 'Bengal' was more an archive and project, akin to, and far exceeding, what Wales was for David Jones or Northumberland for Basil Bunting—a place that was local, with an organic folk and rural vivaciousness, upon which converged the Sanskritic legacy and metre of Kalidasa, the musical systems of Indian antiquity, Scottish and Irish melodies, the European sense of the individual, anti-colonial exacerbation, and an unprecedented, very modern phenomenology of space and time, of nothingness. Nowhere is this 'Bengal' more explicit as a project than in the letters he wrote to his niece Indira Devi from 1887 to 1895, when he was travelling up the river in a houseboat through his estates in Shilaidaha, desultorily performing his duties as a landlord, and composing the letters as a sort of notebook or journal in which the everyday becomes a resilient, palpable presence, and both the intellectual and the eternal constant intrusions into consciousness. At around this time, he also begins to write his first great stories, based on this long excursion into a place he owns, and where he's also strangely homeless and adrift. 'The Postmaster', about a young Calcutta man transferred to a village, bored by nature and beauty and uncannily desirous to be reunited with concrete, but reluctantly, if superficially, drawn to the young village girl who works for him, was published in 1893—not so much later, then, than the appearance of Kipling's first astonishing collection.

When Kipling published his stories, however, they were treated as if they were almost unique in having contemporary India as their subject, and this notion persists, quite commonly, in Britain and America. Indeed, no one reading Kipling would suspect that Tagore and Bankimchandra Chatterjee might be living in the same world as Kim, Mehboob Khan, Shere Khan, and Mowgli. So profound was the effect of British colonial policy on post-Mutiny India, so fiercely was the division between the races enforced, that it is still difficult to reconcile the neighbouring worlds of modern, Renaissance India and Kipling's fiction. If there's a lacuna that sometimes persists in our view of that crowded universe which Kipling engendered, it's the one that inadvertently endures from the politics of late nineteenth-century Empire: the absence of modern India, with what would later be called its regional literatures and languages, such as Bengali, Tamil, and Urdu, an India in which Kipling was situated, and which he (unlike, say, Parker from an earlier period) did his best to ignore, and which nevertheless left its imprint on his writing. Not that I advocate a clearer view of these neighbouring worlds, or places, or regions, for a comparative purpose; or in order to increase or swell our knowledge of modernity. Quoting Goethe in a letter written on the houseboat in a city-shunning mood, Tagore exclaimed: 'I want more light, more space!'[19] In other words, it's always possible to long for a greater amount of nothingness—this is curiously in keeping with Tagore's phenomenology—but, on the other hand, perhaps it's hard to increase what we think we already know. My purpose in laying out the configuration I have is simply to understand better what we believe we know already.

★

What is meant by 'regional'? In this context—Kipling on the one hand, India on the other—the word must possess a double, possibly conflicted, significance. I've already mentioned Eudora Welty, and I have partly in mind the way the word 'regional' might be used to describe writing about certain principalities, such as the American South, but also to approximate a particular temperament in a writer—say, William Carlos Williams, and his Indian disciple, Arun Kolatkar. And I'm thinking, among others, of the three great Banerjees of the early to mid-twentieth century, Bibhutibhushan, Tarashankar, and Manik, who all make an imaginative symbol of their territories. But I'm also using the term more loosely, as a counter to the notion that writing about place is either subsumed under the category of the nation, or, alternatively, expresses local identity. My understanding of the regional is idiosyncratic and specific, and is counter to both nationalism and community: for me, it represents a very specific approach to the unfamiliar.

In India, 'regional', as I've pointed out, has a certain kind of political and cultural definition, encompassing interests that are distinct from the nation's, as well as possessing a sort of authenticity that, say, a foreign or colonial tongue such as English doesn't. To my knowledge, the 'regional' isn't discussed in India, even by its major writers, in conjunction with what it has actually been inextricable from in that country—the modern, the modernist, the avant-garde, a particular intimation of the strange. The perceived defeat of the regional literatures by Indian writing in English after globalization is seen, depending on which side you come from, either as a defeat of 'authentic' India, or the coming into its own, with *Midnight's Children*, of the postcolonial nation—but not connected, as it might be, to the retreat of avant-gardes and modernisms everywhere. The 'regional', despite the evidence of oeuvres, canons, and individual works, is hardly ever seen in India for what it has often been—an elite, 'high', counter-cultural project, imperiously overturning the conventions of nationalism and identity. In fact, even acute commentators such Dipesh Chakrabarty must see the 'regional' within that old context of nationalism, or as a variety of sub-nationalism. Chakrabarty, indeed, compares the historians Niharranjan Ray and Dinesh Chandra Sen's passionate apostrophes to Bengal and its landscape to the poet Jibanananda Das's great sonnet-sequence, *Rupasi Bangla* (*Bengal the Beautiful*), as expressions of 'romantic nationalism'. In further support of this position regarding Das's mysterious, incantatory sonnets, Chakrabarty cites the fact that soldiers involved in the war of liberation that created Bangladesh in 1971 were constantly reading, and deriving sustenance from, those poems. No mention is made of the fact that the particular apotheosis of place that Das's poems represent involves a constant, repetitive opening up to the foreign and the strange. Das uses 'Bengal' or 'Bangla' in that magical way, as an occasion for conjuring up a world, as well as opening it up to the faraway. Besides expressing a disarmingly straightforward desire for the homeland, Das's sonnets contain an experience that the soldier facing extinction might also be susceptible to: of being simultaneously at home and in a fundamentally strange place—the world.

There's no way of comprehending the impact 'place' and 'region' have on us without taking into account their constant teetering towards the foreign. This paradox is the paradox of modernity, and modernism. And the inversions between the natural or native and the strange or faraway that the 'regional' depends upon is referred to constantly by Kipling, in throwaway remarks such as, 'England is the most marvellous of foreign countries I've ever been in',[20] or suggested by the disorienting English pidgin and the peculiar insight he gives to his soldiers in the story, 'On Greenhow Hill', where, fighting the Aurangabadis on the lower slopes of the Himalayas, Pvt. Learoyd watches 'the bare sub-Himalayan spur that reminded him of his Yorkshire moors'.[21] Speaking 'more to himself than his fellows', Learoyd observes that 'Ay... Rumbolds Moor stands up ower Skipton town, an' Greenhow Hill stands up ower Pately Brig. I reckon you've never heard tell o' Greenhow Hill, but yon bit o' bare stuff if there was nobbut a white road windin' is like ut; strangely like.'[22] The category of 'strangely like' is what creates the contours of the regional and the modern; it is not merely comparative, but a moment of unsettlement, and would work without the element that the scene is compared to being revealed to us—in the metaphor of place or region, the tenor would still be lit up without the vehicle. After all, as Learoyd admits to his friends, 'I reckon you've never heard tell o' Greenhow Hill'.[23] 'Strangely like' is maybe what those other soldiers, the Bangladeshi liberation fighters, encountered in Das's sonnets, without necessarily *knowing* what the 'Bengal' in them was 'strangely like'. The 'regional' is neither about unambiguous love and affiliation nor about a complete memory of one's past; it is an intimation of the unlike.

This intimation nudges, all the time, Welty's Jackson and New Orleans, as it did, before her, Bibhutibhushan Banerjee's Nischindipur, and, even further back, it did *Plain Tales from the Hills*. Welty is always encountering the unfamiliar, the foreign, within the boundaries and parameters of the known; as, in a more histrionic way, is Flannery O'Connor, not only with her courting of the extreme and peculiar, but in her upkeep of peacocks. The American South, in the work of these writers, is not just a record of itself, but of the faraway and bizarre it's oddly reminiscent of. That faraway, usually, is never as baldly articulated as Learoyd articulates it to his companions. But the intimation of the 'strangely like', or the unlike, causes to crumble that dichotomy that separates 'regional' from 'migrant' literature, Welty from Jean Rhys. In her first novel, *Voyage in the Dark*, Rhys's West Indian narrator describes her rented London room with the intimacy and desperation of one for whom the room and boarding-house is as much personal terrain as Jackson, Mississippi is to Welty. But Rhys brings to the writing also the silent, observant attention that a new, foreign place provokes, the very quality of foreignness that also excites Welty—for the latter's characters have seldom been far; remoteness defines where they already live. In this way, the 'regional' and 'migrant' often become each other, in a flow and convergence that finds its precursors both in Kipling and in the young letter-writing Tagore, discovering his estates in solitude on his houseboat.

*

One might make a related claim about the regional which is appropriate to my context here: that it derives some of its energy and creative character through elision. The 'regional' pertains to a world that's secret and concealed; but it's also a sort of imagination that conceals and elides. With Kipling, the elision that gives his region, his microcosm—I hesitate to call it something as banal as 'his India'—its particular texture is his erasure of modernity, especially the modern Indian, who is either absent, or available for vivid satire, as Hurree Chunder Mookerjee in *Kim*, or is mutilated and put to death, as is the Bengali member of the Indian Civil Service in the grotesquely eponymous story, 'The Head of the District'. But the satire, even when it rewrites history to suit Kipling's purposes and prejudices, is deeply observant and telling; perhaps more revealing than a liberal affinity would have been. And though the contemporary Indian is largely missing in them, in the best of his fictions Kipling lets in through the back door what he seems to keep out of his busy but timeless narratives—the modern, the historical, the contingent. For instance, for the English family in 'Rikki-Tikki-Tavi', the India of snakes, mongooses, and tailor-birds is a fabulous and dangerous place, a world in which to keep handy both the pen (for there's much to write about and report on) and the gun (for one must rule and protect one's domain). For the narrator, the actual scene of action and narration seems to be where the animals are, which is a kind of India special to Kipling, where English notions of valour and honesty and the English suspicion of the sly Oriental are enmeshed with the garrulous, wise, and foolish animals of the Indian fables, of the spiritual tales of the *Jatakas*, and the armies of devotee-animals in the *Ramayana*—resources that Kipling either didn't mention openly, or distanced himself from. These elisions and insertions are inseparable from the story's enchantment. Then, there's the world of modernity itself, as glimpsed by the mongoose Rikki-Tikki: it's where, like a migrant, he resolves to make his place of domicile:

> 'There are more things to find out about in this house,' he said to himself, 'than all my family could find out in all their lives. I shall certainly stay and find out.'
>
> He spent all that day roaming over the house. He nearly drowned himself in the bath-tubs, put his nose into the ink on a writing-table, and burnt it on the end of the big man's cigar, for he climbed up in the big man's lap to see how writing was done.[24]

Kipling introduces a Shklovsky-like 'defamiliarization' in the story, peculiar to animal actors, in order to explore the comedy of scale—so that the slightly banal world of colonial modernity, with its bathtubs and cigars, begins to look gigantic and immense, indeed mythic, without losing any of its ordinariness and tactility, and the mythic world of the *Jatakas*, with its talking creatures, tiny enough to drown or hide in the modern. This inversion, one suspects, had still not occurred for John Lockwood Kipling, or for the Curator in the *Jadughar* in *Kim*, and in their view of the place of myth and legend in the Orient and their own relationship to it. Modernity, Rikki-Tikki finds, is hospitable and indecipherable: and, despite the very intellectualized, nationalistic approach to the colonial legacy that agitates the surface of Kipling's consciousness, we can see, from the figure of the mongoose, that the pleasure he takes in the features of colonial modernity is physical, and has mostly to do with touch and sensation: the mongoose is all body. The action shifts constantly from inside to outside, from interior to crevasse to garden, as the war between the snake and the mongoose is rapidly recounted, so that we're not sure where the setting is—just as Parker wasn't quite certain, upon arrival, if Calcutta was a 'city of palaces', the Oriental city itself, or just a 'scummy tank'. Parker's 'scummy tank' in Kipling's story is the bathtub, where a crucial episode in the action unfolds: 'Then he was battered to and fro as a rat is shaken by a dog... his eyes were red, and he held on as the body cart-whipped over the floor, upsetting the tin dipper and the soap-dish and the flesh-brush, and banged against the tin side of the bath.' Despite the decisive closure at the end of the story, where, after the mongoose's victory, we're assured that 'never a cobra dared show its head inside the walls', the consequence of these battles, with their agile evasions, ferocious lunges, and swift disappearances, is that we're left undecided as to what's being left out and what let in. That mixture of elision and truthfulness indefatigably at work here, where the foreign and unlike are at once being given a home (as in Rikki-Tikki's and the English family's cases), opposed (where the cobra is concerned), and surreptitiously engaged with, is also what defines a particular notion of the 'regional'.

★

The matter of elision, when it comes to the modern regional literatures of India that are contemporary with Kipling and also survive him into the present, is a two-way traffic. Kipling and other colonial writers by and large confer invisibility upon the modern in India; and, in the regional canons in question, the modern in India largely confers invisibility upon the colonizer. It's one way of creating a region that runs counter to the stream of nation and history while participating angularly in both; of engendering the inner weather and excitement, the strangeness, with which the very ordinariness and the everyday in these writings are marked. In that early story by Tagore, 'The Postmaster', the figure of the Englishman appears in the third sentence, 'There was an indigo planter's home nearby, and the sahib had made every effort to get a post office established in its environs',[25] and then vanishes forever. Exactly eighty years after that story was written, Shiva Naipaul published a novel, *The Chip-Chip Gatherers*, about a very different part of the world, Trinidad; in the novel, colonial history and strangeness are all-pervasive, but the colonial himself is mentioned only once. The young Wilbert Ramsaran is visiting his father's estates with the caretaker, a relative, and discovers there a failed idyll, a kind of parody of Tagore's Shelidah, and the antithesis of the populated, buzzing world of the *Jungle Book*: 'At the back they found the ruins of outhouses: the stables and servants' quarters, dank, dark cells with the subterranean atmosphere of caves and carpeted with velvet moss.'[26] This is neither the Orient nor even the New World that Parker's English critics might have envisioned; it's something different. The sort of figure that touched and shaped this history definitively is mentioned explicitly only once: ' "Who used to live here, Singh?" "Some Scotsman or the other. He used to own not only your father estate but nearly all the land you see around here." '[27] In brushing aside that figure, Shiva Naipaul is continuing in a deliberate imaginative tradition embarked upon by the Indian regional literatures, and perhaps by 'regional' writing elsewhere. The act of elision is what gives this body of writing its particular magic and unexpected freedom, its air of play: the condition of invisibility is crucial to the artist pursuing his or her idiosyncratic project, but so is the act of bestowing invisibility. One feels this while reading Tagore, his contemporaries, and his successors; that we're witnessing a form of play which Sartre hinted at when he noted that the French may have been most free during Nazi occupation, and when, in an earlier age, Tolstoy observed: 'Freedom consists in my not having made the laws.' In lieu of making the laws, it was possible to make a world, or simply to recognize the laws without acknowledging the lawmaker. This agreement to both notice and ignore generates a momentum that also impels Kipling's stories, and contributes to their restless, transmuting playfulness. In Bengali, the play translates often into an unlikely situational comedy, when the invisible is being made visible fleetingly. In 'Blue Star', the great humorist Parusuram's short story about Sherlock Holmes's visit to Calcutta, the event is contextualized simultaneously in colonialism and in Bengali literary history: 'I am talking about a time sixty years behind us, during the reign of Queen Victoria. In those days Calcutta did not have electric lights, motor cars, radios or loud-speakers;

aeroplanes did not fly in the sky; Tagore was not yet famous; and Hemchandra was called the best poet.'[28] There's the disorienting instant when what's been both taken for granted and left unaddressed in Bengali fiction—what Bankimchandra termed the 'immeasurably superior' English—appear to the narrator's eye in the incarnation of Holmes and Watson: 'One of the Europeans was tall and thin, clean-shaven, the cheeks a little sunken, his receding hairline making his forehead look bigger than what it was. The other man was of medium build, neither fat nor thin, had a moustache and limped a little.'[29] The protagonist, Rakhal, confesses to the two visitors that he's unable to procure copies of *Strand* magazine, but subsists on Bengali journals like *Bangabasi* and *Janmabhumi*. But such an avid follower is he of Holmes's method that he's able to tell them that they're newly-arrived (from the fact that they address him as 'Sir', unlike hardened colonials), that they've slept badly (from the mosquito bites on their skin), and that Holmes ate chillies the previous night (from the way he sticks out the tip of his tongue repeatedly while smoking). Somewhere in the midst of this, Holmes makes a crucial inference: 'Do you see, Watson? This Bengali gentleman is well-versed in the science of deduction. No, Sherlock Holmes won't be able to attract many clients in this country.'[30] Holmes has seen himself through the point of view of Bengali regional literature, from a writing engaged in what was defined by Bankimchandra as the 'subordinate task', and noticed the curious fact of his redundancy to his cherisher.

This odd strategy of simultaneously eliding and producing foreignness would, whenever it was nodded at openly, lead to further comedies of the absurd—as in Bibhutibhushan's story 'Einstein o Indubala', where the people of a Bengali small town have ignored the arrival of the archetypal scientist, and have gone, instead, to attend a recital by their favourite singer, the ample and sweet-voiced and historically verifiable Indubala. Bibhutibhushan took the business of erasing one reality and generating another to a new terrain when he wrote *Chaander Pahar* (*The Moon Mountain*), an adventure set in Africa, creating a colonial region which he had never seen. These peculiar gestures have their echoes in the universe of the French surrealists and especially their reluctant fellow-travellers, such as Raymond Roussel, who wrote *Impressions of Africa* and *New Impressions of Africa* without ever having travelled to that continent, and who often visited places like

Egypt in a *roulette*, a luxurious, caravan-like vehicle, in which he was accompanied and attended to by his staff, and from which he hardly emerged. To fashion a region, you must either never travel, or return home to claim that you are abroad, as Kipling repeatedly did, or, like Roussel, stage your ignorance of the place you're visiting.

2011

★ ★ ★

16

Possible, not alternative, histories

A literary history emerging from sunlight

I'm looking back at the title to remind myself of what it is. 'Possible, not alternative, histories'. I want to do something here that's reckless because it's very ambitious. I want to tell you about my reading. And, in the process, I wish to describe or allude to glimpses or hiccups or revisions that are germane to a discussion on reassessment.[1] And also talk about not only my history, but a possible literary history. By 'possible' I don't mean a history that doesn't exist, but possible *ways* of looking at history. I also wish to distance myself from the term 'alternative history': it feels exhausted. Certainly, if somebody of my ethnic and cultural background spoke about it, they'd inevitably do so with a particular inflection and emphasis. I'm distancing myself from the idea of 'alternative histories' in order to inquire into what histories it might be possible to speak about and describe, and in what way.

In order to do this, one must first create and explore a space that one might call, for convenience's sake, a 'fictional' space. This 'fictionality' facilitates a critique, a certain way of speaking, which wouldn't be possible in a sombre piece of academic writing. Let me try to give you an example. I'm obviously not referring, when I say 'fictional', to writing about characters or telling stories. I mean a particular tone which you can't reduce to irony, a tone that's serious but at the same time indeterminate, and most profound when parodying itself. Borges was a great practitioner of this register; it's moot as to whether his most significant critical insights occur in his mock-essays or in his essays proper. What is the difference between the first and the second? The instances of type 1 and type 2 that come almost randomly to mind from his oeuvre are 'Pierre Menard, the Author of the Quixote' and 'The

Argentine Writer and Tradition'. In 'Pierre Menard', the narrator points out that the eponymous author 'did not want to compose another *Quixote*—which is easy—but the *Quixote* itself. Needless to say, he never contemplated a mechanical transcription of the original; he did not propose to copy it. His admirable intention was to produce a few pages which would coincide—word for word and line for line—with those of Miguel de Cervantes.'

Famously, this mock-narrator goes on to quote from Cervantes's *Don Quixote* and then from Pierre Menard's, to analyse their differences, and showcase the latter's originality:

> It is a revelation to compare Menard's *Don Quixote* with Cervantes's. The latter, for example, wrote (part one, chapter nine):
>
> ... truth, whose mother is history, rival of time, depository of deeds, witness of the past, exemplar and adviser to the present, and the future's counsellor.
>
> Written in the seventeenth century, written by the 'lay genius'' Cervantes, this enumeration is a mere rhetorical praise of history. Menard, on the other writes:
>
> ... truth, whose mother is history, rival of time, depository of deeds, witness of the past, exemplar and adviser to the present, and the future's counsellor.
>
> History, the *mother* of truth: the idea is astounding. Menard, a contemporary of William James, does not define history as inquiry into reality but as its origin...
>
> The contrast in style is also vivid. The archaic style of Menard—quite foreign, after all—suffers from a certain affectation. Not so that of his forerunner, who handles with ease the current Spanish of his time.[2]

The question of what gives to writing its modern or archaic or national characteristics comes up again in 'The Argentine Writer and Tradition', which, in the collection *Labyrinths*, is classified as an 'essay' rather than, as 'Menard' is, a 'fiction'. Borges, here, makes a series of proclamations that distinguish him from his Argentine contemporaries and what they take to be the attributes of Argentine tradition. Among the better-known of Borges's statements are these: 'What is our Argentine tradition? I believe we can answer this question easily... I believe our tradition is all of Western culture, and I also believe we have a right to this tradition, greater than that which the inhabitants of one or another Western nation might have.'[3] In other remarks to do with the accoutrements of culture, Borges observes: 'Some days past I have found a curious confirmation of the fact that what is truly native can and often does dispense with local colour... Gibbon observes that in the Arabian book *par excellence*, in the Koran, there are no camels; I believe if there were any doubt as to the authenticity of the Koran, this absence of camels would be sufficient to prove it is an Arabian work.'[4]

In both the fiction, 'Pierre Menard', and in this essay, Borges is at his most incisive in complicating the business of cultural and historical markers: he's countering whatever it is we take to be the *visible* characteristics of a seventeenth-century Spanish work (Cervantes's *Quixote*), a modern cosmopolitan text (Menard's recreation of Cervantes's novel), an Arab book (the Koran), and Argentine tradition. For Borges, there are no clear or definite features that proclaim a work to be Spanish or Argentine or Arabic, although each is definitely what it is *because* it's Spanish or Argentine or Arabic. The register in which Borges explores this crucial insight (crucial to him and to the modern reader burdened with an overdetermined notion of culture) is the register of 'fictionality': there's almost no difference, tonally, between the invented scholar who presents the reader with Menard and the 'Borges' who begins his essay with 'I wish to formulate and justify here some sceptical proposals concerning the problem of the Argentine writer and tradition.'[5] Who are we to take more, or less, seriously—the narrator of the Menard 'fiction' or of the essay? It's worth adding here that, like Borges, Roland Barthes, too, is a writer whose work constantly inhabits the peculiar domain of fictionality; his provocations are enabled by tone: 'we know that to give writing its future, it is necessary to overthrow the myth: the birth of the reader must be at the cost of the death of the Author.' It's as wrong to take this sentence from Barthes as a simple declaration, to divorce it from its narratorial voice, as it would be to do something similar with any of the remarks in 'Pierre Menard'. It's appropriate that Barthes, like Borges, must *invent* a particular authorial register in order to debunk the notion of the author's continuing, reassuring presence. To understand Barthes, you need to not only follow the argument, but to be alive to tonality. The tone of fictionality is not ironical; that is, it isn't saying, 'The opposite of what I'm saying is actually true.' It's disruptive. It allows the critic to become fiction-writer, and say what it isn't possible to in academic writing.

*

My use of the word 'possible' is meant to gesture towards 'fictionality'. The foundation and starting point of my account of certain shifts in literature in the last three decades refer to a particular turn in the 1980s that affected us all. This turn was taking place on various levels, and

I will restrict myself to two—the emergence of the global novel, which encompasses what we used to call 'magic realism', novels to do with journeys, novels to do with maps and the way cultures come together. The global novel proposed—I will use a perhaps harshly simplistic binary here—that a bourgeois domestic setting was integral to the conventional Western realist novel, and the non-Western novelistic imagination implied the emigrant's journeys, border crossings, hybridity, and cartography. In other words, it's difficult for the novels of 'other' cultures, generically speaking, to be about a bourgeois apartment. There was also talk of polyphony. Since the global novel opens on to multiple cultures and the manner in which they encounter and mingle with each other, it necessarily must be home to, and echo with, a hubbub of many voices. It *will* be polyphonic.

This wasn't entirely unrelated to the new and largely unprecedented interest in philosophy at the time in literature departments. Here, a particular version of Derrida came into being, with a special style of interpreting his words, drawing attention to, for instance, his first work, *Writing and Difference*, where Derrida introduces the concept of play thus: 'the absence of the transcendental signified extends the play of the signifier to infinity'.[6] This unbridled incarnation of play segues, in fiction, into polyphony, which segues into the global novel of the journey: the extension of 'play' is also a new, political idea of narrative, a moving out from the shackles of realism into the limitlessness of globalization and its historical precursor, the discovery of the New World (the subject of 'magic realism'). I'm not saying that the philosophical and narrative turns are identical; but they come to occupy a particular tone—not only celebratory, but also triumphalist. With 'play' comes the notion of laughter. At this time, laughter emanates from Bakhtin too, with a specific political significance, a significance that immediately adheres to the ludic.

⋆

These developments announced the death-knell of the apartment, and the view from the window. All of that had been rendered imaginatively peripheral by the turn in the 1980s. Oddly, inappropriately, it was at this time (1986, to be precise) that I began to think about moving from poetry to writing my first novel, *A Strange and Sublime Address*, which, in some senses, was a book about a house, and which I conceived of in spatial terms.

I want to give you a brief prehistory of this moment. I grew up in Bombay over the 1960s and 1970s. It was around 1978 that I became a poet-manqué; a modernist-manqué. There must have been a sizeable group of us from the middle and upper-middle classes who, in that period of hormonal transformation, were angst-driven. Theories of misery excited us; there was a buzz around two words in particular. The first was 'existentialism', a term that everybody was familiar with in Bombay, especially leading ladies like Parveen Babi and Zeenat Aman, who'd refer to it in interviews in magazines dedicated to film gossip. The other word was 'absurd'. Of course, we understood these words in the light of teenage self-interest. Life was absurd for us as teenagers. We found a great deal of our experience fell under the purview of the existential, of absurdity: we tended to adopt, at once, an interior and metaphysical way of looking at the world. The moment we engaged with and immersed ourselves in this perspective and its language, we ceased to notice—simply weren't interested in—the physical. I was oblivious, for instance, to Beckett's humour. I was mainly concerned with the word that had associated itself with his oeuvre—'absurdist', which sounded close enough to 'absurd'. There were aspects of his theatre which appeared to confirm that, in the second half of the twentieth century, the contemporary imagination's conception of both the world, stripped to its essentials, and of the proscenium was basically a post-holocaust landscape, minimal, with few physical or living details. Then there were the terms that Sartre had put out there: 'contingency', for instance, which led back urgently to Camus's 'absurdity'. Existence was contingent rather than pre-ordained; its lack of meaning or purpose made it 'absurd'. The teenager in me would have seen this statement less as a celebration of the role of chance in creation and creativity than as a confirmation of the acute pointlessness of life that suddenly becomes clear to a seventeen-year-old. (Both Camus and Sartre were Frenchmen and literary writers, with the Surrealists as part of their intellectual antecedents: so the idea of the contingency of existence carrying an echo of the joyously accidental provenances of creativity can't be entirely dismissed. What in Camus and Sartre is tragic affirmation is preceded, in Breton and Aragon, by a sense of release regarding the same conditions of chance in relation to creativity.)

Much of the academic interpretative apparatus around modernism still carries that teenage passion: it sees fragmentariness of form,

Beckett's minimalism, and Kafka's parables—to take three examples—as allegories of the twentieth century human condition. That is, its readings are mimetic, its meanings metaphysical. It largely ignores the physical.

★

The scenario I've sketched above would vanish by the mid-1980s with the upsurge of the ludic. Theory, postmodernism, the global novel: these would render the absurd and the existential obsolete, just as it had made a particular spatial sub-tradition within modernism—the view from the window in the apartment—marginal.

In my life, too, a change was taking place: it coincided with my parents moving to St Cyril Road in Bandra after my father's retirement. It led to me discovering, during my visits back home from London and then Oxford, the flowering in these lanes on the outskirts of Bombay. For me, too, it became necessary, by the time I was twenty-three or twenty-four, to leave the absurd behind. Thinking back, it wasn't as if I was really aware, from the early to mid-1980s, of the changes to do with the postmodern novel, or with the poststructuralist conception of play. But I needed to abandon a world defined by a sense of the self and its penumbral shadow subsuming everything in its interiority. For me, this interiority was partly the legacy of a teenage misreading of modernism and Continental philosophy. I had to step out. This resulted in a remaking of myself, whose consequence was my first novel, *A Strange and Sublime Address*, a book unlike the poems I'd been composing from my late teens to the beginnings of my twenties, quasi-modernist testimonies to the tragedy of the contemporary world. The subjects of my novel were not only a house and a street in Calcutta, but joy.

In spite of this embrace of joy and play, my turn was unconnected to the cultural untrammelling I delineated earlier, which characterized the new fiction and philosophy. For me it had to do with reading D. H. Lawrence's *Sons and Lovers*. Lawrence's novel gave me what I hadn't found in my own misreadings of modernism. At that time—the early 1980s—T. S. Eliot was still to fall into disrepute. He was viewed as the founding father of modernism in Anglophone poetry, but, as importantly, his work contained features that could be misread, and which lent themselves to, and, in my mind, converged with the melancholic history to do with the existential and absurd. His use of Dante in the epigraph to 'The Love Song of J. Alfred Prufrock' as well as in strategic insertions in *The Waste Land* provided an impetus for an allegoric reading of modernist poetry—formally, verbally, thematically—as if it were somehow a metaphysical representation of the human condition. The epigraphs and quotations, especially as they derive from the *Inferno*, set a frame for reading. So did remarks such as these, where Eliot invokes a cultural mimesis that makes us see modernism as a symptom, an allegory, of historical or personal extremity: 'We can only say that it appears likely that poets in our civilization, as it exists at present, must be *difficult*. Our civilization comprehends great variety and complexity, and this variety and complexity, playing upon a refined sensibility, must produce various and complex results.'[7]

When I was sixteen, and until I was twenty-three, I believed modernism was, on one level, a formalist representation of the fragmenting of human, of Western, civilization, and the tragedy of that fragmenting ('These fragments I have shored against my ruins'). This reading was inextricable from a metaphysical position on value: that it, like meaning or meaningfulness, must come from elsewhere (in this case, it emanated from a unitary Western civilization that was now lost). In *Sons and Lovers*, I found no attempt to summon an extraneous source of value; there was no civilizational sense of loss. I was astonished by it. *Sons and Lovers* carried within it a polemic which emerged from its anti-metaphysical position: its writing returned me radically to the significant fact of physicality, the fact of living in the 'here and now', and of living this life. *Sons and Lovers* is an early work, but its polemics are prescient of the provocative claims Lawrence made in a work he wrote not long before he died: *Apocalypse*, his eccentric gloss on the Revelations, which begins: 'Whatever the unborn and the dead might know, they cannot know the beauty, the marvel of being alive in the flesh.'[8] *Sons and Lovers* is saying the same thing many years before he formulated those words in *Apocalypse*. The 'unborn and the dead' is, among other things, Lawrence's euphemism for Western tradition and its inheritance; 'being alive in the flesh' a reference to a moment in literary history that's ameliorated by a radical idea of value. This arc is important to me; it enacts an ongoing rejection on behalf of the physical which I first accessed through Lawrence and which I could not access in my misunderstanding of modernism or the existential. This refutation of interiority has to be distinguished from the postmodern and poststructuralist turn.

★

Now, where did Lawrence get this from? Possibly from the Nietzsche of *The Gay Science*. How important *The Gay Science* is to literature, as is the Nietzsche that says 'yes' to life, who exhorts us, 'Embrace your fate'![9] Why is he saying this? Perhaps it might be connected to the fact that—like Lawrence, for whom the encounter with Italy and sunlight was a transformative experience—for Nietzsche too, the idea of Italy and the encounter with it comprise a revaluation. In *The Gay Science*, Nietzsche speaks repeatedly of Italy, and Genoa. He also refers to the luxury of a summer afternoon. In other words, Nietzsche's sense of the release from interiority is happening through sunlight. Sunlight is not a metaphor for the enlightenment; it's a way of speaking about 'being alive in the flesh'—physical existence—but it's also a way of broaching the dissolution of the self upon its encounter with sunlight. When, in *Apocalypse*, Lawrence exhorts us that 'whatever the dead or the unborn might know, they cannot know the marvel of being alive in the flesh', he's rejecting an extraneous meaning that comes from 'elsewhere', and derives its validity from a source, universe, or epoch outside our own. He's rebutting the kind of superstructure on which not only is religion built, but the idea of meaning too. There are overlaps here with what Derrida made a case for in, say, *De la Grammatologie*. But what's happening with Nietzsche and Lawrence is quite specific and singular, because it involves a particular physical encounter with the sun. Lawrence reminds us in *Apocalypse*, when pointing out that 'the mind has no existence by itself, it is only the glitter of the sun on the surface of the waters', of what the encounter involves: dissolution.

The tradition or lineage of renewal I'm establishing here includes Goethe. *Italian Journey*, Goethe's record of his wanderings in and around Rome, Naples, and the Italian countryside, is not only an account of architecture but of weather and of the sun, of the difference of the European South from the Nordic darkness from which value is supposed to derive. The memory of Italy never leaves him. He's reported to have asked, before he died, for 'more light, more light'. Apparently, his actual words were closer to: 'Could you pull down the second shutter so that more light might come in?'[10] That's a very specific instruction. Tagore, in the 1890s, when he's in his thirties and journeying up and down the Padma on a houseboat, overlooking his father's estates, writes to his niece Indira Devi, 'Like Goethe, I want more light, more space'. Goethe is probably invoking Italy on his deathbed, attempting to return to that sunlit moment. Tagore's memory adorns

Goethe by adding space. 'More light, more space'—space takes us back to the self's dissolution into emptiness. So light (which we can only perceive within space) and emptiness are connected both to each other and to the self's dissolution, while simultaneously affirming physical existence. This is an unrecovered tradition in the West which counters Western metaphysics. Its origins are uncertain, but it goes back at least to Diogenes. Here is a philosopher who instructs Alexander (when he goes to him to honour him and asks, 'What can I give you?'), 'Could you stand back? You're blocking the sunlight.' This is a gesture towards all the traditions to which sunlight is not a pure metaphor for enlightenment but a reiteration of the immediacy of the physical now and the dissolution of the psychological world of value ('What can I give you?'). Diogenes's response is unhesitant because the rejection of the metaphysical, of meaning that comes from another source (and which other source of meaning might be more powerful than the Emperor?), is an urgent matter before the unmediated quality of sunlight.

In Tagore, the exclamation to do with 'more space, more light' must be viewed in the context of what's often, where he's concerned, a Nietzschean position on saying 'yes' to life. The first two lines of his song '*jagate ananda jagnye amar nimantran, / dhanya holo, dhanya holo manaba jiban*' ('I've been invited to the world's festival, / Human life has been blessed')[11] appear to contain a startlingly egotistical observation: they actually comprise an assertion. There's an odd implicit hiatus between the first and the second lines, so that they could function as independent statements about 'embracing [one's] fate': 'I've been invited . . . '; 'Human life is blessed'. Tagore doesn't even bother to use 'so' or 'therefore'—*tai* in Bengali—at the beginning of the second line to connect it, explanatorily, to the first (ah, so *that's* why human life is blessed—because I'm here); he could have, easily. Both lines become standalone proclamations about the miraculous contingency of 'being here', 'alive in the flesh . . . only for a time'. But to believe that one's been invited to participate in existence, and to call existence a 'festival of joy' (Tagore composed the song in 1909), is an extraordinary as well as an extraordinarily obdurate thing to say for a man who'd suffered many untimely bereavements in his family. There was his wife Mrinalini's death in 1902, his daughter Renuka's in 1903, and his younger son Samindranath's in 1907 of cholera at the age of ten. Tagore's song is the most unexpectedly Nietzschean instance of poetry saying 'yes' to life. (So, in *Thus Spoke Zarathustra*: 'Have you ever said

Yes to a single joy? O my friends, then you have said Yes too to *all* woe. All things are entangled, ensnared, enamoured . . .'. In another song by Tagore that I know because it was my mother's first recording, something like Nietzsche's disorienting insight—'then you have said Yes too to *all* woe'—is presented in a variation: '*dukhero beshe esechho bole tomare nahi doribo he. / jekhane byathha tomare sethha nibido kore dharibo he*'—'I won't fear you because you've come to me in the guise of sorrow. / Where there's pain, there I'll clutch you intimately'.)[12]

★

A great number of Tagore's songs, in one form or another, praise light. Light is not only synonymous with consciousness, but with the contingency—the chance occurrence—of being alive. To acknowledge light is also an act of affirmation. How does this love of light come to one who belongs to a climate in which it's freely available? Shouldn't one, in such a context, cease to notice it? Maybe we who live in countries such as the one Tagore and I belong to—where there's more of the sun than where Nietzsche or Goethe or Lawrence lived—still develop, at a certain point in our lives, the same sense of being a migrant, a visitor, in the way Nietzsche did when he was in Italy. That is, we, who live in climates that are less dark, still can't take the sun for granted. Maybe it's just the interruption of night—I can't vouch with certainty for the reason—but, at some point, like migrants, we become *aware* of the sun. Historically, as we notice in the early Sanskrit texts, the poets began to praise it in direct relation to the fact of existence.

I place myself in that tradition. Unlike the global novelists who left behind the melancholy of the absurd—often in the interests of the 'play' which was so wonderful in Derrida but took on a slightly sterile expression in postmodernity—for me there was something else: I was allying myself with another lineage by the mid-1980s (possibly because my student days in London hardly had any summer days in them), involving sunlight.

★

This brings me, finally, to two shifts in fiction and in reading—instances of critique—that defined the 1990s. These were significant shifts, I think, but never clearly mapped or described.

The first had to do with nostalgia. I think that, in the time of the global novel, there grew in many a longing for a value that emanated not from the energy of globalization and the free market, and the fiction it was generating, or from the polyphony of the postcolonial novel, but from a European idea of seriousness. Let me discuss, very briefly, three novelists whose reputations represent this longing; then move swiftly to three other writers connected to what I have been saying about sunlight. All of this happened from the 1990s to the early twenty-first century. The first three novelists—W. G. Sebald, J. M. Coetzee, and Roberto Bolaño—emerged in a particular way, the reputations occasionally related to posthumousness, untimely death, or silence: in concordance with our desire for something from the prehistory of the global novel. To be perfectly clear, I'm not talking about their achievements, but the manner in which they were often read and valued.

Sebald seems to be prized primarily as an impossibility: that antediluvian beast, the European modern. Susan Sontag sets the tone in the two questions with which she begins an essay—an act of championing crucial to the shift mentioned above—published in 2000 in the *Times Literary Supplement*: 'Is literary greatness still possible? Given the implacable devolution of literary ambition, and the concurrent ascendancy of the tepid, the glib, and the senselessly cruel as normative fictional subjects, what would a noble literary enterprise look like now? One of the few answers available to English-language readers is the work of W. G. Sebald.'[13] The adjective she uses to describe the ill-fitting nature of his enterprise is 'autumnal'. It's no surprise, then, that, for Sontag, Sebald is powerful at this moment within the flurry of global Anglophone publishing because he's 'both alive and, if his imagination is the guide, posthumous'.[14] His provenance is decidedly European in a classic twentieth-century sense: his 'passionate bleakness' has a 'German genealogy'. This essay is a vivid testament to Sontag's own millennial yearning. Her essays on other Europeans—Barthes, Benjamin—are extraordinary portraits of temperament: both of personality and of an age they might embody without intending to. Her piece on Sebald is as much about the impossibility of Sebald as it is about him. It articulates an anachronistic need—unaddressed by the triumphalism of the postmodern and the postcolonial—for the European's sense of tragedy. Of course, Europe is actually irrelevant. Unlike Sontag's other essays, she's less concerned with Sebald's 'genealogy' than—through the compulsions of her need—with his singularity.

J. M. Coetzee satisfied a different, and equally profound, requirement, and one that seemed to have no place in the ethos of the literature of globalization: that of a person who, in the midst of extreme politics, should either be completely silent or speak only in figurative language. Coetzee is, for us, Coetzee precisely because he's not André Brink or even Nadine Gordimer, because he refuses to speak in their language and terms, or in a directly interventionist way. Asked to address a crowd of more than a thousand at the Jaipur Literature Festival, Coetzee refused to either say anything or engage in conversation. Instead, he read out a story before the rapt audience. Coetzee satisfies the crowd's deep longing—a residue of modernity—for silence and allegory in a literary universe that, since the 1980s, gives a political meaning to polyphony, to the act of 'giving voice' to something. The value of the kind of gesture now synonymous with Coetzee is extraneous to his actual work. It's seemingly out of sync with the time, and appeals to a seriousness within ourselves that's out of sync with globalization.

The third figure, Roberto Bolaño, reminds us—inappropriately, in the new millennium—of a tradition to do with failure, elusiveness, and a resistance to the sort of 'boom' that Marquez and other practitioners of the global novel came to represent. Bolaño's world—often to do with obscure little magazines and the intensity of the literary in marginal locations—descends from Borges and Pessoa, weird Anglophile writers, whose tonality, as I said at the beginning, is unclassifiable, cannot be part of any boom, and actively militates against participating in a tradition of national characteristics. Pessoa, of course, remained largely invisible as a poet during his lifetime; and even his posthumous fame is based on the invisibility of Pessoa, since we can't say who this seemingly ordinary person, divorced from the heteronyms through which he wrote poetry, might be. Bolaño became famous in Latin America just when he was dying in 2003 at the age of fifty. His fame in the Anglophone world—related to this anomalous need for invisibility in the midst of visibility, for failure where writing was newly, and exclusively, in union with success—came later. According to Larry Rohter in the *New York Times*, 'Bolaño joked about the "posthumous", saying the word "sounds like the name of a Roman gladiator, one who is undefeated" '.[15]

In what way these writers' works perform in the traditions they're implicitly or openly associated with is another matter, and not my concern here. Nor am I going to dwell on whether they bring back to the contemporary world the legacies of Benjamin, Kafka, or Borges. Their reputations satisfy a counter-need in the ethos of the global novel; and those reputations exist in the space in which the global novel does. They now exemplify a type of singularity, prickliness, and recalcitrance—very different from the loquaciousness of a Rushdie or the exuberance of Marquez—created within, and fashioned by, globalization.

*

I end this 'possible history' with four people connected, for me, with a quiet reassessment that took place in the world, or at least in me, in the 1990s. It was a time (we have forgotten this now) when we discovered that some artists—especially those we hadn't thought of in that way—loved sunlight. The first comes from the very centre of that older tradition, and carries my sense—maybe misprision—of what the absurd is. The occasion was the posthumous publication of *The First Man* by Camus. The book appeared in France in 1994, and in Britain in the following year. It was out of place in at least three spheres: his own sphere of stoic despair; in the dominant tone set in the 1980s by Grass, Marquez, Kundera, and Rushdie of textual, cultural, and political exuberance (and play); and in the alternative tone of a paradoxically postmodern modernism being established then by Sebald and Coetzee (Bolaño would come almost a decade later), of melancholy, reticence, and posthumousness. The posthumous nature of *The First Man* couldn't be fetishized: it confirmed not the author's tragic attitude to existence (as Sebald's death did) but a startling refutation of the deep metaphysical unease that was synonymous for many with his work. The refutation had less to do with poststructuralism's critique of 'Western metaphysics' than with the sun. It was extraordinary to find that Camus had a body, and that he was aware of it. The awareness arose in *The First Man* the moment—as with Diogenes—sunlight touched the skin. This is an acknowledgement of the sun quite different from—in fact, it's a rebuttal of—the allegorical colonial 'heat' of *The Stranger*: 'It was a blazing hot afternoon.' In *The First Man*, sunlight makes the narrator conscious of Paris (the home of the human as intellectual) as a place of exile, of his homesickness for Algeria and his love of existence, and the consciousness comes to him as he approaches Algiers again, just as Nietzsche was moved to embracing his fate after his experience of Italy:

Jack was half asleep, and he was filled with a kind of happy anxiety at the prospect of returning to Algiers and the small poor home in the old neighbourhood. So it was every time he left Paris for Africa, his heart swelling with the secret exultation, with the satisfaction of one who has made good his escape and is laughing at the thought of the look on the guards' faces. Just as, each time he returned to Paris, whether by road or by train, his heart would sink when he arrived, without quite knowing how, at those first houses of the outskirts, lacking any frontier of trees or water and which, like an ill-fated cancer reached out its ganglions of poverty and ugliness to absorb this foreign body and take him to the centre of the city, where a splendid stage set would sometimes make him forget the forest of concrete and steel that imprisoned him day and night and invaded even his insomnia. But he had escaped, he could breathe, on the giant back of the sea he was breathing in waves, rocked by the great sun, at last he could sleep and he could come back to the childhood from which he had never recovered, to the secret of the light, of the warm poverty that had enabled him to survive and to overcome everything.[16]

To read this passage in 1995 was to register, with shock, what it had made newly available. 'His last novel luxuriates in the . . . sensuality of the sun,' said Tony Judt in *The New York Review of Books*. 'Nowhere else in Camus's writing is one so aware of his pleasure in such things, and of his ambivalence toward the other, cerebral world in which he had chosen to dwell.'[17] Judt hints at, but doesn't fully explore, what the 'escape' from Paris described above constitutes, and what it means both to the legacy of Continental philosophy and to the ubiquity, at the time, of the global novel. I'm not dismissing the latter, and nor am I negating the importance of the Derridean critique I so admire. But here is something else, which I'd encountered when I'd read *Sons and Lovers*; a lineage opened up surreptitiously in the 1990s with the discovery of *The First Man*.

The second node in this lineage resurfacing at the millennium's end is represented by Orwell's essays. Their rediscovery qualified the allegorical Orwell: it took our gaze away from the metaphysical terrain that dominated our idea, from school onward, of the 'Orwellian', as exemplified by the slightly absurdist proscenium space of *Animal Farm* and especially *1984*. With the essays, it's not only a question of sunlight—it's a question of love. I suppose this is the word I've kept out of my discussion, which Camus mentioned in the context of his numbness in Paris and his love for Algeria and for the sun. Orwell's *love* of everyday aspects of English culture included even its food. At one time, to champion English food was to take up a shockingly provocative position that, in Orwell, becomes an embrace of the physical and the un-grandiose, of 'all things . . . entangled, ensnared, enamoured'.[18] English tea, English food, English second-hand bookshops, 'dirty' postcards on an English beach—the very joyous absurdity of Englishness becomes an argument against the absurdist, metaphysical, parable-like shape of *1984*. As with Camus, the reappraisal of Orwell, who expended no more than five to six or seven hundred words on these subjects, was unexpected and sank in slowly. Its significance to the post-globalization era is still not clearly delineated.

My third reassessment is a personal one, related once more to my search for a refutation of the metaphysical, but in a way that had little connection to the various critiques raised by Derrida, Said, and postmodernism. I realized—again, in the 1990s—that Ingmar Bergman, whose cinema, when I was a teenager, seemed integral to the penumbral darkness we took so seriously in the 1970s, was not so much a proponent of allegory as an artist of physical existence. I had seen *Smiles of a Summer Night*, but somehow not noticed it. When you're responding to allegories of the human condition, you fail to see the physical. It was as if I'd watched *Smiles of a Summer Night* daydreaming about what the word 'Bergman' signified, and missed the carnality and mischief, Bergman's promiscuous love of sunlight and joy. Once I began to notice these details in the film in the 1990s, it was if the lineage of the sun, and of physical, sensory experience, had revealed itself—as in Camus—in the heart of the metaphysical and of the dark. I saw how much of a presence sunlight, and the joy it bestowed upon the moment, had been in *Wild Strawberries*; again, it had passed me by completely when I'd viewed it, in the late 1970s, as the work of an agonized allegorist dealing in symbols. Even *The Seventh Seal*, about death, medieval mythology, and the winter, was, I now saw, essentially a comic work, its bleak but clear light illuminating the dance of death at the end as it might a dance of life.

My final example of reassessee is the author who was recruited, from the start, ever since his posthumousness defined the twentieth century, as the arch parable-writer and prophet of absurdity: Kafka. It's only in the last fifteen years that I've paid more attention to the anecdote that relates how the friends who listened to him read from his stories doubled up in laughter at what they heard. About two decades ago, revisiting 'Metamorphosis', I marvelled at Kafka's devotion to physical detail. I marvelled, too, that I'd ignored these details on earlier readings of Kafka's writing as allegory. The appeal of the metaphysical had made his exactness redundant. Here is an account of Gregor's sister trying to figure out *what* might appeal to her brother after his appalling transformation:

> She brought him, evidently to get a sense of his likes and dislikes, a whole array of things, all spread out on an old newspaper. There were some half-rotten vegetables; bones left over from dinner with a little congealed white sauce; a handful of raisins and almonds; a cheese that a couple of days ago Gregor had declared to be unfit for human consumption; a piece of dry bread, a piece of bread and butter, and a piece of bread and butter sprinkled with salt.[19]

The juxtaposition of bones, sauce, bread, and newspaper, the dry and understated poetry of the list, the hilarious but wrenching double-edged positioning of the cliché, 'unfit for human consumption', comprise, together, an example of how a sentence might embrace fate. Once I discovered it, I found Kafka untethering himself from the remnants of teenage interiority.

2017

* * *

17

Starting from scratch

Buddhadeva Bose and the English language

Buddhadeva Bose's writings—their sophistication and range—firmly entered my consciousness when I was editing an anthology, the *Picador Book of Modern Indian Literature*. I was still in England for much of the year. I had few friends or literary acquaintances in Calcutta. My parents lived here; so did my parents-in-law. In my asocial life in the city at that time (in the mid-1990s), I got to know a journalist who was older than me and who had once interviewed me for a Bengali paper—the late Ashok Sen, a widower who too was leading a life fairly solitary and asocial, if not obscure. Asociability, notwithstanding the British Council parties at which I'd spot him, entailed, for Mr Sen, a retreat into books and a certain moment in modern Bengali culture which for his generation was probably formative and of which Bose was emblematic. It was he who urged me to consider extracts from Bose's wonderful novel *Tithidore* for the anthology I was then thinking of, and who spoke with much zeal of Bose's critical writings in English, especially of the essays collected in *An Acre of Green Grass*.

I had heard of Bose (1908–74) before, of course. My mother, an impassioned advocate of Bengali literature, admired his writing greatly, as did an idiosyncratic maternal uncle, who loved his children's stories. Bose was also mildly infamous in the annals of Indian poetry in English for having dismissed the enterprise harshly, as a folly, and the body of work it comprised as a 'curio shop'. It was a viewpoint that should have made the likes of me—I'd just published my first novel—uncomfortable. The reason it didn't was because by 1992–3, when I began to discover Bose's English essays, the authority of the tradition that he represented had faded in a way that would have been difficult to predict even in 1974, when Bose died. The reason why Bose—this extraordinary writer—appeared so marginal in 1993, when all the 'literary' talk centred on the publication of *A Suitable Boy*, was because the idea of literature and modernity that enlivened such a figure seemed unexpectedly peripheral at the time.

There was another reason why the jibe about the 'curio shop' felt irrelevant. It was the encounter with the work itself. It was a fraction of the oeuvre, admittedly, and the part of it that was written in a language with which Bose wouldn't have wanted to be identified. Yet it was difficult not to feel the impact of the intelligence, the vitality of the thinking. And then there was the fact that Bose's constant preoccupation with the shape of the literary tradition he belonged to, and the nature of his own relationship with it, spoke to me much more than the maxims about 'writing back to the Empire', 'Orientalism', and 'Indian writing's coming-of-age' that were freely circulating in the domain I then belonged to. Maybe I didn't actually belong to it. My new-found interest in Bose was a reminder of this. Much of this interest emerged from the fact that Bose evidently refused to take anything—Tagore's achievement, say, which had been crucial to every writer of his generation, including himself; the literatures of Europe and Britain, and their place in the Bengali imagination; his contemporaries; the place of Sanskrit—as a given. When writing and thinking, Bose began from scratch, querying what he'd been educated in and the values he'd inherited. It's as if he understood instinctively, and robustly, that ideas, like reputations, are historically contingent. To grasp this as a principle of intellectual exploration rather than as a pedagogical piety is as unusual today as it was then. It's why Bose seemed important to me in the 1990s, and why he is important now.

No writer can articulate their creative project without addressing their place in the present moment and in history. And no writer occupies a position that's 'natural', or that's already been fashioned for them. Tagore argued for his project via Kalidasa: by second-guessing the Sanskrit poet; by reading and rereading him; by immersing himself in the work; by admitting to the anguish of not being able to wholly inhabit and revisit Kaildasa's world. Bose does it by constantly returning to Tagore, and to the paradox of his generation's relationship with him: 'It was impossible not to imitate Rabindranath, and it was impossible to imitate Rabindranath.'[1] Much of his English writing is devoted to sorting this paradox out. But the writing on Tagore is different from

Tagore's own essays on Kalidasa in an important way. It is in English. Tagore, in Bengali, is a modern, and must address the problems that most acutely assail or define his modernity as a creative practitioner; in English, he's an 'Indian', and writes accordingly. Occasionally, he's an explainer—the English language will push this responsibility upon Indian writers, who must resist or succumb to whatever degree they choose. To engage with Tagore's debates around a complex and secret modernity, to turn from the Indian to the Bengali, we'll have to consult the Bengali writings. Bose, interestingly, doesn't become 'Indian' when he writes in English. He continues to be beset by the problem of being Bengali, and, therefore, of being a 'modern'. He never translates himself into the arena of timelessness. In this sense, he is, in this other language, more self-aware and critical than Tagore was. Although he's speaking to a wider audience, and an audience that often won't know the nuances of his subject-matter, he's not an explainer in English. He's still working out the intellectual problem of defining himself as a Bengali writer.

This tone of constant self-interrogation—Bose is only secondarily critical of others; he's primarily critical of his own assumptions—leads to the complexity, humour, and unexpectedness of his style. He begins *An Acre of Green Grass*, his magnificent collection of essays on Bengali writers, with a claim about Tagore that seems characteristic of the familiar drum-beating about the poet: 'Rabindranath Tagore is a phenomenon. If Nature, manifest in the even light of the sun, forsook the form of hills and fields and trees, and flowered in words, that, indeed, were he. There has not been a greater force, a force like Nature's, expressing itself in literature.'[2] This is the opening paragraph: a clash of cymbals. On first reading, it's embarrassing. Then you come to the second paragraph, and the self-distancing immediately opens up a range of meanings:

This sounds fantastic, but is true. I do not mean that he is the greatest writer or poet in my experience, or even the greatest modern. If I had not read Shakespeare, I would not have known to what extreme heights (and depths) the spirit of man can travel. If I had not read Yeats, I would have been left with only an imperfect notion of the capacity of the lyric: knowing him, I have known the uttermost meaning that a poem of twenty words may contain. What I am thinking of as Rabindranath's unique merit is his quantity, his immense range, his fabulous variety. It would be trite to call him versatile; to call him prolific very nearly funny. The point is not that his writings run into a hundred thousand pages of print, covering every form and aspect of literature, though this matters: he is a source, a waterfall, flowing out in a hundred streams, a hundred rhythms, incessantly. Yet in his boyhood or youth he displayed no prodigious talents, no revolutionary fire; he obeyed conventions and followed his elders; he was rather slow, rather dim and timid. If he had died at Keats's age, he would have been a minor poet of the anthologies, taking his turn with twenty others; at Shelley's, a fascinating figure whom poets and scholars would be constantly 'discovering'; if his life had closed at fifty, or seventy even, he would not have meant to us as much as he does. His death, at eighty, has been premature, for he was still changing, still growing.[3]

You now begin to see what Bose was doing in that first paragraph; he was (cleverly) not so much refuting Tagore's publicists as mimicking them, borrowing their phrases—'force of nature'—in order to take the discussion to a different place. Which place is that? It's where a strong judgement is being arrived at even while the language of judgement is being subjected to scrutiny, and its usefulness weighed: 'I do not mean that he is the greatest writer or poet in my experience, or even the greatest modern.' These—particularly the first half of the sentence—are the terms in which Bengalis described Tagore, both echoing and challenging the terms in which the English spoke of Shakespeare: 'the greatest writer or poet'. It's a formulation that's of limited use to Bose. What Bose is concerned with is changing the terms. When he says, 'What I am thinking of as Rabindranath's unique merit is his quantity',[4] you stop short for an instant—as you are meant to; it's another distancing device—and wonder if this is faint praise. Bose is playing with the idea of 'quantity'—a term with subterranean negative connotations in literary history (bad writers overwrite, or write too much)—opening up onto a register of meaning that flows into his against-the-grain advocacy.

One of the ways Bose achieves this is through his brilliant, compressed, and very idiosyncratic sense of the biographical. Literary lives and achievements—Keats, Yeats, Shakespeare, Tagore—are at once interconnected, relative, and singular to Bose; Tagore may be 'a force of nature', but that only defines the particularity of his temperament in comparison to Yeats's mastery of the lyric and Shakespeare's explorations of human nature. It doesn't comprise an absolute. The hidden element of this biographical configuration, underlining specificity and movement, is Bose himself. Notice, too, the transition the paragraph makes from claiming that Tagore's 'unique merit is his quantity' to '[h]is death, at eighty, has been premature, for he was still changing, still growing'.[5] At what point has Bose moved from Tagore's completeness and volume ('his quantity') to his unfinishedness ('still changing, still growing')? It happens very subtly. He's gestured towards this already by inserting shrewd observations that contradict our full possession of Tagore: 'Yet in his boyhood or youth he displayed no prodigious talents, no revolutionary fire; he obeyed conventions and followed his elders; he was rather slow, rather dim and timid.'[6] Beginning by suggesting Tagore is 'nature', and as a result abundant and always around us, Bose ends by instructing us that the notion that Tagore can be known in entirety is illusory ('he was still changing'). This peculiar biographical drift reasserts that, for Bose, neither the literary life nor the work is a given.

★

Bose is a remarkable close reader—almost too ingenious at times, as when, in his defence of the English *Gitanjali*, he makes a persuasive claim for discovering verbal nuance even where none exists. But, unlike the American New Critic, he isn't disdainful of referring to the author's life. Nor does Bose, like the biographical critic, believe the life to be a source of information that might clarify the artist's work. For Bose, both the life and the work are fascinating for their hidden value. Their facets and details don't add up to what we know about these writers and works; instead, they signal to Bose that he must start from scratch.

No wonder, then, that he was drawn to the poet Jibanananda Das: 'shy, sombre, and a little frightened of what is popularly known as life'.[7] Bose's championing of Das is notable for the case he makes for the reticent, the eccentric, the not-immediately-familiar. But his view of Tagore, whose facets are always on display (the life, the written work, the art, the educational activism, the music, the art, the politics), is oddly similar. In his brief monograph, *Tagore: Portrait of a Poet* (1962), which comprises a series of lectures delivered at Bombay University, he reminds his audience of his unfitness for the task: 'it is both an honour and an embarrassment to address a learned audience on one of the most *elusive* poets of the modern times' (my emphasis).[8] After a conventional Bengali eulogy—'he was a marvel of a man, a peer of da Vinci and Goethe, handsome, powerful in physique, abundant . . . a veritable god among men'[9]—he tackles the conundrum of who Tagore really was: 'I have said he *was* a marvel; I mean he *made* himself one'.[10] Here's that self-distancing again; Bose is always listening to his own pronouncements. This leads him from the man, whom he had 'the privilege of seeing . . . in the flesh', to two pictures of the poet, 'sketches . . . dated 1877 and 1881, drawn by his brother Jyotirindranath'. 'Both of these show Tagore in the weakness of early youth,' Bose tells us. The first is 'Shellyean in its appearance of vulnerability'; in the second, 'the nose looks sharper, the chin more firm; he has already a sprouting beard, but the parted lips seem to give away a secret: he is still nervous, irresolute, unsure'.[11] Why? Bose explains to us, and makes immediate, Tagore's moment of anonymity: 'On this picture Jyotirindranath inscribed the name of his favourite younger brother—"Rabi" And that was what he was then, merely "Rabi", a fourteenth child, fruit of a weary womb, apparently an unworthy addition to a family of outstanding brilliance.'[12] Although the facts that Tagore's education and upbringing were unusual and that it took a while for him to 'settle down' are part of Bengali literary lore, I find Bose's visualization of the unknowable in the poet—not the Tagore of incredible achievements, but the possible Tagore—estranging and revealing. Sometimes the only way of getting to a culture's features is by returning to the nascent, the inchoate—of which Bose is a connoisseur. 'Young Rabi, acutely self-conscious, must have felt what his family did—that he still lacked a vocation, or if he had one, that the people around him did not know what it was. This, apart from the influence of adolescence and his innate romanticism, is possibly a reason of his early melancholy.'[13] The problem of the undiscovered and apparently directionless Tagore is also a problem of Bengaliness: a problem of interpretation when there are no obvious signs to declare that the thing is what it is. It's what draws a certain kind of reader to that melancholic juncture of uncertainty. Bose's approach here is prescient of Susan Sontag's eighteen years later when, at the beginning of her essay 'Under the Sign of Saturn', she reviews Walter Benjamin's achievement by studying a series of photographs ('In most of the portrait photographs he is looking down, his right hand to his face'[14]). 'In his youth he seemed marked by "a profound sadness,"[15] Scholem wrote.' For Sontag, like Bose, looking at pictures is an attempt at reading. With Benjamin, the photos suggest a narrative because both the life and work were unfinished. The figure Sontag confronts in the pictures is one *we* must invent. With Tagore, the invention has taken place, in a collaboration between the poet and the world. But Bose, by focusing briefly, decisively, on the 'nervous, irresolute, unsure' boy who was to *become* 'Tagore', is shifting the responsibility of creating Tagore: he wants us to start from scratch.

*

To the Indian who wishes to divest themselves of accumulated concepts so that they may start from scratch, identity must be frequently jettisoned or unravelled. (For Bose, 'identity' is both 'Indian' and 'Bengali', and being 'Bengali' takes on the characteristics of a fluid range of cultural experiences rather than a static fixity, inasmuch as it's an escape from being 'Indian'.) In his extraordinary essay, 'Bengali Gastronomy', Bose states: 'There is no such thing as "Indian food"; the term can only be defined as an amalgamation of various food-styles, just as "Indian literature" is the sum-total of literatures written in a dozen or more languages. And I think it is no less difficult to eat each other's food than to speak each other's tongues . . . '.[16] This is a man who writes, at once, as a food critic and a literary critic; for whom the act of reading and the act of tasting involve proximate sensations and responses. That opening sentence sets up an equation that allows Bose to suggest that 'There is no such thing as "Indian literature"' without actually making that declaration; we're in the presence of someone to whom the 'idea of India' has no real use. This doesn't mean that Bose isn't fascinated by the eclectic, or the admixture: it's just that his approach isn't that of the ethnographer or the professional. He sets aside stating for tasting. In fact, stating is, for Bose, a form of tasting, and integral to the persona he embraces—of connoisseur and inspired amateur. What Sontag says of Bose's almost exact contemporary, Roland Barthes, applies equally well to him: 'Throughout his late writings Barthes repeatedly disavows the, as it were, vulgar roles of system-builder, authority, mentor, expert, in order to reserve for himself the privileges and freedoms of delectation . . . '.[17] Tasting, for Bose, supplants interpretation, and opens up fresh lines of inquiry—regarding, for instance, the place of bitter foods in Bengali cuisine: 'What I mean is that Bengali food is designed to cover the entire range of the palate and satisfy every need of human body-chemistry. The Chinese eschew bitters and avoid milk or sweets; in the Occident, you may find the bitter or sour taste only in alcoholic drinks, but never the hint of either in any food. The thought that whole areas of sensation should be expelled from the art of cooking would have pained the ancient Hindus . . . "From shukto to payesh", was Rabindranath's phrase for a complete Bengali meal, and this is only another way of saying that one must begin with bitters and end with sweets.'[18] Constant realignment of value, then, is what this sensory inclusiveness entails: an attack on the hierarchy of the intellect in favour of 'completeness' of sensation. Bose, speaking of tasting food, is paraphrasing, here, what the anti-metaphysical D. H. Lawrence (a poet he greatly admired) said of 'thought', that it isn't a product of the mind ('Thought, I love thought. / But not the juggling and twisting of already existent ideas. / I despise that self-important game'[19]), but of 'a man in his wholeness, wholly attending'.

★

Bose's English essays would have been enriching to read had he simply been an English writer, or a writer in English. What we do know about him—that he was one of twentieth-century Bengali literature's great prose writers and poets; that 'Bengali literature' itself had emerged as a legitimate body of writing only a generation ago; that he was, among other things, an interrogator of legitimacy; that he believed that the creative usage of English by Indians was a mistake; that he was consistently receptive to, and a champion of, other literatures—means that his experiments in English ('essays', in the true sense) are without plausible parallels in literature. Also, for a man whose antennae are attuned to the finer vibrations, he's strikingly un-attuned to hierarchy—to do with the iconic poet, say; or of the West over the East, or vice versa. It's as if he chose to inhabit a domain in which intellectual or cultural hierarchy didn't exist, and to unwittingly exemplify what a way of thinking that has no capacity for that mode of assigning meaning might be like.

It's odd—but maybe not that odd—that these writings should take so long to find a wider readership. Their historical circumstances (which are our historical circumstances), besides their intelligence, have made them resistant. Our history is perhaps far too complex for us to deal with. As Bose said—partly ironically, partly with regret—of Bengali food, it 'suffers from one serious drawback: it cannot be publicized or commercialized'. The same, alas, is true of who we are. He then goes on to admit that this might not be a drawback. What's resistant (because it's new; because it's close to ourselves) offers the possibility of discovery.

2017

★ ★ ★

18

On the paragraph

I don't subscribe to the idea of the strong opening sentence. Since the novel isn't a sprint to a finishing line, the first sentence is not necessarily about making a 'strong beginning' similar to the athlete responding with instinctive release to the pistol shot. At best, it might establish a kind of magic. But other sentences must do the same: no sentence, in this regard, is more equal than the other.

I should add that an early reader of *Friend of My Youth* in India sent me a text saying: 'What a wonderful opening sentence! It gave me goosebumps!' I thanked her, and pointed out that it was by Walter Benjamin. In the novel the first paragraph (the quotation from Benjamin's *One-Way Street*) appears without acknowledgement of source or author, though it's in quotation marks. The paragraph is meant to be incorporated in the main narrative, rather serve as an epigraph. This means that we're not reading Benjamin's words as if they were informing the narrative from the outside, but as part of the author's recounting. The act of recounting really begins with the title, which is also borrowed (from a title from an Alice Munro story), and the borrowing only dwelt upon in the last third of the short novel. The narrator, at the start, is thinking of his friend, who is now in rehab in Alibag and absent from the Bombay he's visiting; remembering is indistinguishable, at this point, from the memory of other people's words.

For me, though, the paragraph—the first one in particular—is the significant unit rather than the first sentence. How do you characterize the first paragraph? I would say that it's marked by a quality of 'opening out' on to something—not to the story, necessarily, but our sense of existence, which the story can hint at but never represent, since our 'sense of existence' is transient and without resolution. As stories never begin at the beginning, but in *medias res*, the first paragraph has not so much the fixity of being point A in a narrative, but the air of buoyancy that all initial utterances have, as well as the irresolution of moments in which many strands are hanging, when you still lack clarity about where you're headed. This absence of fixity is what I mean by 'opening out'. Occasionally this irresolution and its accompanying excitement characterizes the first page of a novel, or even the first chapter. These first paragraphs, pages, or chapters often have little in terms of event, and may be a meditation on place, or space, or any category that exists in lieu of narrative or story. Then, in the novel, that sense of arrest is painstakingly removed, and the 'opening out' is tamed, as it were, by the discipline of narrative. This taming is a skill peculiar to the novelist; she or he must put their intimation of abeyance in the first paragraph or page itself into abeyance, and attend to the exigency of telling us what happened next. The other reason for this taming is, of course, that it isn't easy—some would even say, desirable—to sustain the 'opening out' over an entire novel.

For me, each paragraph is like a first paragraph. It's probably an impossible aim—to want the paragraph, because of its peculiar enchantment, to be the primary unit; to want it to stand alone, available, at any point, for rereading; to give individual paragraphs primacy over the superstructure of narrative itself; to view the novel as an assemblage of paragraphs and, in a sense, quotations.

I say 'quotation' because the paragraph and the quote are to me almost interchangeable. I spent my years as a reader and apprentice writer devoted to poetry. I was first drawn to novels in the 1980s through quotations in critical essays. I remember encountering *A House for Mr Biswas* in that way—as a paragraph in an essay describing Mr Biswas's early days as a sign painter in Trinidad. Mr Biswas can't decide which letter in the English language he adores more, the R or the S. I recall marvelling at the paragraph and reading it repeatedly. It seemed to contain the wonder and humour, the irresolution and opening out into existence, that I would from now take to be the paragraph's domain. I thought it was a shame that I would have to read the novel. The superstructure—the narrative and plot—was made almost redundant by comparison.

The quotation, like the paragraph, is for me not a sample of writing, or a taster, or a representative of the narrative; inasmuch as it's an 'opening out', it's of the narrative and not of it. It has its independent existence.

It can be revisited for its own sake, in a way that has little to do with the cumulative picture the book presents us with. Ideally, I'd like a book to be composed of such paragraphs only, which both belong and don't belong to the story, and, in themselves, comprise multiple instances of opening up, each, individually, with their own form and integrity. In which case, development and progression in such a narrative must be an illusion. We *think* we've moved from one point to another, while we've been actually been lingering over these entrances and exits.

⋆

In the early 1990s, there was hardly any creative writing teaching in Oxford. I, having completed my graduate work there, became Creative Arts Fellow at Wolfson College, a job without either much of a stipend or responsibilities. An exchange student called Ted Scott from Yale—a maths student spending a year at Oxford—tracked me down through my designation and asked me if I'd read his stories and give him creative writing advice. I'd never done this before. The idea didn't appeal—but I said yes.

A year later, he said he'd read my first novel. He made a perspicacious observation: 'The paragraphs don't *really* have to follow each other in the sequence you've put them, right? I mean—the paragraph that follows the earlier one could just as easily have come before it.'

He was shrewd to have noticed this. Revising *A Strange and Sublime Address* had been nightmarish. I'd found that I couldn't keep much of the first half. Revision became what it often is: an act of salvaging—the sentence that works, the paragraph that works. The second phase of revision involved some writing, but I eschewed composing joins between one salvaged bit and another. I arranged paragraphs that had no innate sequentiality in order to give them an appearance of linearity. Each participated in, and ignored, the onward current. You could move from one to the other; but there was also the option of not moving if you chose.

⋆

Two months ago, a French philosopher and dramaturge, Jean-Frédéric Chevallier, who lives in a village outside Calcutta for much of the year, told me this about *Friend of My Youth*: 'Your novel is about the present moment. But this "present moment" doesn't just capture the process of writing, it's about reading too.' It's how he saw the repetitions of phrases and sentences in the book—as the narrator not only writing again what he's already written, but reading (and possibly recounting) what he'd said a few moments ago.

Perhaps this is what the second paragraph of the novel does. Referring to the first paragraph, the quote from Benjamin, the narrator says, 'I think of Ramu when I read these lines. It's of him I think when I reread them.'[1] A journalist in Calcutta said to me that, having finished reading this second paragraph, she went back to the first one to read it in the light of what the second one had said.

*

The 'friend of my youth' on whom I reflect in this novel escaped the punitive rehab in Alibag after two years. I began to see him again in Bombay. I describe a few of these post-rehab meetings in the last two sections of the book. What I don't mention is that the idea for the novel was already in my head at the time, and that I'd begun warning my friend that I was going to write about him. He told me that he expected a substantial percentage of royalties. More seriously, he asked me to ensure that his name was changed. Thus 'Ramu'.

Just before publication he was bristly, but, as he began to learn more about the book from newspaper reports and from friends—some of whom had a history of addiction—he relaxed. I would even say that, when I went to Bombay to launch the book in late April, he was happier than I've usually seen him. His mood was more celebratory than mine. He didn't investigate the novel by reading it himself because he didn't read books. He didn't have the patience.

But, the day after the launch, I caught him, sitting on a sofa in the club room I was staying in, reading paragraphs from *Friend of My Youth* with a faint smile on his face: now from the middle, now the end, and now the beginning. 'You could read it from start to finish,' I said. 'It's not very long.' 'I know,' he said. 'But I've never been able to read a book that way. I get bored.' Our minds may have gone back then to how he'd struggled in school, despite his intelligence and his gifts as a sportsman, and even failed twice—which is how we got to be in the same class (though he's two years older than me) when I was twelve years old. 'To succeed in life, you have to be able to read from start to finish,' he acknowledged. 'You might be an average person, but you can be successful if you can do that. I can't.'

This is one among various traits we share—a restiveness to do with narrative, a short attention span. It's why I've always preferred reading poems to novels. I remember when I first became an 'avid reader'. It was in school, in the fourth standard. I was miserable and alienated. During lunch break, I sometimes stayed on in class. I became curious about the library that occupied a small bookshelf on the right. I recall looking at illustrations on the pages of a book—pictures of animals—and reading from somewhere in the middle. The teacher, a young woman who'd lately grown kindly towards me, said, 'Why don't you start at the beginning? You'll be able to enjoy the story.' I complied, and learnt how to read books.

Notwithstanding this advice from school, which I inadvertently repeated to my friend the day after the launch, I'm still easily distracted. A sound will take me away from a book; a thought might come to me. My wife tells me that it's because I'm more interested in life than in stories—in comparison, say, to her. This may be true. I probably find life, when I become aware of it, unpredictable in a way that I don't narratives. Storylines tend to fatigue me. While watching TV, my mind will wander, making associations from the way a street looks. A scene in which nothing is ostensibly happening will absorb me; so will a paragraph that contains no vital piece of information.

When I described Ramu's manner of reading my novel to the journalist I've mentioned above, by choosing random paragraphs and admitting to his failure to start at the beginning, she said, 'But is it possible that the book *can* be read in that way—that one can start at a point of one's choosing, and then move to another?' She was echoing Ted Scott, the student from Yale. I admitted that there was probably something in my writing—given how I'd been first drawn to novels, through singular, free-standing paragraphs—that was conducive to Ramu's approach.

2017

* * *

19

'*I* am Ramu'

The important European novelist makes innovations in the form; the important Indian novelist writes about India. This is a generalization, and not one that I believe in. But it represents an attitude that may be unexpressed but governs some of the ways we think of literature today. The first half of the sentence can be changed in response to developments in the millennium to include 'American'; in fact, to allow 'American' to replace 'European'. The second half should accommodate, alongside India, Africa and even Australia. Arguably, we go to an Australian novel primarily because it asserts Australian characteristics, and those characteristics are related to what we already know to be the newly discovered worlds and continents of the last two hundred years. If an Australian novel is formally innovative, the innovations will be related to its Australian or New World or postcolonial or vivid non-metropolitan features. The innovations of a European novel, on the other hand, are not an assertion of European particularity, but have to do with the form of the novel itself. The sequence of deduction moves here in the opposite direction—a major European novelist effects formal innovations on the novel; pure formal innovation is a characteristic of European culture (rather than a political expression of Europeanness). If we find formal innovations in a non-European novelist, modulations on form unrelated to, say, identity, difference, or colonial history, we might say, 'This novelist has a European air.' We could say the same about the more formally ambitious of the recent American writers, whose innovations are unrelated to Americana: that they are, in some ways, Europeans from, say, Brooklyn. At the moment, though, because of the centrality in the Anglophone world of the USA and of New York, we don't think of innovations in fiction emerging from these locations as being primarily connected to what it means to be a New Yorker, or an American—we think of them as formal innovations in themselves. The American writer has succeeded the European writer. The rest of us write of where we come from.

What does formal innovation mean at this moment? Firstly, it probably has something to do with a reclamation of modernism, and a slightly uncomfortable cluster of symptoms and signifiers: the slowing down of narrative; Proust's madeleine; involuntary memory. Proust's return felt subversive at first, a shorthand for introducing a discussion of the subconscious in a fictional landscape that, over the 1980s to the early 2000s, had little overtly to do with the randomness of memory, and saw the global or postcolonial novel as a receptacle of the world's exuberant multiculturalism. By now, however, Proust risks being industrialized; the madeleine today is probably as much a part of a literary history of memory and sensation as it is of a contemporary lived history of artisanal gentrification. On some levels, you feel, Proust has been loosed from modernism's difficult history.

The other mark of innovation that preoccupies us now involves a questioning, and extension, of generic boundaries. It reshapes the novel in the light of the essay, and, in doing so, not only challenges those obvious antinomies, 'fiction and non-fiction', 'the creative and the critical', but asks us to rethink what the novel might *be*. This innovation is related to the first one. Both ask a set of related questions. Does the novel have to contain an event, or series of events? Is novel-writing a way of organizing and fictionalizing such events? What exactly does 'fictionalizing' mean? Does the novel have to be a 'made-up story' (Naipaul's term for what had begun to bore him in fiction)? If it doesn't, then what replaces the 'made-up story' in fiction? It's important to note that those who are making a break here with the conventional novel aren't offering something 'natural' in opposition to the novel's artifice. If anything, the kind of novel I'm trying to describe is marked by a certain self-consciousness. Again, one must make further distinctions here. I'm not referring to the ironical self-consciousness of postmodernism. I'm thinking, instead, of the self-consciousness of the essay—its simultaneous uncovering of its subject (which might be food, art, childhood, social class, or something else) and its awareness of itself, at every moment, as a piece of writing. The 'self' in the essay's self-consciousness might also include autobiography: that is, personal detail or reminiscence. But autobiography in the essay is only one element in its pervasive formal self-consciousness.

★

I feel connected to these relatively recent preoccupations and departures. Finally, I feel, the delineation of the kind of novel I embarked on in the late 1980s (my first novel was published in 1991) is becoming clearer to others; is actually finding a place in the discussion. When I started out, there was the legacy of the nineteenth-century novel to contend with, and the presence of the Latin American novel. Both made the novel identical with compendiousness.

The moment I completed *A Strange and Sublime Address* in 1988, I became aware of its brevity. In fact, brevity was the shape it had assumed after revision; it was not what I'd aimed for. But, among other things, I was aiming for beauty—not just beauty of description, but beauty of form and its inner progression—and it seemed that brevity accentuated both form and beauty. I mean that the novel is not generally thought of in abstract, formal terms (form, after all, is a kind of abstraction, and has no extraneous meaning), but in relation to its content, to the life of the society, time, and human beings it represents. With the short novel, though, you are as aware of its finitude as of the life narrated within it. You can't be completely immersed in the story, as you can in a long conventional novel whose end is nowhere in sight, because you're partly conscious, from the sheer lack of pages and the negligible physical weight of what you hold in your hand, that this story is also a piece of writing, and the pages are finite. In other words, you're aware of form, in the way that, as you start reading a poem, you're already conscious that there are only a limited number of stanzas after the first one. This determines not only how you read the first stanza, but each line. One can never forget, in the more formal genres, that writing, like a musical composition, is a finite creation, and not to be confused with life and its sprawl and unendingness. Finitude is a feature of beauty and of form.

Having typed out my novel in 1988, I realized at once that, in the Anglophone world at least, I was, if not alone, a member of a very tiny minority. I had to deal with publishers—who had earlier been enthusiastic about seeing the finished work after reading a chapter in the *London Review of Books*—suddenly having second thoughts. The lack of a conventional story contributed to their nervousness, certainly; but size did too. The novel was around 35,000 words. In the period of waiting (two and a half years) between finishing the book and the month of its publication, I would walk into Blackwell's bookshop in Oxford to spot the brief, attenuated volumes in the Fiction section and identify their authors. I discovered that only two writers—both women—had pursued this form as an ongoing project, and distanced themselves from the long novel: Muriel Spark and Jean Rhys. I check the shelves even today (but only occasionally, as bookshops have become abhorrent in a way I couldn't have foreseen in the 1980s) to see if anything has changed, and because, after twenty-six years, it turns out that most of my fiction is still the size of my first book: as is my new novel, *Friend of My Youth*. Glancing at the shelves for short books is one approach to excavating a tradition. It's largely absent from Anglophone writing, while in every other modern culture—German, French, Urdu, Bengali—this beautiful form appears 'normal', and practitioners whose existence one knew nothing of keep appearing on the horizon, like Clarice Lispector.

★

When a cousin's Belgian wife read my first novel, her response wasn't, as it might have been: 'I know these people, literally.' She might well have said so: the characters in the novel were people she'd come to know in Calcutta on her visits from America, then Denmark, in the first decades of her marriage. Her relatives through marriage were my relatives on my mother's side. They were *in* the small novel. Instead, she said to my cousin, 'It reminds me of Proust.' This was in 1991. I don't recall Proust being commonly mentioned then in reference to the contemporary novel.

She may have meant that Proust too wrote of people he knew without little conventional fictional adornment. In fact, for certain readers, like Roland Barthes, who believed that the character Baron de Charlus in *À la recherche du temps perdu* was not based on Robert de Montesquiou but that Montesquiou modelled himself on Charlus, Proust had reversed the sequence by which we understand life's relation to art: that the novel is a fictionalized version of the life we know. That this may not be necessarily so became evident to me even before I'd encountered Barthes's observation, with the publication of *A Strange and Sublime Address*, when I noticed that my maternal uncle, who had his counterpart in the narrative as 'Chhotomama', was studying my work meticulously to find out what he would do next.

But I think my cousin's wife had in mind, when she made that remark, a slowing down of time as a consequence of the confluence of sensation and memory. I hadn't read Proust except in fragments, mainly because of my reluctance to read long books. But the name came up again, when the Indian writer Khushwant Singh described my second novel, *Afternoon Raag*. Then again, in the citation for the *Los Angeles Times* Book Prize; then, in a review by Hilary Mantel in the *New York Review of Books*. And I remember being surprised and moved when the philosopher Charles Taylor introduced himself to me at the Wissenschaftskolleg in Berlin in 2005 and said: 'Your writing gives me the kind of pleasure Proust does.' This was at a juncture when I was beginning to wonder if the sort of novels I wrote were at all publishable—a question I have to reconsider periodically.

I speak of this background not to aggrandize myself (though the charge of self-aggrandizement may be inescapable), but to put on record the fact that the mention of Proust was unusual once, and to address, today, what it means to the literary history of a writer like myself. The name 'Proust' began really to gain renewed currency in Anglo-American publishing circles around 2012–13, with the English translation of Karl Ove Knausgaard's *My Struggle* series of novels—though there was some undecidedness about whether the books were fiction or memoir. I heard that Knausgaard's work demonstrated an exaggerated preoccupation with how language engages with the mundane. Unlike me, who'd resisted Proust, Knausgaard, in the first volume of *My Struggle*, makes a direct and eloquent claim on his antecedents: 'I not only read Marcel Proust's novel *À la recherche du temps perdu* but virtually imbibed it.'[1] There was reportedly more than a hint of the scandalous in the novels, mainly to do with how Knausgaard had portrayed his family members, but I suspected this account of the work had less to do with Knausgaard's emphases than an interpretation imposed on it by contemporary culture. I pricked up my ears. It seemed to me that Knausgaard might be a member of my species: that is, one who found deeply boring what others found fundamentally interesting (story) and deeply interesting what others found fundamentally boring (the everyday and its poetics).

It's one thing when Proust is retrieved from the cupboard in relation to a relatively young Norwegian novelist, and another when he's alluded to in conjunction with an Indian writer. In the first case, the comparison extends a lineage to do with the European novel's formal characteristics. It's a fresh turn, or a re-turn. In the second, it comprises an anomaly in the terms in which the Indian novel in English is usually discussed. In what sense could Proust and the sort of narrative we call 'Proustian' constitute my inheritance? This question can only be investigated to a point. The markers of Knausgaard's writing are part of the unfolding of the form. In my case, the fact that I'm working within the history of the form is necessarily secondary to the fact that I'm writing about India.

*

In the 1990s, there was an opening up in the form of the novel, not unrelated to the Proustian refusal to make a distinction between the imagined, the remembered, and the real. This involved a breaking down of the demarcation between the invented narrative of fiction and the ruminative tone and content of the essay. It made obsolete the speculation about how 'autobiographical' a work might be. This new kind of novel didn't tap into the author's life for the purposes of fiction; it rephrased this relationship by making the novel essayistic—that is, by turning it into a form that was not primarily meant to tell stories, but to express a writerly self-consciousness. Again, even in terms of this word, 'self-consciousness', it represented a departure from the postmodernism of the 1980s. There are many differences between the former and the latter, but maybe the chief among them is the relative lack of interest in narrative in this new form; its courtship, often, of a poetic arrest, in contrast to postmodernism's ironic investment in the tricks of storytelling.

The awareness of such a development in the form—a development away from postmodernism, but not towards a renewed faith in realism (such as, say, Vikram Seth's *A Suitable Boy*, published in 1993, seemed to exemplify), nor a wholesale recuperation of modernism—came into being around 1996, with the English publication of W. G. Sebald's *The Emigrants*. It had been published in Germany in 1992. A very well-known English critic asked me to read this book: 'I think you'll like it.' Maybe he'd spotted a commonality of purpose. Sebald's practice appeared to look back to Walter Benjamin, and perhaps further back, to Baudelaire the essayist, and bring to the domain of fiction in the newly-globalized world an eclectic critical mind whose perceptions were determined by desultory physical exploration: by flânerie. Sebald's brief but productive six-year-old career in the Anglophone world (he died in 2001) and its aftermath inaugurated, in the new millennium, a way of placing the novel on the cusp of the essay and of fiction. Much of the discussion of this positioning began to take place in this century in America, especially in Brooklyn and Manhattan. I never finished *The Emigrants* myself, or read any of the other work, though I wish to: there's a time for everything. In New York, Sebald's putative descendants (according to commentators) included Teju Cole, whose *Open City* was published in 2011, and David Shield, whose highly-publicized 'manifesto', *Reality Hungers*, came out a year earlier. More recent writers in this line might include Ben Lerner. Susan Sontag's championing of Sebald pointed to the essential Europeanness of this practice and temperament. Sebald's retrospective interest in the German writer Robert Walser (also brilliantly endorsed by Sontag, and reassessed absorbingly in 2013 in the *New Yorker* by Lerner) confirmed that the radical preoccupation with this particular formal and generic shift had originated in Europe and migrated to Brooklyn. A British variation in this line was provided by Geoff Dyer's hilarious extended essay with novelistic first-person narrator features, *Out of Sheer Rage* (1997).

It took me a while to comprehend the trajectory and nature of this development, from 1996 to roughly 2013, when people began to become conscious of it as a category, and publishers employ complacent terms like 'genre-bending'. It pleased me that my unease with both the nineteenth-century and the postmodern, postcolonial novel, my attempts, from 1991, to make a place for the kind of writing that I was doing, should be echoed and recognized, at long last, by this shift. Because it had felt like I was working in isolation. But it remained to be seen if the isolation had ceased. To be an Indian writer means, after all, that you're writing about India. What you're doing to and with the form won't determine the terms of critique where you're concerned; least of all from Indian commentators.

My own feeling is that the break was made well before Sebald appeared on the Anglophone's horizon, with the publication of V. S. Naipaul's novel *The Enigma of Arrival* in 1987. It was well-received, but puzzled many. The puzzlement was related to the recognizability, or lack of it, of the genre. I think it was Bernard Bergonzi who wondered why Naipaul had called it a novel, and not an autobiography. This missed the fact that the book was not only about the narrator's life in Wiltshire, but about *wanting* to write a novel about the life of a Trinidadian writer in Wiltshire. Writerly self-consciousness had, in a very different way from postmodernism, placed autobiography at one remove. Naipaul didn't look into a mirror to get a sense of his own story, but at a painting by a European, Giorgio de Chirico, of a ship sailing into the harbour of a city. This painting became both mirror and the image, the crystallization, of a moment. From the painting Naipaul borrowed the title, *The Enigma of Arrival*, again putting the theme of the personal arrival into Wiltshire at a slight distance.

It's taken time to for us to see Naipaul's book as a significant innovation in form. Instead, it's taken to be a document that attests to the postcolonial's life in the heart of the former imperial centre. It's difficult for the postcolonial, or Indian, artist's contribution to be discussed in formalist terms, because everything they do—the life they describe, the language they use—becomes the testimony of postcolonial history. Teju Cole's *Open City* has been saved from this; maybe enough time has passed for a certain kind of novel to be read not just as a Nigerian's effort to negotiate a Western metropolis—in this case, New York. Or maybe New York's position as a post-globalization Paris allows us to situate one history—that of the Nigerian immigrant—within another—that of flânerie and the essay.

The other artist, besides Naipaul, who opened things up in generic terms was the filmmaker Abbas Kiarostami. In 1987, Kiarostami made a feature film called *Where is the Friend's Home?* set in the Iranian village of Koker. Nothing ostensibly happens in the film except a schoolboy attempting to return a notebook to a friend in a neighbouring village. In 1990, there was an earthquake in Iran. In 1992, the year that *The Emigrants* was published in Germany, Kiarostami released a film called *And Life Goes On*, in which a director sets out in a car with his son to look for the child actors who'd worked in his previous film and been displaced by the earthquake. The film isn't about the impact of the earthquake; it records how the process of filmmaking, impinged upon unexpectedly by an event, might constitute its own story. *And Life Goes On* explores what it is to make a film on an earthquake's impact on filmmaking, on both the auteur's vocation and that of the side-players, just as *The Enigma of Arrival* explores the desire to write *The Enigma of Arrival*. Wikipedia's filmography for Kiarostami lists it as both 'documentary' and 'fiction' (this reminded me of a sentence in James Wood's generous essay on my work in the *New Yorker*: 'The effect is closer to documentary than to fiction; gentle artifice—selection, pacing, occasional dialogue—hides overt artifice').[2] The confusion is a productive one. Kiarostami's self-awareness (the film was made at a time when our understanding of 'self-awareness' was still mediated by postmodernism) embraces references to the exigencies of filmmaking as well as random significances, during the journey to Koker, reminiscent of neo-realism.

The difference is this: neo-realism employed non-professional actors to play characters in the story, giving cinema a register at once ramshackle and lyrical. In Kiarostami's films, actors and ordinary people often play themselves. We are in the realm of a productive confusion without abjuring neo-realism's evanescence and lyricism.

*

When *A Strange and Sublime Address* was published in 1991, critics noted that 'nothing happens' in it, strictly speaking. Whether a novel was the proper vehicle for conveying 'nothing happening' was open to question. I personally thought that a great deal was happening in the book, things that people may or may not usually notice. When it won a prize in the UK, I was told confidentially by a judge that another judge, a literary journalist, had disagreed with the decision on the grounds that my book wasn't a 'proper novel'. This began to be said about my early fiction in different ways even by those who were generous to me and liked what I was doing. *Afternoon Raag* (1993), my second novel, was called a 'prose poem' by Karl Miller in a British newspaper.[3] In an interview to an Indian paper, the novelist and critic Paul Bailey said he admired the book, and added, 'But it isn't a proper novel, is it?'[4]

In retrospect, these remarks seem prescient. They gesture towards a vocabulary that was still unavailable and would come into existence only after 1996 and Sebald. The gradual creation of such a vocabulary was, and is, something of a reassurance for me. But it's a limited reassurance, as I remain an onlooker in relation to the history of the form. I'm an Indian, so of course I write about India. But then, again, I don't write about India. I'm not interested in writing about India. This means I'm not entirely, or comfortably, a part of the history of the Indian novel in English either. Nor can I be part of a history that's now been appropriated by literary journalism and publishing houses: of the form of the novel. It's not that I'm resistant to appropriation. I'm unfit for appropriation. This may be a good place to be in.

*

It's while writing this essay that I remembered that Naipaul's book, like my new novel, had a borrowed title. I knew this, but it had never sunk in. Naipaul was clearly obsessed with de Chirico's painting; it meant something to him. But the shape and sound of the title must have meant something too. In relation to my novel, 'Friend of My Youth' is actually the title of an Alice Munro story I never read. Titles point to two things. The first is the book that it faintly conjures up. The second is the reader, to whom the title suggests what the book might possibly be. In imagining this possibility, the reader partly becomes a writer: he or she has started to create the book for themselves. In Naipaul's book and mine, I realize a bit belatedly, the act of reusing a title covers the duality in us of reader and writer. Both books are also—again, I spot this coincidence now—about *wanting* to write a novel, and then becoming caught up, implicitly, in writing about wanting to write the book that's being written. *Out of Sheer Rage* is at once a parody and a poetic embodiment of such a project. Dyer wants to write a book on Lawrence; he can't write the book; he writes a book about being unable to write that book. The narrative is Sisyphean, a version of Beckett's 'I can't go on, I'll go on.' And yet it's infected with Lawrentian exuberance. Maybe there's a name to such a pursuit.

Long ago—perhaps when I was in the midst of my third novel—I noticed that 'writing' doesn't begin when one puts pen or ballpoint to paper. (I wrote longhand and still do.) Writing a novel simultaneously happens in the midst of lived life, expresses a relationship with lived life, and is a departure from, a hiatus in, lived life. It may or may not be synonymous with the time spent putting words on paper. The time of writing really begins before one has written anything. This time is not really one of gathering material or preparation. You haven't picked up a pen or notebook but are in a slightly altered state; you are writing. It isn't absolutely certain either when the writing ends. When I set out to discuss my book, I meant not the story or the hardbound or paperback copy, but a dilation in time in relation to writing and rereading it.

In this context, let me tell a story that may belong inside the novel as much as it exists outside it. The book is about a writer called Amit Chaudhuri who visits Bombay in early 2011 to read at an event from his last novel, *The Immortals*. He grew up in Bombay, but no longer has a home there. He's staying in a room in a club in Malabar Hill, opposite, as it happens, the building in which he spent most of his childhood. The other unsettling thing about this visit, besides the knowledge that he no longer has a home in this city, is the encounter with a Bombay that was attacked on 26 November 2008, a Bombay still fresh in the narrator's mind from reports and TV footage, but which has been restored to normalcy. Bombay *looks* more or less the same, but it's changed completely. The third source of unsettlement is the absence of the narrator's school friend, Ramu. Ramu, the 'friend of my youth', is a recovering drug-addict. He is now in Alibag in a punitive rehab that's closed off his access to the world. The narrator is surprised at the effect Ramu's absence has on him. Most of the novel covers the two-day visit in 2011. Two short sections follow, in which the narrator revisits the city of his childhood twice. Ramu is back in Bombay in these sections.

None of this is different from things that have happened in my life. 'My life' became, at one point, the book I was writing. Since then the life and the writing have been compelled to diverge, as if pulled by separate destinies. But, again, the two from time to time meet. Some of this has to do with my ongoing interactions with the friend who is Ramu's prototype, who lives, like him, in Bombay, and, like him, was an addict. Even when I was beginning the novel, I was nervous of his response, as one would be of the response of a famous and abrasive critic, or, alternatively, of one's most trusted reader. Of course, Ramu hardly read. He'd told me many times that he lacked the patience. Yet he had informers. I'd referred to him in a piece of writing in the past, and not changed his name, because, frankly, I thought I was paying tribute to him. (I see my writing as a tribute, rather than portrayal or analysis.) His informer had told him that I should have given him a cut from my royalties. My friend mentioned this half in jest; but he was a bit aggrieved too. 'You could have changed my name,' he admonished me. I had no defence. I wasn't sure he cared for immortality.

After starting work on this book, I'd tell him from time to time that I was writing about him. He said: 'Just change my name' (which I had); 'And don't forget my share of the royalties'. A few months before the novel came out in India, a long extract appeared in a British magazine, and I went to Bombay in February to read from it at a literary festival. The evening before, walking through the dark arcades in Kala Ghoda, not far from the college he'd been educated at and where I'd studied for a year, we had a long conversation, sometimes standing on the pavement in the intensity of our exchanges, about *why* he was in the book. Of course, he wasn't going to read it. The idea of reading the book—any book—was more repellent to him than figuring in it.

At the actual event the following evening, he sat at the back with another friend of mine, a scientist. He was complaining to him about various things, when I started to read. My other friend the scientist alerted him with, 'This is about you.' I'd chosen paragraphs in which he hardly made an appearance. I'm told he grumbled later: 'What—I'm mentioned only once?'

I returned to Bombay in a few months for the publication of the novel. My friend called me soon after I'd got out of the airport. The book launch event was to take place that afternoon, at a venue not far from where he lived. He was in good spirits. It emerged quickly that his informants had read reports about *Friend of My Youth* in the press. They'd said good things about it. 'He's your truest friend', one of them had told him—about me. Inebriated with these exaggerations, he was now happy and at ease. He was looking forward to the evening's launch as an actor might to a lifetime achievement award ceremony.

At the event, crowded with literary readers and well-known people, he sat with a man, a recovered addict, three-quarters into the back rows. By temperament, he hated social occasions and 'pretentiousness'. He also shied away from running into people because of his history. But he enjoyed the launch. When, afterwards, the organizer asked me to join him for a drink at a club nearby, I told them I'd be with him shortly. I hung out with my two guests, and then persuaded them to accompany me to the club.

I found the organizer's party of three on the far side of the bar on the first floor. My two companions said they'd rather sit at a separate table and not intrude. But the organizer went across to them and invited them to join the others. The two ex-addicts said no to the offer of a drink; alcohol can lead back to drugs. I hardly drink. We focused on snacking. I'd introduced my friend as an old friend from school. The conversation turned to my novel—its inception; how *true* it was. And then it turned to my friend: how long he'd known me; what he did. Suddenly, he said expansively, '*I* am Ramu.' He wasn't looking at me. I was irrelevant. Everybody was silent. Then the organizer said, as you would to one who's made a large claim at a party: 'Really?' I marvelled at my friend: at the loss of reticence and subterfuge about his social identity. It was as if he'd finally decided to endorse the relationship between writing and life. The others looked at him with scepticism, and with some of the disbelieving awe characters in Woody Allen films display when they run into fictional characters.

I felt moved by my friend's statement that night. Partly it had to do with the fact that its shape reminded me of something. It came to me later. It was the words attributed to Flaubert: 'Madame Bovary, c'est moi'.

What, if indeed he'd said such a thing, did Flaubert mean? In what way could you be a character you'd created; especially a character you knew was doomed? However difficult Ramu's life might seem to me or, particularly, to himself, I wanted to firmly separate him in my mind from Madame Bovary. Yet Flaubert's words don't seem to me fundamentally hopeless, but shrewdly obdurate: an affirmation of something, and as much a confirmation as my friend's statement was. The author produces a work; but the work too produces the author's life. The author is a reader, and vice versa. The writing isn't finished as long as we continue to believe, rightly or wrongly, that it is about *us*.

★ ★ ★

Notes

INTRODUCTION

1. Personal correspondence.
2. Roland Barthes, *The Eiffel Tower and Other Mythologies* (Berkeley and London: University of California Press, 1997).
3. W. B. Yeats, 'What Then?', in *The Collected Works of W. B. Yeats*, ed. Richard J. Finneran (Upper Saddle River, NJ: Prentice Hall, 1997).
4. T. S. Eliot, 'Tradition and the Individual Talent', in *Selected Essays* (London: Faber and Faber, 1999).
5. T. S. Eliot, 'The Love Song of J. Alfred Prufrock', in *Prufrock and Other Observations* (London: Faber and Faber, 2001).
6. D. H. Lawrence, 'Thought', in *The Poems* (Cambridge: Cambridge University Press, 2013).
7. Amit Chaudhuri, *Small Orange Flags* (Calcutta: Seagull Books, 2003).
8. Matthew Arnold, *Essays in Criticism Second Series* (London: Macmillan, 1888).
9. Amit Chaudhuri, *A Strange and Sublime Address* (London: Heinemann, 1991).
10. Jacques Derrida, *Dissemination* (Chicago: University of Chicago Press, 1981).
11. Matthew Arnold, *Essays in Criticism First Series* (London: Macmillan, 1865).
12. Juan Mascaró, *The Upanishads* (Harmondsworth: Penguin, 1965).
13. Ibid.

CHAPTER 1

1. D. H. Lawrence, 'Introduction to These Paintings', in *Phoenix* (London: Heinemann, 1961).
2. Harold Bloom, *The Anxiety of Influence* (Oxford: Oxford University Press, 1973).
3. John Keats, letter to John Taylor, 27 February 1818, in H. E. Rollins (ed.), *The Letters of John Keats, 1814–21*, 2 vols., vol. 1 (Cambridge: Cambridge University Press, 1958).
4. John Berger, *Ways of Seeing* (London: Penguin Classics, 2008).
5. Ibid.

6. Ibid.
7. Ibid.
8. Ibid.
9. Ezra Pound, 'A Pact', in Ezra Pound, *New Selected Poems and Translations* (New York: New Directions, 2010).
10. Ezra Pound, *Confucian Analects* (London: Peter Owen, 1956).
11. Lawrence, *Phoenix*.
12. Berger, *Ways of Seeing*.
13. Walter Benjamin, 'Theses on the Philosophy of History', in *Illuminations* (New York: Harcourt, Brace & World, 1968).
14. Virginia Woolf, *Mr Bennett and Mrs Brown* (London: L. and Virginia Woolf, 1924).
15. Roland Barthes, *Writing Degree Zero* (London: Jonathan Cape, 1967).
16. Ibid.
17. William Dalrymple, *The Last Mughal: The Fall of a Dynasty, Delhi 1857* (London: Bloomsbury, 2006).
18. Heiner Mueller, 'The Walls of History', *Semiotexte: The German Issue*, No. IV, 1982.
19. Rabindranath Tagore, 'Dream', in *I Won't Let You Go: Selected Poems*, trans. Ketaki Kushari Dyson (Newcastle upon Tyne: Bloodaxe, 1991).
20. Rabindranath Tagore, 'The Meghdut', *Selected Poems*, trans. William Radice (Harmondsworth: Penguin, 1985).
21. Ibid.
22. Rabindranath Tagore, *Selected Writings on Literature and Language*, ed. Sukanta Chaudhuri and Sukanta Chaudhuri (New Delhi: Oxford University Press, 2010).
23. Tagore, 'The Meghdut'.
24. Junichiro Tanizaki, *A Portrait of Shunkin* (Tokyo: Hara Shobo, 1965).
25. Junichiro Tanizaki, *Seven Japanese Tales* (New York: Vintage, 1963).
26. Kazuo Ishiguro, *An Artist of the Floating World* (London: Faber and Faber, 2013).

CHAPTER 2

1. Benjamin Kunkel, 'How Benjamin Kunkel Went from Novelist to Marxist Public Intellectual', *Vulture*, March 2014.
2. Clark Blaise, 'A Novel of India's Coming of Age', *New York Times Book Review*, 19 April 1981.
3. A. E. Housman, *The Name and Nature of Poetry* (New York: Macmillan, 1933).
4. Arvind Krishna Mehrotra, 'The Emperor Has No Clothes', in *Partial Recall and Other Essays* (Ranikhet: Permanent Black, 2012).
5. Personal correspondence.
6. Ezra Pound, *Hugh Selwyn Mauberley* (London: Ovid Press, 1920).

7. Arvind Krishna Mehrotra, 'Bharatmata: A Prayer', *Poetry India*, Vol. 2, Number 2, April–June 1967.
8. Arvind Krishna Mehrotra, *Middle Earth* (Delhi: Oxford University Press, 1984).
9. Arvind Krishna Mehrotra, 'Borges', in *The Transfiguring Places* (New Delhi: Ravi Dayal, 1998).
10. Personal correspondence.
11. Personal correspondence.
12. John Walsh, 'She told him to get lost, he asked her to imagine them making love . . .', *The Independent*, 27 April 2009.
13. 'Profile: Derek Walcott: A Smear Silences the Colonial Bard', *The Sunday Times*, 17 May 2009.
14. 'Oxford Professor of Poetry Ruth Padel Resigns after Smear Allegations', *The Guardian*, 25 May 2009.
15. 'Poetic Machinations', *The New York Times*, 26 May 2009.

CHAPTER 3

1. D. H. Lawrence, *Apocalypse* (London: Heinemann, 1972).
2. Dan Pagis, 'Written in Pencil in the Sealed Railway-Car', in *The Selected Poetry of Dan Pagis*, trans. Stephen Mitchell (Berkeley, Los Angeles, and London: University of California Press, 1989).
3. Rabindranath Tagore, my translation.
4. Jorge Luis Borges, *Ficciones* (New York: Grove Press, 1962).
5. Quoted in Rabindranath Tagore, *The Essential Tagore*, ed. Fakrul Alam and Radha Chakravarty (Cambridge, MA and London: Belknap Press, 2011).
6. Rabindranath Tagore, *Selected Writings on Literature and Language*, ed. Sisir Kumar Das and Sukanta Chaudhuri (New Delhi: Oxford University Press, 2010).
7. Ibid.
8. Rabindranath Tagore, trans. Amit Chaudhuri, in *The Essential Tagore*.
9. Rabindranath Tagore, my translation.
10. Rabindranath Tagore, my translation.
11. Rabindranath Tagore, *Gitanjali* (New Delhi: Penguin Books India, 2011).
12. Ibid.
13. Rabindranath Tagore, trans. Amit Chaudhuri, in *The Essential Tagore*.
14. Jibanananda Das, trans. Clinton B. Seely, *A Poet Apart* (Newark: University of Delaware Press, 1991).
15. Tagore, *Selected Writings on Literature and Language*.
16. Jibanananda Das, trans. Joe Winter, *Naked Lonely Hand* (Manchester: Carcanet, 2003).
17. Jibanananda Das, trans. Seely, *A Poet Apart*.
18. Rabindranath Tagore, trans. Fakrul Alam, in *The Essential Tagore*.
19. Ibid.

20. Ibid.
21. Quoted in Rabindranath Tagore, *The Essential Tagore.*

CHAPTER 4

1. Chad Harbach, *MFA vs NYC: The Two Cultures of American Fiction* (New York: n+1/Faber and Faber, 2014).
2. Kirsty Gunn, quoted in personal correspondence.
3. 'The SRB Interview: Kirsty Gunn', *Scottish Review of Books*, 14 September 2013.
4. Dubravka Ugrešic, *Thank You For Not Reading: Essays on Literary Trivia* (Normal, IL: Dalkey Archive Press, 2001).
5. Franz Kafka, trans. Michael Hofmann, 'The Hunger Artist', in *Metamorphosis and Other Stories* (London: Penguin, 2007).
6. Ugrešic, *Thank You For Not Reading.*
7. Ibid.
8. Walter Benjamin, *Illuminations* (New York: Harcourt, Brace & World, 1968).
9. Marina Warner, 'Diary', *London Review of Books*, Vol. 36, No. 17, 11 September 2014.
10. Personal correspondence.
11. Ramachandra Guha, *Caravan*, 7 March 2015.

CHAPTER 5

1. 'Henry Green, 'The Art of Fiction No. 22', *The Paris Review*, Issue 19, Summer 1958.
2. Henry Green, *Loving; Living; Party Going* (London: Pan Books, 1978).
3. Ibid.
4. Ibid.
5. Ibid.
6. Ibid.
7. Ibid.

CHAPTER 6

1. Juan Mascaró, *The Bhagavad Gita* (Harmondsworth: Penguin, 1962).
2. Ibid.
3. Ibid.
4. William Wordsworth, 'Lines Composed a Few Miles Above Tintern Abbey', *Collected Poems.*
5. Mascaró, *The Bhagavad Gita.*
6. Ibid.
7. Ibid.
8. Ibid.

9. T. S. Eliot, 'Tradition and the Individual Talent', in *Selected Essays* (London: Faber and Faber, 1999).
10. Georg Wilhelm Friedrich Hegel, *On the Episode of the Mahabharata Known by the Name Bhagavad-Gita by Wilhelm von Humboldt* (1826; New Delhi: Munshiram Manoharlal, 1995).
11. Matthew Arnold, *Culture and Anarchy and Other Writings*, ed. Stefan Collini (Cambridge: Cambridge University Press, 1993).
12. Juan Mascaró, *The Bhagavad Gita* (Harmondsworth: Penguin, 1962).
13. Samuel Taylor Coleridge, *The Complete Works of Samuel Taylor Coleridge* (New York: Harper & Brothers, 1868).
14. Flaubert, letter to Louis Colet.
15. James Joyce, *A Portrait of the Artist as a Young Man* (London: Jonathan Cape, 1924).
16. Hegel, *On the Episode of the Mahabharata.*
17. Roland Barthes, *A Barthes Reader*, ed. Susan Sontag (London: Vintage, 2000).

CHAPTER 7

1. Partha Mitter, *The Triumph of Modernism: Indian Artists and the Avante-Garde, 1922–1947* (London: Reaktion, 2007).
2. Stella Kramrisch, quoted in Mitter, *The Triumph of Modernism.*
3. Cynthia Ozick, *Art and Ardour: Essays* (New York: Knopf, 1983).
4. Ibid.
5. Ibid.
6. Ibid.
7. Ibid.
8. Ibid.
9. Ibid.
10. Ibid.
11. T. S. Eliot, 'Lines for Cuscuscaraway and Mirza Murad Ali Beg', in *Collected Poems 1909–1962* (London: Faber and Faber, 1974).
12. Ozick, *Art and Ardour.*
13. Susan Sontag, *Under the Sign of Saturn* (1981; London: Penguin, 2013).
14. Walter Benjamin, *Selected Writings, Volume 2, Part 2, 1931–1934*, ed. Michael W. Jennings, Howard Eiland, and Gary Smith (Cambridge, MA and London: Belknap Press, 1999).
15. Nissim Ezekiel, *Collected Poems 1952–1988* (New Delhi: Oxford University Press, 1989).

CHAPTER 8

1. Quoted in *The Concise Cambridge History of English Literature*, ed. George Sampson (Cambridge: Cambridge University Press, 1961).

2. Nadeem Aslam, *The Wasted Vigil* (London: Faber and Faber, 2008).
3. Fredric Jameson, *Fables of Aggression: Wyndham Lewis, The Modernist as Fascist* (Berkeley: University of California Press, 1979) and 'Third-World Literature in the Era of Multinational Capitalism', *Social Text*, No. 15 (Autumn, 1986).
4. Aslam, *The Wasted Vigil.*
5. 'An open letter to the Prime Minister of India from Mr. Rushdie, a novelist', *The New York Times*, 19 October 1988.
6. Aslam, *The Wasted Vigil.*
7. Ibid.
8. James Buchan, 'Between Two Worlds', *The Guardian*, 20 September 2008.
9. Adam Mars-Jones, 'Anything to See Those Paper Eyes', *The Observer*, 12 October 2008.
10. Lorraine Adams, 'Torch Song for Afghanistan', *The New York Times*, 11 October 2008.
11. Aslam, *The Wasted Vigil.*
12. Salil Tripathi, 'A New East-West Symphony', *Mint*, 23 July 2009.
13. Fahmida Riaz, 'Some Misaddressed Letters', in Aamer Hussein (ed.), *Hoops of Fire: Fifty Years of Fiction by Pakistani Women* (London: Saqi Books, 1999).

CHAPTER 9

1. Satyajit Ray as quoted in Stephen Teo, *The Asian Cinema Experience: Styles, Spaces, Theory* (London: Routledge, 2014).
2. Satyajit Ray, 'Calm Without, Fire Within', in *Our Films, Their Films* (Bombay: Orient Longman, 1976).
3. Ibid.
4. Ibid.
5. Ibid.
6. Ibid.
7. Ibid.
8. Chandak Sengoopta, 'Tracking Shots', *Outlook*, 16 November 2009.
9. Max Lerner, *New York Post*, 1961.

CHAPTER 10

1. Raghubir Singh, *River of Colour: The India of Raghubir Singh* (London: Phaidon Press, 1998).
2. Ibid.
3. Rosinka Chaudhuri, 'Modernity at Home: A Possible Genealogy of the Indian Drawing Room', in *Freedom and Beef Steaks: Colonial Calcutta Culture* (Delhi: Orient Black Swan, 2012), 120–55.
4. Ibid.
5. Ibid.

6. Ibid.
7. Amit Chaudhuri, *A Strange and Sublime Address* (London: Heinemann, 1991).
8. Singh, *River of Colour.*
9. Ibid.
10. Ibid.
11. Ibid.
12. Ibid.
13. Ibid.
14. Philip Larkin, *An Interview with The Observer* as quoted in *Required Writing: Miscellaneous Pieces 1955–1982* (London: Faber and Faber, 1983).
15. Chaudhuri, *A Strange and Sublime Address.*

CHAPTER II

1. Arvind Krishna Mehrotra, *Partial Recall and Other Essays* (Ranikhet: Permanent Black, 2012).
2. Ibid.
3. Ibid.
4. Quoted in Arvind Krishna Mehrotra, 'The Emperor Has No Clothes', in *Partial Recall.*
5. 'A Novel of India's Coming of Age', *The New York Times*, 19 April 1981.
6. Steiner, quoted in Mehrotra, 'The Emperor Has No Clothes'.
7. Philip Sidney, 'Astrophe and Stella', in *The Poems of Sir Philip Sidney* (London: Oxford University Press, 1962).
8. T. S. Eliot, 'The Metaphysical Poets', in *Selected Essays* (London: Faber and Faber, 1999).
9. T. S. Eliot, *After Strange Gods* (London: Faber and Faber, 1934).
10. T. S. Eliot, 'The Love Song of J. Alfred Prufrock', in *Prufrock and Other Observations* (London: Faber and Faber, 2001).
11. Matthew Arnold, 'The Study of Poetry', *Essays in Criticism Second Series* (London: Macmillan, 1888).
12. T. S. Eliot, *The Use of Poetry and the Use of Criticism* (Cambridge, MA: Harvard University Press, 1986).
13. Mehrotra, *Partial Recall.*
14. Ibid.
15. Ibid.
16. Ramanujan, quoted in Mehrotra, 'The Emperor Has No Clothes'.
17. Ibid.
18. Foreword by Tom Paulin in Amit Chaudhuri, *D. H. Lawrence and 'Difference'* (Oxford: Oxford University Press, 2003).
19. Jorges Luis Borges, 'The Argentine Writer and Tradition' (1951), trans. Esther Allen, in *Selected Non-Fictions*, ed. Eliot Weinberger (New York: Penguin, 2000).

20. Ibid.
21. Ibid.
22. Rosinka Chaudhuri, *The Literary Thing: History, Poetry, and the Making of a Modern Literary Culture* (New Delhi and Oxford: Oxford University Press, 2013).
23. Arun Kolatkar, quoted in Arvind Krishna Mehrotra, 'Death of a Poet', introduction to *Collected Poems in English* (Newcastle upon Tyne: Bloodaxe 2010).
24. Arun Kolatkar in Eunice de Souza, *Talking Poems: Conversations with Poets* (Oxford: Oxford University Press, 1999).
25. Ibid.
26. Jorges Luis Borges, 'Kafka and his Precursors', in *Labyrinths: Selected Stories and Other Writings* (Harmondsworth: Penguin, 1970).
27. T. S. Eliot, 'Tradition and the Individual Talent', in *Selected Essays*.
28. Octavio Paz, *Alternating Current* (New York: Arcade Publishing, 1990).
29. Mehrotra, *Partial Recall*.
30. Eliot, 'The Metaphysical Poets'.
31. Arvind Krishna Mehrotra, *Nine Enclosures* (Bombay: Clearing House, 1976).
32. Ibid.
33. Mehrotra, 'The Emperor Has No Clothes'.
34. Quoted in de Souza, *Talking Poems*.
35. Mehrotra, *Partial Recall*.
36. Arvind Krishna Mehrotra, *Collected Poems, 1969–2014* (New Delhi: Ravi Dayal, 2014).
37. Arvind Krishna Mehrotra, 'Partial Recall', in *Partial Recall*.
38. Arvind Krishna Mehrotra (ed.), *The Oxford India Anthology of Twelve Modern Indian Poets* (Calcutta: Oxford University Press, 1992).
39. Nissim Ezekiel, *Collected Poems 1952–1988* (New Delhi: Oxford University Press, 1989).
40. Ibid.
41. Ibid.
42. Quoted in NGMA catalogue, Bhupen Khakhar retrospective.
43. Ibid.
44. *India Today*, 16 September 2002.
45. Mehrotra, *The Oxford India Anthology*.
46. Quoted in Amit Chaudhuri, *Clearing a Space: Reflections on India, Literature and Culture* (Oxford: Peter Lang, 2008).
47. Mehrotra, *Partial Recall*.
48. G. H. Hardy, *A Mathematician's Apology* (Cambridge: Cambridge University Press, 2012).
49. Ezra Pound, *Confucian Analects* (London: Peter Owen, 1956).
50. Vladimir Nabokov, *Lectures on Literature* (New York: Harcourt, 1980).

CHAPTER 12

1. Rabindranath Tagore, *Rabindranath Tagore: Selected Writings on Literature and Language*, ed. Sisir Kumar Das and Sukanta Chaudhuri (New Delhi: Oxford University Press, 2010).
2. The *Charyapad* was a twelfth-century manuscript fragment believed to be the earliest extant specimen of Bengali literature. A collection of short songs by Buddhist teachers of the Sahajiya cult, it was discovered by Haraprasad Sastri in 1916 and edited under the title *Bauddha Gan o Doha*. Its discovery pushed back the history of Bengali literature by several centuries and it was incorporated in the Bengali syllabus as the starting point of Bengali literature in Calcutta University. It remains a prescribed text for university students of Bengali to this day.
3. Tagore, *Selected Writings on Literature and Language*.
4. Ibid.
5. Ibid.
6. Ibid.
7. Ibid.
8. Ibid.
9. Ibid.
10. Ibid.
11. Ibid.
12. Ibid.
13. Percy Bysshe Shelley, *A Defence of Poetry* (Indianapolis: Bobs-Merrill, 1901).
14. William Wordsworth, *The Prelude 1799, 1805, 1850*, ed. Jonathan Wordsworth, M. H. Abrams, and Stephen Gill (New York: Norton, 1979).
15. A. K. Ramanujan, *The Collected Essays of A. K. Ramanujan*, ed. Vinay Dharwadker (New Delhi: Oxford University Press, 2004).
16. Ibid.
17. Quoted in Prasanta Kumar Pal, *Rabi Jibani*.
18. Rabindranath Tagore, quoted in Ranajit Guha, *History at the Limit of World-History* (New York: Columbia University Press, 2003).
19. Arun Kolatkar, *Collected Poems in English*, ed. Arvind Krishna Mehrotra (Newcastle upon Tyne: Bloodaxe, 2009).
20. Ibid.
21. Ibid.
22. Ibid.

CHAPTER 13

1. As quoted in Adam Drozdek, *Greek Philosophers as Theologians* (New York: Routledge, 2016).
2. This piece was written for the *Telegraph*, Calcutta.

3. Ritwik Ghatak, *Ajantrik*, 1958.
4. Gilles Deleuze, *Cinema 1: The Movement Image* (London: Continuum, 2005).
5. Ritwik Ghatak, *Ajantrik*, 1958.
6. 'Dada, I had wanted to live!'

CHAPTER 14

1. Philip Larkin, *Required Writing: Miscellaneous Pieces 1955–1982* (London: Faber and Faber, 1983), 175.
2. Philip Larkin, *Collected Poems* (London: Faber and Faber, 1988), 165.
3. Ibid., 84.
4. Ibid., 136.
5. Ibid., 152.
6. Nissim Ezekiel, *Collected Poems 1952–1988* (New Delhi: Oxford University Press 1989), 181.
7. Larkin, *Required Writing*, 65.
8. Larkin, *Collected Poems*, 81.
9. T. S. Eliot, *Collected Poems 1909–1962* (London: Faber and Faber, 1974).
10. Ezekiel, *Collected Poems*, 8.
11. D. J. Enright (ed.), *Poets of the Nineteen-Fifties* (Tokyo: Kenkyusha, 1955).
12. Arvind Krishna Mehrotra (ed.), *The Oxford India Anthology of Twelve Modern Indian Poets* (New Delhi: Oxford University Press 1992), 9.
13. Ibid.
14. Gilles Deleuze and Félix Guattari, *Kafka: Toward a Minor Literature* (Minnesota: University of Minnesota Press, 1986).
15. James Joyce, *A Portrait of the Artist as a Young Man* (London: Jonathan Cape 1924), 172.
16. Theodore Douglas Dunn (ed.), *The Bengali Book of English Verse* (London: Longman, Green, and Co, 1918), 5.
17. Ibid., 82.
18. Fredoon Kabraji, *A Minor Georgian's Swan Song* (London: The Fortune Press, 1944), 8.
19. Ezekiel, *Collected Poems*, 41.
20. Ibid., 117.
21. Ibid., 118.
22. Ibid.
23. Ibid.
24. Ibid., 129.
25. W. B. Yeats, 'The Fisherman', in *Selected Poetry* (London: Macmillan, 1974), 71.
26. Ezekiel, *Collected Poems*, 129.
27. Ibid.
28. Ibid., 135.

29. Ibid.
30. Ibid., 137.
31. Ibid., 138.
32. Ibid.
33. Ibid., 161.
34. Ibid.
35. Ibid., 162.
36. Ibid.
37. Ibid., 181.
38. Ibid.

CHAPTER 15

1. I began to write this essay—or lecture, as it was at first intended to be—out of another I had already written, on Kipling, for the *London Review of Books*, which was later collected in *Clearing a Space*. Sections of that earlier piece can be found in this one, but the present essay took on a life of its own as it began to dwell on questions distinct from the preoccupations of the previous one. I have left its form as it was when I wrote it.
2. See Rosinka Chaudhuri's account of this world in *Gentlemen Poets in Colonial Bengal* (Calcutta: Seagull Books, 2002) and *Freedom and Beef Steaks* (Delhi: Orient Black Swan, 2013).
3. Rudyard Kipling, 'The Ballad of East and West', in *A Choice of Kipling's Verse*, ed. T. S. Eliot (London: Faber and Faber, 1941).
4. Rudyard Kipling, *Stories and Poems*, ed. Daniel Karlin (Oxford: Oxford University Press, 2015).
5. D. H. Lawrence, *Selected Critical Writings*, ed. Michael Herbert (Oxford: Oxford University Press, 1998).
6. D. H. Lawrence, *Studies in Classic American Literature*, ed. Ezra Greenspan (Cambridge: Cambridge University Press, 2003).
7. Ibid.
8. Rosinka Chaudhuri, 'Young India: A Bengal Eclogue; Meat-Eating, Race and Reform in a Colonial Poem', *Interventions*, Volume 2, Issue 3 (2000).
9. Henry Meredith Parker, *Bole Ponjis* (London, 1851).
10. Ibid.
11. Walter Benjamin, *Selected Writings* (1999).
12. Walter Benjamin, *Selected Writings, Volume 2, Part 2, 1931–1934*, ed. Michael W. Jennings, Howard Eiland, and Gary Smith (Cambridge, MA and London: Belknap Press, 1999).
13. Harry Ricketts, *The Unforgiving Minute: A Life of Rudyard Kipling* (London: Chatto & Windus, 1999).
14. Rudyard Kipling, *The City of Dreadful Night* (Rockville, MD: Wildside Press, 2009).

15. Ibid.
16. Bankimchandra Chatterjee, 'A Popular Literature for Bengal', in *Bankim Rachanavali, Volume 3: English Writings* (Calcutta: Sahitya Samsad, 1998).
17. Ibid.
18. Rabindranath Tagore, *Selected Letters of Rabindranath Tagore*, ed. Krishna Dutta and Andrew Robinson (New York: Cambridge University Press, 1997).
19. Ibid.
20. Letter to Charles Eliot Norton, in *The Letters of Rudyard Kipling, Volume 3: 1900–10*, ed. Thomas Pinney (Iowa City: University of Iowa Press, 1996).
21. Kipling, *Stories and Poems*.
22. Ibid.
23. Ibid.
24. Rudyard Kipling, 'Rikki-Tikki-Tavi', in *The Jungle Books*, ed. W. W. Robson (Oxford: Oxford University Press, 2008).
25. Rabindranath Tagore, *Selected Short Stories*, ed. William Radice (London: Penguin, 2005).
26. Shiva Naipaul, *The Chip-Chip Gatherers* (London: Penguin, 2012).
27. Ibid.
28. Parasuram, trans. Ketaki Kushari Dyson, *The Picador Book of Modern Indian Literature*, ed. Amit Chaudhuri (London: Picador, 2001).
29. Ibid.
30. Ibid.

CHAPTER 16

1. This piece was first delivered as a talk at a symposium on 'Reassessments'.
2. Jorge Luis Borges, *Labyrinths: Selected Stories and Other Writings* (Harmondsworth: Penguin, 1970).
3. Ibid.
4. Ibid. Whether or not Borges knew this, there *are* camels in the Koran, evidently. This error—if that's what it is—in his assumption doesn't detract from the tone of 'fictionality' I'm talking about.
5. Ibid.
6. Jacques Derrida, *Writing and Difference* (Chicago: University of Chicago Press, 1978).
7. T. S. Eliot, 'The Metaphysical Poets', in *Selected Essays* (London: Faber and Faber, 1999).
8. D. H. Lawrence, *Apocalypse* (London: Heinemann, 1972).
9. Friedrich Wilhelm Nietzsche, *The Gay Science* (New York: Vintage Books, 1974).
10. K. W. Müller, *Goethes letze literarische Thätigkeit* (Jena, 1832).
11. Tagore, *Gitobitan*, my translation.
12. Ibid.

13. Susan Sontag, 'A Mind in Mourning', *Times Literary Supplement*, 25 February 2000.
14. Ibid.
15. Larry Rohter, 'A Writer Whose Posthumous Novel Crowns an Illustrious Career', *New York Times*, 9 August 2005.
16. Albert Camus, *The First Man* (London: Penguin, 1996).
17. Tony Judt, 'Albert Camus; The Best Man in France' (1995), reprinted in Judt, *Reappraisals: Reflections on the Forgotten Twentieth Century* (London: Vintage, 2009).
18. Friedrich Wilhelm Nietzsche, *Thus Spoke Zarathustra* (Oxford: Oxford University Press, 2009).
19. Franz Kafka, trans. Michael Hofmann, *Metamorphosis and Other Stories* (London: Penguin, 2007).

CHAPTER 17

1. Buddhadeva Bose, *An Acre of Green Grass* (Calcutta: Papyrus Publishing House, 2006).
2. Ibid.
3. Ibid.
4. Ibid.
5. Ibid.
6. Ibid.
7. Ibid.
8. Buddhadeva Bose, *Tagore: Portrait of a Poet* (Bombay: University of Bombay, 1962).
9. Ibid.
10. Ibid.
11. Ibid.
12. Ibid.
13. Ibid.
14. Susan Sontag, *Under the Sign of Saturn* (1981; London: Penguin, 2013).
15. Ibid.
16. Buddhadeva Bose, 'Bengali Gastronomy', *Hindustan Standard* (Diwali Edition, Calcutta), to be included in *The English Writings of Buddhadeva Bose*, forthcoming from Oxford University Press in 2018.
17. Susan Sontag (ed.), *A Barthes Reader* (London: Vintage Books, 2000).
18. Bose, 'Bengali Gastronomy'.
19. D. H. Lawrence, *Complete Poems*, ed. Vivian de Sola Pinto (London: Heinemann, 1972).

CHAPTER 18

1. Amit Chaudhuri, *Friend of My Youth* (London: Faber and Faber, 2017).

CHAPTER 19

1. Karl Ove Knausgaard, *A Death in the Family: My Struggle* (London: Vintage Books, 2013).
2. James Wood, 'Circling the Subject', *The New Yorker*, 4 May 2015.
3. Karl Miller, "Long, short and beautifully formed: 'Afternoon Raag' - Amit Chaudhuri: Heinemann; 'The Grandmother's Tale' - R K Narayan: Heinemann", *The Independent*, 10 July 1993.
4. Paul Bailey, interview in *The Statesman* (Calcutta).

Select Bibliography

Ananthamurthy, U. R., *Samskara* (Delhi: Oxford University Press, 1976).

Arnold, Matthew, *Essays in Criticism First Series* (London: Macmillan, 1865).

Arnold, Matthew, *Essays in Criticism Second Series* (London: Macmillan, 1888).

Arnold, Matthew, *Culture and Anarchy and Other Writing*, ed. Stefan Collini (Cambridge: Cambridge University Press, 1993).

Aslam, Nadeem, *The Wasted Vigil* (London: Faber and Faber, 2008).

Aurobindo, Sri, *Savitri* (Pondicherry: Sri Aurobindo Ashram, 1993).

Barthes, Roland, *Writing Degree Zero* (London: Jonathan Cape, 1967).

Barthes, Roland, *The Eiffel Tower and Other Mythologies* (Berkeley and London: University of California Press, 1997).

Barthes, Roland, *A Barthes Reader*, ed. Susan Sontag (London: Vintage, 2000).

Benjamin, Walter, *Illuminations* (New York: Harcourt, Brace & World, 1968).

Benjamin, Walter, *Selected Writings, Volume 2, Part 2, 1931–1934*, ed. Michael W. Jennings, Howard Eiland, and Gary Smith (Cambridge, MA and London: Belknap Press, 1999).

Berger, John, *Ways of Seeing* (London: Penguin Classics, 2008).

Borges, Jorge Luis, *Ficciones* (New York: Grove Press, 1962).

Borges, Jorge Luis, *Labyrinths: Selected Stories and Other Writings* (Harmondsworth: Penguin, 1970).

Borges, Jorge Luis, *Selected Non-Fictions*, ed. Eliot Weinberger (New York: Penguin, 2000).

Bose, Buddhadeva, *Tagore: Portrait of a Poet* (Bombay: University of Bombay, 1962).

Bose, Buddhadeva, *An Acre of Green Grass* (Calcutta: Papyrus Publishing House, 2006).

Bose, Buddhadeva, *The English Writings of Buddhadeva Bose* (Oxford: Oxford University Press, 2018).

Burckhardt, Jacob, *The Civilisation of the Period of the Renaissance in Italy* (London: C. K. Paul & Co., 1878).

Camus, Albert, *The First Man* (London: Penguin, 1996).

Chatterjee, Bankimchandra, *Bankim Rachanavali, Volume 3: English Writings* (Calcutta: Sahitya Samsad, 1998).

Chaudhuri, Amit, *A Strange and Sublime Address* (London: Heinemann, 1991).

Chaudhuri, Amit (ed.), *The Picador Book of Modern Indian Literature* (London: Picador, 2001).

Chaudhuri, Amit, *D. H. Lawrence and 'Difference'* (Oxford: Oxford University Press, 2003).

Chaudhuri, Amit, *Clearing a Space: Reflections on India, Literature and Culture* (Oxford: Peter Lang, 2008).

Chaudhuri, Amit, *On Tagore* (Oxford: Peter Lang, 2012).

Chaudhuri, Amit, *Friend of My Youth* (London: Faber and Faber, 2017).

Chaudhuri, Rosinka, *Freedom and Beef Steaks: Colonial Calcutta Culture* (Delhi: Orient Black Swan, 2012).

Chaudhuri, Rosinka, *The Literary Thing: History, Poetry, and the Making of a Modern Literary Culture* (New Delhi and Oxford: Oxford University Press, 2013).

Coleridge, Samuel Taylor, *The Complete Works of Samuel Taylor Coleridge* (New York: Harper & Brothers, 1868).

Dalrymple, William, *The Last Mughal: The Fall of a Dynasty, Delhi 1857* (London: Bloomsbury, 2006).

Day, Lal Behari, *Folk Tales of Bengal* (London: Macmillan, 1883).

Deleuze, Gilles, *Cinema 1: The Movement Image* (London: Continuum, 2005).

Deleuze, Gilles and Félix Guattari, *Kafka: Toward a Minor Literature* (Minnesota: University of Minnesota Press, 1986).

Derrida, Jacques, *Writing and Difference* (Chicago: University of Chicago Press, 1978).

Drozdek, Adam, *Greek Philosophers as Theologians* (New York: Routledge, 2016).

Dunn, Theodore Douglas (ed.), *The Bengali Book of English Verse* (London: Longman, Green, and Co., 1918).

Durant, Will, *The Story of Philosophy* (Garden City, NY: Garden City, 1943).

Eliot, T. S., *Collected Poems 1909–1962* (London: Faber and Faber, 1974).

Eliot, T. S., *Selected Essays* (London: Faber and Faber, 1999).

Eliot, T. S., *Prufrock and Other Observations* (London: Faber and Faber, 2001).

Eliot, T. S., *The Waste Land* (London: Faber and Faber, 2015).

Enright, D. J. (ed.), *Poets of the Nineteen-Fifties* (Tokyo: Kenkyusha, 1955).

Ezekiel, Nissim, *Collected Poems 1952–1988* (New Delhi: Oxford University Press, 1989).

Ford, Richard, *The Sportswriter* (London: Bloomsbury, 2006).

Germain, Edward B., *English and American Surrealist Poetry* (Harmondsworth: Penguin, 1978).

Green, Henry, *Loving; Living; Party Going* (London: Pan Books, 1978).

Harbach, Chad, *MFA vs NYC: The Two Cultures of American Fiction* (New York: n+1/Faber and Faber, 2014).

Hardy, G. H., *A Mathematician's Apology* (Cambridge: Cambridge University Press, 2012).

Heaney, Seamus, *The Government of the Tongue* (New York: Farrar, Straus & Giroux, 1976).

Heaney, Seamus, *The Redress of Poetry* (Oxford: Clarendon Press, 1990).

Hegel, Georg Wilhelm Friedrich, *On the Episode of the Mahabharata known by the name Bhagavad-gita, by Wilhelm von Humboldt* (New Delhi: Munshiram Manoharlal, 1995).

Housman, A. E., *The Name and Nature of Poetry* (New York: Macmillan, 1933).
Hyder, Qurratulain, *River of Fire* (New Delhi: Kali for Women, 1998).
Ishiguro, Kazuo, *An Artist of the Floating World* (London: Faber and Faber, 2013).
James, William, *The Principles of Psychology* (New York: Henry Holt, 1890).
Jameson, Fredric, *Fables of Aggression: Wyndham Lewis, The Modernist as Fascist* (Berkeley: University of California Press, 1979).
Jameson, Fredric, 'Third-World Literature in the Era of Multinational Capitalism', *Social Text*, No. 15 (Autumn, 1986): 65–88.
Joyce, James, *A Portrait of the Artist as a Young Man* (London: Jonathan Cape, 1924).
Judt, Tony, *Reappraisals: Reflections on the Forgotten Twentieth Century* (London: Vintage, 2009).
Kabraji, Fredoon, *A Minor Georgian's Swan Song* (London: The Fortune Press, 1944).
Kafka, Franz, *Metamorphosis and Other Stories*, trans. Michael Hofmann (London: Penguin, 2007).
Keats, John, *The Letters of John Keats, 1814–1821*, ed. Hyder Edward Rollins, 2 vols. (Cambridge: Cambridge University Press, 1958).
Kipling, Rudyard, *A Choice of Kipling's Verse*, ed. T. S. Eliot (London: Faber and Faber, 1941).
Kipling, Rudyard, *The Jungle Books*, ed. W. W. Robson (Oxford: Oxford University Press, 2008).
Kipling, Rudyard, *The City of Dreadful Night* (Rockville, MD: Wildside Press, 2009).
Kipling, Rudyard, *The Man Who Would Be King: Selected Stories of Rudyard Kipling* (New York: Penguin Books, 2011).
Kipling, Rudyard, *Stories and Poems*, ed. Daniel Karlin (Oxford: Oxford University Press, 2015).
Knausgaard, Karl Ove, *A Death in the Family: My Struggle* (London: Vintage Books, 2013).
Kolatkar, Arun, *Jejuri* (London: Peppercorn, 1978).
Kolatkar, Arun, *The Boatride and Other Poems*, ed. Arvind Krishna Mehrotra (Mumbai: Pras Prakashan, 2009).
Larkin, Philip, *Required Writing: Miscellaneous Pieces 1955–1982* (London: Faber and Faber, 1983).
Larkin, Philip, *Collected Poems* (London: Faber and Faber, 1988).
Lawrence, D. H., *Apocalypse* (London: Heinemann, 1972).
Lawrence, D. H., *Complete Poems*, ed. Vivian de Sola Pinto (London: Heinemann, 1972).
Lawrence, D. H., *Selected Critical Writings*, ed. Michael Herbert (Oxford: Oxford University Press, 1998).
Lawrence, D. H., *Studies in Classic American Literature*, ed. Ezra Greenspan (Cambridge: Cambridge University Press, 2003).
Lawrence, D. H., *The Cambridge Edition of the Works of D. H. Lawrence: The Poems*, ed. Christopher Pollnitz (Cambridge: Cambridge University Press, 2013).
Mascaró, Juan, *The Bhagavad Gita* (Harmondsworth: Penguin, 1962).

Mascaró, Juan, *The Upanishads* (Harmondsworth: Penguin, 1965).
Mehrotra, Arvind Krishna, *Nine Enclosures* (Bombay: Clearing House, 1976).
Mehrotra, Arvind Krishna, 'The Emperor Has No Clothes', *Chandrabhaga*, Number 3 (Summer, 1980).
Mehrotra, Arvind Krishna, *Middle Earth* (Delhi: Oxford University Press, 1984).
Mehrotra, Arvind Krishna (ed.), *The Oxford India Anthology of Twelve Modern Indian Poets* (Calcutta: Oxford University Press, 1992).
Mehrotra, Arvind Krishna, *The Transfiguring Places* (New Delhi: Ravi Dayal, 1998).
Mehrotra, Arvind Krishna, *Partial Recall and Other Essays* (Ranikhet: Permanent Black, 2012).
Mehrotra, Arvind Krishna, *Collected Poems, 1969–2014* (New Delhi: Ravi Dayal/ Penguin, 2014).
Michelet, Jules, *Histoire de France* (Paris: Chamerot, 1855).
Mitter, Partha, *The Triumph of Modernism: Indian Artists and the Avante-Garde, 1922–1947* (London: Reaktion, 2007).
Morrissey, *Autobiography* (London: Penguin Classics, 2013).
Muldoon, Paul (ed.), *The Faber Book of Contemporary Irish Poetry* (London: Faber and Faber, 1986).
Müller, F. Max, *The Upanishads* (Oxford: Clarendon Press, 1879–84).
Naipaul, Shiva, *The Chip-Chip Gatherers* (London: Penguin, 2012).
Nietzsche, Friedrich Wilhelm, *The Gay Science* (New York: Vintage Books, 1974).
Nietzsche, Friedrich Wilhelm, *Thus Spoke Zarathustra* (Oxford: Oxford University Press, 2009).
Ozick, Cynthia, *Art and Ardour: Essays* (New York: Knopf, 1983).
Pagis, Dan, *The Selected Poetry of Dan Pagis*, trans. Stephen Mitchell (Berkeley, Los Angeles, and London: University of California Press, 1989).
Parker, Henry Meredith, *Bole Ponjis* (London, 1851).
Parthasarathy, R., *Ten Twentieth Century Indian Poets* (Delhi: Oxford University Press, 1976).
Paz, Octavio, *Alternating Current* (New York: Arcade Publishing, 1990).
Pound, Ezra, *Hugh Selwyn Mauberley* (London: Ovid Press, 1920).
Pound, Ezra, *Confucian Analects* (London: Peter Owen, 1956).
Pound, Ezra, *New Selected Poems and Translations* (New York: New Directions, 2010).
Rabaté, Jean-Michel, *The Cambridge Companion to Lacan* (Cambridge: Cambridge University Press, 2003).
Ramanujan, A. K., 'Is There an Indian Way of Thinking? An Informal Essay', *Contributions to Indian Sociology*, 23, 1 (1989): 41–58.
Ramanujan, A. K., *The Collected Essays of A. K. Ramanujan*, ed. Vinay Dharwadker (New Delhi: Oxford University Press, 2004).
Ray, Satyajit, *Our Films, Their Films* (Bombay: Orient Longman, 1976).
Rhys, Jean, *Wide Sargasso Sea* (Harmondsworth: Penguin, 1968).
Riaz, Fahmida, 'Some Misaddressed Letters', in Aamer Hussein (ed.), *Hoops of Fire: Fifty Years of Fiction by Pakistani Women* (London: Saqi Books, 1999).

Ricketts, Harry, *The Unforgiving Minute: A Life of Rudyard Kipling* (London: Chatto & Windus, 1999).
Roy, Arundhati, *The God of Small Things* (London: Flamingo, 1997).
Rushdie, Salman, *Midnight's Children* (London: Jonathan Cape, 1981).
Ruskin, John, *The Stones of Venice* (London: Smith, Elder, 1851–3).
Sampson, George (ed.), *The Concise Cambridge History of English Literature* (Cambridge: Cambridge University Press, 1961).
Sarkar, Susobhan, *Bengal Renaissance and Other Essays* (New Delhi: People's Publishing House, 1970).
Schlegel, August Wilhelm von, *Bhagavad-gita id est [Thespesion melos] sive Almi Crishnae et Arjunae colloquim de rebus divinis* (Bonnae: E. Weber, 1846).
Seth, Vikram, *The Golden Gate* (London: Faber and Faber, 1986).
Seth, Vikram, *A Suitable Boy* (New York: HarperCollins, 1993).
Shelley, Percy Bysshe, *A Defence of Poetry* (Indianapolis: Bobbs-Merrill, 1901).
Singh, Raghubir, *Calcutta: The Home and the Street* (London: Thames and Hudson, 1988).
Singh, Raghubir, *Bombay: Gateway of India* (New York: Aperture, 1996).
Singh, Raghubir, *River of Colour: The India of Raghubir Singh* (London: Phaidon Press, 1998).
Sontag, Susan (ed.), *A Barthes Reader* (London: Vintage Books, 2000).
Sontag, Susan, *Against Interpretation and Other Essays* (London: Penguin Classics, 2009).
Sontag, Susan, *Under the Sign of Saturn* (London: Penguin, 2013).
Sydney, Philip, *The Poems of Sir Philip Sidney*, ed. William A. Ringler (Oxford: Oxford University Press, 1962).
Tagore, Rabindranath, *Selected Letters of Rabindranath Tagore*, ed. Krishna Dutta and Andrew Robinson (New York: Cambridge University Press, 1997).
Tagore, Rabindranath, *Selected Short Stories*, ed. William Radice (London: Penguin, 2005).
Tagore, Rabindranath, *Selected Writings on Literature and Language*, ed. Sisir Kumar Das and Sukanta Chaudhuri (New Delhi: Oxford University Press, 2010).
Tagore, Rabindranath, *The Essential Tagore*, ed. Fakrul Alam and Radha Chakravarty (Cambridge, MA and London: Belknap Press, 2011).
Tagore, Rabindranath, *Gitanjali* (New Delhi: Penguin Books India, 2011).
Tanizaki, Junichiro, *A Portrait of Shunkin* (Tokyo: Hara Shobo, 1965).
Tanizaki, Junichiro, *In Praise of Shadows* (New Haven, CT: Leete's Island Books, 1977).
Tartt, Donna, *The Secret History* (London: Penguin, 1993).
Teo, Stephen, *The Asian Cinema Experience: Styles, Spaces, Theory* (London: Routledge, 2014).
Ugrešić, Dubravka, *Thank You For Not Reading: Essays on Literary Trivia* (Normal, IL: Dalkey Archive Press, 2001).
Updike, John, *Rabbit, Run* (Harmondsworth: Penguin, 1964).

Wilkins, Charles, *The Bhăgvăt-gēētā, or dialogues of Krĕĕshnă and Ărjŏŏn* (London: printed for C. Nourse, opposite Catherine-Street, in the Strand, 1785).
William, Wordsworth, *The Prelude 1799, 1805, 1850*, ed. Jonathan Wordsworth, M. H. Abrams, and Stephen Gill (New York: Norton, 1979).
Woolf, Virginia, *Mr Bennett and Mrs Brown* (London: L. and Virginia Woolf, 1924).
Yeats, W. B. *Selected Poetry* (London: Macmillan, 1974).
Yeats, W. B., *The Collected Works of W. B. Yeats*, ed. Richard J. Finneran (Upper Saddle River, NJ: Prentice Hall, 1997).

General Index

Note: Page numbers in italics refer to illustrations.

Index of Names

Note: Page numbers in italics refer to illustrations.